FUTURISM
AND THE INTERNATIONAL AVANT-GARDE

THIS CATALOGUE AND EXHIBITION WERE SUPPORTED BY A GRANT FROM THE PEW MEMORIAL TRUST

Luigi Russolo Carlo Carrà F. T. Marinetti Umberto Boccioni Gino Severini

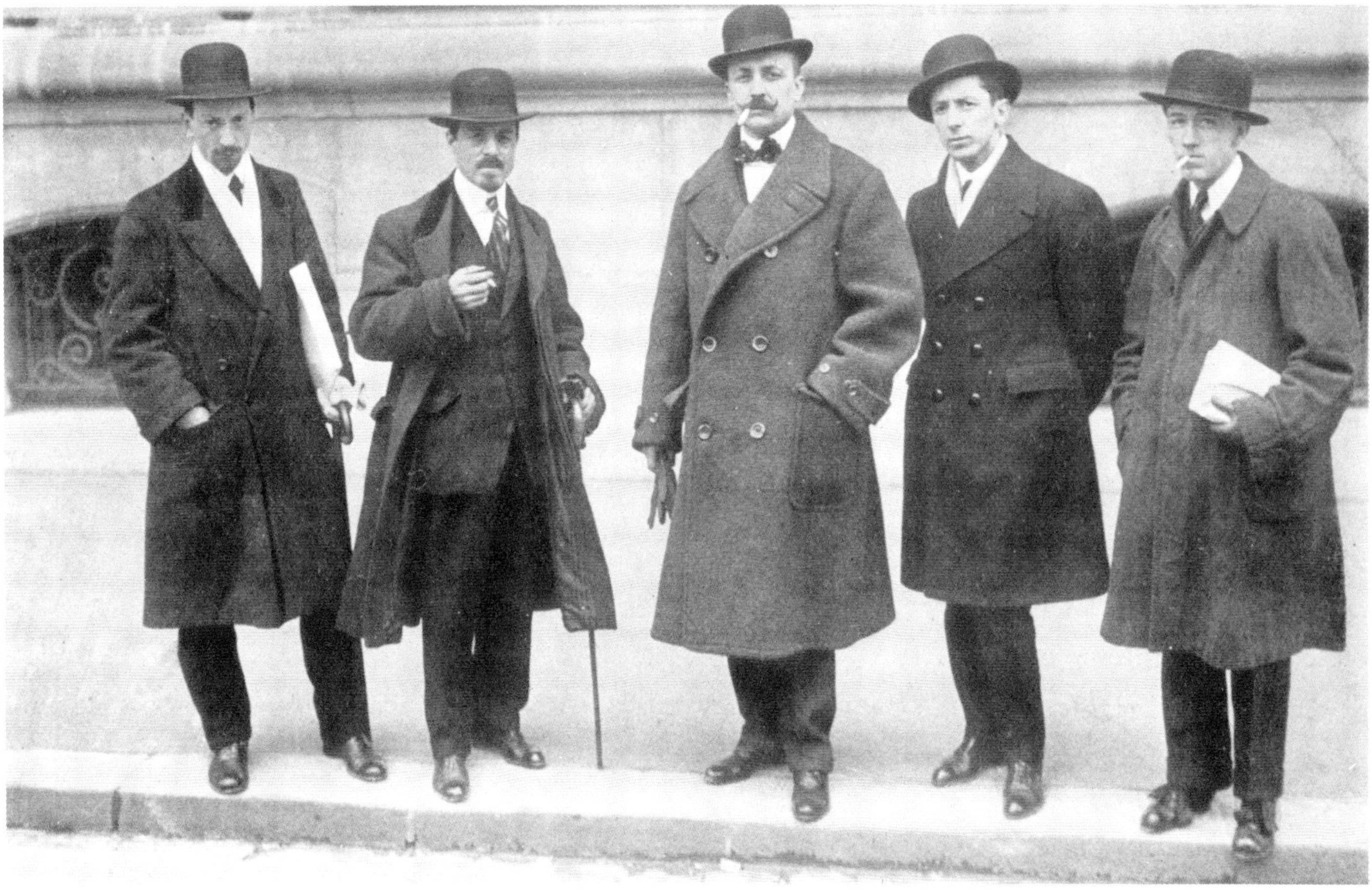

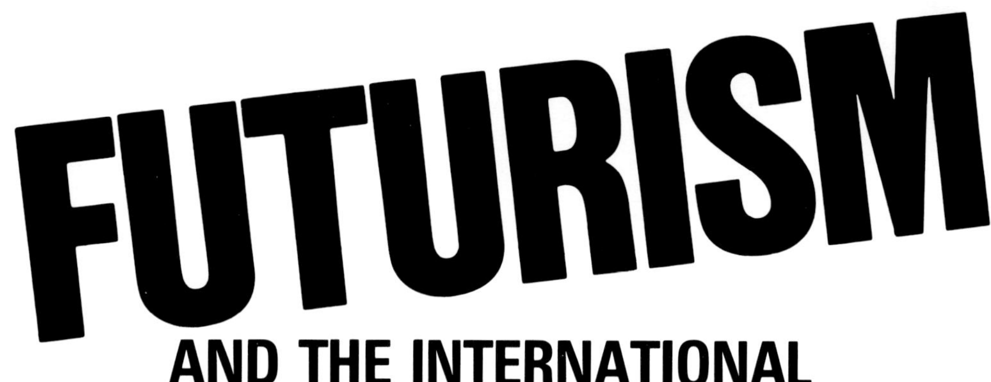

AND THE INTERNATIONAL AVANT-GARDE

BY

ANNE d'HARNONCOURT

WITH ESSAY BY GERMANO CELANT

OCTOBER 26, 1980 TO JANUARY 4, 1981

PHILADELPHIA MUSEUM OF ART

cover: Giacomo Balla, *The Injection of Futurism,* c. 1918 (no. 14)

frontispiece: Five Italian Futurists in Paris, February 1912; Luigi Russolo, Carlo Carrà, Filippo Tommaso Marinetti, Umberto Boccioni, and Gino Severini (left to right)

Edited by Jane Iandola Watkins

Designed by Russell Rollins

Printed by Eastern Press, Inc., New Haven

Photographs courtesy of the owner, except the following
Plates: E. Irving Bloomstrann, no. 80; Will Brown, nos. 12, 44, 48, 65, 74; Geoffrey Clements, nos. 72, 123, 129; Lew Gilcrest Studios, nos. 1, 2, 3, 8, 9, 10, 11, 13, 38, 51, 58, 61, 68, 73; Leonard Hutton Galleries, no. 120; Jacqueline Hyde, nos. 63, 103; Robert E. Mates, no. 104; Eric E. Mitchell, no. 59; O. E. Nelson, no. 60; Nathan Rabin, nos. 89, 90; John D. Schiff, no. 118; Duane Suter, no. 94; Joseph Szaszfai, nos. 49, 122, 130; Charles Uht, no. 107; *Figures:* Will Brown, figs. 2, 52; Brunel, fig. 13; Barbara Goldner, courtesy Ronald Feldman Fine Arts Inc., fig. 48; Lynn Goldsmith Inc., fig. 47; Leonard Hutton Galleries, fig. 14; Jacqueline Hyde, fig. 9; Steven Izenour, fig. 56; Robert E. Mates, figs. 11, 17, 31, 37; Mario Perotti, fig. 20; Petersen, fig. 8; Joseph S. Rychetnik, courtesy Photo Researchers, Inc., fig. 54; Sunami, fig. 7

Library of Congress catalog card number: 80-83095
Library of Congress Cataloging in Publication Data
Main entry under title:
Futurism and the international avant-garde.
Bibliography: p. 43
1. Futurism (Art)—Addresses, essays, lectures. 2. Art, Modern—20th century—Addresses, essays, lectures. 3. Avant-garde (Aesthetics)—Addresses, essays, lectures. I. d'Harnoncourt, Anne, 1943- II. Celant, Germano. III. Philadelphia Museum of Art.
N6494.F8F86 709'.04'033 80-83095
ISBN 0-87633-037-5

CONTENTS

LENDERS TO THE EXHIBITION

Albright-Knox Art Gallery, Buffalo

Art Gallery of Ontario, Toronto

The Art Institute of Chicago

Dr. and Mrs. James F. Bing, Baltimore

The Cleveland Museum of Art

Delaware Art Museum, Wilmington

The Detroit Institute of Arts

Anthony d'Offay Gallery, London

Mme Marcel Duchamp, Villiers-sous-Grez

Fogg Art Museum, Harvard University, Cambridge, Massachusetts

The Solomon R. Guggenheim Museum, New York

Hirshhorn Museum and Sculpture Garden, Smithsonian Institution, Washington, D.C.

Mr. and Mrs. Dan Johnson, New York

The Metropolitan Museum of Art, New York

Mr. and Mrs. N. Richard Miller, New York

Musée National d'Art Moderne, Centre Georges Pompidou, Paris

Museum of Art, Carnegie Institute, Pittsburgh

The Museum of Modern Art, New York

Philadelphia Museum of Art

Private collections (five)

Miss Barbara Slifka, New York

The Tate Gallery, London

Thyssen-Bornemisza Collection, Lugano

Mrs. Louise Varèse, New York

Wadsworth Atheneum, Hartford

Whitney Museum of American Art, New York

The Lydia and Harry Lewis Winston Collection
(Dr. and Mrs. Barnett Malbin, New York)

Yale University Art Gallery, New Haven

Richard S. Zeisler Collection, New York

FOREWORD

The Philadelphia Museum of Art has superb examples of avant-garde painting in Europe from before World War I because of the Louise and Walter Arensberg and A. E. Gallatin bequests. For some reason, neither the Arensbergs nor Gallatin acquired Futurist works—perhaps because their collecting was done after the war when Italian Futurism had withdrawn from Paris. Since most of the artists represented in strength in Philadelphia's early twentieth-century collection—Marcel Duchamp, Picasso, Delaunay, Léger, Jacques Villon—were interested in Futurist ideas and Futurist artists, an exhibition of Futurist art seemed desirable—not only to show material rarely seen in Philadelphia, but to be able to present the Futurists in relation to the other art of their own time, which this Museum does possess.

The desire for the exhibition existed and the opportunity came with the expansion and construction program at the Museum of Modern Art in New York. That museum was particularly happy to lend groups of works in exchange for generous loans to its exhibition *Pablo Picasso: A Retrospective*. It not only agreed to lend all its Futurist works that could safely travel to Philadelphia, but it secured a grant from the National Endowment for the Arts to cover some of the costs of such an exchange. We should like to thank Richard E. Oldenburg, Director of the Museum of Modern Art, William S. Rubin, its Director of Painting and Sculpture, John Elderfield, its Director of Drawings, and Richard Palmer, its Coordinator of Exhibitions, for their collaboration, particularly with Anne d'Harnoncourt, the organizer of the exhibition for Philadelphia.

The opportunity to show a fine group of Futurist works expanded into an exhibition with the willingness of Dr. and Mrs. Barnett Malbin to lend from the Lydia and Harry Lewis Winston Collection, surely the finest private collection of Futurist art ever assembled outside Italy. Mrs. Malbin has not only been gracious in lending, but has given Anne d'Harnoncourt every encouragement, including access to her invaluable library and archives. The Museum of Modern Art and Dr. and Mrs. Malbin were joined as lenders by museums and private collectors in this country and abroad, to whom we are enormously grateful. We must also express our great appreciation for the generous grant from the Pew Memorial Trust, without which this exhibition would not have been possible.

Anne d'Harnoncourt, Curator of Twentieth-Century Art, took on the exhibition with very little notice, but with her customary zeal and sense of responsibility has pulled it together into a coherent exhibition of which we can be very proud. We should like to thank the provocative Italian critic of contemporary art Germano Celant for his contribution of an essay for this catalogue. In bringing this exhibition and catalogue about in a relatively short time, we have every reason to be grateful to the faithful and enterprising members of the staff in the offices of the Registrar, Library, Installations, and Publications.

JEAN SUTHERLAND BOGGS
Director

ACKNOWLEDGMENTS

Any project that spans international boundaries in a field teeming with scholars and students exploring new aspects of modernism inevitably owes much to the generous assistance of many colleagues. Particular and profound thanks are due to Marianne W. Martin, author of one of the most distinguished studies of Futurism in any language, who gave unstintingly of her time and knowledge in reviewing the information on the Futurist works included in the exhibition as well as responding to innumerable queries. Any increase in the accuracy of recording Futurist achievements is attributable to her vigilance. A new resource in the United States for the study of Futurism is the Marinetti Archives at Yale University. Marianne Martin oversaw the translation of a group of letters from Gino Severini to F. T. Marinetti, which sheds new light on the Futurists' relationships to each other and to their colleagues in other countries. Anyone concerned with the international ramifications of Futurism must be in debt to Dr. Martin's scholarship, and many facets of this project benefited from her wise counsel.

For thoughtful advice and helpful suggestions during the preparation of this exhibition we are also grateful to Susan P. Compton, Edward F. Fry, Robert L. Herbert, Joan M. Lukach, Daniel Robbins, Angelica Rudenstine, and Joshua C. Taylor. Many other scholars graciously answered questions or pursued elusive information: Zeno Birolli, Mary Chamot, Margaret B. Clunie, Emily Wallace Harvey, Linda D. Henderson, Michel Hoog, Giovanni Lista, Garnett McCoy, Francis Naumann, Simonetta Nicolini, Mark Rosenthal, Roberta K. Tarbell, and Judith Zilczer. For their kind assistance in obtaining photographs and in making available archival material in their collections we are indebted to Eleanor Apter of the Société Anonyme archives, Yale University Art Gallery, Suzanne Foley and Eugenie Candau of the San Francisco Museum of Modern Art, Geneviève Lacambre of the Musée d'Orsay, Paris, Jean Lacambre and Nadine Pouillon of the Musée National d'Art Moderne, Centre Georges Pompidou, Paris, Gail Levin of the Whitney Museum of American Art, New York, Richard Morphet of the Tate Gallery, London, Clive Phillpot and Pearl L. Moeller of the library at the Museum of Modern Art, New York, Margit Rowell of the Solomon R. Guggenheim Museum, New York, Elizabeth S. Wrigley of the Francis Bacon Library, Claremont, California, and Marjorie G. Wynne of the Beinecke Rare Book and Manuscript Library, Yale University. John Hand, now of the National Gallery of Art, Washington, D.C., generously consented to allow us to consult his unpublished master's thesis on the spread of information about Futurism within the United States. Laurie A. Shepard, supervised by Marianne Martin, ably translated the group of letters by Gino Severini in the Marinetti Archives at Yale University. For their help in seeing important Futurist material in Italy, I am most grateful to Dr. Mercedes Garberi, Director of the Civiche Raccolte d'Arte, Milan, and Dr. Carlo Bertelli, Director of the Pinacoteca di Brera, Milan. Special thanks for assistance are also due to Jean Chauvelin, Andrew Crispo, Mr. and Mrs. Leonard Hutton, and Signora Franca Mancini, whose efforts on behalf of the exhibition are greatly appreciated. For their very generous consent to share their knowledge of the art and artists of this period, I am also deeply grateful to Mrs. Herbert Bayer, Mme Marcel Duchamp, Mrs. Nikifora Iliopoulos, Signora Angela Maria Boneschi Mattioli, N. Richard Miller, Signora Laura Mattioli Rossi, and Beatrice Wood.

Colleagues in all the museums that have lent to the exhibition have been extremely helpful, and I would particularly like to thank Jay Belloli of the Detroit Institute of Arts, A. James Speyer of the Art Institute of Chicago, and Stephen Nash, formerly of the Albright-Knox Art Gallery, Buffalo, for their support of this project. It is difficult to acknowledge sufficiently the enthusiastic cooperation on the part of so many colleagues at the Museum of Modern Art, which has lent its Futurist treasures to the exhibition; the staffs of the Department of Painting and Sculpture and the Department of Drawings have been extraordinarily helpful, and special thanks must go to Cora Rosevear and Beatrice Kernan, who handled so many details. The friendly assistance of the Museum of Modern Art's Department of Rights and Reproductions and their Registrar's office was invaluable in the preparation of the catalogue and the complex transportation arrangements for the exhibition itself.

The realization of this project depended upon the enthusiastic efforts of many on this Museum's staff, and warm thanks are due to more colleagues than can be named here. Barbara Sevy and Carol Homan in the Library and Fernande E. Ross and Judith Brodie in the Registrar's office spent many extra hours of work on the exhibition. The Department of Publications was particularly patient and inventive under pressure: George H. Marcus, Jane Iandola Watkins, and Sherry Babbitt of the editorial staff, and Russell Rollins, designer, and his assistant, Andrea Legg. Finally, the exhibition and catalogue could not have been realized without the patience, good humor, and energetic efforts of the staff in this Museum's Department of Twentieth-Century Art: Ann Hitchins and Sylvia Hamerman, volunteers, Margaret Kline, departmental assistant, and Anne Schuster, special assistant for this project.

A.d'H.

MANIFESTE

DU

FUTURISME

(Publié par le « Figaro » le 20 Février 1909)

Nous avions veillé toute la nuit, mes amis et moi, sous des lampes de mosquée dont les coupoles de cuivre aussi ajourées que notre âme avaient pourtant des cœurs électriques. Et tout en piétinant notre native paresse sur d'opulents tapis persans, nous avions discuté aux frontières extrêmes de la logique et griffé le papier de démentes écritures.

Un immense orgueil gonflait nos poitrines, à nous sentir debout tous seuls, comme des phares ou comme des sentinelles avancées, face à l'armée des étoiles ennemies, qui campent dans leurs bivouacs célestes. Seuls avec les mécaniciens dans les infernales chaufferies des grands navires, seuls avec les noirs fantômes qui fourragent dans le ventre rouge des locomotives affolées, seuls avec les ivrognes battant des ailes contre les murs !

Et nous voilà brusquement distraits par le roulement des énormes tramways à double étage, qui passent sursautants, bariolés de lumières, tels les hameaux en fête que le Pô débordé ébranle tout à coup et déracine, pour les entraîner, sur les cascades et les remous d'un déluge, jusqu'à la mer.

Puis le silence s'aggrava. Comme nous écoutions la prière exténuée du vieux canal et crisser les os des palais moribonds dans leur barbe de verdure, soudain rugirent sous nos fenêtres les automobiles affamées.

— Allons, dis-je, mes amis ! Partons ! Enfin la Mythologie et l'Idéal mystique sont surpassés. Nous allons assister à la naissance du Centaure et nous verrons bientôt voler les premiers Anges ! — Il faudra ébranler les portes de la vie pour en essayer les gonds et les verrous !... Partons ! Voilà bien le premier soleil levant sur la terre !... Rien n'égale la splendeur de son épée rouge qui s'escrime pour la première fois, dans nos ténèbres millénaires.

Nous nous approchâmes des trois machines renâclantes pour flatter leur poitrail. Je m'allongeai sur la mienne comme un cadavre dans sa bière, mais je ressuscitai soudain sous le volant — couperet de guillotine — qui menaçait mon estomac.

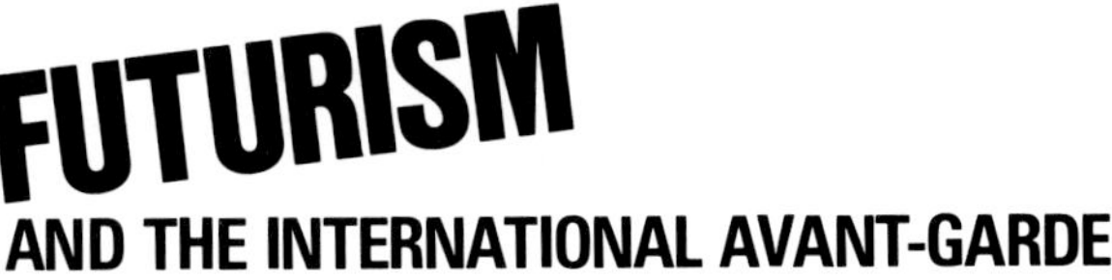

FUTURISM AND THE INTERNATIONAL AVANT-GARDE

ANNE d'HARNONCOURT

Thank you and bravo, poet!

Thanks for your sublime and sumptuous review *Poesia* . . . .

Bravo for the force with which you sing, for your enthusiasms, which are grandly lyric and which I admire intensely.

I have read your violent manifesto, shrieking and incendiary, which appeared in our French press and in which you glorify dangers, energy, bold audacity, revolt, and I agree with you completely, without restriction.

R. Delaunay [1909][1]

Sir,

You predict that in ten years you will be thrown in the wastebasket; in my opinion one could do so now!
Unleash the forces of the *unknown!*
Open the flood gates of the impossible!
Add to the fervor of primordial elements!
All this rigamarole is perfectly ridiculous and I beg you not to continue sending me your review. I fear the fisticuffs which you extol; I am seventy years old and I wish to die in peace.

C. Saint-Saëns [1909][2]

For the young French poet Delaunay, the founding Manifesto of Futurism, published in Paris on the front page of *Le Figaro* on February 20, 1909, was a vital clarion call; to the irritable sensibilities of the composer Saint-Saëns, it simply heralded cacophony. Both responses were typical of the uproar in which Filippo Tommaso Marinetti delighted (he claimed to have received 9,500 letters provoked by his manifesto) and which accompanied the presentation of so many of the accomplishments of the Italian painters, poets, and musicians with whose works he promoted his movement during the years from 1909 to 1915. Amid the intentional tumult of a Futurist "evening" in Turin (March 8, 1910), the opening of the extraordinary exhibition of Umberto Boccioni's sculpture in Paris (June 20, 1913), or a performance of "noise intoners" at the London Coliseum (June 15, 1914), it must have been difficult to discern the impact of the occasion upon the startled audience. It is an equally difficult matter to trace the complex interaction between the art and theories of the Italian Futurists and the artists of other countries whom they sought to impress, even to overwhelm, with their own work while eagerly absorbing what they saw around them.

The very word "Futurism" instantly acquired the distinction of being at once a specific term and the blowsiest of categories. On the one hand, the Futurists were a chosen band of avant-garde Italians who joined the poet F. T. Marinetti in his effort to destroy the dead weight of past culture and to launch an aggressive search for new forms of expression. But to a bewildered public and sensation-seeking press, "Futurism" rapidly came to mean any sort of modern manifestation. In choosing his catchword (Dynamism and Electricism were also considered),[3] Marinetti provided the world with a single, explosive epithet that summed up the creative energy and feverish optimism of a society shortly to be irrevocably altered by the devastation of a vast war.

The impact of Italian Futurism on the visual arts was from its inception a matter for hot debate. The English artist Wyndham Lewis voiced his own strict definition in November 1913: "Futurism, one of the alternative terms for modern painting, was patented in Milan. It means the Present, with the Past rigidly excluded, and flavoured strongly with H. G. Wells' dreams of the dance of monstrous and arrogant machinery, to the frenzied clapping of men's hands. But futurism will never mean anything else, in painting, than the art practised by five or six Italian painters grouped beneath Marinetti's influence."[4] Those five painters were Giacomo Balla, Umberto Boccioni, Carlo Carrà, Luigi Russolo (who was also a musician), and Gino Severini. The mysterious sixth in Lewis's summary was the Florentine critic Ardengo Soffici, who joined the others briefly between 1912 and 1914. Across the Channel one month later, Guillaume Apollinaire echoed Lewis rather peevishly in an article in *Les Soirées de Paris:* "From what I have read, the philosophers confuse all new painting with futurist painting. Now, in France, there is not a single futurist painter as defined by the manifestos published in Milan."[5] And, he added triumphantly, "from an artistic point of view, futurism bears witness to the worldwide influence of French painting, from impressionism to cubism." This pronouncement, however, followed by several months Apollinaire's proposal to Severini (roundly rejected by the patriotic Marinetti) that the term Futurism be adopted to describe "all of modern art."[6]

If anyone was aware of the intricacy of international relationships between artists and artistic movements during the years 1909 to 1915, it was Apollinaire. Son of a Polish mother and an Italian army officer, raised in Monte Carlo, fluent in Italian as well as French, intimate with innumerable painters and poets in prewar Paris, he extended his friendship and lively critical interest to the

Filippo Tommaso Marinetti
Founding Manifesto of Futurism, 1909
The Lydia and Harry Lewis Winston Collection
(Dr. and Mrs. Barnett Malbin, New York)

Futurists (and later to the Russian Rayonists), well aware that he courted the jealousy of his French confreres.

Lewis and Apollinaire were sophisticated, if hardly objective, observers of the international scene, and their own efforts had a dramatic effect on the history of avant-garde art, but they both acknowledged with mingled admiration and dismay the extraordinary powers of Marinetti. No other movement of modern art had such an impresario. Some were envious (the Russian painter David Burliuk wrote to the poet Benedikt Livshits in the fall of 1912: "Be our Marinetti!"[7]) and others were appalled, but Marinetti's brilliant promotional tactics gave the Futurists an instant international notoriety that kept their activities and their writings on the front pages in Paris, New York, Berlin, and Tokyo. A truly international figure himself, wealthy and well-informed, Marinetti was fond of stressing his exotic early years in the city of Alexandria. He studied literature in Paris and law in Milan, and most of his early poetry was written in French. Sarah Bernhardt had recited one of his prize-winning poems to an admiring French audience in 1898, but by all accounts he himself was to become one of the most dazzling and persuasive orators of this century. By 1902 the scale of his ambitions began to emerge in the epic poem *Conquest of the Stars,* and in 1905 he founded the international literary journal *Poesia* in Milan, which he sought to fill with contributions from the most celebrated writers in France and the most adventurous spirits in Italy. A devotee of the motor car and later an amateur pilot, he sounded a thoroughly modern note in a 1905 poem dedicated to the automobile: "Vehement god of a race of steel/Automobile drunk with space . . ."[8]

It has been pointed out that in 1906 and 1907 Marinetti was a frequent visitor to the Abbaye de Créteil, a community of artists and writers several miles outside Paris, which was founded by Henri-Martin Barzun, the painter Albert Gleizes, and the poet René Arcos, among others.[9] The Abbaye marked a transition in twentieth-century French thought from the pervasive Symbolism of the previous decades to a modern vision based on the new reality of industrial machinery, scientific advances, and vast cities. Perhaps its most significant publication was Jules Romains's extended poem of 1904–7, *La Vie Unanime,* which celebrated the exhilarating experience of communal urban life in phrases prophetic of the Futurists:

The city yearns to burst forth
Like fireworks, a great rebellious people of sparks. . . .
It desires to expand but not to dissolve,
To mingle space and wind with its houses,
To make the sky flow down its widened streets,
To remain one, and to become boundless. . . .[10]

It is vital to remember that the sources for many of Marinetti's ideas and images were common to the intellectual vanguard of Europe at the time. The poetry of Walt Whitman, the metaphysics of Henri Bergson, the philosophy of Friedrich Nietzsche, and the absurd theater of Alfred Jarry, to cite only a few examples, each had a bearing on the violent exuberance of his manifestos as well as upon the thought of many of his European colleagues. Similarly, the excitement created by scientific and technical discoveries—the X-ray, airplane, wireless telegraph—was clearly not an exclusively Futurist preoccupation.[11] (Apollinaire wrote a poem to "L'Avion" and Picasso jokingly referred to Braque as "Wilbur," after the celebrated aviator.) It was Marinetti's genius to seize upon the elements that most characterized the experience of modernity and to project them into a form that captured the attention of a larger public than had ever shown interest in the arts.

Aside from the scathing denunciation of the past and the praise of aggressive action (the fisticuffs that had alarmed Saint-Saëns), the founding manifesto often burst into poetry:

We affirm that the world's magnificence has been enriched by a new beauty: the beauty of speed. A racing car whose hood is adorned with great pipes, like serpents of explosive breath—a roaring car that seems to ride on grapeshot is more beautiful than the *Victory of Samothrace.*

We will sing of great crowds excited by work, by pleasure, and by riot; we will sing of the multicoloured, polyphonic tides of revolution in the modern capitals; we will sing of the vibrant nightly fervour of arsenals and shipyards blazing with violent electric moons; greedy railway stations that devour smoke-plumed serpents; factories hung on clouds by the crooked lines of their smoke; bridges that stride the rivers like giant gymnasts, flashing in the sun with a glitter of knives; adventurous steamers that sniff the horizon; deep-chested locomotives whose wheels paw the tracks like the hooves of enormous steel horses bridled by tubing; and the sleek flight of planes whose propellers chatter in the wind like banners and seem to cheer like an enthusiastic crowd.[12]

It seems clear why Marinetti attracted the attention of visual artists; this celebrated passage abounds with images for the painter and the sculptor, and he soon found friends eager to translate them into visual form.

Marinetti's mission was nothing less than to revivify the arts in his beloved Italy, that "land of the dead, a vast Pompeii, white with sepulchres,"[13] and to electrify the rest of the world with the brilliant innovations of Futurism. Although the founding manifesto spoke primarily of poets, it threatened to flood the museums as well as to burn down the libraries: "Oh, the joy of seeing the glorious old canvases bobbing adrift on those waters, discoloured and shredded!"[14] The Futurist painters were ready to present *their* first manifesto in February 1910, and by 1915 the publication of over twenty-six manifestos had extended the Futurist adventure into a multitude of media, including the least traditional, photography and cinema. Marinetti's insistence that the movement embrace all the arts and expand into the political arena as well was perhaps the most revolutionary and controversial aspect of Futurism. Intermingling of the arts was promoted: poets painted, painters wrote poetry and directed plays, and even Marinetti tried his hand at sculpture. Boccioni exulted in 1912: "There is neither painting, nor sculpture, nor music, nor poetry. The only truth is creation!"[15] Although close friendship and interaction between poets and painters were particularly characteristic of this period—Blaise Cendrars and the Delaunays, Ezra Pound and the Vorticists, Picasso and his succession of poet-confidants—perhaps only the extraordinary alliances between artists and writers in Russia at this time surpass those of the Italians in creative energy. Among Marinetti's most brilliant and prophetic conceptions was his celebration of "The Variety Theatre," which he saw as incorporating every form of human and mechanical invention in a hilarious interaction between actors and audience. In his manifesto of 1913 Marinetti transformed the music-hall stage into a vast metaphor for Futurist aspirations:

> The Variety Theatre, born as we are from electricity, is lucky in having no tradition, no masters, no dogma, and it is fed by swift actuality.
>
> The Variety Theatre is absolutely practical, because it proposes to distract and amuse the public with comic effects, erotic stimulation, or imaginative astonishment.
>
> The authors, actors, and technicians of the Variety Theatre have only one reason for existing and triumphing: incessantly to invent new elements of astonishment.

After a breathless enumeration of music-hall delights (athletes, daredevils, magicians, mind readers, ballerinas, trained birds, "musical jugglers and eccentric Americans"), he concluded:

> Finally, the Variety Theatre offers to every country (like Italy) that has no great single capital city a brilliant résumé of Paris considered as the one magnetic centre of luxury and ultrarefined pleasure.[16]

Marinetti was determined to awaken Italy, but it was on the front page of the distinguished French newspaper *Le Figaro* that he published his founding manifesto. Despite his ardent patriotism, he saw that the battle had to be won or lost in Paris, the universally acknowledged center of the artistic and literary world. It is impossible to overestimate the attraction of Paris before World War I for artists and intellectuals of every nationality. Everything was exciting: the huge, annual salons mingling established and conventional art with the new, private galleries showing the experimental, a profusion of theaters and cabarets, cafés and dance halls, and above all the vibrant, stimulating life of the great metropolis. The beauty of the city itself was overwhelming—the graceful Seine and the broad boulevards, the Eiffel Tower and the great Ferris wheel, the myriad lights that magically transformed Paris nights. Boccioni was twenty-four, on his first extended visit to Paris in 1906, when he sent home a long, incoherent letter fairly sputtering with statistics:

> In all of Italy there is only one telegraph agency . . . in Paris there are 17! 100 matrimonial agencies which perform an average of 10,000 marriages per year.
> 3,000 architects!
> 12 nocturnal shelters which house 52,000 men! and 4,000 women!
> 1,500 practicing lawyers!!!
> 500 factories for footwear each of which makes 300 pairs of shoes per day!
> 180,000 resident foreigners! Not including me, who just arrived.
> 400 dentists! Good for me! [17]

Boccioni returned to Milan, but in November 1906 his friend Severini settled in Paris, which was to welcome an astonishing array of painters and sculptors during the next decade. Some came for brief forays, others established studios, but all absorbed new ideas and, perhaps most importantly, enjoyed an encouraging atmosphere. Alexandra Exter, Liubov Popova, Nadezhda Udaltzova, and Vladimir Tatlin came from Russia (Alexander Archipenko,

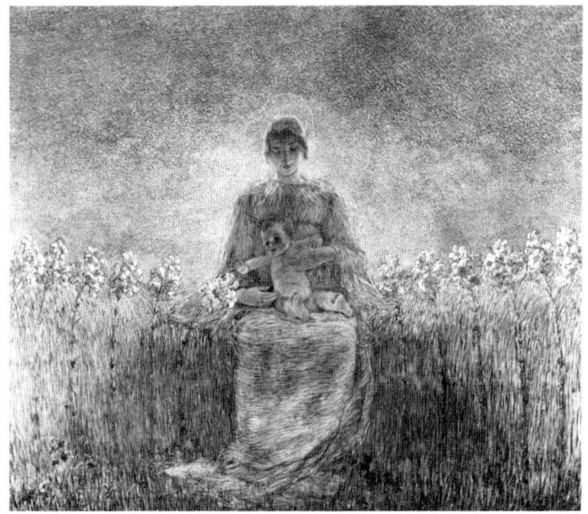

1

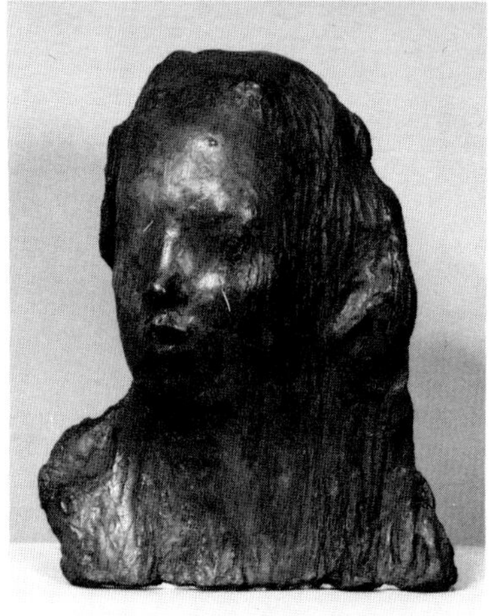

2

Marc Chagall, and Jacques Lipchitz formed part of a more permanent Russian colony); Paul Klee, August Macke, and Franz Marc, from Germany, and Piet Mondrian, from Holland. English visitors included Roger Fry as well as Wyndham Lewis, David Bomberg, and Christopher Nevinson; and, of course, there came a swarm of eager Americans: Max Weber, Joseph Stella, the Stieglitz group, and the Synchromists, all painfully conscious of the thousands of miles of ocean to be traversed between home and the studio of Henri Matisse or the legendary apartment of Gertrude Stein. It was by the standard of Paris that any new proposition in the visual arts would be judged.

The history of the Futurist painters between 1909 and 1915 is a perplexing and still far from perfectly known sequence of interactions between the Italians and their colleagues. Given Marinetti's penchant for the manifesto as a means of spreading the word as rapidly and widely as possible and his desire to be first to announce any important innovation, Futurist theories often preceded the actual creation of the works which they describe. Lewis's crisp description of Futurism as the "art practised by five or six Italian painters" must be amplified to incorporate the distinctly individual approaches taken by each artist (differences of which Lewis was well aware). If Futurism had a coherence imposed by Marinetti's relentless pressure to present a united front, there are nevertheless few artistic movements which have produced such visually diverse works as Severini's *Bal Tabarin* (no. 66), Boccioni's *Matter (Materia)* (see fig. 23), and Balla's *Girl Running on a Balcony* (see fig. 18), all from mid-1912. While the paintings of Picasso and Braque were virtually indistinguishable during the heroic period of analytical Cubism in late 1911 (when these artists described themselves "rather like being roped mountaineers"[18]) and the Rayonist paintings and drawings of Mikhail Larionov and Natalia Gontcharova in 1912 and 1913 come very close in appearance as well as intention, the Futurists shared no common style after their early works and grew steadily more, rather than less, divergent.

The Futurist painters were not ready to present their visual case in Paris until their large exhibition at the Bernheim-Jeune gallery in February 1912. However, they issued two manifestos on painting which preceded the exhibition by almost two years.

The first Manifesto of Futurist Painters, dated February 11, 1910, was aimed clearly at an Italian audience and apparently was not published in France. This manifesto announced little but scorn for the art of the past and support for "all attempts at originality, however daring, however violent." The admiration for the Divisionist painters Giovanni Segantini and Gaetano Previati (fig. 1) expressed in this pronouncement underlines the fact that the finest achievements of that group of late nineteenth-century Italian artists, who combined separate strokes of pure color with expressionist style and symbolic or pastoral subject matter, served as the major visual source of inspiration for the Futurists within Italy. The remarkable sculpture of Medardo Rosso (fig. 2), fusing the human form with light and atmosphere, was also singled out as worthy of notice amidst the general "hotchpotch of encrusted rubbish" that constituted conventional art.[19]

The early development of each of the Futurist painters[20] reflected the inchoate and fragmentary state of the visual arts in Italy at the beginning of the century. By 1910 Balla was the only established figure among the Futurists. The respected teacher of Boccioni and Severini during their years in Rome, he was familiar with Impressionism from a trip to Paris in 1900 and practiced a methodical Divisionist style applied to idiosyncratic subjects. His ominous lamp in the painting *Work* of 1902 (no. 1) and the vertiginous viewpoint of *Stairway of Farewells* of c. 1908 (no. 3) are uncanny premonitions of Futurist themes. Balla's isolation in Rome, his age, and his rigorous personality set him apart even within such a disparate group; ironically, he was the only one of the five Futurist painters to carry the movement with vigor into the postwar decades. Severini was also a special case; his exposure to the French capital after 1906 sharply distinguished his elegant and geometric Neo-Impressionism from the undulating lines and hot Divisionist colors that characterized several early works of Boccioni, Carrà, and Russolo, who continued to live in Milan. Severini's expressed admiration for the French Impressionists (see fig. 3) and his passion for the carefully ordered art of Georges Seurat (fig. 4) clearly affected his work and also played a part in Boccioni's theories, but exerted little influence on the latter's paintings or on those of Carrà and Russolo.

The Technical Manifesto of Futurist Painting was published in Paris on May 18, 1910 (accompanied by mocking caricatures), before any of the five who signed it had completed a Futurist picture. Unlike the painters' first statement, it included a wealth of striking concepts and images, which surely proved inspiring to others as well as

fig. 1 Gaetano Previati (Italian, 1852–1920)
The Madonna of the Lilies, 1893–94
Oil on canvas, 71½ x 86¾" (182 x 220 cm)
Civica Galleria d'Arte Moderna, Milan

fig. 2 Medardo Rosso (Italian, 1858–1928)
Ecce Puer, 1906–7
Wax over plaster, 15⅞ x 9½ x 6¾"
(40.32 x 24.1 x 17.1 cm)
Philadelphia Museum of Art. Purchased:
Membership Fund

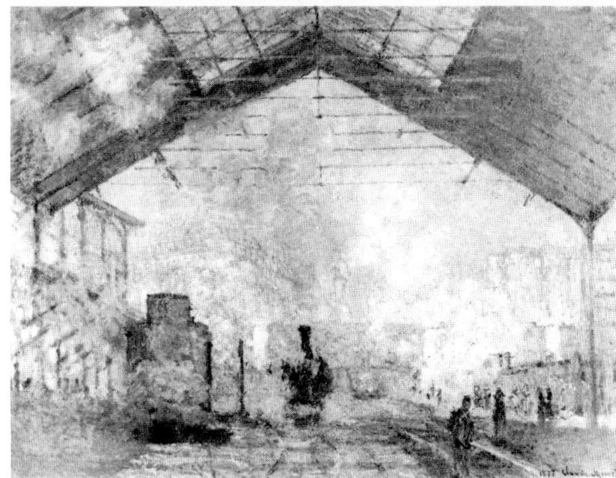

3

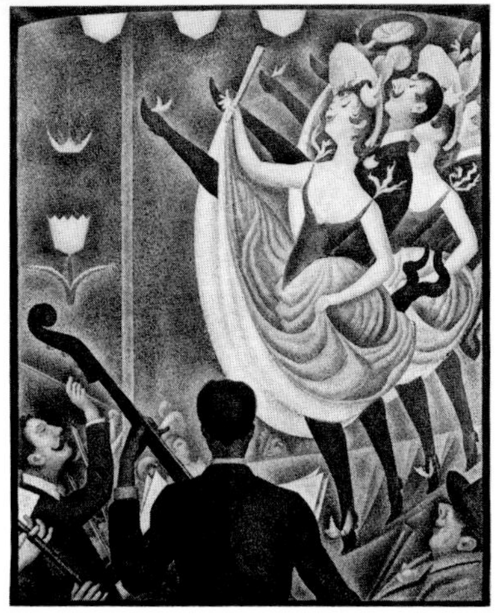

4

to the budding Futurists. The manifesto declared, in phrases destined to reverberate from Moscow to New York, that the chief aim of painting was to capture "the dynamic sensation" of life, and to "put the spectator in the centre of the picture." Citing recent advances of science as support, the Technical Manifesto presented a series of the now famous formulas:

> Indeed, all things move, all things run, all things are rapidly changing. A profile is never motionless before our eyes, but it constantly appears and disappears. On account of the persistency of an image upon the retina, moving objects constantly multiply themselves; their form changes like rapid vibrations, in their mad career. Thus a running horse has not four legs, but twenty, and their movements are triangular.
>
> To paint a human figure you must not paint it; you must render the whole of its surrounding atmosphere.
>
> Space no longer exists: the street pavement, soaked by rain beneath the glare of electric lamps, becomes immensely deep and gapes to the very centre of the earth. Thousands of miles divide us from the sun; yet the house in front of us fits into the solar disk.
>
> How often have we not seen upon the cheek of the person with whom we are talking the horse which passes at the end of the street.
>
> Our bodies penetrate the sofas upon which we sit, and the sofas penetrate our bodies. The motor bus rushes into the houses which it passes, and in their turn the houses throw themselves upon the motor bus and are blended with it.
>
> Our renovated consciousness does not permit us to look upon man as the centre of universal life. The suffering of a man is of the same interest to us as the suffering of an electric lamp, which, with spasmodic starts, shrieks out the most heartrending expressions of colour.
>
> Your eyes, accustomed to semi-darkness, will soon open to more radiant visions of light.[21]

Adding a few strong exhortations as to the importance of Divisionism and the "innate" use of complementary colors (which they compared to "free metre in poetry or polyphony in music"), the Futurist painters concluded with a parting shot aimed at banning the nude as a subject in painting for the next ten years, not as immoral but (far worse) as monotonous.

In the twenty months that elapsed between the publication of the Technical Manifesto and the opening of the Futurists' exhibition in the large and prestigious Bernheim-Jeune gallery in Paris on February 5, 1912, the Italians worked feverishly to realize their new visions. Only a handful of paintings included in that exhibition could be said to reveal a common style: Carrà's *Leaving the Theater*, Russolo's *Hair of Tina* and *Memories of a Night* (no. 62), and Boccioni's *Modern Idol*.[22] These were preoccupied with a sensuous rendering of night life and femininity that characterizes the most romantic, and least deliberately "modern," aspect of Futurism, but none suggests exposure to Parisian innovations, an exposure Severini insisted upon when he saw his friends' work in Milan in the summer of 1911. Beginning in October of that year, when Boccioni, Carrà, and possibly Russolo[23] visited Paris with Severini as a guide, the Futurists became part of the Paris art world. Apollinaire reported their presence in a chatty article[24] and began to keep close track of their activities, no doubt assisted by a steady barrage of letters and manifestos from Marinetti. Severini took his friends to the studios of Braque and Picasso, as well as to those of painters who were exhibiting the most radical work in the 1911 Salon d'Automne. There the Milanese artists had the opportunity to study Jean Metzinger's *Tea Time* (Philadelphia Museum of Art), Albert Gleizes's *Portrait of Jacques Nayral* (Tate Gallery, London), Fernand Léger's huge *Essay for Three Portraits* (Milwaukee Art Museum), and Marcel Duchamp's *Portrait* (no. 91), whose close relationship to their own declared interests the Futurists may not have detected. There is no evidence that they met any of the Duchamp brothers or that they went to see Robert Delaunay, of whose Eiffel Tower paintings Boccioni was already aware.[25] After his return to Milan in fall 1911, Boccioni sent pompous but wistful greetings to Picasso through Apollinaire, and for the next few years vacillated between a desperate longing to live in Paris and a proud affection for the "loneliness" of his Milan studio.[26]

It is perhaps not surprising that the three Futurists most responsive to Parisian developments should focus on Picasso, who in turn seems to have regarded them with a certain affection. At home in his adopted city, Severini divided his loyalty among a number of painters and poets, but for Boccioni and Carrà there was no doubt that Picasso was the genius with whom they must contend. It seems likely that the Italians, particularly Boccioni, with his clumsy French and passionate desire to revolutionize first painting and then sculpture, would have appealed to Picasso's interest in outsiders. Picasso took them to see Gertrude

fig. 3 Claude Monet (French, 1840–1926)
La Gare Saint-Lazare, 1877
Oil on canvas, 29¾ x 40⅞" (75.5 x 104 cm)
Musée du Louvre, Galerie du Jeu de Paume, Paris

fig. 4 Georges Seurat (French, 1859–1891)
Le Chahut, 1889–90
Oil on canvas, 66½ x 54¾" (169 x 139 cm)
Rijksmuseum Kröller-Müller, Otterloo, Holland

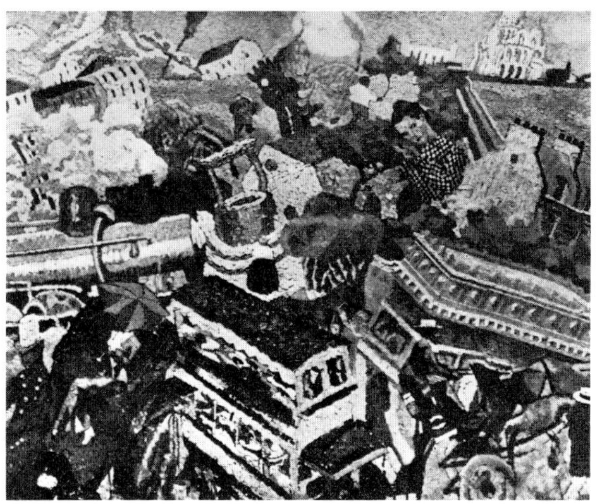

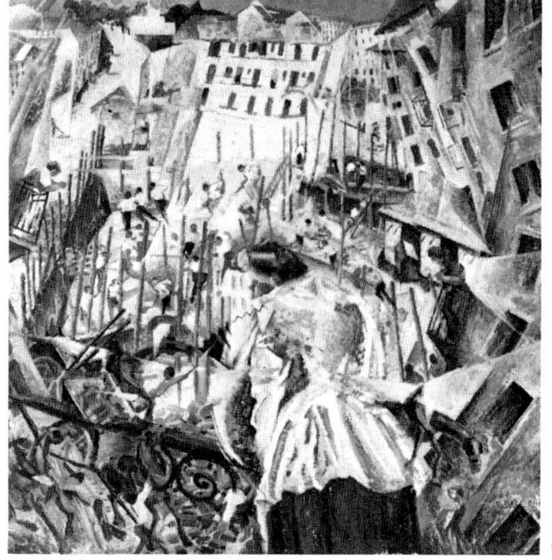

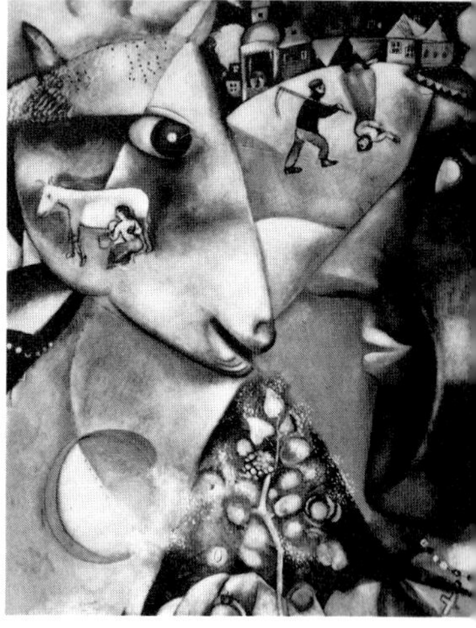

Stein (who found them boring), and later he used the bold cover of the Futurist journal *Lacerba* in a handsome collage of 1914 (The Peggy Guggenheim Collection, Venice). Never completely part of the French art world and far more closely allied with poets than with theoretically minded artists like Gleizes or Metzinger, Picasso probably found the exaggerated vehemence of Boccioni a welcome relief after sober French logic.

After a few months of frantic work in Italy, the Futurists returned to Paris in February 1912 and presented at the Bernheim-Jeune gallery not only a remarkable group of paintings but also a catalogue complete with illustrations, their Technical Manifesto, and a new theoretical preface entitled "The Exhibitors to the Public." Coupled with Marinetti's volume of texts and manifestos entitled *Le Futurisme* published in Paris in the fall of 1911, the catalogue and exhibition constituted an unusually organized aesthetic venture at a moment when theoretical writings were only beginning to accumulate around the Cubist painters. The Futurist paintings themselves were a vital, if uneven, mixture of Italian ideas and methods amended by several of the latest French innovations. Many of the pictures shown had been in process for several years, some had been included in the Free Exhibition of Art in Milan in May 1911, and very few could be said to look Cubist, with the possible exception of the most recent work by Carrà. Boccioni had made prodigious strides since the Paris studio tour, however; the schematic views of wineglasses in *The Laugh* (no. 29) and the bold numerals floating in the center of *The Farewells* (no. 31) testify to his ability to absorb what he wanted from Metzinger's and Picasso's newest work.

Boccioni's role as an independent theorist had already been established in a lecture given on May 29, 1911, in Rome,[27] paraphrased in length in the preface of the catalogue of the 1912 Futurist exhibition. Accompanied by a certain amount of bombast (deplored by the peacemaker Severini) and with a stiff bow to the Cubists, the preface contrasts the Futurists' search for a "style of motion" and an "emotive ambience" with the French persistence in painting objects as "motionless, frozen." The Impressionists are introduced as worthy of being surpassed rather than opposed, perhaps due to the influence of Severini and his admiration for paintings such as Claude Monet's *Gare Saint-Lazare* (fig. 3), which addresses a modern subject and fuses object and environment, albeit with Impressionist "atmosphere" rather than with Futurist interpenetrating planes. In the preface Boccioni stressed the individual and intuitive nature of art and propounded his celebrated demand for "the simultaneousness of states of mind in the work of art." Rephrased, this becomes a new Bergsonian law: "The picture must be the synthesis of *what one remembers* and of *what one sees*." Added to the previous insistence upon Divisionist strokes of complementary colors is a newly phrased call for "force-lines," derived from the inner nature of the object and its dynamic interaction with its environment. Abstraction is adumbrated, but the subject remains all important: "We declare . . . that there can be no modern painting without the starting point of an absolutely modern sensation, and none can contradict us when we state that *painting* and *sensation* are two inseparable words."[28]

Supported by this stimulating, if inconsistent, theoretical framework, the Futurists' Paris exhibition offered a wild mixture of subjects and personal styles. Since widespread, international publicity accompanied its opening, and many paintings were reproduced on front pages or in color newspaper supplements around the world, this particular group of pictures came to stand for the Futurist achievement. This was exaggerated by the extended tour which Marinetti arranged for the show, producing the odd result that while the public of Munich or Budapest exclaimed over early or tentative works in 1912, the Futurists themselves by that time had gone on to produce more sophisticated and mature paintings.

Among the pictures shown in the Bernheim-Jeune gallery in 1912 were four very large canvases in which each artist addressed major Futurist themes of insurrection, urban dynamism, or night life: Russolo's *Revolt* (Gemeentemuseum, The Hague), Carrà's *Funeral of the Anarchist Galli* (no. 56), Boccioni's *The City Rises* (fig. 8), and Severini's *Pan-Pan Dance at the Monico* (fig. 26). Although these were spectacular efforts, and therefore may have had the widest impact, several of the smaller pictures struggled to solve highly original pictorial problems. Russolo's *Memories of a Night* (no. 62) is a literal translation of several images in the Technical Manifesto, expressed awkwardly but compellingly. It is unfortunate that Severini's *Travel Memories* (fig. 5) has not survived, since its improbable juxtaposition of geographical landmarks (the Arc de Triomphe, the Eiffel Tower, and a village well from his home in Cortona) with a tram and a locomotive was perhaps the first bold, if clumsy, attempt to summarize the kaleidoscopic experience of modern travel. Balla did not

fig. 5 Gino Severini (Italian, 1883–1966)
Travel Memories, 1911
Oil on canvas, dimensions unknown
Lost

fig. 6 Umberto Boccioni (Italian, 1882–1916)
The Street Enters the House, 1911–12
Oil on canvas, 39½ x 39½" (100.3 x 100.3 cm)
Kunstmuseum Hannover mit Sammlung Sprengel, Hanover

fig. 7 Marc Chagall (French, born Russia, 1887)
I and the Village, 1911
Oil on canvas, 75⅝ x 59⅝" (192.1 x 151.4 cm)
The Museum of Modern Art, New York. Mrs. Simon Guggenheim Fund

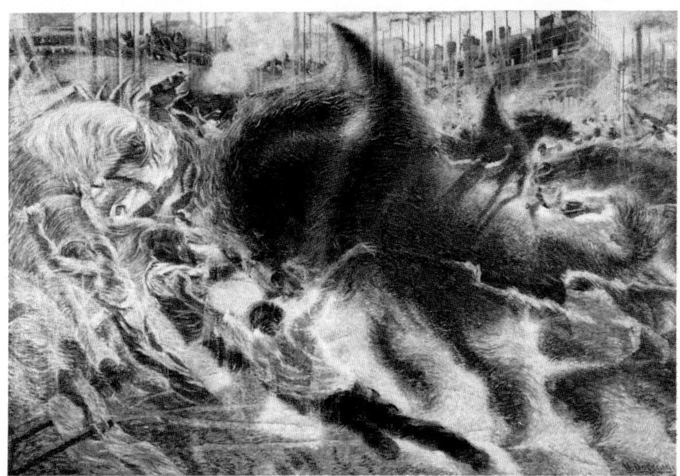

send a picture to Paris in 1912, although his *Street Light* (no. 6) was listed in the catalogue—nor apparently did he exhibit with the group until early 1913 in Rome. In light of the frequent contemporary criticism of the Futurists as "cinematographic," an adjective that applied much more appropriately to Balla's work of 1912 than to that of his colleagues, it is startling to realize that Balla's contribution to Futurist iconography probably went unperceived internationally until May 1913, when he participated in a group exhibition in Rotterdam.

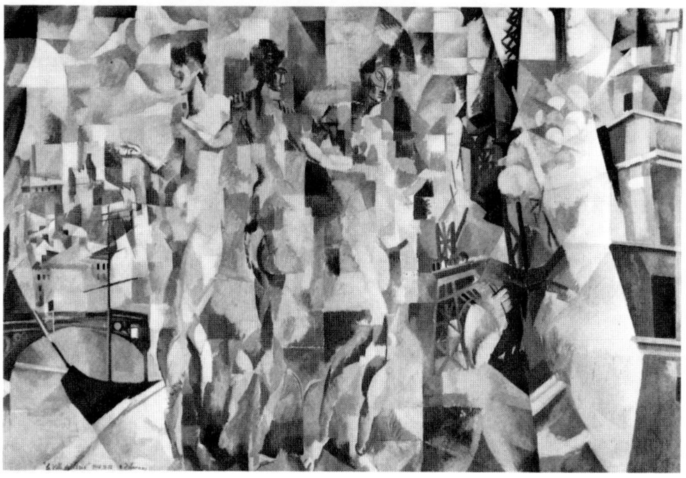

At the moment when the 1912 Futurist exhibition opened in Paris, the French avant-garde painters and sculptors could by no means be distinguished as constituting unified groups, nor could their differences be clearly defined. It seems probable, in fact, that the noisy arrival of the Futurists in their midst helped to bring their ideas into sharper focus. By February 1912 Picasso and Braque had advanced their investigation of form to its most hermetic phase, in which only little, coded references to specific subjects (still-life arrangements or human figures) permitted the interpretation of their apparently abstract scaffolding of lines and luminous planes (see Picasso's *Man with a Violin*, no. 111). The word "Cubism" itself had recently come into wide use, and a number of artists preoccupied with epic themes as well as new formal means (Gleizes, Metzinger, Delaunay, and, briefly, Léger, among others) were preparing for a major presentation in the Salon des Indépendants to open in March 1912. In the Paris suburb of Puteaux, the master printmaker Jacques Villon was beginning to take a more profound interest in painting and Raymond Duchamp-Villon was pondering the relationship of sculpture to modern architecture, while their brother Marcel Duchamp had already begun to explore his own interest in the representation of motion and "states of mind." It continues to be extremely difficult to determine to what extent any of these artists were affected by the Futurists' texts (which they scarcely could have avoided reading) or by the sight of Futurist paintings in the Bernheim-Jeune gallery, but it has been suggested that the large exhibition called the Salon de "La Section d'Or," held in Paris in October 1912, was at least in part organized in response to the Futurist challenge.[29] The exhibition title, invented by Jacques Villon and deriving from a classical formula for harmonious proportions, was a clear reference to the French artists' continuing preoccupation with artistic tradition—directly opposed to the Italians' violent rejection of "passatist" cultural values. Yet the "Section d'Or" exhibition included a number of paintings such as Duchamp's *King and Queen Surrounded by Swift Nudes* (no. 93) and Villon's *Young Girl* and *Puteaux: Smoke and Trees in Bloom* (nos. 112, 113) that displayed striking equivalents to Futurist notions of form disintegrated by speed and light as well as the intermingling of a figure with its environment. Between the fall of 1911 and the fall of 1912, the paintings of a number of artists in Cubist circles revealed a gradual shift away from tightly organized, rigid structure toward a more fluid and rhythmic composition in which forms appeared to vibrate or commingle. This shift was due at least in part to the gradual absorption of Futurist ideas or of notions latent in French thought, which were aroused by the Futurist invasion.

The generalized concepts of "universal dynamism" and "simultaneity" emphasized in the Futurists' 1912 Paris exhibition catalogue were familiar to the Parisian avant-garde, in part surely because of exposure to previous Futurist writings. Each artist meant something different when he described a picture as "simultaneous." Metzinger had used the term in October 1910 to describe Picasso's multiple views of a single object;[30] Delaunay developed his own fiercely defended sense of the word as referring strictly to simultaneous contrasts of color that render the movement of light. The Futurists themselves provided a multitude of pictorial interpretations of simultaneity, from the fusion of exterior and interior space in Boccioni's *The Street Enters the House* (fig. 6), to the juxtaposed mental images in Russolo's *Memories of a Night* (no. 62), to the mingling of landmarks widely separated in space in Severini's *Travel Memories*. The complexity of possible cross-references is obvious from just one example: Does Marc Chagall's celebrated vision of 1911, *I and the Village* (fig. 7), owe a debt to the Futurists' striking phrase of 1910: "How often have we not seen upon the cheek of the person with whom we are talking the horse which passes at the end of the street"? Or is the Russian painter's whimsical variation on Russolo's interpretation of the same passage in *Memories of a Night* simply coincidence?

Whatever their attitudes toward the brash young Italians, there were probably few avant-garde artists in Paris who did not visit the 1912 Bernheim-Jeune exhibition. Apollinaire reported that Picasso was amused by Boccioni's *The Laugh* ("C'est plutôt le Pêle-Mêle.")[31] and André Salmon mocked the Futurists' aim to put the spectator in the center of the picture: "They were overwhelmed before Russolo's *Memories of a Night*; they

fig. 8 Umberto Boccioni (Italian, 1882–1916)
The City Rises, 1910
Oil on canvas, 78½ x 118½" (199.4 x 301 cm)
The Museum of Modern Art, New York. Mrs. Simon Guggenheim Fund

fig. 9 Robert Delaunay (French, 1885–1941)
The City of Paris, 1912
Oil on canvas, 105⅛ x 159⅞" (267 x 406 cm)
Musée National d'Art Moderne, Centre Georges Pompidou, Paris

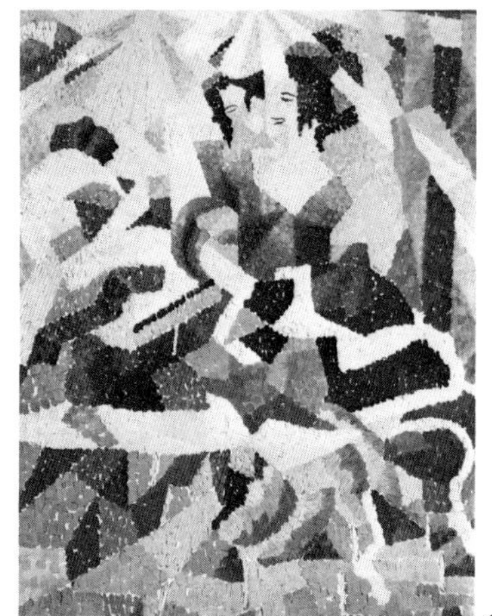

10

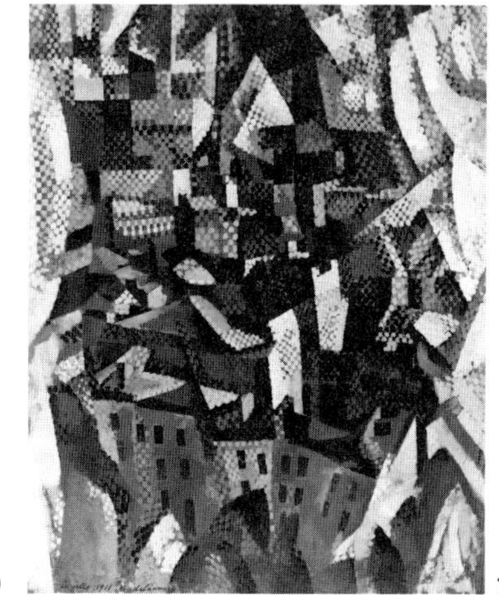

11

stamped their feet with rage in front of the *Funeral of the Anarchist Galli* by Carrà; they shrieked in front of *Pan-Pan Dance at the Monico* by Severini."[32] But the impact of the Futurists' ideas and their audacity in trying to paint them was profound; the reverberations carried far beyond France. The contemporary subject matter—cities under construction, riots, train and tram journeys, dance halls blazing with electric lights—predominating in their Paris exhibition contributed much to its force. No other group of painters had addressed themselves to painting the newest additions to their environment, and surprisingly few followed their lead. Chief among the Futurists' detractors was Robert Delaunay, whose name was frequently linked with theirs, to his intense irritation. But his wife, Sonia Delaunay, was fascinated by the phenomenon of crowds and the new brilliance of electricity, while Robert Delaunay himself incorporated airplanes into his cosmic visions. On the other hand, Léger, who proved among the most sympathetic of the Parisian artists to Futurists aims, resisted tackling their favorite themes, noting that "locomotives and other modern engines . . . are difficult to pose in one's studio."[33] But he agreed that the experience of rapid travel fundamentally altered ways of seeing, and therefore ways of painting: "If pictorial expression has changed, it is because modern life has necessitated it. . . . When one crosses a landscape by automobile or express train, it becomes fragmented; it loses in descriptive value but gains in synthetic value. . . . A modern man registers a hundred times more sensory impressions than an eighteenth-century artist; so much so that our language, for example, is full of diminutives and abbreviations. The compression of the modern picture, its variety, its breaking up of forms, are the result of all this."[34]

Duchamp took a more convoluted approach. A car trip through the Jura mountains with Apollinaire and Francis Picabia in October 1912 appears to have had a profound effect upon his thinking, inspiring his first extended preparatory note for his major project *The Large Glass*, but the automobile makes only one literal appearance in his work, as a mysterious shape gliding between two human figures (see no. 90). Picabia shared Marinetti's passion for fast cars and even spoke about painting his favorite subject in terms clearly borrowed from Futurist writing: "From my pictures of an automobile race you will be able to achieve the same suggestions of wild desire for speed, the excitement of that hundred mile an hour rapidity, that the driver himself feels. I can throw colors, the idea of movement on a canvas that will make you feel and appreciate that."[35] However, both Picabia and Duchamp used the machine ultimately as a complex metaphor for human behavior, rather than exploring its dynamic or pictorial qualities further.

Not all the Futurist painters, of course, took up every visual idea offered by Marinetti or promoted in their own manifestos. As has often been remarked, Boccioni clearly felt more at ease conveying the "dynamic sensation" of a running horse or a cyclist rather than the trajectory of a speeding car, which so fascinated Balla and which inspired one of Russolo's most powerful paintings (see no. 63). Natalia Gontcharova was one of the few artists to concentrate on the subject of the machine, painting both its effect on human experience and the fascinating new array of forms it provided. She seems to have pursued her interest with method, according to a reviewer of her Moscow exhibition in 1913: "What meticulous effort has she not expended to study machines, to execute purely technical sketches (also shown in the exhibition) before painting her *Steam Machine*, the *Dynamo* or the *Loom + Woman (sic)*. It is true that there is art even in this chaos of wheels, axles, shafts and *étonnoirs*, but does one need this lesson of a factory?"[36] Gontcharova's "technical sketches" do not seem to have survived but together with Balla's precise studies of cars in motion and the ironic machine diagrams by Picabia and Duchamp, they constituted a rare group of early twentieth-century works applying a mechanical style of rendering to a machine subject.

Like most of her Russian colleagues, Gontcharova would have learned about Futurism only second hand and in translation. Whereas, in Paris the Futurists' paintings and writings directly confronted artists whom the Italians most admired, all anti-Cubist bombast notwithstanding. The situation was quite different in England, Russia, or Germany, where Futurism arrived along with other creative innovations emanating from Paris. Surprisingly, the English public was exposed to stronger doses of Futurist art than any other country except Italy, and had proportionately less opportunity to see Cubist painting. Marinetti's lectures and recitations had considerable success in London and he managed to publish a manifesto entitled "Vital English Art" in June 1914, which infuriated many English artists who had admired Futurism up to that point.[37] On the other hand, painters in Moscow and Saint Petersburg never saw an original Futurist picture in all the large and varied exhibitions of modern art held in Russia between 1910 and 1915.

fig. 10 Gino Severini (Italian, 1883-1966)
The Milliner, 1910-11
Oil on canvas, 25⅜ x 18⅞" (64.5 x 48 cm)
Mr. and Mrs. Joseph Slifka, New York

fig. 11 Robert Delaunay (French, 1885-1941)
The City, 1911
Oil on canvas, 57⅛ x 44½" (145.1 x 113 cm)
The Solomon R. Guggenheim Museum, New York

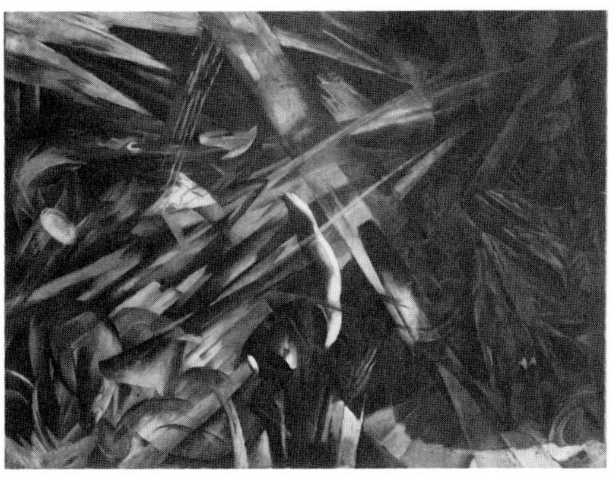

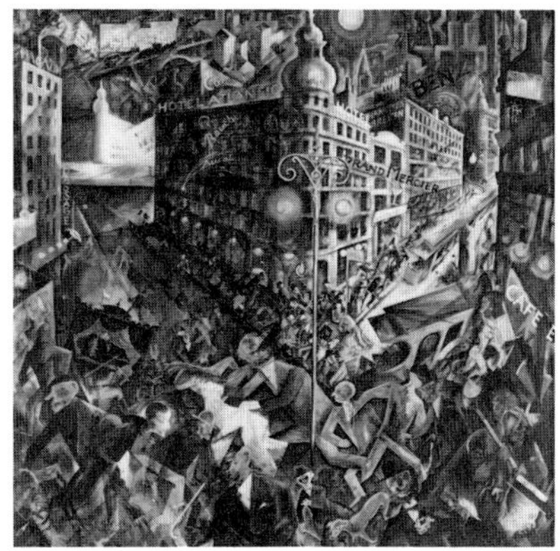

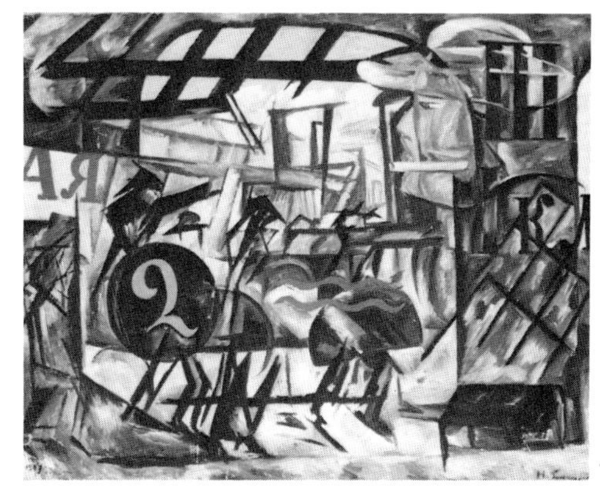

But David Burliuk's aggressive manifesto "A Slap in the Face of Public Taste," published in January 1913, as well as "Rayonists and Futurists: A Manifesto" by Larionov and Gontcharova, which appeared the following July, gave ample evidence that the Russian avant-garde was well-informed but independent.[38] In Germany, Marinetti found a fellow promoter in Herwarth Walden, who not only snapped up the Futurist exhibition for his second offering in the new Der Sturm gallery in Berlin but also sent it on tour, arranged for the sale of many of the paintings, and published the most important manifestos and texts in translation during 1912 and 1913. German artists had such a rich diet of exhibitions and such relatively easy access to Paris between 1910 and 1914 that the impact of Futurism seems to have been widespread although diluted by other influences.

The two and a half years between the Futurists' Paris exhibition and the outbreak of war in August 1914 was one of the most fecund periods in the history of art. The Futurists themselves achieved masterpieces of painting and sculpture far more sophisticated, if not more ambitious, than the works they had shown in February 1912. Braque and Picasso invented collage and *papier collé*, and began to reintroduce vivid color into their brilliantly simplified compositions. In Munich, Wassily Kandinsky painted his unprecedented series of large, abstracted *Compositions*, and the Czech artist Frantisek Kupka exhibited a very large, fully abstract painting in the Paris Salon d'Automne of 1912. Kasimir Malevich hit upon the conception of the "black square" as part of his revolutionary stage design for the opera *Victory over the Sun*, produced in Moscow in December 1913, although he did not fully recognize its importance to his art until 1915. In the privacy of his studio and in notes jotted at café tables, Duchamp began to plot the strategy that would lead him out of "art" altogether and into the arcane realm of *The Large Glass*.

New movements were born in profusion, several in what appear to be deliberate attempts to supercede Futurism. Apollinaire invented the term "Orphic Cubism" during a lecture in November 1912, and described as Orphist not only the lyric paintings of Delaunay, but also the ebullient abstractions of Picabia, the highly individual Cubism of Léger, and the last idiosyncratic paintings of Duchamp. The Synchromist movement consisted of two American painters, Morgan Russell and Stanton MacDonald-Wright, determined to surpass the Cubists, Futurists, and Delaunay, and their movement was announced in June of 1913 with an exhibition of their work at the Neue Kunstsalon in Munich. Synchromism also arrived in Paris and was presented at the Bernheim-Jeune gallery in October. Rayonism did not have a Paris debut until June of 1914, but its exponents, Gontcharova and Larionov, began to exhibit paintings and drawings in their new style in the winter of 1912–13. Larionov issued a text on Rayonist painting in April 1913[39] expressing their desire to depict the sum of the intersecting rays emanating from objects: a kind of suprasensory vision derived in part from Futurist dynamism but more abstract in its results (see no. 121). The last major movement that clearly sprang from a reaction to Futurism was Wyndham Lewis's Vorticism, announced in London in the first issue of his magazine *Blast* (July 1914) but drastically curtailed by the war, which Marinetti had hailed so optimistically as "the world's only hygiene."

The same brief period saw the publication of an extraordinary number of important theoretical texts. Kandinsky's *Concerning the Spiritual in Art* was published after some delay in January 1912, followed by the *Blaue Reiter Almanach* in May. Gleizes's and Metzinger's treatise *Du Cubisme* appeared in December, several months before Apollinaire's *Les Peintres Cubistes* in the spring of 1913, while Boccioni struggled over his book *Pittura Scultura Futuriste* during virtually the whole of that year, coming to grips with several of Kandinsky's ideas as well as describing his own case against the Cubists. At the same time the flood of information on recent developments in the visual arts increased steadily. Not only were paintings illustrated and described in widely read journals and newspapers but postcards and photographs were available through galleries and publishers. Perhaps most crucial, and most difficult to document, were the direct contacts between artists. Letters flew back and forth between the Futurists testifying to their eagerness for contact with each other and their sensitivity to new developments within the Paris art world. Paris, the great meeting place, was itself increasingly made up of groups divided along national, geographical, or aesthetic lines. Leo Stein remarked in a letter dated October 11, 1913: "Every one has a program and none have any critical sense—never saw so many little cliques. Russell and Wright find virtue in each other's work and in none other. Picasso and Braque are a world apart, and the six Futurists form an independent system. Delaunay stands in lonely grandeur on a mountain top."[40] Alliances formed and reformed. Metzinger, who had been close to Delaunay in 1906 and shared his Neo-Impressionist interests, was an

fig. 12 Franz Marc (German, 1880–1916)
The Fate of Animals, 1913
Oil on canvas, 76¾ x 103¾" (195 x 263.5 cm)
Kunstmuseum Basel

fig. 13 George Grosz (German, 1893–1959)
The City, 1916–17
Oil on canvas, 39½ x 40¼" (100 x 102 cm)
Thyssen-Bornemisza Collection, Lugano

fig. 14 Natalia Gontcharova (Russian, 1881–1962)
Railway Station, 1912
Oil on canvas, 28⅜ x 36⅝" (72 x 93 cm)
Private collection

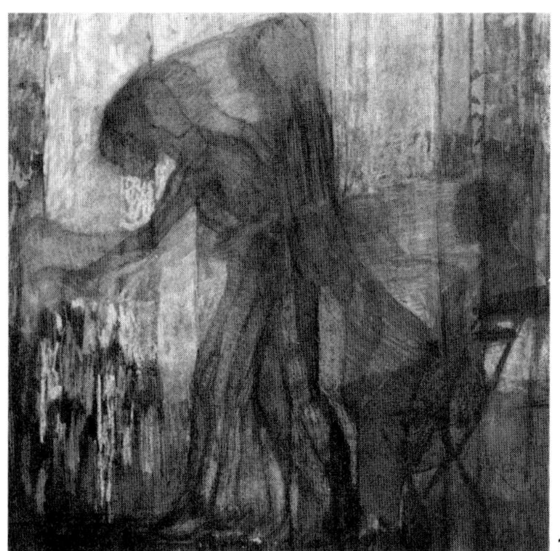

15

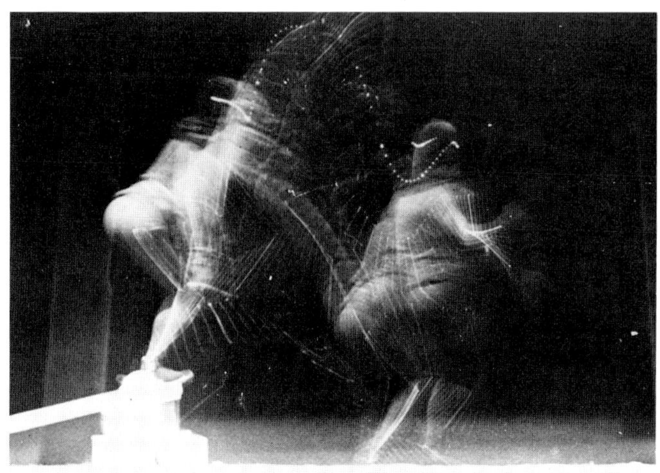

16

intense admirer of Picasso by 1910 and became linked with Gleizes in 1912. Delaunay, as Leo Stein noted, broke with all the other movements. (He officially resigned from Cubism in the summer of 1912.) Apollinaire flitted like a buoyant, exotic bird from studio to studio: arguing late into the night with Marinetti and Picasso, advising Severini on collage, living with the Delaunays, swept off in a fast car by Picabia, attending a performance of Raymond Roussel's *Impressions d'Afrique* with Picabia and Duchamp.

The Futurists were never to be as much an "independent system" as Marinetti might have wished. Severini felt deeply attached to his friends in the Paris art world, who included Braque, Raoul Dufy, and Picasso, and somewhat later, Metzinger, Léger, and Juan Gris. On the other hand, Balla scarcely moved from Rome between 1910 and 1915: his major excursions were two visits to Düsseldorf in 1912 to execute a decorative commission, with a pause en route to visit Boccioni in Milan. Carrà increasingly resented Boccioni's tendency to dominate the group, and grew closer to the Florentine circle which published the Futurist journal *Lacerba*. Boccioni's letters to Severini and Vico Baer attest to his hunger for information and his desire to be at the center of the action.

The Futurists' belligerent approach to their colleagues and their vaunting ambition clearly account for much of the negative reaction of other artists, particularly in Paris. Delaunay responded with fury and Jacques Villon (much later) with irritation, when their work was linked with Futurism, despite the fact that they clearly had interests in common with the Italian painters. Very few artists in Western Europe would have echoed the permissive attitude of Larionov and Gontcharova in their manifesto of July 1913: "We acknowledge all styles as suitable for the expression of our art, styles existing both yesterday and today—for example, cubism, futurism, orphism, and their synthesis, rayonism, for which the art of the past, like life, is an object of observation."[41] For the majority of the Parisian avant-garde, their "style" and their "art" were synonymous, and the two Russian painters' ability to paint a crude image drawn from folk tradition on one day and a highly abstracted Rayonist composition the next would have been incomprehensible. The fact that Futurism displayed no uniform style must have seemed proof of immaturity to its detractors. And yet during 1912 and 1913 the confluence of ideas and even techniques of painting within a broad spectrum of the European avant-garde makes more sense of the Rayonist manifesto statement than it may have appeared to have at the time. The Erster Deutscher Herbstsalon, which opened in Berlin on September 20, 1913, presented a remarkable cross section of advanced painting. Besides a large gallery devoted to the Delaunays, it included important recent works by each of the Futurists (joined by Balla at last), and major pictures by Léger, Picabia, Gleizes, Metzinger, Mondrian, Marc, Kandinsky, and Chagall, as well as contributions sent by Larionov, Gontcharova, and the Burliuk brothers from Russia. Apollinaire called the Berlin exhibition the "first salon of orphism"[42] and claimed victory for the French, but in retrospect it is clear that French, German, Italian, and Russian tendencies mingled there with influences and crosscurrents flowing in every direction.

REFLECTIONS ON THE PAINTINGS THEMSELVES

Of the paintings shown in the Futurists' 1912 Bernheim-Jeune exhibition, Boccioni's *The City Rises* (fig. 8) remains one of the most powerful and successful. As he struggled with the picture over the course of a year, he described it as "a great synthesis of work, of light and of movement."[43] Its origins in the Symbolist attitudes and Divisionist techniques of Previati and Segantini are evident, but the violence of action and the frenzied vibration of form disintegrated by light go beyond anything in their work. Nothing of the Neo-Impressionist painters would have prepared the French for this expression of the "dynamic sensation." Boccioni's painting makes a striking contrast to Delaunay's vast canvas on a similar theme, *The City of Paris* (fig. 9), exhibited at the Salon des Indépendants, which opened one month after the Futurist show closed. In the Italian's vision of a city under construction, "all things run, all things move": the great draft horse surges forward, men strain against it, shafts of light dissolve solid shapes into fluid, flaming strokes. But Delaunay's *City* is a balanced and classical composition, with three Cubist Graces poised between the river Seine and Montmartre on the left and the Eiffel Tower on the right. In his praise for Delaunay's achievement, Apollinaire saw a precedent in the "great Italian painters" of the Renaissance,[44] a reference which must have infuriated Boccioni.

Delaunay's modern allegory was a departure for the French painter, whose earlier Eiffel Tower and city window series clearly had been vehicles for intensive study of form and light. *The City of Paris* seems particularly reactionary in view of Apollinaire's article "On the Subject in Modern

fig. 15 Frantisek Kupka (Czechoslovakian, 1871–1957)
Woman Picking Flowers, I, 1909–10
Pastel on paper, 17¾ x 18¾" (45 x 48 cm)
Musée National d'Art Moderne, Centre Georges Pompidou, Paris

fig. 16 Etienne Jules Marey (French, 1830–1904)
Man Jumping off a Stool
Chronophotograph
Cinémathèque Française, Paris

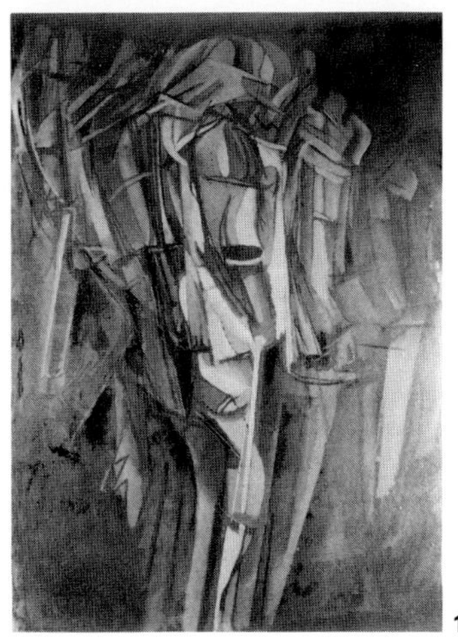

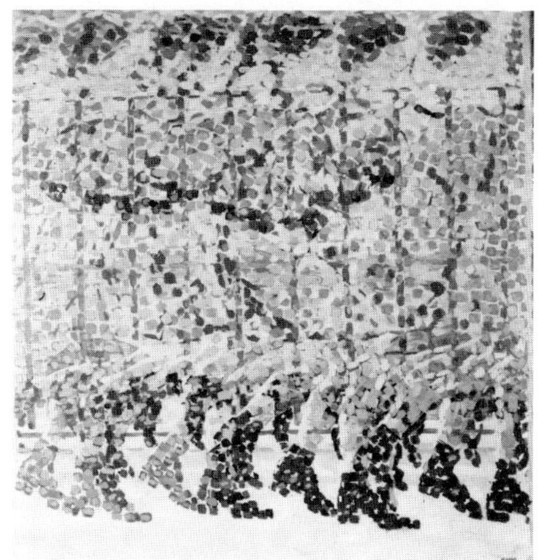

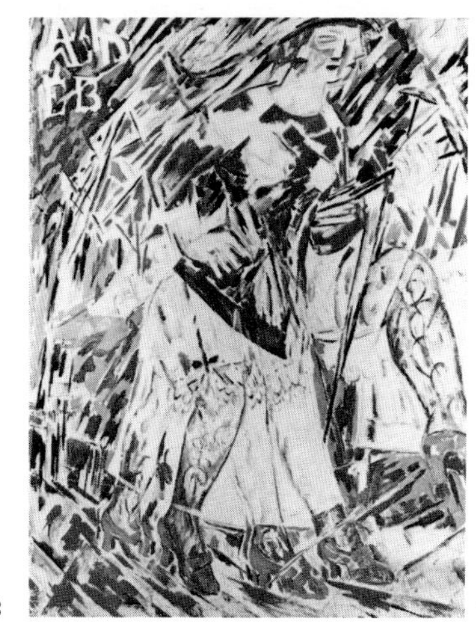

Painting," published on February 1, 1912, in which the poet stressed the modern artist's new freedom from the need to represent the human figure and natural scenery and went on to state that "the subject no longer counts, or if it counts, it counts for very little."[45] However, the Futurists' exhibition, which opened four days later, revealed a wealth of modern subject matter, and their preface to the catalogue denounced the use of allegorical nude figures as "evidence of a traditional and academic mentality."[46] It is tempting to believe that Delaunay prepared his huge "machine" (larger than any of the Futurists' canvases) for the Salon des Indépendants in deliberate answer to the Italian challenge. Although *The City of Paris* includes the Eiffel Tower as a symbol of modernity, it is a patriotic salute to the eternal values of French culture as opposed to the chaotic vicissitudes of contemporary life.

Delaunay and the Futurists launched polemical writings at each other in the press, but their paintings appear to take part in a dialogue that is more creative than their words would suggest. Discussing one of Delaunay's early Eiffel Tower paintings in June 1911, the critic Roger Allard made reference to its "futurist" aspect,[47] a remark surely based on Allard's reading of the manifestos rather than on the sight of any Futurist canvas. In turn, Boccioni's interest in the reproduction of Delaunay's Eiffel Tower in Allard's article seems to underlie his own *The Street Enters the House* of late 1911–1912 (fig. 6). There is also a fascinating parallel between the 1910–11 paintings of Severini such as *The Milliner* (fig. 10) or *Yellow Dancers* (no. 64) and Delaunay's views of Paris through a window (fig. 11) in their use of the same firm Neo-Impressionist touches within an overall triangular grid pattern. Both artists were profound admirers of Seurat and were familiar with his color theories and his ideas for compositional structure. It is as yet unclear what Severini and Delaunay knew of each other's work prior to early 1912, when Delaunay's first retrospective at the Galerie Barbazanges in Paris coincided with the Futurist exhibition. Perhaps Jean Metzinger provided a link between them, since he was a devout Neo-Impressionist and a close friend of Delaunay (before he became attracted to Picasso's early Cubist work) and he was one of the French artists Severini often saw. Metzinger's own *Dancer in a Café* of 1912 (no. 106), with its delicate color and lighthearted subject, is difficult to imagine without the suggestive presence of Severini's dancers, a favorite theme of the Italian expatriate since 1909.

Carrà's *Funeral of the Anarchist Galli* (no. 56), a painting clearly revised late in 1911 for presentation to a Parisian public at the Bernheim-Jeune exhibition, proved to be one of the pictures that most impressed the German artists who saw the exhibition as it traveled to Berlin, Cologne, and Munich. Klee noted in his diary in 1913 that Carrà impressed him as having the greatest talent and compared his handling of color and paint to that of Tintoretto and Delacroix.[48] Marc, who was of all his German colleagues perhaps the most deeply affected by the Futurists' ideas and images, painted his own masterpiece in 1913. *The Fate of Animals* (fig. 12), very close in size to Carrà's large canvas, depicts not a specific human experience such as the 1904 riot which Carrà had witnessed in Milan, but rather an apocalyptic vision. The violently expressive lines and colors represent not the vibrating trajectories of flags and lances of Carrà's *Funeral* but more generalized forces of destruction which penetrate the spirits as well as the bodies of the animals with whom Marc felt such empathy. Marc's vivid palette of colors of the spectrum derives in part from Delaunay, whom he admired and knew, but his tragic subjects and empathetic approach have no equivalent in the lyrical compositions of his French friend. Although he abhorred modern technology, crying "Airplanes—can they serve any spirit?,"[49] Marc displayed increasing fascination with the same aspects of science that preoccupied Boccioni: "Today . . . we can see through matter and the day is not far off when we shall move through its oscillating mass as we now move through the air."[50] Other German painters were to pursue the apocalyptic side of Futurist painting and theory in savage depiction of cities torn asunder by violence or depravity, such as George Grosz's works of 1916–17 (fig. 13), which look back at the converging composition of Carrà's *Funeral* or Boccioni's *The Street Enters the House* through the blood-red filter of several years of war.

To Boccioni's great delight, his triptych *States of Mind* (nos. 31, 33, 35) was the subject of much discussion and controversy during the 1912 Bernheim-Jeune exhibition in Paris. Apollinaire quickly noted his debt to analytical Cubism and his use of numerals as independent compositional elements.[51] There is no doubt that Boccioni's visits with Picasso and Braque in October 1911 had impressed him deeply. Yet the fusion of Symbolist "soul states," undulating Art Nouveau line, and the multiple viewpoints and grid structure of Cubism with the sensation of speed and dislocation of modern train travel produced an extraor-

fig. 17 Marcel Duchamp (American, born France, 1887–1968)
Sad Young Man in a Train, 1911
Oil on canvas, mounted on board, 39⅜ x 28¾" (100 x 73 cm)
The Peggy Guggenheim Collection, Venice.
The Solomon R. Guggenheim Foundation

fig. 18 Giacomo Balla (Italian, 1871–1958)
Girl Running on a Balcony, 1912
Oil on canvas, 49¼ x 49¼" (125 x 125 cm)
Civica Galleria d'Arte Moderna, Milan

fig. 19 Mikhail Larionov (Russian, 1881–1964)
Woman Walking on the Boulevard, c. 1912
Oil on canvas, 45⅝ x 33⅞" (116 x 86 cm)
Private collection

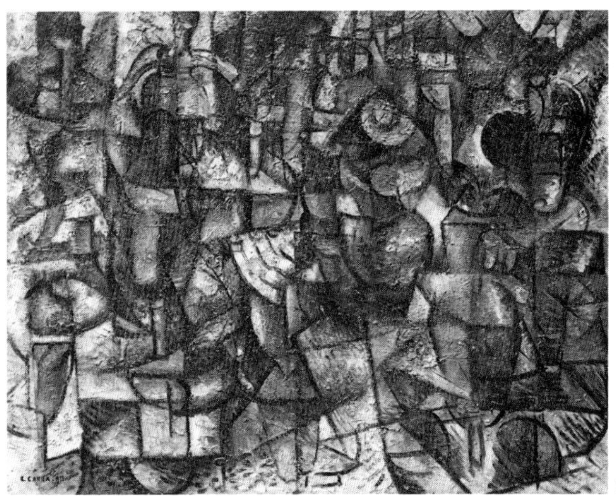

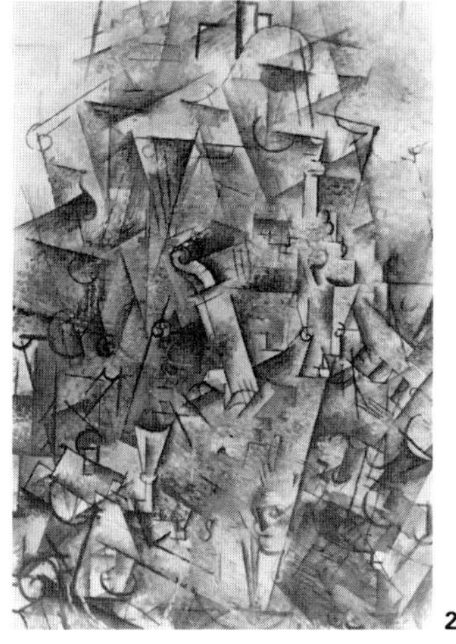

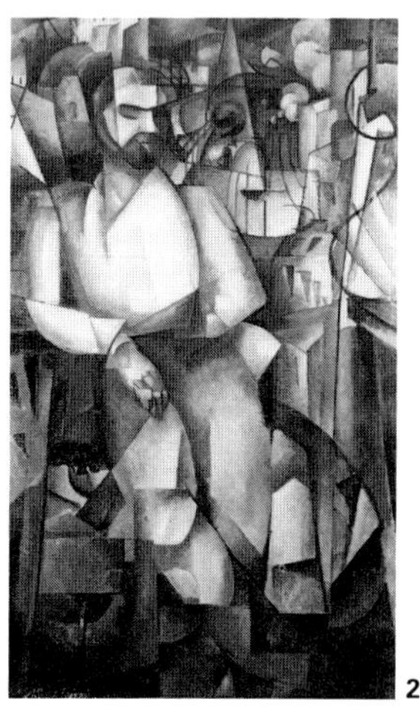

dinarily fresh vision. The gray-green embracing couples whirling around the central image of the smoking engine in *The Farewells* have no prototypes in earlier Cubist painting, but they appear to be close kin to the bluish forms that stream across the canvas in Duchamp's *King and Queen Surrounded by Swift Nudes* (no. 93), painted a few months later, and they may serve as ancestors to Picabia's flesh-colored ribbons of abstract energy in his *Physical Culture* of 1913 (no. 108). In fact, Boccioni's triptych may prove to have many unruly progeny which take after it in various ways: Gontcharova's *Railway Station* of 1912 (fig. 14) appropriates the subject and the bold red numbers, although rejecting fluid, graceful motion in favor of stick figures and staccato rhythms.

Marcel Duchamp's relationship to the Futurists is typically obscure and the chronology of events remains puzzling. Although he characterized them neatly as "urban Impressionists,"[52] he knew Severini, admired Boccioni and Marinetti, and admitted to an interest in a number of their ideas, which were occasionally so close to his own. Marinetti's proto-Dada rejection of the art of the past and his willingness to back any experiment would have appealed to Duchamp, but the Futurists' essentially romantic celebration of the emotions was foreign to his dry, Cartesian wit. While Boccioni, Carrà, and Severini could have seen one of Duchamp's first ventures into multiple imagery and "mental" motion in *Portrait* (no. 91), which depicts a young lady in progressive stages of undress and was exhibited in the Salon d'Automne of 1911, Duchamp surely did not know any of their paintings until the February 1912 Bernheim-Jeune exhibition. Duchamp's *Portrait of Chess Players* (see no. 89), *Sad Young Man in a Train* (fig. 17), and the first study of *Nude Descending a Staircase* (see no. 92) had apparently been completed by the previous Christmas. The *Chess Players*, with its attempt to portray a mental exercise, bears an odd affinity with Russolo's programmatic translation of Futurist theory in *Memories of a Night* (no. 62), while the *Sad Young Man* moving slowly away on his train is obviously a close relative of Boccioni's anxious passengers in *Those Who Go* (no. 33). The case of the *Nude Descending a Staircase* is more mysterious. Painted during the month of February, while the Futurist exhibition was held in Paris, but visually unlike anything shown there in its brown tones and precise rendering, the *Nude Descending* was completed in time for the Salon des Indépendants, which opened on March 20, but was rejected by the organizers of the Cubist contributions. There is every reason to believe that its rejection was due to its "Futurist" aspect, which would have irritated and unnerved Duchamp's French colleagues.[53] Yet the title of the picture is itself a mocking challenge to the Italians' brash prohibition of the nude as a subject in art for ten years. Duchamp further confused the issue of artistic interchanges by referring several times to his interest in seeing Balla's *Dynamism of a Dog on a Leash* (no. 7) at the Futurists' exhibition, although that picture was not shown in February 1912; it was not even painted until the following May.

The first painter to venture into representing a figure in motion by a sequence of successive, overlapping images appears to have been Frantisek Kupka, whose series of prismatic pastels entitled *Woman Picking Flowers* (fig. 15) has been dated 1909–10. Kupka's early interest in the chronophotography, or photography of successive phases of motion, of Etienne Jules Marey (fig. 16) is now well documented, and it is believed that the publication of the Futurist manifestos gave Kupka the impetus to explore his ideas further.[54] Duchamp's *Sad Young Man in a Train* and the more explicit and schematic *Nude Descending a Staircase* followed in late 1911 and early 1912. It seems very likely that Duchamp knew of Kupka's experiments because his brothers shared their garden in suburban Puteaux with the older Czech painter. Balla's three famous studies of sequential motion were almost certainly an entirely independent venture. The celebrated little dachshund was painted in May, followed by *Girl Running on a Balcony* (fig. 18) and his study of a violinist in *Rhythms of a Bow*, probably completed by the late fall.[55] All three pictures were shown for the first time in Rome in February 1913. The flickering paint strokes of Balla's Divisionist period are still vital to the composition of *Dynamism of a Dog on a Leash* (no. 7), which superimposes a layer of color onto what might otherwise seem an exercise in black and white. Not only do the dog's legs, ears, and tail multiply themselves in a diminutive flurry of energy which echoes his mistress's more dignified stride, but the road on which they walk appears to be a moving surface that streams away beneath them. Whereas Duchamp's *Nude* is an elegant diagram of motion, "without our knowing if a real person is or isn't descending an equally real staircase,"[56] as Duchamp put it, Balla's dog gives the spectator a truly Futurist "sensation" of a world in which all things move at varying speeds.

Never having visited Paris, yet in some ways far

fig. 20 Carlo Carrà (Italian, 1881–1966)
Rhythm of Objects, 1912
Oil on canvas, 20⅛ x 26" (51.1 x 66 cm)
Pinacoteca di Brera, Milan

fig. 21 Georges Braque (French, 1882–1963)
Still Life with Harp and Violin, 1912
Oil on canvas, 45⅝ x 31⅞" (116 x 81 cm)
Kunstsammlung Nordrhein-Westfalen, Düsseldorf

fig. 22 Albert Gleizes (French, 1881–1953)
Man on a Balcony (Portrait of Dr. Morinaud), 1912
Oil on canvas, 76¾ x 45¼" (194.9 x 114.9 cm)
Philadelphia Museum of Art. The Louise and Walter Arensberg Collection

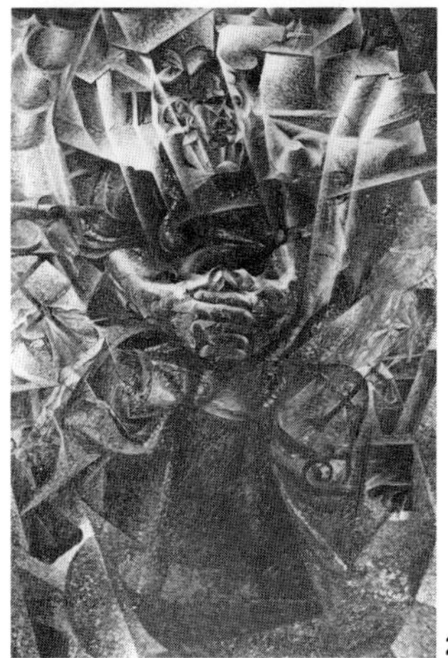

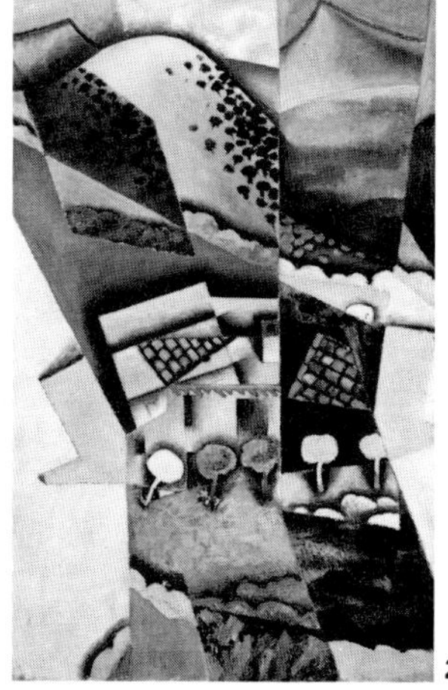

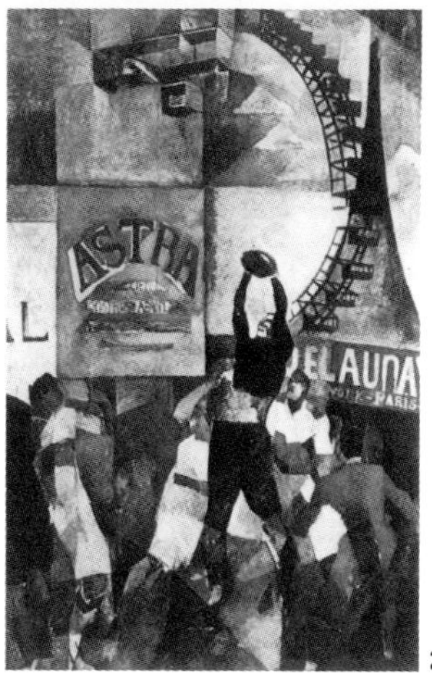

more in touch with the international avant-garde than was Balla in his Roman studio, Kasimir Malevich in Moscow examined both human and mechanical motion in *The Knife Grinder* (no. 122), first shown in 1913. The painting was part of a remarkable sequence of paintings and drawings in which Malevich deliberately explored Cubist and Futurist pictorial means, and which culminated in his abstract Suprematist compositions of 1915. Unlike either Duchamp's *Nude* or Balla's *Dog, The Knife Grinder* does not suggest chronophotography as a specific visual source. Its bright patchwork of colors and simplified, shaded volumes suggest the action of a robot rather than a man. Clearly aware of Futurist ideas by mid-1912 and interested in several of the scientific theories and non-Euclidean geometry, which also intrigued Duchamp, Malevich pursued a sharply divergent course. *The Knife Grinder* combines the consciously crude vigor of his earlier paintings of peasants with a sophisticated concern to activate every section of the canvas. The presence of a flight of stairs, which begins with a banister at the upper left and proceeds down the right side of the canvas in a series of jerky stages, appears to be an uncanny coincidence in light of Duchamp's *Nude Descending a Staircase*. Could Malevich have gotten wind of the Frenchman's ironic title? The precise, investigatory nature of this group of paintings by Duchamp, Balla, and Malevich is brought into sharper focus when they are compared to a lighthearted variation on the theme of sequential motion by Larionov. His exuberant *Woman Walking on the Boulevard* of c. 1912 (fig. 19) was probably painted without direct knowledge of Duchamp's or Balla's work, but Larionov certainly had read the Futurist manifestos. This Russian lady prancing along the boulevard, her two plump legs multiplied to seven and her red dress becoming coyly transparent to permit a glimpse of pink breast and a flutter of petticoats, epitomizes the ease with which Futurist concepts could be absorbed by a painter who did not share the analytical concerns of Balla or the passionate identification of Boccioni with his subject. Although it was the Futurists' interest in representing motion in successive images that was often criticized by other artists as being too mechanical or too simplistic, this aspect of their theories surprisingly was not emphasized in their joint exhibitions until 1913 when Balla showed his three variations on that theme and Severini exhibited his paintings of blue and white dancers. Boccioni himself found Balla's studies of movement too "truthful" and was unhappy about their obvious links to photography.[57]

Balla's little dog, Duchamp's descending nude, and Malevich's mustachioed knife grinder stand out as remarkable, isolated examples of early twentieth-century artists contending with a distinctly unpainterly modern theme. Each of the three used his study of motion to penetrate beyond what Duchamp described as the "retinal" vision of surface impressions and to arrive at a schematic vocabulary with which to express a new view of the world. Meanwhile Boccioni and Carrà remained deeply immersed in a dialogue with French painting, although after February 1912 their pictures never again appeared in Paris to confront their rivals directly. Both artists, particularly Boccioni, developed an elaborate critique of Cubist painting, which they saw as essentially static, analytical, and cold, in contrast to the synthetic, dynamic equivalent of sensation that they sought in their own work. Carrà's paintings of 1912–13 come very close to the analytical Cubism of Picasso and Braque, and he adopted their restricted palette of silvery tones, which Boccioni continued to decry. The title of Carrà's *Rhythm of Objects* of 1912 (fig. 20) for example, suggests a Futurist approach to an archetypal Cubist still-life arrangement, but the picture itself is not more "dynamic" than, for instance, a 1912 painting by Braque (fig. 21) or Jacques Villon's vibrating forms in *The Set Table* of 1912–13.[58]

Another pair of paintings clearly reveals the gulf between Boccioni and French avant-garde painting late in 1912. Albert Gleizes's *Man on a Balcony (Portrait of Dr. Morinaud)* (fig. 22), exhibited at the Salon d'Automne of that year, which Boccioni presumably saw,[59] presents startling points of comparison to the Italian's portrait of his mother entitled *Matter (Materia)* (fig. 23). The two pictures are roughly similar in scale and each presents a full-length figure posed on a balcony against an urban background, seen from a vantage point within a room. The French Cubist Gleizes constructed his figure out of graceful curves and shallow planes, consciously rhyming the lines of the cast-iron guardrail with the head and torso of Dr. Morinaud. The subject of the portrait is ultimately a pretext for a handsome arrangement of formal elements in a balanced composition. But Boccioni's mother is an overwhelming presence, seated at the center of a mysterious and pulsating world. Behind her head, chimneys belch smoke and houses unfold, rays of unearthly light are shed across her massive body, which is in turn pierced by the spectral form of a horse plunging past in the street below. *Materia* is appropriately built up of layers and particles of paint, and

fig. 23 Umberto Boccioni (Italian, 1882–1916)
Matter (Materia), 1912
Oil on canvas, 59 x 88½" (150 x 225 cm)
Mattioli Collection, Milan

fig. 24 Juan Gris (Spanish, 1887–1927)
Céret Landscape, 1913
Oil on canvas, 36¼ x 23⅝" (92 x 60 cm)
Moderna Museet, Stockholm

fig. 25 Robert Delaunay (French, 1885–1941)
Third Representation, Cardiff Team, 1912–13
Oil on canvas, 128⅜ x 81⅞" (326 x 208 cm)
Musée d'Art Moderne de la Ville de Paris

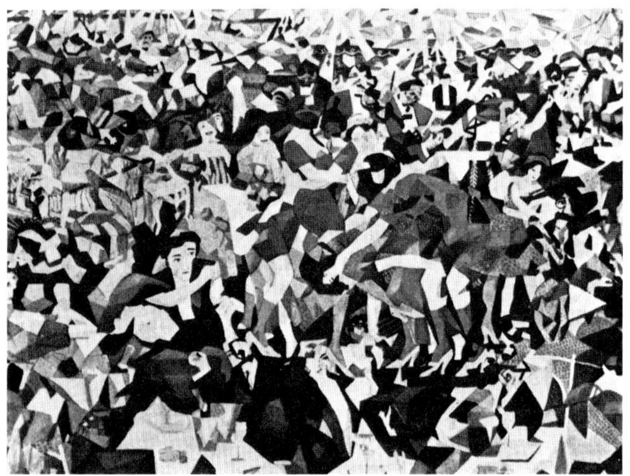

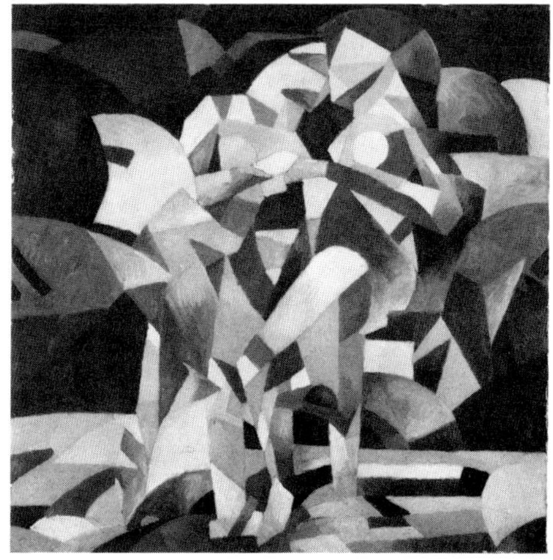

dark but radiant touches suggest the molecular structure of life which so fascinated Boccioni. On the other hand, Gleizes presented a profoundly rational world, with man tranquil and assured above a city he appears to dominate; the two are harmoniously juxtaposed within the structure of the painting.[60] But Boccioni allowed each element its vital force. We experience his picture as a bewildering interplay of different sensations: the brilliance of light, the hardness of an iron railing, the speed of a horse, the fleshy solidity of the huge clasped hands. The structural lessons of Cubism, still evident in the vigorously distorted planes of his mother's face, are subsumed into the dynamic imbalance of a Bergsonian world in constant flux which can be grasped only by intuition, never fully comprehended by intellect.

Despite its distance from any Cubist aesthetic, Boccioni's *Materia* provokes fresh reflection upon one of the masterpieces of Juan Gris's career, his *Still Life Before an Open Window (Place Ravignan)* of 1915 (no. 101). The complex analytical processes in Picasso's and Braque's work of 1910–12 had led them to restrict their subjects to single figures or arrangements of objects in a shallow space. The Futurists' extraordinarily audacious desire to mingle objects and their surroundings on a grand scale may have affected the Cubists' cautious expansion of these self-imposed restrictions, although that expansion does not really occur in Picasso's work until the summer of 1915. But the unearthly blue light irradiating Gris's picture, the crisply delineated foliage rustling into the room, and the mysterious marriage of wallpaper pattern with balcony railing all contrive to make this as lyrical a vision of the interpenetration of objects and surroundings as Boccioni's is disturbing. Gris was probably unaware of Boccioni's work produced after the 1912 Bernheim-Jeune exhibition in Paris, which he would have seen just as he was about to present his own first major contribution to the Salon des Indépendants that year, but his paintings over the years 1912 to 1915 occasionally suggest curious affinities to Futurist ideas. Links between his neatly dislocated portraits of 1912 and those of Severini have been suggested,[61] and the Céret landscapes which Gris painted in the fall of 1913 (fig. 24) have a dynamic structure that allows them to unfold like the narrow planes of a fan. If there is evidence that Boccioni looked at Gris's early work for inspiration for his relief sculpture of a woman's head,[62] there is also a possibility that the Spanish Cubist found in Futurist ideas stimulating impetus to his own desire to express the hidden poetry of ordinary objects.

Some months after *Materia*, Boccioni achieved another astonishing expression of energy in his *Dynamism of a Soccer Player* of 1913 (no. 50), the last picture he was to complete on such a grand scale. As the figure of the athlete hurtles forward in undefined space, the sense of speed and weight is almost palpable. There is an uneasy tension between the advanced degree of abstraction and the oppressive physicality of the image, a conflict Boccioni was to resolve brilliantly in his sculpture *Unique Forms of Continuity in Space* (no. 48). Delaunay's vast painting depicting the same popular sport, *Cardiff Team* of 1912–13 (fig. 25), reveals how distant the two artists' aims had become several months before they clashed in a fierce battle in the press over their claims to the term "simultaneity."[63] The weightless, flat figures of Delaunay's team hover amidst symbols of the modern age: the Eiffel Tower, the Ferris wheel, billboards, and a biplane. Broad areas of color give Delaunay's painting a formal poise and resolution, while Boccioni's persistent Divisionist touch is once again at the service of his desire to "show the living object in its dynamic growth." When Delaunay's painting was exhibited in London in the fall of 1913, the critic Clive Bell compared it unfavorably to Wyndham Lewis's large composition called *Kermesse*, which showed three energetic figures in motion. The powerful, abstracted lines of Lewis's lost work probably placed it midway between what Bell described as the gay, posterlike effect of Delaunay's picture[64] and the sensual urgency of Boccioni's. Delaunay stressed vision and the importance of "seeing"; Boccioni craved intuition and the vital force of "feeling." Both *Materia* and *Dynamism of a Soccer Player* were begun on smaller canvases, which Boccioni apparently enlarged as he painted—as if under the inexorable pressure of the expanding physical and psychic energies he was trying to convey.

Severini did not share Boccioni's fascination with matter and its inner life; influenced by his years in France and certainly true to his own more balanced temperament, he produced a series of canvases in which movement is expressed in witty dislocations of form, brought under control in a coherent structure. His vast *Pan-Pan Dance at the Monico* (fig. 26) is a patchwork of colored angular shapes carefully constructed to synthesize the noise, lively action, and bright lights of a Paris dance hall. *The Bal Tabarin* of 1912 (no. 66) takes up the same theme with virtuoso elegance, allowing myriad, tiny details to catch the eye without compromising the overall pattern. Severini's

fig. 26 Gino Severini (Italian, 1883–1966)
Pan-Pan Dance at the Monico, 1910–12
Oil on canvas, dimensions unknown
Destroyed

fig. 27 Francis Picabia (French, 1879–1953)
Dances at the Spring, 1912
Oil on canvas, 47½ x 47½" (120.7 x 120.7 cm)
Philadelphia Museum of Art. The Louise and Walter Arensberg Collection

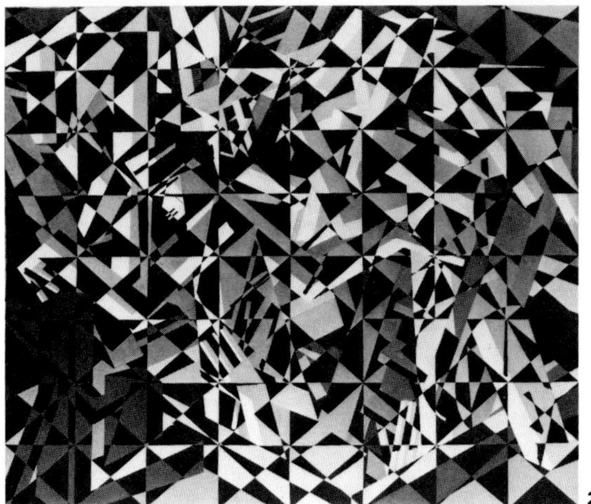

28

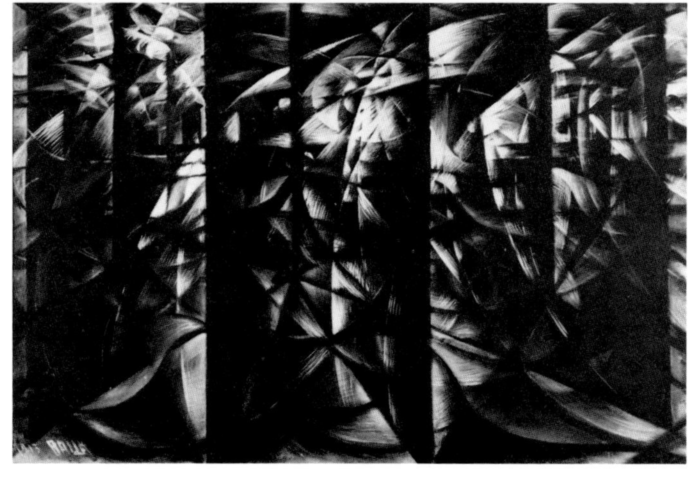

29

dance pictures strike a balance between abstraction and representation that seems to have proved very suggestive to other European painters. The two versions of Picabia's *Dances at the Spring* (see fig. 27) appear to owe a debt to Severini's crisply formal but dynamic patterns, while David Bomberg's impressive painting *In the Hold* (fig. 28), completed when the artist was only twenty-four, may reflect his absorption of works by Severini shown in London in 1912 and 1913. For his representation of men in action, Bomberg chose to use a rigid grid structure and reduced agitated movement to purely abstract geometric shapes; his picture makes a striking (if imperfect) parallel to Balla's studies of velocity (see fig. 29) which were exhibited in London shortly after Bomberg's masterpiece went on view for the first time.[65] Balla had several English admirers, and it is still not clear what connections exist between Wyndham Lewis's Vorticist movement (Ezra Pound had used the word "vortex" as early as December 1913) and Balla's drawings of spiral "force-lines" (see no.11) executed presumably in 1914–15.

Although Boccioni could be said to have flirted with pure abstraction and certainly discussed the possibility in his writings, the dynamic and sensuous nature of his subjects remained too central to his concerns for him to pursue it. Both Balla and Severini, however, produced abstract paintings and studies in the years 1912 to 1914. Severini's *Spherical Expansions of Light* (see no. 72), although modest in scale, bear comparison with Léger's extended series *Contrasts of Form* of 1913–14 (fig. 30). Both artists evolved their abstract compositions from a sequence of studies of the human figure and its surroundings. The comparison is perhaps most apt in a work such as *Dancer = Sea* (fig. 31), where Severini retained traces of the subject (and therefore of suggested volume), since Léger never relinquished his clearly modeled volumes, essential to his theory of dynamic contrasts. Delaunay's 1912 series of *Windows* (see no. 85) and his solar and lunar paintings of 1913, Severini's *Spherical Expansions*, and Léger's *Contrasts of Form* all achieve highly individual effects of abstraction without the deliberate and programmatic intentions that Malevich and Piet Mondrian were later to pursue into the nonobjective world.

FUTURISM IN THREE DIMENSIONS

Despite their praise of the sculptor Medardo Rosso in the first Manifesto of the Futurist Painters of February 1910, none of the Futurists appears to have given serious thought to sculpture until early 1912.[66] Triumphant after the heady controversy over the Futurists' Bernheim-Jeune painting exhibition, Boccioni looked about him, drew a deep breath, and decided that there was yet another world to conquer. After a brief trip to London he wrote to Vico Baer from Paris on March 15: "I am obsessed these days by sculpture! I think I can perceive a complete renewal of this mummified art!"[67] In fact, there was a revolution brewing in the field of sculpture, in which Boccioni's role was certainly to be catalytic. Several sources of his inspiration are evident. Rosso's Paris studio was filled with his mysterious experiments in fusing the human figure with the light and shadow of its surroundings. Severini visited Rosso with Ardengo Soffici; it is probable that Boccioni also paid homage in person to the fifty-four-year-old sculptor, but by that time Rosso was too deeply rooted in the French art world to find the Futurists' strident program appealing.[68] More challenging to Boccioni's pride, Picasso's magisterial *Head of a Woman* of 1909 (no. 109), clearly visible in contemporary photographs of his studio, was the most significant Cubist sculpture yet created, until then without immediate offspring even in Picasso's own work. (Apollinaire was to note Picasso's *Head* as a source for Boccioni in his review of the latter's exhibition in 1913.[69])

During the spring of 1912 Severini took his friend Boccioni to visit the most advanced sculptors in Paris: Alexander Archipenko, the elusive Spaniard August Agero, of whose work so little survives, Raymond Duchamp-Villon, and Constantin Brancusi. Lively discussions took place, in which Boccioni somehow failed to mention that he was planning another manifesto—an omission resented by the Parisian sculptors and wounding to Severini. Boccioni would have seen Duchamp-Villon's *Torso of a Young Man* of 1910 (no. 94), severely simplified to express controlled energy, and might have seen sketches of the architectural project for the facade and interiors of the "Cubist House," to be constructed in the Salon d'Automne (an exhibition he was also to see). Duchamp-Villon's conviction that sculpture should be architectural in conception and his passionate admiration for the modernity of the Eiffel Tower, "living its strange life, animated by an

fig. 28 David Bomberg (English, 1890–1957)
In the Hold, 1913–14
Oil on canvas, 77¼ x 91" (196 x 231 cm)
The Tate Gallery, London

fig. 29 Giacomo Balla (Italian, 1871–1958)
Speed of an Auto + Light + Sound, c. 1913
Oil on canvas, 34¼ x 51⅛" (87 x 130 cm)
Kunsthaus Zürich

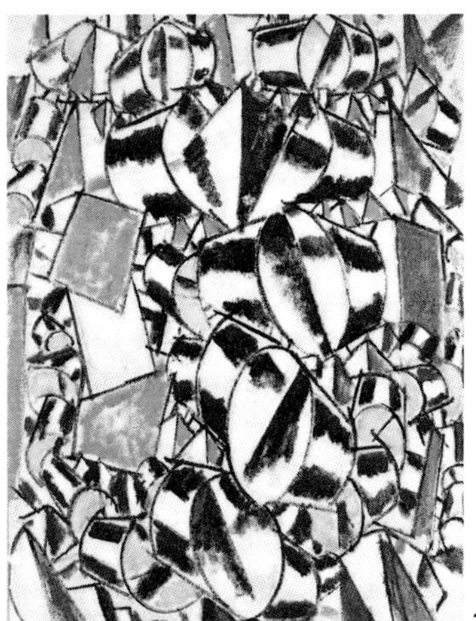
30

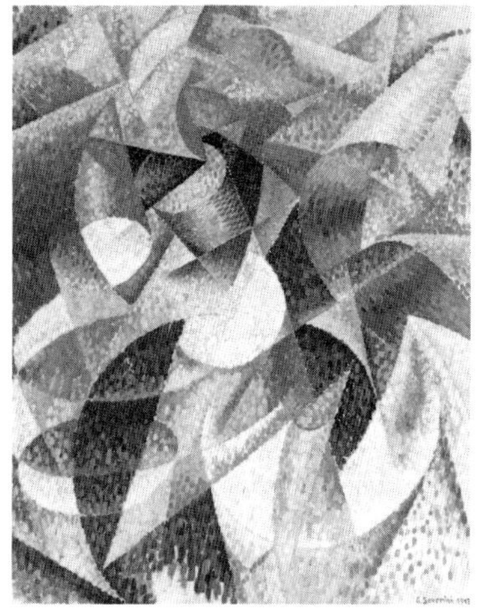
31

imperceptible oscillation,"[70] would have struck sympathetic chords in his Italian visitor. Brancusi's intensely concentrated forms in *The Kiss* and *Prometheus* (both Philadelphia Museum of Art), shown in the Salon des Indépendants of 1912, clearly fell outside the scope of Boccioni's interest. Archipenko, however, was beginning to hollow and pierce his stone figures. His curious *Walking Woman* of 1912[71] occupies a place halfway between Duchamp-Villon's *Torso* and Boccioni's striding figures of 1913. Of all the Cubist sculptors, Archipenko seems to have been closest to the Futurists. It is unfortunate that the precise sequence of his work of 1912–13 is still too little known. Although there is no mention of a visit to Henri Matisse, an artist admired by the Futurists but apparently less relevant to their concerns, it should be noted that Matisse's series of five portrait heads of Jeannette was in progress; the powerful and intuitive distortions of *Jeannette V* find few parallels as apt as Boccioni's *Anti-Graceful* (no. 44).

The precise date of Boccioni's Technical Manifesto of Futurist Sculpture remains in doubt, despite continuing efforts to establish a precise chronology for Futurist publications. Bearing the date of April 11, 1912, but cited by Severini as appearing five months after the Bernheim-Jeune exhibition (which would put it in July), the manifesto apparently was not noticed in the French press until mid-September.[72] Turning his "Futurist eye" away from the "lamentable . . . spectacle of barbarism and lumpishness," as he described most contemporary sculpture, Boccioni lingered briefly over Constantin Meunier, Antoine Bourdelle, and Auguste Rodin before sweeping on to proclaim new laws for *"a sculpture of environment."* In rolling phrases and vivid, specific terms, he demanded that the sculptor begin by penetrating to the inner core of an object, and make it "live" by translating "those atmospheric planes that link and intersect things." He pleaded for a new sculptural whole, uniting object and environment in dynamic interaction "outside of and despite all logic of appearances," and as technical means to this end he proposed a breath-taking array of new methods and materials:

> A figure can have an arm clothed and the rest of the body nude. The different lines of a vase of flowers can follow one another nimbly while blending with the lines of the hat and neck.
>
> Transparent planes of glass or celluloid, strips of metal, wire, interior or exterior electric lights can indicate the planes, the tendencies, the tones and half-tones of a new reality.
>
> It is necessary to destroy the pretended nobility, entirely literary and traditional, of marble and bronze, and to deny squarely that one must use a single material for a sculptural ensemble. The sculptor can use twenty different materials, or even more, in a single work, provided that the plastic emotion requires it. Here is a modest sample of these materials: glass, wood, cardboard, cement, concrete, horsehair, leather, cloth, mirrors, electric lights, etc.

Boccioni even provided for elements in mechanical motion, remarking that "a valve opening and closing creates a rhythm as beautiful but infinitely newer than that of a living eyelid."[73]

Nothing in the work of the established avant-garde sculptors even suggested such a riot of possibilities, but it must be remembered that the spring of 1912 was a critical period in the work of Picasso, who was in the process of obliterating once and for all the delicate boundary between painting and sculpture. In May he glued a piece of oilcloth onto a canvas to produce the first collage, *Still Life with Chair Caning* (Musée Picasso, Paris). In his continuing exploration of form, Picasso was also to use paper, cardboard, and metal to construct in three dimensions the guitars that he had been painting for two years. In *The Rise of Cubism*, published in 1920 but written during the war, his dealer Daniel-Henry Kahnweiler noted in a passage critical of Futurism that Picasso had also toyed with radical ideas of introducing actual motion into his art. According to Kahnweiler, "clock mechanisms" were to be used to animate paintings or sculpture, and Picasso also considered painting successive images on transparent sheets of material and showing the results with a cinematographic projector.[74] By this report, Picasso had contemplated a foray into the field explored by Balla (and Duchamp) as well as that proposed by Boccioni.

Even without motors, collage and assemblage proved sufficiently revolutionary to arouse hostility among the avant-garde. In a letter to a Russian friend drafted in 1912 and reworked in 1918, Robert Delaunay fulminated against what he perceived as an infuriating challenge to pure painting, and he had no doubt as to the identity of the chief villains: "Certain people tried to smuggle in as French art (made in Paris) some pastiched lucubrations from old primitive sculpture, while others introduced the newspaper, nails, broken glass bottles—all the way to Italian futurism, which has framed bologna sausage, hair, and all

fig. 30 Fernand Léger (French, 1881–1955)
Contrast of Forms, 1913
Oil on burlap, 51⅜ x 38½" (130.5 x 97.8 cm)
Philadelphia Museum of Art. The Louise and Walter Arensberg Collection

fig. 31 Gino Severini (Italian, 1883–1966)
Dancer = Sea, 1913
Oil on canvas, 39¾ x 31¾" (100.1 x 80.6 cm)
The Peggy Guggenheim Collection, Venice.
The Solomon R. Guggenheim Foundation

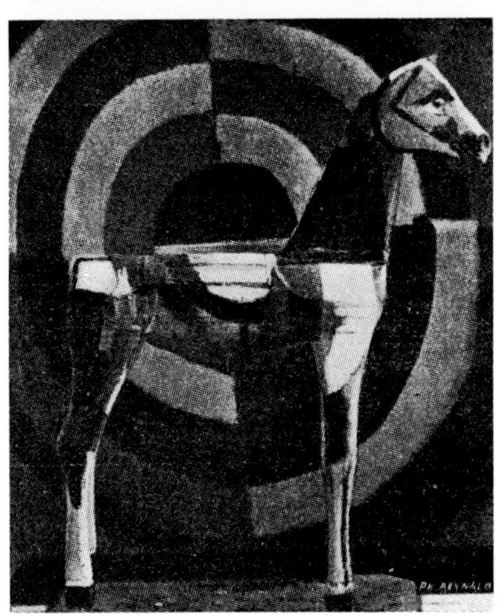
32

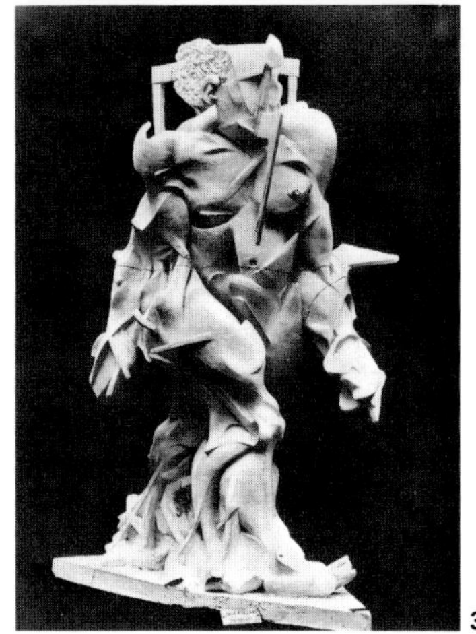
33

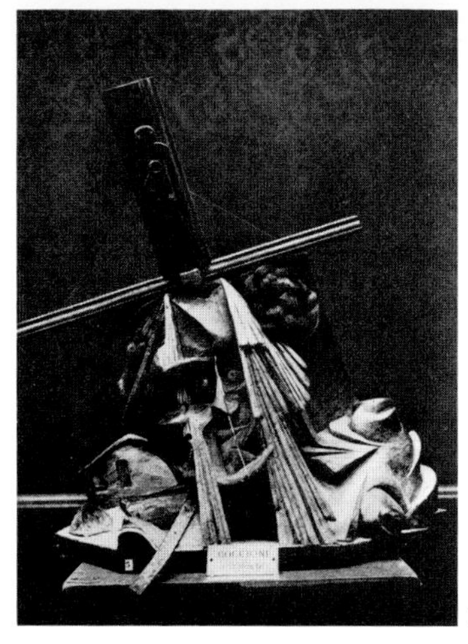
34

sorts of eccentric objects . . . . These incoherent trends had Picasso, Boccioni as their leaders."[75]

By the time Boccioni's exhibition opened in Paris on June 20, 1913, there had been advances on many fronts. Apollinaire, who must have been involved in many a studio discussion of collage and advanced sculptural ideas, referred to Picasso's use of real objects in an article of March 14, 1913, and declared himself ready to accept any new material: "Mosaicists paint with pieces of marble or colored wood. Mention has been made of an Italian painter who painted with fecal matter; at the time of the French Revolution, someone who painted with blood. They can paint with whatever they wish—pipes, postage stamps, postcards or playing cards, candelabras, pieces of oilcloth, starched collars."[76] Apollinaire appears to have made a vigorous effort to outmaneuver Boccioni by suggesting the idea of a "simultaneous sculpture" to Delaunay, Gleizes, Léger, Duchamp-Villon, and Duchamp three months before Boccioni's exhibition, but he was to note wistfully in a review of the Berlin Herbstsalon which opened in September 1913 that only Delaunay (of all unlikely people) had taken his advice.[77] Of Delaunay's three simultaneous sculptures exhibited in that salon, only one is known through a photograph (fig. 32), and bears witness to the painter's discomfort with a mixture of media.

Boccioni's 1913 Paris exhibition included eleven sculptures and twenty-two drawings, all presumably produced in the fifteen months after March 1912. Although the three pieces that survive (nos. 44, 45, 48) are at once the most successful in formal terms and the least experimental in materials (monochrome plaster, cast into bronze after the artist's death), the overall effect of the exhibition, dominated by large, dynamic figures penetrated by real objects and architectural fragments (see fig. 33), must have been bizarre and overwhelming. Apollinaire was duly impressed[78] and made particular note of the drawings Boccioni had grouped under unusual headings: "I wish to model light and atmosphere," or "I wish to extend objects into space." The sculptures in which Boccioni achieved his most aggressive aims of splitting open the closed figure and inserting the environment into it, such as the lost *Fusion of a Head and Window* (fig. 34; see no. 43) were painfully ugly, flying in the face of all canons of classical beauty. They have no direct heirs, proving undigestible to the subsequent history of sculpture. But the splendid dynamic distortions of *Anti-Graceful* (no. 44) have an expressive power to be equaled only by Picasso years later in paintings of weeping women. Boccioni's intense admiration for, and envy of, Picasso seems to establish at least a partial dialogue in their work, so dramatically different in many ways. The Italian's most elegant sculpture, *Development of a Bottle in Space* (no. 45), achieves an almost classical balance despite its upward, spiral motion, enclosing and liberating space in a continuous arabesque. Picasso's witty little bronze *Glass of Absinthe* (no. 110), with its real slotted spoon and gaily colored pointillist dots, could have served as a reminder to Boccioni of his own rebellion against the "dignity" of traditional sculpture.

Boccioni was a brilliant artist at the mercy of his tendency to swing wildly between opposites: his letters reveal him alternately at the height of creative energy and in the depths of depression, torn between pure color and line and his desire to express experience concretely, filled with a fine contempt for the past and haunted by its triumphs. *Unique Forms of Continuity in Space* (no. 48) has nothing to do with Boccioni's quest for new materials or for new subject matter. It is a modern resolution of the same problem tackled by the sculptor of the Victory of Samothrace—the human form in motion. As Duchamp-Villon transformed the horse into a dynamic symbol of the machine age, Boccioni expressed the fusion of outer reality and inner experience in the muscular sensations of a striding man. For Boccioni, as for Duchamp-Villon, man was still the measure of a world increasingly dominated by the machines for which they both expressed admiration. Jacob Epstein's literal fusion of man and machine in his *Rock Drill* of 1913–15 (fig. 35) represented a step they were not prepared to take. Epstein also contemplated, but never executed, the idea of setting his drill in motion with pneumatic power.

While Boccioni turned his attention again to painting, producing only one more remarkable sculpture, *Dynamic Construction of a Gallop: Horse + Houses* of 1914 (The Peggy Guggenheim Collection, Venice), other Futurists made daring experiments and artists in several countries took up the challenge of new materials. Sometime during 1913, Duchamp fastened a bicycle wheel upside down on a stool, creating a kinetic object purely for his own enjoyment. Vladimir Tatlin arrived in Paris in the spring of 1913[79] and his famous visits to Picasso's studio heralded the production of a radical group of relief sculptures in Russia during 1914–15 (see fig. 36). In the Salon des Indépendants of 1914 Apollinaire singled out Archipenko and a fellow Russian émigré, Vladimir Baranoff-Rossiné, for their "poly-

fig. 32 Robert Delaunay (French, 1885–1941)
Horse Prism Sun Moon, 1913
Mixed media, dimensions unknown
Lost

fig. 33 Umberto Boccioni (Italian, 1882–1916)
Synthesis of Human Dynamism, 1913
Plaster, dimensions unknown
Destroyed

fig. 34 Umberto Boccioni (Italian, 1882–1916)
Fusion of a Head and Window, 1912
Mixed media, dimensions unknown
Lost

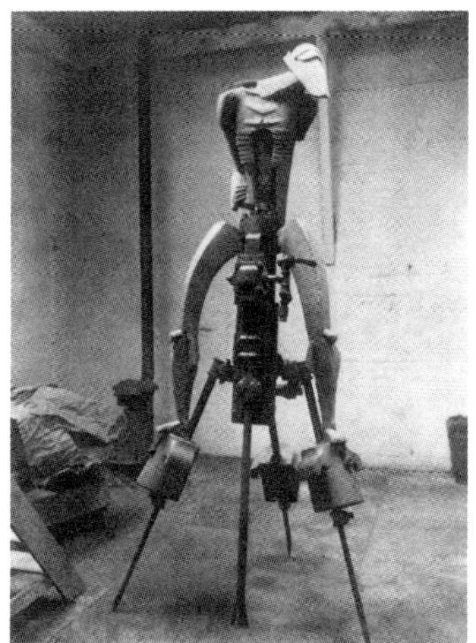
35

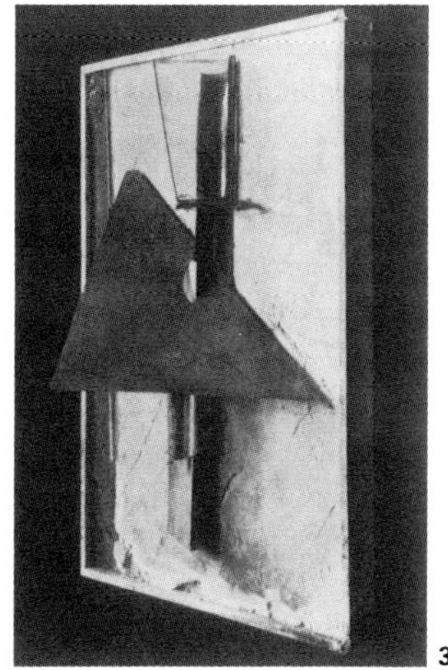
36

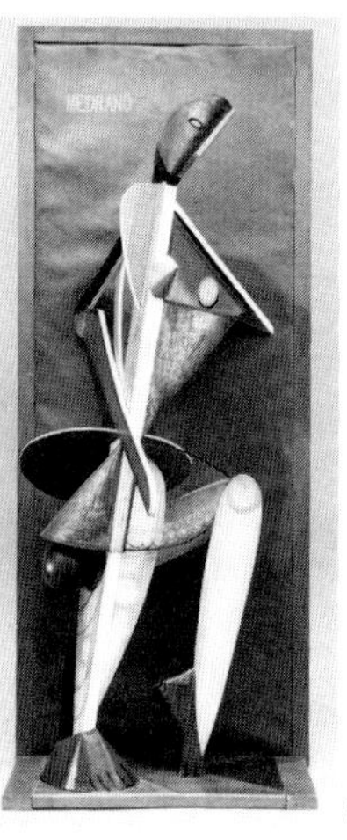

37

chrome sculptures in various materials."[80] Archipenko confronted Boccioni in two directions: his *Medrano* (fig. 37) playfully juxtaposes colored parts of the body with planes of metal and glass, but his *Boxing (Struggle)* (no. 83) addresses the problem of dynamic "force-lines" and interpenetration of planes in a more dignified vein. Like many of his compatriots, Archipenko delighted in combining radical innovations with images and colors drawn from the rich tradition of Russian folk art. Although his gay constructions seem to have offended Boccioni, who deplored their "Byzantine dryness, archaic, skeletal, rigid and jerky silhouettes characteristic of all primitives in all epochs,"[81] Archipenko remained linked to the Futurists and sent five works to the Free Exhibition of International Futurists in Rome in April 1914.

That same exhibition included what must have been among the first "dynamic constructions of objects" produced by Marinetti and the poet Francesco Cangiullo. Boccioni's intense seriousness was replaced by high jinks, evident in the titles of Cangiullo's lost sculptures *Head of a Passatist Philosopher + Futurist Slaps* or *Miss FlicFlic ChiapChiap*. Marinetti's ungainly *Self-Portrait*, a running stick figure composed of "frames brushes handkerchiefs tin cans,"[82] was preserved in a photograph in the London *Sketch* (fig. 38), and belongs to that class of irreverent objects which includes Jean Crotti's 1915 portrait of Marcel Duchamp (with glass eyes and a wig) and Picabia's 1920 assemblage of a toy monkey surrounded by crude letters reading "Portrait de Cézanne Portrait de Renoir Portrait de Rembrandt Natures Mortes."[83] More elaborate constructions were produced during 1914 and 1915 by Balla and Fortunato Depero, a newcomer to Futurist ranks. None of the original "plastic complexes" reproduced in their joint manifesto "Futurist Reconstruction of the Universe" of March 11, 1915, appears to survive (figs. 39, 40), but their "complex, constructive, noise-producing abstraction" is remarkable even as a written proposal. Anticipating the assemblages of Robert Rauschenberg, they call for: "Strands of wire, cotton, wool, silk of every thickness and coloured glass, tissue paper, celluloid, metal netting, every sort of transparent and highly coloured material. Fabrics, mirrors, sheets of metal, coloured tin foil, every sort of gaudy substance. Mechanical and electrical devices; musical and noise-making elements, chemically luminous liquids of variable colours; springs, levers, tubes, etc."[84] All these heterogeneous elements were to be combined into abstract constructions and set rotating on one or more axes; better yet, they were to "decompose, talk, produce noises and play music simultaneously," or to appear and disappear "with unexpected explosions." As a sideline, Balla and Depero proposed several varieties of "the futurist toy," to delight and instruct the child and refresh adults (keeping them "young, agile, jubilant, spontaneous, ready for anything, inexhaustible, instructive and intuitive"). Finally, they summed it all up in "the metallic animal," the miraculous "fusion of art and science" which will "speak, shout and dance automatically." They promised to construct millions of these new creatures for a vast battle, which readers in the 1980s will readily recognize as an episode in *Star Wars!*

Casting a severe glance at future art historians, Balla and Depero concluded by staking their claim: "The inventions contained in this manifesto are absolute creations, integrally generated by Italian Futurism. No artist in France, Russia, England or Germany anticipated us in perceiving anything similar or analogous." Their claim appears to stand, judging from the photographs of their works, and considering that Tatlin's constructions were not intended to move and that Naum Gabo did not create his first kinetic sculpture, *Standing Wave*, until 1920.[85] But it was Russia that provided the most substantial competition in the fields of abstract sculpture and proto-Dada assemblage. Tatlin's intensely serious reliefs and constructions were made of ordinary materials, emphasizing their specific physical properties but removing them from the context of daily life. A review of the exhibition "Year 15" in Moscow gives a humorous account of what followed:

> Larionov—the most enterprising of the scandal-makers—quickly took Tatlin's caprice ad notam and gave birth to "plastic Rayonism" for the exhibition, tacking together a composition of pieces of wood, planks, rope, coloured paper, bits of cloth, bottles etc.
>
> The others we can pass over in silence. They nail together absolutely anything: soiled gloves, a bit of cheap top hat—and call it "self-portrait of Mayakovsky" or similar.
>
> On the piece of wall assigned to Larionov, there happened to be a fan. Someone started it up. Larionov was called to admire the new effect given to his construction. He approved hugely and set some extra strings and nails on the fan. The other brethren sighed with jealousy.[86]

fig. 35 Jacob Epstein (English, 1880–1959)
The Rock Drill, 1913–15
Plaster model mounted on an actual drill, photographed in the artist's studio, 1913–15
Dismantled

fig. 36 Vladimir Tatlin (Russian, 1885–1953)
Assemblage of Materials, 1914
Mixed media, dimensions unknown
Lost

fig. 37 Alexander Archipenko (American, born Russia, 1887–1964)
Medrano II, 1913
Painted tin, wood, glass, and oilcloth, height 50" (127 cm)
The Solomon R. Guggenheim Museum, New York

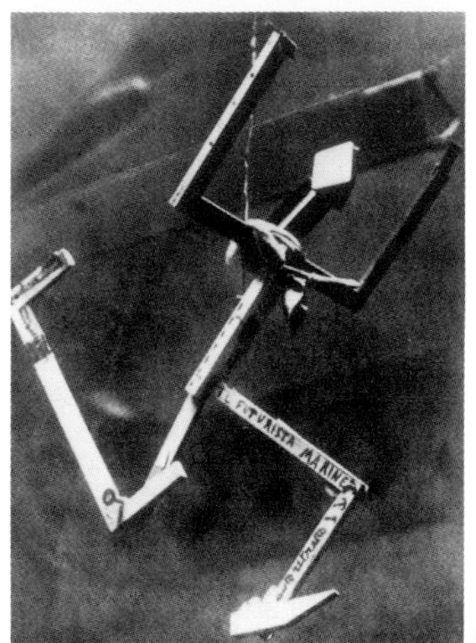
38

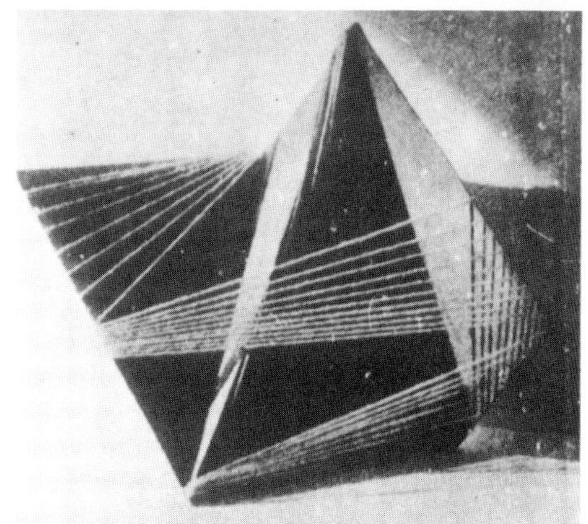
39

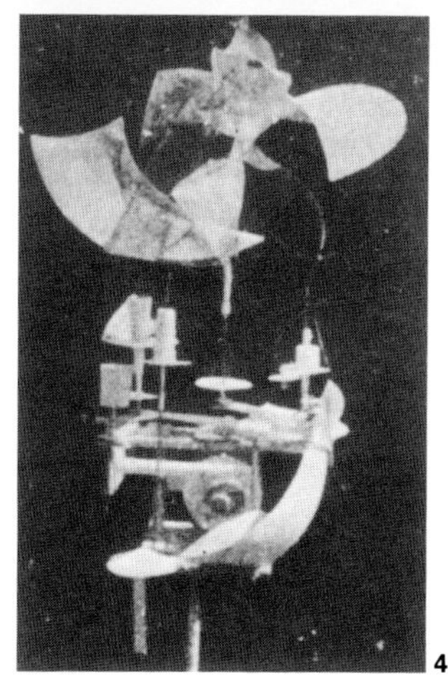
40

Balla's major construction to survive from those years was kinetic only in spirit, but spectacularly so. The *Fist of Boccioni* (no. 12) is a dynamic and graceful combination of cardboard curves and wedges, painted vivid orange-red. It is a calligraphic sculpture, cutting into space with an abstracted image of such speed and force that Marinetti adapted a drawing of it for the official stationery of the Futurist movement. Even Severini was briefly tempted into the field of mobile relief construction in the year 1915, which is proving to be an *annus mirabilis* for radical work created in the very shadow of war and since lost to us. Severini had made skillful use of collage since 1912, when he first applied sequins to the fluttering skirts of his painted dancers (see no. 66), and he glued a bristling black mustache to his 1913 portrait of Marinetti. His most adventurous effort was the *Articulated Dancer*, exhibited in early 1916: a painted canvas in front of which hung two colored planes on a pivot and a series of elements, which could be manipulated with gentle tugs on a string.[87]

The subsequent disappearance, destruction, or alteration of many fragile and transient works of 1912 to 1915 renders the early history of avant-garde sculpture particularly difficult to trace. But the profusion of radical proposals and remarkable objects produced by the Italians in those years played a vital role in launching an international revolution whose end is not yet is sight. Balla continued to experiment with mixed media and a second generation of Futurists (notably Depero and Enrico Prampolini) carried on a lively exploration of collage and assemblage in Italy after the war.

THE PRINTED WORD

Books and journals have often proved to have a better chance of survival than works of art. The history of early twentieth-century typographic design and the intermarriage of words and images were profoundly affected by Futurist theory and practice. Marinetti's innovations as a poet were frequently borrowed by his painter-friends; both Boccioni and Severini used his concepts of "words-in-freedom" and "immense nets of analogy" for their pictorial purposes. Influences traveled in both directions, as Marinetti proposed a visual revolution for the printed word: "On the same page . . . we will use three or four colours of ink, or even twenty different typefaces if necessary."[88] Severini's drawing made up of words, *Serpentine Dancer* (fig. 41), and Carrà's famous *Free-Word Painting (Patriotic Celebration)*[89] were published in the summer of 1914. Although they were preceded by Sonia Delaunay's multicolored unfolding design for Blaise Cendrars's poem "La Prose du Transsibérien" (no. 87) and their appearance coincided with the first publication of Apollinaire's figurative *Calligrammes* (see fig. 42),[90] the Futurists' efforts were once again matched in audacity only by the collaborative achievements of the Russian painters and poets. Many of the artists' books published between 1910 and 1916 in Russia confirm the interest in folk art and a consciously "primitive" style on the part of the most sophisticated painters. But influences of Cubism and Western art were swiftly absorbed as well. Malevich's book illustrations provide rare clues to his own development. His untitled drawing of September 1913 (fig. 43) combines letters, numerals, musical notes, and mechanical elements in a "transrational" portrait of a pilot, which actually anticipates Futurist practice, although it may reflect exposure to Marinetti's ideas.[91] Typographical innovations were transmitted swiftly from country to country. The two issues of Wyndham Lewis's *Blast* not only reverberated with criticisms of Marinetti expressed in Marinettian terms but made brilliant use of huge, black letters and dynamic arrangements of words. In New York during 1915 Marius de Zayas published a daring magazine entitled *291*. Its large, handsome pages were essentially individual "ideagrams" (fig. 44), in which the proportion of images to words varied according to the whim of the creators.

fig. 38 Filippo Tommaso Marinetti (Italian, 1876–1944)
Self-Portrait (Dynamic Combination of Objects), 1914
Mixed media, dimensions unknown
Lost. Reproduced in *Sketch* (London), May 13, 1914

fig. 39 Giacomo Balla (Italian, 1871–1958)
Colored Plastic Complex of Force-Lines, c. 1914–15
Construction: cardboard, wool, red and yellow thread, dimensions unknown
Lost

fig. 40 Fortunato Depero (Italian, 1892–1960)
Colored Plastic Motor—Noisemaking Complex of Equivalents in Motion, c. 1914–15
Construction: colored cloth, cardboard, tinfoil, wire, wood, pipes, pulleys, etc., dimensions unknown
Lost

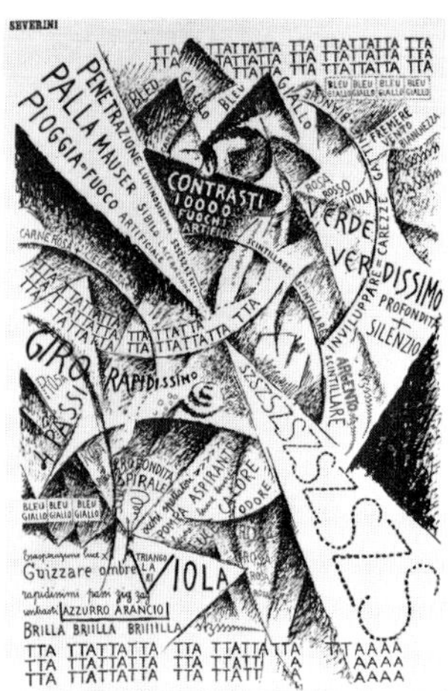

41

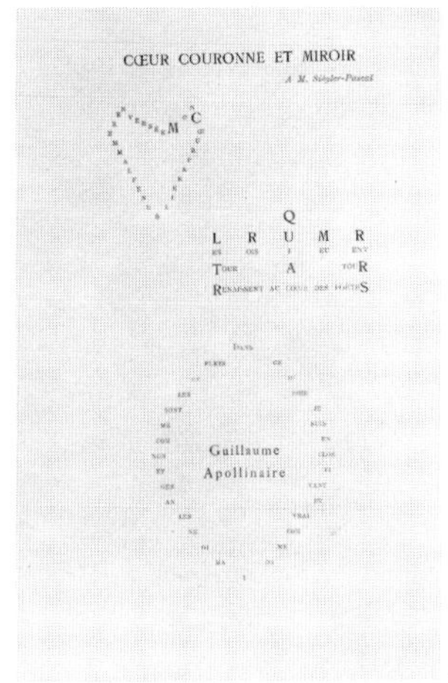

42

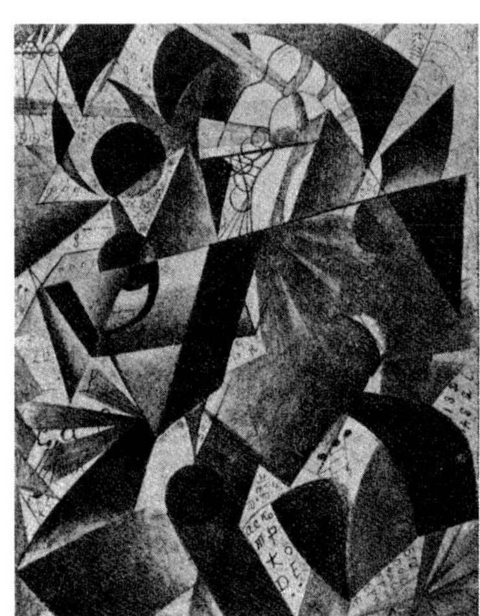
43

FINALE

By the time the long-delayed ship *Jason* reached San Francisco in April 1915 with its cargo, including fifty works by the five Futurist painters for the Panama-Pacific International Exposition,[92] the first vital phase of Futurism was essentially over. Italy entered the war on May 24, 1915; Marinetti volunteered for service in a cyclist unit, together with Boccioni, Russolo, and the architect Sant'Elia. As early as the spring of 1914, signs of the imminent disintegration of the movement were evident amidst its vigorous expansion. The crowd of recruits to Futurist ranks was swelling, with Marinetti's encouragement, but the original members of the movement were in disaccord. The publication of Boccioni's book *Pittura Scultura Futuriste* in March 1914 had exacerbated a deepening rift between Boccioni and Carrà, and even the equable Severini was irritated by Boccioni's tendency to claim all Futurist innovations as his own. Two exhibitions in Italy emphasized the decline of the old order of Futurism and the rise of the new. The Free Exhibition of International Futurists was held in Rome at the gallery of Dr. Giuseppe Sprovieri in April 1914.[93] Of the five original Futurist painters only Balla was represented, but sixteen new Italian adherents were joined by an odd assortment of colleagues from other countries: four well-established Russian artists (Archipenko, Alexandra Exter, Olga Rosanova, and Nicolai Kulbin), the British poetess Mina Loy, the obscure Belgian painter J. Schmalzigaug, and an elusive American named Frances Simpson Stevens, who contributed eight pictures. In May of the same year another large exhibition, in Milan, announced the first manifestation of a group calling itself Nuove Tendenze (New Tendencies). It included sixty-two works by nine Italian artists, most notably the painter Leonardo Dudreville and Sant'Elia, whose contribution to the catalogue was to be revised and published by *Lacerba* in August as the Manifesto of Futurist Architecture. A potential candidate for the Futurist movement as early as 1910,[94] Dudreville was a friend of Russolo and deeply interested in analogies between painting and music. His huge canvas *Daily Domestic Arguments* (no. 59) was derived in part from an interpretation of Richard Strauss's *Domestic* Symphony and was clearly related to Boccioni's theory of states of mind. Dudreville was also one of the first Italian painters to join Balla and Severini in attaining pure abstraction with two works of 1913. Although Dudreville did not refer to himself as a Futurist, his paintings of 1912–14 have more in common with the theories and even the works of the original group than do many of those by artists who eagerly followed Marinetti's lead and became the second generation of Futurists carrying the movement on in Italy after the war.

The remarkable period of international contacts between artists approached an end in 1914 as Europe moved into the first of four disastrous years of conflict. Poets and painters volunteered or were conscripted; by 1918 the grim list of casualties included Boccioni, Duchamp-Villon, Marc, and Apollinaire. Larionov, Gontcharova, and Chagall joined the throng of those who returned to Russia from Paris; Kandinsky left Munich after eighteen years in the West. Commissions for Diaghilev's Russian ballet provided a brief, curiously poignant reunion of international figures in Italy during 1917. (A photograph showing Picasso, Gontcharova, and Larionov with Marinetti in Rome, during the preparations for the ballet *Parade*, evokes a sense of unreality.[95]) A band of expatriate Frenchmen settled in New York, and Duchamp found himself a fellow exile with Gleizes, who had so disapproved of his *Nude Descending a Staircase,* now the scandalous darling of the American press. While the visible influence of Futurist ideas waned in Europe, and both Severini and Carrà moved gradually toward a renewed interest in the art of the past, a number of painters in the United States continued to explore dynamic modes of composition for contemporary subject matter. Joseph Stella celebrated the hurly-burly of Coney Island, while Max Weber conveyed the turmoil of the subway at rush hour or Grand Central Station. For not a few Europeans, exposure to the City of New York was itself a heady Futurist experience. Picabia had expressed this excitement as early as February 1913 when he arrived for the opening of the Armory Show,[96] and even the sober Gleizes was to fall under the spell of the electric signs and billboards of Broadway in 1915.

For many of the avant-garde, the war years were to cause, or at least to coincide with, a major shift in their artistic development. The innovations which followed each other with such breathless rapidity between 1910 and 1914 were absorbed, synthesized, or denied. Picasso moved toward the triumph of late Cubism in *The Three Musicians* of 1921 and simultaneously returned to a ponderous, classical style. Wyndham Lewis forsook his interest in abstraction, while Delaunay fell into uninspired repetition of his earlier themes. The Russian Revolution of 1917 carried

fig. 41 Gino Severini (Italian, 1883–1966)
Serpentine Dancer, 1914
Drawing reproduced in *Lacerba* (Florence), July 1, 1914

fig. 42 Guillaume Apollinaire (French, 1880–1918)
Coeur Couronne et Miroir, 1914
Calligramme reproduced in *Les Soirées de Paris*, nos. 25 and 27 (July and August 1914)

fig. 43 Kasimir Malevich (Russian, 1878–1935)
Drawing reproduced in V. Khlebnikov, A. Kruchenych, E. Guro, *The Three* (Saint Petersburg, 1913), opp. p. 82

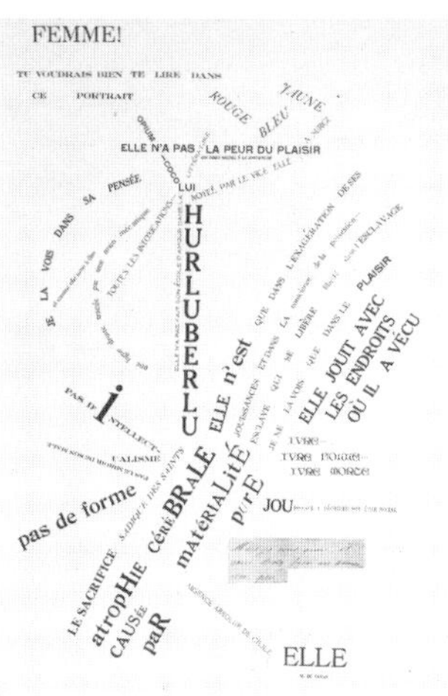

44

vanguard artists to a short-lived but exciting period of creative effort in the service of a new society. In Zurich, the Cabaret Voltaire opened on March 5, 1916, and the lively, disruptive phenomenon of Dadaism was born. While Futurism itself expired as an international movement, Dada, with its penchant for nonsense poetry and collage, chaotic "evenings," and subversive satire, appropriated a number of Futurist techniques. The first issue of the Dada review *Cabaret Voltaire*, published in June 1916, contained a free-word poem by Marinetti, but by July 1918 the Dadaist Tristan Tzara was neatly turning the Italian impresario's tactics against him: "I write a manifesto and I don't want anything, however, I say certain things, and I am on principle against manifestos as I am also against principles . . . . I write this manifesto to show that one can do opposed actions together, in a single fresh breath; I am against action; for continual contradiction for affirmation too, I am neither for nor against and I don't explain because I hate good sense. . . ."[97] Dada was not only against the past, it was also against the future, and Marinetti's violent optimism was out of date.

The legacy of the first heroic phase of Futurism in part resides in a number of powerful works of art by the Futurists themselves and others affected by their ideas or their images. In part it lingers in ongoing developments in theater, music, and the increasingly rich domain of "performance art." Futurism drew upon many of the sources that nourished other avant-garde movements in the early twentieth century, and their histories are inextricably entwined. Marinetti's founding manifesto of 1909 had prophesied that one day Futurism too would be overtaken by its successors: "Sniffing doglike at the academy doors the strong odour of our decaying minds, which will already have been promised to the literary catacombs."

But we won't be there . . . . At last they'll find us—one winter's night—in open country, beneath a sad roof drummed by a monotonous rain. They'll see us crouched beside our trembling aeroplanes in the act of warming our hands at the poor little blaze that our books of today will give out when they take fire from the flight of our images.[98]

Malevich observed the "flight" of Futurist images with a keen eye. He was never to traverse the vast distance between Moscow and Paris, but his awareness of contemporary European developments was intense and his study of them profound. Although the existence of a distinct Futurist movement in Russia must be taken into account in reading Malevich's texts, he clearly knew the Italian Futurist manifestos well and responded directly to many of their ideas. His impassioned yet rigorous statements in *From Cubism and Futurism to Suprematism: The New Painterly Realism* of 1916 may serve as the valediction to Futurism from one of its most intelligent contemporary critics:

Futurism opened up the "new" in modern life: the beauty of speed.
And through speed we move more swiftly.
And we, who only yesterday were futurists, have reached new forms through speed, new relationships with nature and objects.
We have reached suprematism, abandoning futurism as a loophole through which those lagging behind us will pass.
We have abandoned futurism, and we, bravest of the brave, *have spat on the altar of its art*.

We rejected futurism not because it was outdated, and its end had come. No. The beauty of speed that it discovered is eternal, and the new will still be revealed to many.
Since we run to our goal through the speed of futurism, our thought moves more swiftly and whoever lives in futurism is nearer to this aim and further from the past.

Malevich had passed beyond Futurism to the absolute abstraction of his "black square." He proposed a world of art which is "new, nonobjective, pure," leaving the representation of nature, even distorted and accelerated as it appears in Futurist pictures, far behind. But his final words retain a familiar ring:

Hurry up and shed the hardened skin of centuries, so that you can catch up with us more easily.
I have overcome the impossible and made gulfs with my breath.
You are caught in the nets of the horizon, like fish!
We, suprematists, throw open the way to you.
Hurry!
For tomorrow you will not recognize us.[99]

fig. 44 Marius de Zayas (American, 1880–1961)
Femme!, 1915
Drawing reproduced in *291* (New York), no. 9
(November 1915)

NOTES

1. R. Delaunay to Filippo Tommaso Marinetti, [1909], Marinetti Archives, The Beinecke Rare Book and Manuscript Library, Yale University (hereinafter referred to as Beinecke Library) (author's translation). Delaunay was an obscure French poet not to be confused with the artist Robert Delaunay.
2. Charles Camille Saint-Saëns to Marinetti, [1909], Marinetti Archives, Beinecke Library [written on the reverse of a copy of Marinetti's founding Manifesto of Futurism] (author's translation).
3. See Pär Bergman, *"Modernolatria" et "Simultaneità"* (Uppsala, 1962), pp. 52–53.
4. Wyndham Lewis, "Room III. The Cubist Room," forward to Brighton, Public Art Galleries, *Exhibition of English Post-Impressionists, Cubists and Others* (November 1913–January 1914); reprinted in Wyndham Lewis, *Wyndham Lewis on Art: Collected Writings 1913–1956,* ed. Walter Michel and C. J. Fox (New York, 1969), p. 56.
5. Guillaume Apollinaire in *Les Soirées de Paris,* December 15, 1913, translated as "The Salon d'Automne," in Guillaume Apollinaire, *Apollinaire on Art: Essays and Reviews 1902–1918,* ed. LeRoy C. Breunig and trans. Susan Suleiman (New York, 1972), p. 334.
6. Gino Severini, *La Vita di un Pittore* (Milan, 1965), p. 140.
7. Quoted in Benedikt Livshits, *The One and a Half-Eyed Archer*, ed. and trans. John E. Bowlt (Newtonville, Mass., 1977), p. 108.
8. Quoted in Bergman, *"Modernolatria" et "Simultaneità,"* p. 45 (author's translation).
9. For discussions of the Abbaye and Unanimism, see Daniel Robbins, "From Symbolism to Cubism: The Abbaye de Créteil," *The Art Journal,* vol. 23 (Winter 1963–64), pp. 111–16; and Marianne W. Martin, "Futurism, Unanimism and Apollinaire," *The Art Journal*, vol. 28 (Spring 1969), pp. 258–68.
10. Jules Romains, *La Vie Unanime: Poèmes 1904–1907* (Paris, 1934), 7th ed., p. 106 (author's translation).
11. See Bergman, *"Modernolatria" et "Simultaneità,"* pp. 1–33 passim.
12. Filippo Tommaso Marinetti, Manifesto of Futurism [1909], in Umbro Apollonio, ed., and Robert Brain et al., trans., *Futurist Manifestos* (New York, 1973), pp. 21–22.
13. Manifesto of Futurist Painters [1910], translated in Apollonio, ed., *Futurist Manifestos*, p. 25.
14. Marinetti, Manifesto of Futurism [1909], translated in Apollonio, ed., *Futurist Manifestos*, p. 23.
15. Umberto Boccioni, Technical Manifesto of Futurist Sculpture [1912], in Robert L. Herbert, ed. and trans., *Modern Artists on Art: Ten Unabridged Essays* (Englewood Cliffs, N.J., 1964), p. 55.
16. Filippo Tommaso Marinetti, "The Variety Theatre" [1913], in *Marinetti: Selected Writings*, ed. R. W. Flint and trans. R. W. Flint and Arthur A. Coppotelli (New York, 1972), pp. 116, 120.
17. Umberto Boccioni to his mother and sister, April 17, 1906, in Umborto Boccioni, *Gli Scritti Editi e Inediti*, ed. Zeno Birolli (Milan, 1971), p. 334 (author's translation).
18. Georges Braque, quoted in New York, The Museum of Modern Art, *Pablo Picasso: A Retrospective* (May 22–September 16, 1980), p. 123. Catalogue edited by William Rubin.
19. Manifesto of Futurist Painters [1910], translated in Apollonio, ed., *Futurist Manifestos*, pp. 25, 26. This document, like many Futurist manifestos, was signed by several artists; its exact authorship is not certain. Signed by Boccioni, Carrà, and Russolo as well as two other Milanese painters (see n. 20 below), the text was probably greatly influenced by Marinetti.
20. The painters Romolo Romani and Aroldo Bonzagni signed the first Manifesto of Futurist Painters but hurriedly resigned when the fireworks started. Balla had joined by May 1910 and Severini soon followed. See Marianne W. Martin, *Futurist Art and Theory 1909–1915* (Oxford, 1968), pp. 71–72.
21. Technical Manifesto of Futurist Painting [1910], translated in Apollonio, ed., *Futurist Manifestos*, pp. 27–31. This manifesto, previously issued in Italy in mid-April 1910, was published in France with the signatures of Balla, Boccioni, Carrà, Severini, and Russolo. It was probably written chiefly by Boccioni and Carrà, since Balla and Severini were latecomers to the movement.
22. The Carrà and Russolo paintings are reproduced in Apollonio, ed., *Futurist Manifestos*, pls. 5, 7. For Boccioni's *Modern Idol* see Aldo Palazzeschi, *L'Opera Completa di Boccioni* (Milan, 1969), pl. 37.
23. Russolo's presence on that 1911 Paris visit is still debated, although Severini mentioned him as being present. Gino Severini to Filippo Tommaso Marinetti, April 17, 1930, Marinetti Archives, Beinecke Library.
24. Guillaume Apollinaire, "Peintres Futuristes," *Mercure de France* (Paris), November 16, 1911; reprinted in Guillaume Apollinaire, *Anecdotiques*, ed. Marcel Adéma (Paris, 1955), pp. 49–50.
25. One of Delaunay's Eiffel Tower paintings was reproduced in Roger Allard, "Sur Quelques Peintres," *Les Marches du Sud-Ouest* (Paris), June 1911, pp. 57–64. Allard's description of Delaunay's work as "futurist" caught Boccioni's attention. For excerpts and discussions of Allard's article, see Edward F. Fry, ed., *Cubism* (New York, 1966), pp. 63–64; and Umberto Boccioni, *Dynamisme Plastique*, ed. Giovanni Lista and trans. Claude Minot and Giovanni Lista (Lausanne, 1975), p. 152.
26. See Umberto Boccioni to Vico Baer, [June 1913], translated in New York, The Museum of Modern Art, *Futurism* (May 31–September 5, 1961), p. 134. Catalogue by Joshua C. Taylor.
27. For draft of that lecture, see Umberto Boccioni, "La Pittura Futurista (Conferenza Tenuta a Roma nel 1911)," in Umberto Boccioni, *Altri Inediti e Apparati Critici*, ed. Zeno Birolli (Milan, 1972), pp. 11–29.
28. "The Exhibitors to the Public" [February 5, 1912], preface to London, Sackville Gallery, *Exhibition of Works by the Italian Futurist Painters* (March 1912); in Apollonio, ed., *Futurist Manifestos,* pp. 45–50.
29. See Virginia Spate, *Orphism: The Evolution of Non-Figurative Painting in Paris 1910–1914* (Oxford, 1979), p. 36.
30. Jean Metzinger, "Note sur la Peinture," *Pan* (Paris), October–November 1910, pp. 649–51; translated in Fry, ed., *Cubism*, p. 60.
31. "It's actually helter-skelter." Guillaume Apollinaire, "A L'Exposition des Peintres Futuristes," *Mercure de France* (Paris), February 16, 1912; reprinted in Apollinaire, *Anecdotiques*, p. 64.

32. André Salmon, "Les Futuristes," *Paris-Journal*, February 6, 1912; quoted in Bergman, *"Modernolatria" et "Simultaneità,"* pp. 159–60 (author's translation).
33. Fernand Léger in *Les Soirées de Paris*, June 15, 1914, translated as "Contemporary Achievements in Painting," in Fernand Léger, *Functions of Painting*, ed. Edward F. Fry and trans. Alexandra Anderson (New York, 1973), p. 17.
34. *Ibid.*, pp. 11–12.
35. Quoted in "Picabia, Art Rebel, Here to Teach New Movement," *New York Times*, February 16, 1913, section 5, p. 9; quoted in Dickran Tashjian, *Skyscraper Primitives: Dada and the American Avant-Garde 1910–1925* (Middletown, Conn., 1975), p. 20.
36. Iakov Tugendhold, "L'Exposition des Tableaux de Natalia Gontcharova," *Apollon*, no. 8 (1913); reprinted in Paris, Musée National d'Art Moderne, Centre Georges Pompidou, *Art et Poésie Russes, 1900–1930: Textes Choisis* (Paris, 1979), p. 85 (author's translation).
37. Filippo Tommaso Marinetti, "Vital English Art," *Observer* (London), June 7, 1914.
38. For the genesis of "A Slap in the Face of Public Taste," see Livshits, *The One and a Half-Eyed Archer*, pp. 106–9. For the Rayonist Manifesto see John E. Bowlt, ed. and trans., *Russian Art of the Avant-Garde: Theory and Criticism 1902–1934* (New York, 1976), pp. 87–91.
39. For Larionov's text as it was published in July 1913, see Bowlt, ed. and trans., *Russian Art of the Avant-Garde*, pp. 93–100.
40. Leo Stein to Lee Simonson, October 11, 1913, Collection of American Literature, Beinecke Library; quoted in New York, The Museum of Modern Art, *Patrick Henry Bruce: American Modernist* (August 22–October 21, 1979), p. 53. Catalogue by William C. Agee and Barbara Rose.
41. Rayonist Manifesto [1913], translated in Bowlt, ed., *Russian Art of the Avant-Garde*, p. 90.
42. Guillaume Apollinaire in *Les Soirées de Paris*, November 15, 1913, translated as "Monthly Chronicle," [Review of the Erster Deutscher Herbstsalon], *Apollinaire on Art*, p. 338.
43. Umberto Boccioni to Nino Barbantini, [September 1910], in Boccioni, *Gli Scritti Editi e Inediti*, p. 343 (author's translation).
44. Guillaume Apollinaire in *Le Petit Bleu* (Paris), March 20, 1912, translated as "New Trends and Artistic Personalities," *Apollinaire on Art*, p. 219.
45. Guillaume Apollinaire in *Les Soirées de Paris*, February 1, 1912, translated as "On the Subject in Modern Painting," *Apollinaire on Art*, p. 197.
46. "The Exhibitors to the Public" [February 5, 1912], preface to London, Sackville Gallery, *Exhibition of Works by the Italian Futurist Painters* (March 1912); in Apollonio, ed., *Futurist Manifestos*, p. 46.
47. See n. 25 above.
48. Paul Klee, *Tagebücher von Paul Klee 1898–1918*, ed. Félix Klee (Cologne, 1957), p. 285.
49. Quoted in Berkeley, University Art Museum, *Franz Marc: 1880–1916* (December 5, 1979–February 3, 1980), p. 59. Catalogue by Mark Rosenthal.
50. Quoted in Basel, Kunstmuseum, *150 Paintings, 12th–20th Century* (1964), p. 232. Catalogue by Georg Schmidt.
51. Guillaume Apollinaire in *L'Intransigeant* (Paris), February 7, 1912, translated as "The Art World: The Italian Futurist Painters," *Apollinaire on Art*, p. 199.
52. Pierre Cabanne, *Dialogues with Marcel Duchamp,* trans. Ron Padgett (New York, 1971), p. 35.
53. See Christopher Green, *Léger and the Avant-Garde* (New Haven, 1976), p. 321 n. 38.
54. See New York, The Solomon R. Guggenheim Museum, *Frantisek Kupka 1871–1957: A Retrospective* (October 10–December 7, 1975), pp. 49–64. Catalogue by Margit Rowell.
55. *Rhythms of a Bow* is reproduced in Martin, *Futurist Art and Theory 1909–1915*, pl. 170.
56. Cabanne, *Dialogues with Marcel Duchamp*, p. 30.
57. See Umberto Boccioni to Gino Severini, January 11, 1913, in Boccioni, *Gli Scritti Editi e Inediti*, p. 364.
58. Reproduced in Cambridge, Mass., Harvard University, Fogg Art Museum, *Jacques Villon* (January 17–February 29, 1976), p. 66 no. 47. Catalogue edited by Daniel Robbins.
59. The Salon d'Automne was held from October 1 to November 8, 1912. Boccioni had been in Paris for some time by November 9. See Umberto Boccioni to Vico Baer, November 9, 1912, in Boccioni, *Gli Scritti Editi e Inediti*, pp. 362–63.
60. In 1922 Marinetti and the French painter André Lhote exchanged letters discussing how a Cubist and a Futurist would depict a person on a balcony; Lhote praised Gleizes's painting. *La Vie des Lettres et des Arts*, no. 16 (1922), pp. 7–13; see New York, The Solomon R. Guggenheim Museum, *Albert Gleizes 1881–1953: A Retrospective Exhibition* (September 15–November 1, 1964), p. 30. Catalogue by Daniel Robbins.
61. See Martin, *Futurist Art and Theory 1909–1915*, p. 140.
62. *Ibid.*, pl. 153.
63. For details of Boccioni's disagreements with Delaunay, see *ibid.*, p. 205.
64. Clive Bell, "The New Post-Impressionist Art Show," *The Nation* (London), October 25, 1913, pp. 172–73.
65. *In the Hold* was shown in the "First Exhibition of the London Group" at the Goupil Galleries in London from March to April 1914. "Exhibition of the Works of the Italian Futurist Painters and Sculptors" opened at the Doré Galleries in London on April 23, 1914.
66. Marianne W. Martin is convinced that Boccioni had some experience with sculpture before 1912, if only in his student days.
67. Umberto Boccioni to Vico Baer, March 15, 1912, translated in New York, The Museum of Modern Art, *Futurism*, p. 134.
68. See Margaret Scolari Barr, *Medardo Rosso* (New York, 1963), p. 78 nn. 168–69. Severini apparently did not mention that Boccioni accompanied him on his visit to Rosso.
69. Guillaume Apollinaire in *L'Intransigeant* (Paris), June 21, 1913, translated as "The Art World: First Exhibition of Futurist Sculpture by the Futurist Painter and Sculptor Boccioni," *Apollinaire on Art*, pp. 320–21.
70. Raymond Duchamp-Villon, "The Eiffel Tower" [1913], translated in George Heard Hamilton and William C. Agee, *Raymond Duchamp-Villon 1876–1918* (New York, 1967), p. 118.

71. Reproduced in Albert E. Elsen, *Origins of Modern Sculpture: Pioneers and Premises* (New York, 1974), pl. 120.
72. See Giovanni Lista, ed., *Futurisme: Manifestes—Proclamations—Documents* (Lausanne, 1973), p. 177.
73. Boccioni, Technical Manifesto of Futurist Sculpture [1912], translated in Herbert, ed., *Modern Artists on Art*, pp. 50–56.
74. See Daniel-Henry Kahnweiler, *The Rise of Cubism*, trans. Henry Aronson (New York, 1949), p. 22 [written during the war and originally published as *Der Weg zum Kubismus* (Munich, 1920)].
75. Robert Delaunay, "Draft of a Letter to Nicolas Maximovitch Minsky (1912; 1918?)," in *The New Art of Color: The Writings of Robert and Sonia Delaunay*, ed. Arthur A. Cohen and trans. David Shapiro and Arthur A. Cohen (New York, 1978), p. 62.
76. Guillaume Apollinaire in *Montjoie!* (Paris), March 14, 1913, translated as "Pablo Picasso," *Apollinaire on Art*, p. 281.
77. Apollinaire in *Les Soirées de Paris*, November 15, 1913, translated as "Monthly Chronicle" [Review of the Erster Deutscher Herbstsalon], *Apollinaire on Art*, p. 337.
78. Apollinaire reviewed Boccioni's exhibition in *L'Intransigeant* (Paris), June 21, 1913, translated as "The Art World: First Exhibition of Futurist Sculpture by the Futurist Painter and Sculptor Boccioni," *Apollinaire on Art*, pp. 320–21.
79. The exact date of Tatlin's important visit remains undetermined. Scholars recently have suggested both spring and late fall 1913. One wonders whether Tatlin saw Boccioni's exhibition.
80. Guillaume Apollinaire in *L'Intransigeant* (Paris), February 28, 1914, translated as "The Salon des Indépendants: Before the Opening," *Apollinaire on Art*, p. 355.
81. Boccioni, *Dynamisme Plastique*, p. 95 (author's translation).
82. Filippo Tommaso Marinetti, "Reciting Poetry while Marching and London Ladies," [from *An Italian Sensibility Born in Egypt*], translated in *Marinetti: Selected Writings*, p. 320.
83. Crotti's lost work is illustrated in Robert Lebel, *Marcel Duchamp*, trans. George Heard Hamilton (New York, 1959), fig. 11. Picabia's assemblage is reproduced in William A. Camfield, *Francis Picabia: His Art, Life and Times* (Princeton, 1979), pl. 184.
84. Giacomo Balla and Fortunato Depero, "Futurist Reconstruction of the Universe" [1915], translated in Apollonio, ed., *Futurist Manifestos*, pp. 197–200.
85. See New York, The Museum of Modern Art, *The Machine as Seen at the End of the Mechanical Age* (November 25, 1968–February 9, 1969), p. 106. Catalogue by K. G. Pontus Hultén.
86. Evg. Adamov in *Kievskaya Mysl* (Kiev), no. 125 (May 6, 1915), p. 2; translated as "Letter from Moscow," in Stockholm, Moderna Museet, *Vladimir Tatlin* (July–September 1968), p. 7. Catalogue by Troels Andersen.
87. Severini, *La Vita di un Pittore*, p. 193.
88. Filippo Tommaso Marinetti, "Destruction of Syntax—Imagination without Strings—Words-in-Freedom" [1913], translated in Apollonio, ed., *Futurist Manifestos*, pp. 98, 104–5.
89. Reproduced in New York, The Museum of Modern Art, *Futurism*, p. 111.
90. *Les Soirées de Paris*, June 1914.
91. See Susan P. Compton, *The World Backwards: Russian Futurist Books 1912–16* (London, 1978), pp. 108–9; and Kasimir Malévitch, *Ecrits*, ed. Andrei B. Nakov and trans. Andrée Robel-Chicurel (Paris, 1975), p. 44.
92. The late arrival of the ship is recounted in "Secret Trip of *Jason* Ended," *New York Times*, April 18, 1915, section 5, p. 20. The Futurist works were not exhibited until September, in an annex to the Fine Arts "Palace" which was constructed to house the overflow. See "Radical Art at Exposition," *American Art News*, October 2, 1915, p. 2.
93. Rome, Galleria Futurista, *Esposizione Libera Futurista Internazionale* (April–May 1914). The catalogue is reproduced in facsimile in Piero Pacini, ed., *Esposizioni Futuriste,* vol. 1, *1912–1918* (Florence, 1977). Although Balla is not listed as an exhibitor, he was a collaborator on a piece of sculpture.
94. See Umberto Boccioni to Gino Severini, [August 1910], in Boccioni, *Gli Scritti Editi e Inediti*, p. 342.
95. See Lista, ed., *Futurisme: Manifestes—Proclamations—Documents*, following p. 320.
96. See Tashjian, *Skyscraper Primitives*, p. 20.
97. Tristan Tzara, "Manifeste dada 1918," *Dada* (Zurich), no. 3 (December 1918); translated in London, Hayward Galleries, *Dada and Surrealism Reviewed* (January 11–March 27, 1978), p. 60. Catalogue by Dawn Ades.
98. Marinetti, Manifesto of Futurism [1909], translated in Apollonio, ed., *Futurist Manifestos*, p. 23.
99. Kasimir Malevich, *Ot Kubizma i Futurizma k Suprematizmu. Novyi Zhivopisnyi Realizm* [From Cubism and Futurism to Suprematism: The New Painterly Realism] (Moscow, 1916); translated in Bowlt, ed., *Russian Art and the Avant-Garde*, pp. 116–35.

GERMANO CELANT

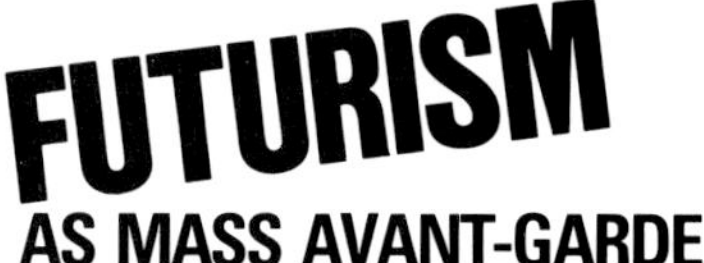

FUTURISM AS MASS AVANT-GARDE

At the beginning of the twentieth century, Italian society was subjected to a number of pressures from coexisting and conflicting forces, both political and economic, each of which tended to impose itself on the others. On the one hand, heavy industry, spurred by technical developments and the increase of new products in the rest of Europe, asked the state for financial aid to sustain the initiatives of entrepreneurs, while urging the workers and rural classes to intensify their labor so as to transform production (read "exploitation") into viable and dynamic capital. On the other hand, the urban middle classes and the peasant population, responding to the call of the international revolutionary movement—whose growth among the proletariat had gained the strength to bring down ancient autocracies—attempted to improve their lot by a libertarian offensive against the bourgeois oligarchy, which had shown itself incapable of coming to grips with social problems. Wavering between anarchy and socialism, the "silent" classes made their anger felt and took to the streets to assert their right to exist. They demanded a process of democratization that would allow the masses to participate in decisions affecting the entire community. It was just this extensive mobilization of those at the bottom that shook up the existing state and brought about a shift of the center of power from the individual to the collective, or rather, to a point somewhere in between. Although their intentions were opposed, both groups demonstrated a desire, if not to overturn, at least to transform, the status quo. In other words, Italian society, with its various forms of poverty and its class dysfunctions, was in need of expansion toward industrialism and technology accompanied by widespread, mass participation in the administration of power.

The push toward technological innovation took place in northern Italy, especially in the Milan-Genoa-Turin triangle—the domain of Futurism—where numerous industrial enterprises carried out experimentation in the fields of machinery and iron and steel manufacturing. The discoveries and inventions of mass communications were widely adapted, and the telegraph, the automobile, and the locomotive became central elements of the new society. Through them a new sensibility, conformist in content but revolutionary in methodology, took on mass proportions. The new media became the instruments used to broaden the foundations of industrial power and at the same time the vehicles for a democratization of culture.

In contrast to the business community where great progress occurred, the masses remained unchanged. If the shipbuilders and industrialists were permeated with the spirit of optimism and profit, the working classes lived in pessimism and poverty. Strikes were provoked and organized to demonstrate their deplorable economic conditions and their lack of voice in the social system. Certainly the so-called mass demonstrations—street rallies, marches, and other forms of struggle—organized by the peasant and working classes from Sicily to Emilia between 1893 and 1908 were one of the characteristics of the growing Italian democracy. In the excitement over new possibilities for work and a better life, the doctrines of socialism spread in the city and countryside. Between 1904 and 1906, from one general strike to the next, a climate of great optimism was ushered in, since financial assets and social values seemed destined to reach new heights, creating a true faith in the "Future."

On this extraordinary and feverish wave, which within the span of the next two years was to demonstrate its inconstancy and fragility, exposing the deficiencies of a crumbling bourgeoisie and an unprepared working class, Futurism made its appearance, its theoretical premises characterized precisely by an enthusiasm for the masses and the new means of communication:

> We will sing of great crowds excited by work, by pleasure, and by riot; we will sing of the multicoloured, polyphonic tides of revolution in the modern capitals; we will sing of the vibrant nightly fervour of arsenals and shipyards blazing with violent electric moons; greedy railway stations that devour smoke-plumed serpents; factories hung on clouds by the crooked lines of their smoke; bridges that stride the rivers like giant gymnasts, flashing in the sun with a glitter of knives; adventurous steamers that sniff the horizon; deep-chested locomotives whose wheels paw the tracks like the hooves of enormous steel horses bridled by tubing; and the sleek flight of planes whose propellers chatter in the wind like banners and seem to cheer like an enthusiastic crowd.
>
> It is from Italy that we launch through the world this violently upsetting incendiary manifesto of ours. With it, today, we establish *Futurism,* because we want to free this land from its smelly gangrene of professors, archaeologists, *ciceroni* and antiquarians.[1]

The excitement of the Futurists and their call for action seized perhaps on the more superficial and obvious aspects of the social and political contradictions that were troubling Italy. Rather than being interested in uniting

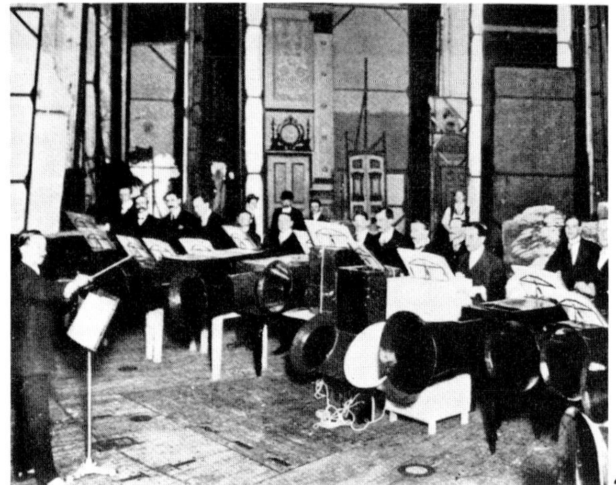

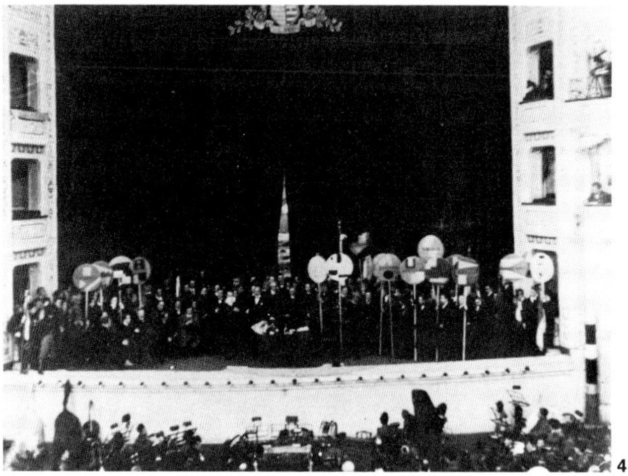

democracy and the working-class movement or even in questioning technology, they seem to have become captivated by technology. They sensed the discontent of the lower classes, but sought to converge with individualistic anarchism and waxed enthusiastic over the doctrine of revolutionary violence of the French philosopher Georges Sorel. They did not take to the streets to demand the reduction of working hours or to protest the exploitation of women and children, but fought instead for the destruction of museums and against academic attachment to the past: "We will destroy the museums, libraries, academies of every kind, will fight moralism, feminism, every opportunistic or utilitarian cowardice."[2] At the same time, they extolled the beauty of industry as the "new expressiveness" of "multiplied man," that is, of the human being identified with the machine. Thus, apart from the strong political ambiguities and increasing connotations of exaggerated masculinity that drove the Futurist movement into the foul den of Italian fascism, Filippo Tommaso Marinetti and his followers created at the beginning of this century a truly "contemporary" cultural phenomenon. Indeed, although it assumed tasks that exceeded its real possibilities, because the ideological and philosophical foundations were lacking, Futurism was the first artistic movement of mass society.[3] It grew out of a period that was experiencing the growth of quantitative and consumer impulses at the expense of qualitative and elitist ones. It was aware of the arrival of the mass media and prophesied the end of an avant-garde destined to be buried—today—under mass creativity.

The effects of "massification," from which society suffers today, include generalized conformity, in accordance with which the area reserved for personal and private choices is greatly reduced. The indoctrination characteristic of mass society tends to repress individual responsibility and exclude convictions not based on momentary emotions or on the passive imitation of the behavior of others. Because of this and the extension of the management of culture, by which a greater number of individuals gain access to the tools of creativity, the avant-garde is destined to perish or to be dissolved in the industry of culture. The Futurists perceived intuitively that it would be ridiculous, as well as unrealistic, to continue to prosper and develop through "diversity" and the abstract principle of experimentation within such restricted fields as painting, sculpture, and poetry. They felt that since each circumstance influences the next, the avant-garde would no longer be able to retain any power, for the revolt of the masses against the elite would sweep it away. Better therefore to step down and in a certain sense transfer aesthetic merit to banal and everyday facts. For this reason Futurism turned its attention more to problems of the total, rather than partial, renewal of sensibility. On the whole, while it did produce alternative modes of poetry and painting, film and theater, it did so by proposing an aesthetic connection with the cabaret, politics, lust, architecture, cooking, and dress. The structure of Futurism, despite its defects, was always "total" and was decided not so much by looking at the taste of the elite as at that of the masses. This then was the reason for its populist dandyism, which let Futurism live intense moments artistically while participating in the active voyeurism of the crowd: "To provoke absolutely improvised words and acts from the spectators, so that every surprise gives rise to new surprises in the orchestra, in the boxes, and in the city."[4] In other words, for the Futurists, the protagonist of culture could not be the abstract category of art or music, theater or film, but the concrete reality of the crowd, which by its impromptu participation, its exchange of remarks and disputes, and its dominance over the actors, became the true defender of freedom of expression, that is, of experimentation "uncontrolled" by the tradition of the avant-garde. Being aware that the demand of the masses for a guarantee of greater freedom was a prelude to the collapse of the privileged freedoms of intellectuals, Marinetti, Umberto Boccioni, Luigi Russolo, Antonio Sant'Elia, Bruno Corra, and the photographer Anton Giulio Bragaglia made a determined effort to nullify the freedom of the avant-garde, true fetish of the upper bourgeoisie, and set out toward a "provocative" affirmation of the presence of the masses.

The revocation of the mandate of the avant-garde may appear debatable, and to historians of international art, will turn out to be indefensible—from their idealist and romantic point of view. Nevertheless, the Futurist formula itself cast doubt on the avant-garde as the representative system of culture in order to bestow that authority on the public, or rather, on the community of consumers of culture. Now if this public demanded a hearing in the streets and in the countryside, it would in time demand one in art and poetry, as well as in cooking and in the cinema. Better therefore to "hear it" in advance and "eliminate, as in the Futurist theater, the physical difference between actors and spectators, so that the

fig. 45 Luigi Russolo's orchestra of "noise intoners" performing at the London Coliseum, June 15, 1914

fig. 46 A Futurist "evening" at the Teatro Fossati in Milan, 1921

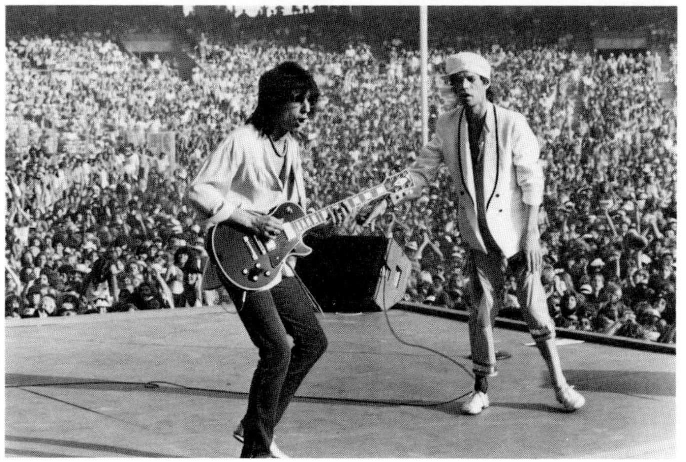

47

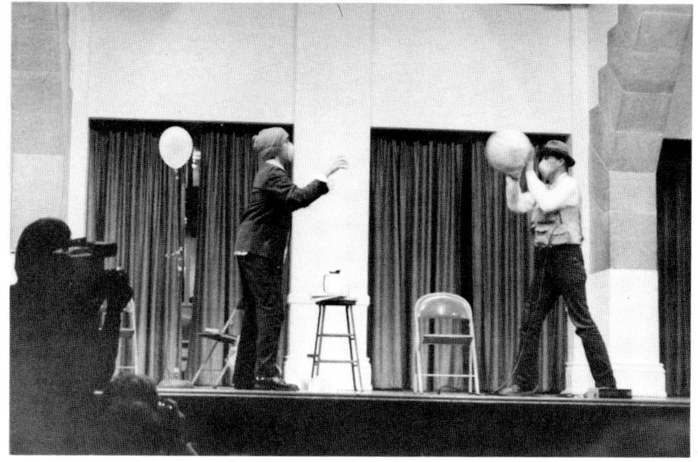

48

auditorium becomes a 'noise-intoner.' At certain moments it would seem to be in a pit of hell: howls, epithets, hisses, laughter, invective, sounds of trumpets and of whistles."[5] Naturally, when this occurred, Futurism defended the freedom and openness of art and the theater, but it also set in motion a mechanism whereby there was a change in position in the hierarchy with the advantage given to the public and not to the individual. In actuality, Futurism presupposed not so much the realization of this transition of power as the discussion of the problem. That is, it took a middle position, between the culture that responds to directives and tastes coming from below and the culture that is detached from society and occupies itself solely with color, form, and volume. In the context of a social organism that was just beginning to function (but would, however, collapse suddenly within a decade), the Futurists had no intention of forming a nucleus apart, distinct from the crowd and their environment. They did not assign themselves a singular or extraordinary task, and thereby did not consider themselves as eccentrics, idlers, or snobs; nor did they wish to be confused with academics and critics. They detached themselves in order to be harmonized, or at least integrated, with the total dynamics:

> The gesture which we would reproduce on canvas shall no longer be a fixed *moment* in universal dynamism. It shall simply be the *dynamic sensation* itself.
> Indeed, all things move, all things run, all things are rapidly changing. . . .
> Our bodies penetrate the sofas upon which we sit, and the sofas penetrate our bodies. The motor bus rushes into the houses which it passes, and in their turn the houses throw themselves upon the motor bus and are blended with it.[6]

The osmosis and mingling of realities emerge from the conviction of a horizontal relationship of languages and persons, the historical comprehension of which can only occur in an interdisciplinary fashion, so that, anthropologically speaking, cultural minorities and majorities have the same function and the same prestige.

The first fifteen years of the twentieth century were marked by consumption, of luxury as well as of life, owing to the rapid acquisition of wealth by the emerging bourgeoisie and the deadly rhythms of work and war. To these were added the speed and mobility of scientific and technological culture, true points of reference in an energetic dynamism in which "Time and Space died yesterday."[7] Out of this lack of concern for the future, Futurism was born, with the intention of transferring its experience into the domain of common usefulness and not restricting it to specialized and specific experimentation. Having been exposed to Symbolism and Cubism during his stay in Paris, Marinetti was in fact aware of the unresponsiveness of the public to an artistic experiment of renewal and at the same time of the difficulty of making it into a central concern for the masses. Art and literature are insignificant "factions" compared to mass demonstrations, which is why he chose to side with the crowd. On the one hand, there was a feeling of isolation, made painful by the conviction that culture must also *do* something; on the other, the detachment of majority public opinion, which despised any artistic or aesthetic product. In this situation, the problem was to constitute a permanent minority, not sterile, but a minority that had a reciprocal relationship with the crowd. This accounts for the disturbing aspects of Futurism, which carried on a divided and schizoid relationship with the masses, whose intense participation it demanded, but to whose scorn it responded with scorn, countering criticism with the "pleasure of being booed."[8] In this way the sterility of the avant-garde was translated into positiveness and sympathy by its relationship with the public. From this emerged the figure of the intellectual as one who refuses to allow himself to wrench approval either from the specialists or from the crowd, and who neither withdraws nor belongs, but is always present where new values are to be found. And these values exist, not on the positive side of art nor the negative side of the masses, but in the dialectic between them. It is an attitude that is not totally passive and which pursues both propaganda and experimentation. In this attitude actions count as such, introduced not only into the lofty fields of art and poetry, but also into furnishings and dress design, cooking and politics. The intransigence of the avant-garde can in fact translate itself into pedantry; hence the call is for a rash sensibility that corresponds to a total consideration of life and is not reduced to the ghetto of artistic expression. In the face of political and social events capable of shaping a new world through the widespread multiplication of objects and persons, what indeed can the role of art be? Almost certainly there is no role, since its function is senseless and marginal. To guarantee a continuity, it would be proper for the avant-garde not to oppose but to facilitate such phenomena.

Futurism was the first movement to promote an

fig. 47 Keith Richards and Mick Jagger of the Rolling Stones in concert, Anaheim, California, July 1978

fig. 48 Impromptu interchange between member of the audience and the artist Joseph Beuys during "An Open Dialogue with Joseph Beuys" at Cooper Union School, New York, January 7, 1980

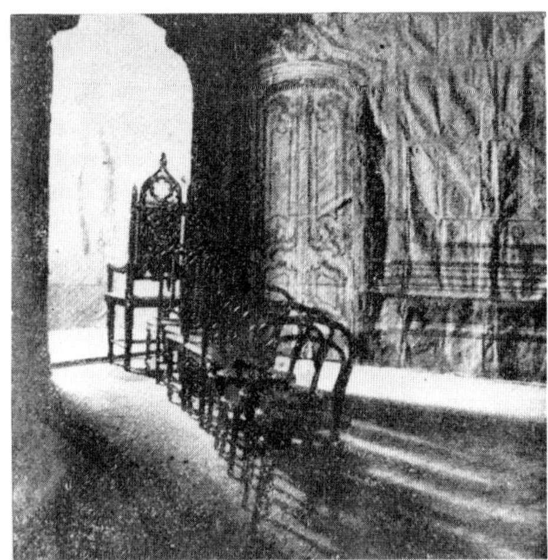

49

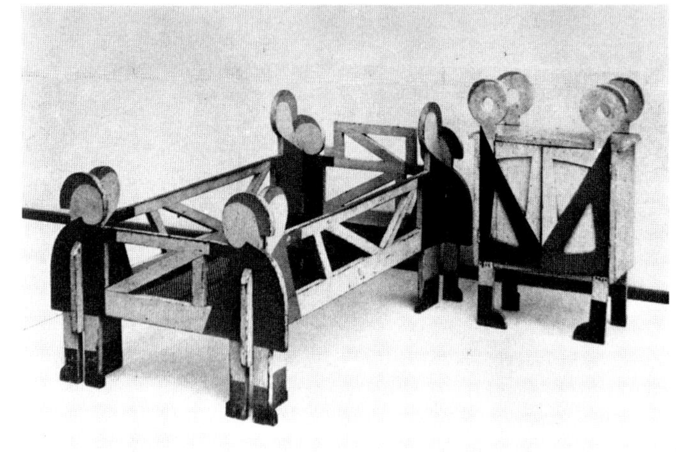

50

aesthetic "abasement" as artistic revolution. Artists immersed themselves in the production of "decor" for interiors and for bodies, and accepted the position of accessories to art when they indulged in typographical experiments, design, interior architecture, publishing, scenography, and orthography. What counted more than conflicts were the combinations and reflections by which art was no longer thought of as active renewal, as stimulation and creative domination over the real (not only the canvas or the bronze, but also the stage, garment, furniture, waistcoat, makeup, sound, food, etc.), but as a "passive counterpart" with regard to the strength of the real. It is at this point that the opposing power of the avant-garde becomes useless. There being no more room for an alternative marginality, since everything is "mass production," art loses its significance and merges with the lampshade or screen, the neckerchief or sideboard, the rug or mural, as demonstrated by the environmental creations of Giacomo Balla and Fortunato Depero. Even toys were required to have artistic responsibility, and like all other everyday objects to participate in the "Futurist Reconstruction of the Universe":

> With plastic complexes we will construct toys which will accustom the child:
> (1) To Completely Spontaneous Laughter (with exaggerated and comical tricks);
> (2) To Maximum Elasticity (without resorting to the throwing of projectiles, whip cracking, pin pricks, etc.);
> (3) To Imaginative Impulses (by using fantastic toys to be looked at through magnifying glasses, small boxes to be opened up at night to reveal pyrotechnic marvels, transforming devices, etc.);
> (4) To The Infinite Stretching And Animation Of The Sensibility (in the unbounded realms of the most acute and exciting noises, smells and colours).[9]

It is obvious that by conceiving toys or metal animals for an artificial landscape, Balla and Depero were conscious of employing techniques of perceptual and sensory persuasion on the eventual users of these Futurist instruments, and yet indoctrination was tied to the banal object, a permanent requirement of cultural consumption. Thus they emerged from the idealist aspiration for the artistic absolute to enter into the taste of the petite bourgeoisie. They placed themselves in the service of a mass that if it had not yet produced "culture," certainly had been its recipient. Their act thus was a provocation, not so much toward the masses as toward all artistic and elite avant-gardes. They turned away from a dead end to accept instead the leveling experience of consumption. The result could only be pure decoration, since in the "effectiveness" of experimentation one object or symbol is as good as another; indeed, they are interchangeable: a painting is equivalent to a sofa, a sculpture to a table. The loss of the effect of culture is accompanied by a loss in artistic stature. No longer is there an underlying meaning, intellectually defined, but one that is apathetic and indifferent, capable of bestowing meaning on "everything," even a suit of clothes. Balla published the "Anti-Neutral Suit. Futurist Manifesto," with the intention of abolishing neutral shades, mediocre balance (that is, "good taste"), symmetry of cut, static lines, and useless buttons to arrive at Futurist clothes, which were to be:

> ASYMMETRICAL. For example, the ends of the sleeves and the front of the jacket will be in circles on the right and in squares on the left. Original clashes of line. . . .
>
> VARIABLE, by means of *modifications* (applications of fabric of different sizes, thickness, pattern, and color) to be placed when and where one likes, at any point on the suit, by suction cups. Anyone can thus invent, at any moment, a new suit of clothes. The modification will be arrogant, jarring, clashing, decisive, warlike, etc.[10]

The shift from what is "striking" in sculpture to what is "refined" in clothing made avant-garde language move toward "mediocrity," which, as Alberto Savinio remarked, is the language of life, since "life in its vastness is mediocre."[11] The old relationship between the elite and masses cracked, and the myths of a heroic avant-garde were shattered into a repertory of banal solutions that produced an incisive effect on the everyday environment. Its orientation to the masses, by which art dissolves into quantity and into anti-artistic vocation (anti-art is in fact an exploit of the leveling of values, where the usual and unusual coexist), marks the importance of Futurism as one of the first examples of mass avant-garde.

Futurism was prophetic of our own time, since it saw in mass meetings and in the banalization of art not the postulate of a negation of culture but the affirmation of a new mode of being, one that became typical of the 1970s, a period in which there occurred an inversion that placed amorality, both stylistic and ideological, as a libertarian scheme. By moral, we mean the political and cultural breakdown of the 1960s. The image of this failure cast a

fig. 49 "The Exit of the Chairs," from F. T. Marinetti's brief Futurist drama *They Are Coming (Vengono)*, 1915

fig. 50 Giacomo Balla's painted wooden bedroom suite for a child, 1928, Collection P. Monachesi, Rome

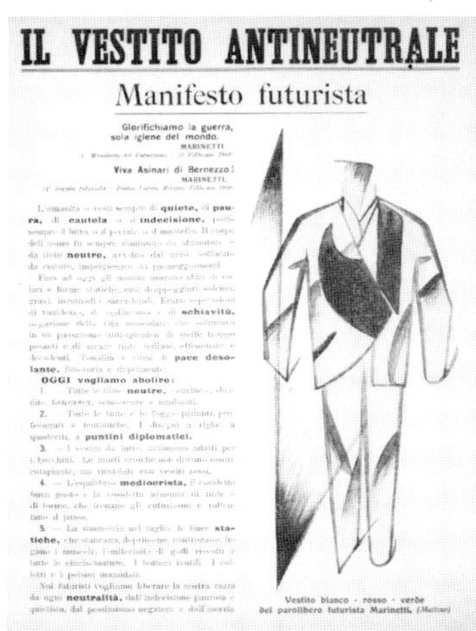
IL VESTITO ANTINEUTRALE

Manifesto futurista

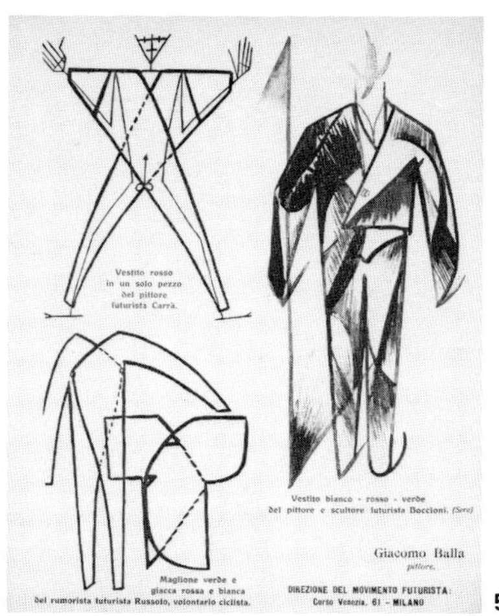

51

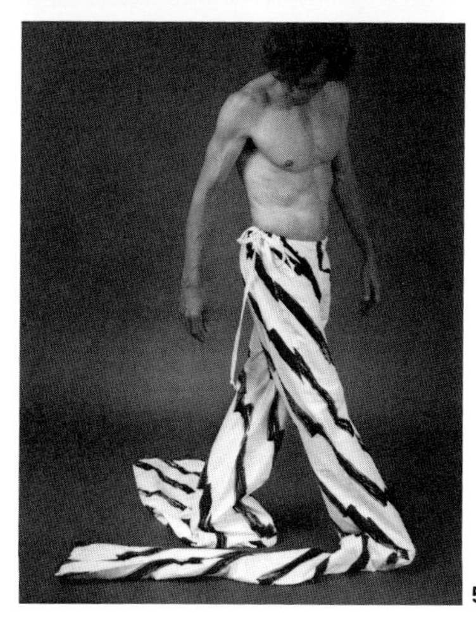
52

pall over experimental planning and made it free territory for all ideologies, so as to give the least possible meaning to things. The last decade in fact, with its decorative art and its mass concerts, took the form of an anti-heroic moment, with one quality inverted: the intensity of the banality of mass existence. Yesterday, like today, the emergence from marginal existence of the petit-bourgeois nuclei, which became increasingly unruly and apparent, so much so as to determine the market and the cultural industry, raised the question of the marginality of art. The marginal becomes useless, since it produces a concept of "absence" at a time when it is political and economic presence that counts.

Futurism, like the consumerist avant-gardes of today from Pop to pattern painting, in order to keep pace with the emergence of a mass society, could not retreat into nihilism and disappear. All that remained was the possibility of currying favor, not of the upper-bourgeois elite, but of the new social orders. Reservations about the generalized application of art faded away, and art once again found itself decorating drawing rooms as frequently as museums, with the difference being that it no longer believed in the charismatic potency of an aesthetic creation, transformed by the need for survival into a "banal sign." No longer did artists impose themselves on the patron, but let themselves be manipulated by his tastes and demands. Art became "socialized," following not the utopian paths of revolution but rather those of consumption and disposability, an attitude that implies the final disappearance of "avant-garde" as value and the advent of a social statute of culture, whereby artistic and literary achievement does not signify the expression of the individual artist or author but the anonymous creation—devoid of originality—of an undifferentiated and undefinable collective.

From 1909 to 1918, the Futurists not only produced manifestos in the sphere of the classic arts, but also took on the themes of lust and politics, in such a way as to lessen their remoteness and make "daily life" the subject and material of expressive language. It is thus no wonder that Futurism, in offering itself as the first opportunity for a mass avant-garde, would be rejected, or would be accepted today only in its narrow definition of painting and sculpture, certainly its least radical moments. And yet its position with regard to mass production and mass communication, because of their attention to the distortions of quantity and mass mediocrity, is more "contemporary" than that of Dada or Surrealism. On close examination, Dada and Surrealism established, in completely different terms, a relationship between culture and the individual, while Futurism instead radicalized that between creativity and the masses. Its hostility was then directed against the focus on "personality" characteristic of Marcel Duchamp and André Breton. In a society of merchandising and consumption, it is necessary to depersonalize and eliminate all originality, since only the banal and mediocre count. In a community of false idolatries (homeland, religion, money), only deception and contempt can find an audience. Thus if the public holds art in contempt, Futurism cannot help but do so also. If the masses demand bad taste, then bad taste is one method of experimental aesthetics. All the central figures of Futurism, from Marinetti to Balilla Pratella, from Severini to Carlo Carrà, tried to take on themselves direct responsibility for everything, that is, for the obscurity of the world, and to distort it in its falsifications, so that pretense and multiplication became the destiny of the avant-garde. One could thus say that Futurism was "a counterfeit avant-garde," and therefore revealed the pretense of all avant-gardes that create the image of an advanced society, despite the fact that the situation remains wretched and closed. One should not therefore create "novelties," but redesign existing signs. Since everything is a setting for the mind, Futurism was not ashamed to work in the world of furnishings and typography. It was conscious of a separation and falsity of the avant-garde, and for this reason worked with falsity and the superficial. Furthermore, it realized that art is a source of power and thus transformed art into a political weapon, that is, into real power. It descended into the streets, it held aesthetic rallies, and bound itself to the social ruin of fascism. It disguised itself with effects because it wanted to strike the public, and it immersed itself in everything, since it was undergoing the crisis over certainties that was tormenting science as well as society. Futurism did not stake out a territory; it spread out. It thus saddled itself with life and through it sought true cultural legitimacy. Instead of taking on the struggle against art (the Futurists had difficulty in hurling themselves against other avant-gardes), it projected itself into real struggles. "First Political Manifesto" (1909); "Against Passatist Venice" (1910); "Against Professors" (1910); "Against Love and Parliamentarianism" (1911); "Manifesto of the Futurist Woman" (1912); "Futurist Manifesto of Lust" (1913); "The Variety Theatre" (1913); "Down with

fig. 51 Giacomo Balla, "Anti-Neutral Suit. Futurist Manifesto," 1914 (front and back of leaflet), The Lydia and Harry Lewis Winston Collection (Dr. and Mrs. Barnett Malbin, New York)

fig. 52 Richard Tuttle wearing the pants he created at The Fabric Workshop, Philadelphia, 1979

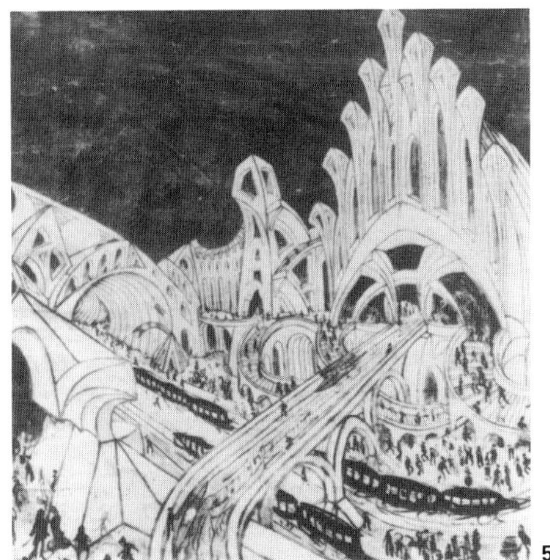

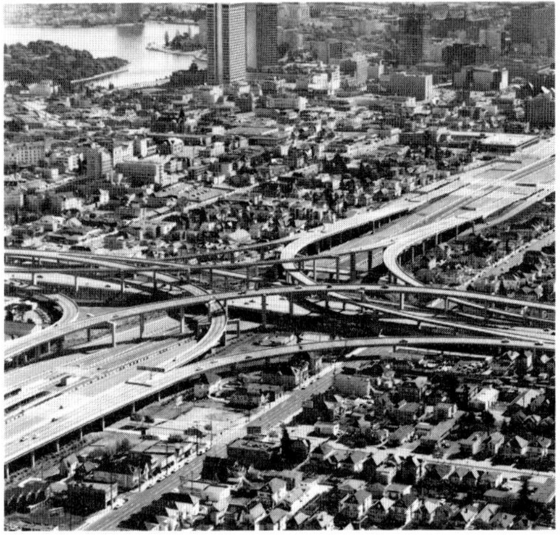

the Tango and Parsifal" (1914); "Futurist Synthesis of War" (1914)—these are only a few of the theoretical statements and manifestos of the movement.

Instead of hiding behind the phantom of art, Futurism interested itself in the effects that art can have on the phantoms of the world. These are summoned up not only by the fears and ghosts of the ego, but by the gradual rise of public opinion, which has dominance over the individual. If the new is linked to quantity, one must recognize the phenomenon and carry it to its greatest consequences by assigning to art as great a presence in order to reach the "greatest number." The founding Manifesto of Futurism was published in *Le Figaro* in Paris on February 20, 1909, while "The Variety Theatre" appeared in the London *Daily Mail* on November 21, 1913. The use of newspapers was not accidental. The philosophy of art is propaganda, and its existence cannot be affirmed in the sophisticated aura of specialized publications, but must come to life through "everyday" means. Thus the manifesto "Against Passatist Venice," drawn up on April 27, 1910, by Marinetti, Boccioni, Carrà, and Russolo, was launched on July 8, 1910, in the form of 800,000 leaflets thrown from the clock tower onto the crowd in the Piazza San Marco, and the "Futurist Synthesis of War" was produced in 300,000 copies "with the plea that it be posted in homes and public places." As soon as the right of assembly and association became recognized, Marinetti, Cangiullo, Bragaglia, and Balla organized Futurist "evenings" and clubs such as the Cabaret del Diavolo and the Casa Bragaglia, which through their indirect creativity became elements in the struggle against the falsifying condition of art. All this contributed to the disintegration and decline of the utopia of an elitist class that declared itself subordinate to the new power of the media and masses. The avant-garde instituted by Futurism was thus actually a "passive" one. It did not impose the transformation through modernization of electric and advertising communication, but allowed it to be imposed. It changed the face of culture in that it did not lead it—and in this way made itself intolerable to later avant-gardes. It violated the right of the avant-garde to change the world by letting itself be trampled by it, making its presence on the cultural scene more necessary than ever.

In seeking to break the closed circle of the avant-garde by involving itself with everything, Futurism also isolated the rhetorical method of art, which had stubbornly defended the old privileges, rejected every interconnection, and exasperated the tension toward life and society, provoking conflicts so as not to undermine its own integrity. Certainly this purpose was taken up by Marinetti and his colleagues in a partial and disconnected way. In general they did not carry out a radical advance, they only alluded to it. Nevertheless, this created a state of relative instability and insecurity that later allowed artistic movements in Germany, France, and Russia to destroy many certainties.

Futurist endeavors thus brought the world to the world. Faced with the rise of mass society, there was no longer anything to propose, except "society" itself, which rejected the faith and message of the few in order to entrust itself to the many. The multiplication of this presence was another of its fundamental constants; it was not sectarian, but affirmed the vision for and by the many. In this, however, there existed much rhetoric, since the experimental quest tried to broaden its bases of support by integrating the collective. The policy of Futurism was still cautious, conducted in a paternalistic way, that is, from above. Even if it reported a possible collapse of the privileges of the avant-garde, which was forced to extend the passage of the aesthetic to new and mass levels in order to make its foundations more secure, this did not disturb the basic initiative. The role of protagonist passed to the crowd: "We create in some way an emotional ambience, creating by strokes of intuition the sympathies and attachments between exterior (concrete) scene and inner (abstract) emotion." Art was no longer capable of entrenching itself; indeed it left the direction of its expression to the public: "It was the public that actually provided the spectacle during Futurist evenings, making a highly comical show of itself."[12]

In the final analysis, the modest proportions of Cubism and Impressionism could not have withstood the invasion of their scene by hundreds of persons. The realization or indiscriminate extension of aesthetic values would in fact have dissolved their private "transactions." Their influence therefore remained specific, limited in scope, while Futurism organized its own discipline in other directions, outside the center of art, because only outside did reality exist, contemporary with mass society. One can understand why Cubism remained dominant. It was the artistic movement that kept alive the myth and illusion of the separate and elite nature of art. It could be controlled by a few with traditional means, since it refused to allow the new quantitative reality to enter its conceptions. Cubism was therefore unripe for transition to the masses;

fig. 53 Virgilio Marchi's vision of a Futurist city, 1919

fig. 54 Complex freeway and rapid-transit systems dominating the city of Oakland, California, 1972

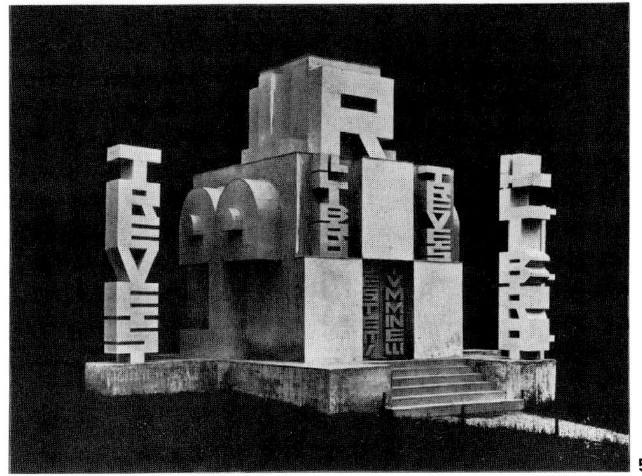

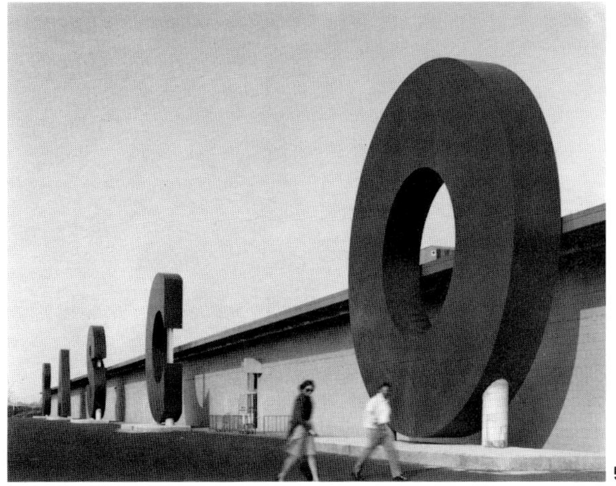

it was incapable of transforming itself, not as language, but as institutional avant-garde.

Futurism, on the contrary, put itself in harmony with the new thrust and sought to carry out the necessary transformations. It is therefore interesting not as a stylistic development, but as an avant-garde development that consecrated the banal to art and thus represented the ascending curve of mass anonymity in the sphere of creativity. When one studies the history of this Italian movement, it becomes clear that it was not born as a reaction to Cubism or Symbolism. For its protagonists, the conflict was not among the various artistic experiments, but between art and life. In this way the power of the masses became real, and therefore present, and if an avant-garde wished to be real and present, it had to let itself be used, almost as though the masses were a magnet and literature, poetry, film, theater, and painting were to become conductors of their meaning, adapted to absorb all their reasons and significance. The arts became "attributes" that attached themselves to everything. This process of inert aggregation was certainly due to the social deficiency that the arts had possessed and demonstrated in the past. Deprived of rules, they had lived by the rule of the positive possibility that called into question all the values of style, but not the crystallized system of the avant-garde. Here thus was content with style, but discontent with a public presence that in no way altered the hierarchical tradition of culture, with its tendency to uphold the precedence of the individual over the masses. The authority assigned to Cubism derived from its opposition to any change that was not formal. This movement was the ideal interpreter of a culture in conflict with society, the clear interpreter of the anxieties of the elite, because it was not ready to go beyond certain limits or to make drastic changes. It was no accident that throughout its history, Cubism let itself be influenced only by images, never by facts. Futurism, on the other hand, was more ambivalent, pragmatic, and indefinite. It always was open to any solution, any reform, any adventure, but at the same time it was opposed to everything organized and established, evidence of a cultural anxiety that saw the unlimited as real. Therefore it was impartial and ready for everything.

Compared to previous avant-gardes, Futurism did not stand apart, but coexisted with the solutions and manifestations of the world. It intuitively grasped the impossibility of a digression in the life of the masses and made itself digress. It thereby became "total." It emerged from the fragmentation of poetry and painting with a determination to observe reality without filters and hierarchies. It resigned itself to dealing with the collective instead of with the individual, on whom it would rather have imposed its own conditions of expression. Nevertheless the surrender of Futurism was forced, the closed, proud, and arrogant surrender of the privileged person who defends his situation and despises the rising masses. It was therefore natural that a challenge to the position of the avant-garde and a claim to be the whole avant-garde should conceal the desire always to maintain the position of the avant-garde, which from then on, however, would appear openly as a career or cultural course of honor. Thus, there was no more preaching to the crowd, for which art had been a moral revolution and a redemption. Suddenly art is no longer a point of reference, but a place for the undistinguished and mediocre, which Futurism came to denote as expression and creativity. It becomes thus the executor of mass imagination, wherein the facts of art become disproportionate and are canceled out in the chance and chaos of the crowd. Does originality still have meaning, or is the battle fought for eclecticism and consumption?

At the beginning of the twentieth century, as today near its end, the avant-garde did not seem equipped to tolerate the exhausting disorder and decoration demanded by the petite bourgeoisie. Although every fact appeared uncertain and unstable, the process continued to be experienced in connection with the fragmentary and particular nature of the individual and the elite. Futurism, of course, did not resolve the difficulties of a transition as yet incapable of being realized, but it tried to get rid of the fascination of a heritage left by tradition, which offered art as the plan for genuine life—masterpiece, utopia, universe, education, ritual, and so forth.

The passive and inert attitude of the Italian movement in the face of the crisis of these simulacra of culture is the final and decisive proof that art no longer corresponds to the interests of society, but only to its trappings, when it mirrors the masses and identifies itself with what they imagine. Art refracts its messages and offers itself as a discredited minority that can be used for national propaganda, as has happened throughout this century with all artistic movements, from Futurism to Minimalism. No longer responding to the tasks that have been assigned to it, the avant-garde reveals itself incapable of resisting new movements created by the masses and by industry. It no

fig. 55 Fortunato Depero's Book Pavilion ("Typographic Architecture"), designed for the publishers Bestetti, Tumminelli, and Fratelli Treves, at the third International Biennial of Monza, 1927

fig. 56 Thirty-foot-high red letters signaling the Basco showroom in Bristol Township, Pennsylvania, designed by Venturi and Rauch, 1979

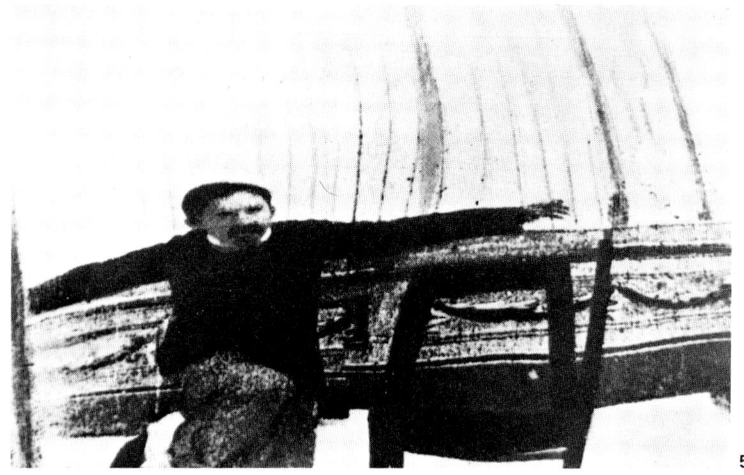

57

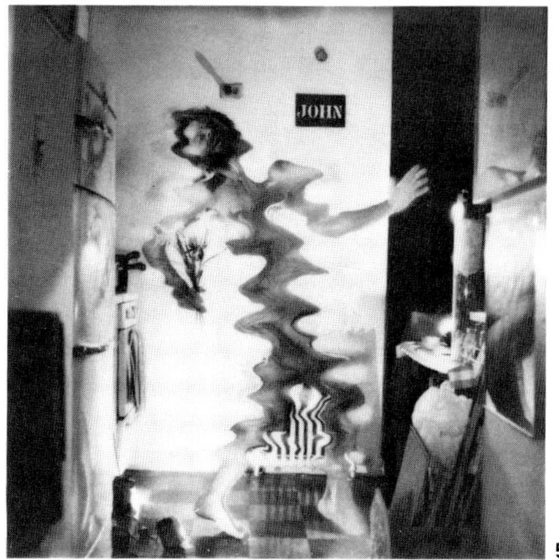

58

longer exiles itself in privileged society but abandons itself to the ebb and flow, becoming silent, precisely because it makes mass noises. It occupies space in the newspapers and fashion magazines so as to respond to public pressures and consumerism. Its space begins to lack perspective, it becomes increasingly generalized, and it tends toward a disappearance from the scene. Thus the aristocrats and idealists are served, originality lies in being everywhere, and the image is nourished by vulgarity (from *vulgus*—the "people"). Rather than humiliate the crowd, it lets itself be humiliated, and it denies itself any plan for the future in order to be truly futurist—i.e., mass.

Translated by John Shepley

NOTES

This essay draws inspiration from the profound and provocative studies on the relationship between Futurist art and theater and mass society by Maurizio Calvesi and Paolo Fossati.

1. Filippo Tommaso Marinetti, Manifesto of Futurism [1909], in Umbro Apollonio, ed., and Robert Brain et al., trans., *Futurist Manifestos* (New York, 1973), p. 22.
2. *Ibid.*
3. See Maurizio Calvesi, *Le Due Avanguardie,* vol. 1, *Studi sul Futurismo,* 2d ed. (Rome, 1975).
4. ·Filippo Tommaso Marinetti and Francesco Cangiullo, "Manifesto of the Theater of Surprise" [1921], reprinted in Marinetti, *Teoria e Invenzione Futurista,* ed. Luciano De Maria (Verona, 1968), p. 143.
5. Francesco Cangiullo, *Le Serate Futuriste* (Milan, 1961).
6. Technical Manifesto of Futurist Painting [1910], translated in Apollonio, ed., *Futurist Manifestos,* pp. 27, 28.
7. Marinetti, Manifesto of Futurism [1909], translated in Apollonio, ed., *Futurist Manifestos,* p. 22.
8. Filippo Tommaso Marinetti, "Manifesto on the Pleasure of Being Booed" [1911], in *Guerra Sola Igiene del Mondo* (Milan, 1915); reprinted in Marinetti, *Teoria e Invenzione Futurista,* p. 266.
9. Giacomo Balla and Fortunato Depero, "Futurist Reconstruction of the Universe" [1915], translated in Apollonio, ed., *Futurist Manifestos,* p. 199.
10. Giacomo Balla, "Anti-Neutral Suit. Futurist Manifesto" [1914], reprinted in Giorgio De Marchis, *Giacomo Balla: L'Aura Futurista* (Turin, 1977), p. 104.
11. See collected articles published posthumously in Alberto Savinio, *Scatola Sonora* (Rome, 1955).
12. Cangiullo, *Le Serate Futuriste.*

fig. 57 Distorted image of Giacomo Balla from Arnaldo Ginna's film *Futurist Life (Vita Futurista)*, 1916

fig. 58 Polaroid self-portrait by Lucas Samaras, one of his series *Photo-Transformations*, 1976, Philadelphia Museum of Art

ITALIAN FUTURISM

Apollonio, Umbrio, ed. *Futurist Manifestos.* Translated by Robert Brain et al. New York: Viking Press, 1973.

Bergman, Pär. *"Modernolatria" et "Simultaneità": Recherches sur Deux Tendances dans l'Avant-Garde Littéraire en Italie et en France à la Veille de la Première Guerre Mondiale.* Uppsala: Svenska Bokförlaget, Bonniers, 1962.

Boccioni, Umberto. *Gli Scritti Editi e Inediti.* Edited by Zeno Birolli. Milan: Feltrinelli, 1971.

__________. *Altri Inediti e Apparati Critici.* Edited by Zeno Birolli. Milan: Feltrinelli, 1972.

Gambillo, Maria Drudi, and Fiori, Teresa, eds. *Archivi del Futurismo.* 2 vols. Rome: De Luca Editore, vol. 1, 1958; vol. 2, 1962.

Kirby, Michael. *Futurist Performance.* New York: E. P. Dutton & Co., 1971.

Lista, Giovanni, ed. *Futurisme: Manifestes—Proclamations—Documents.* Lausanne: L'Age d'Homme, 1973.

Marinetti, Filippo Tommaso. *Teoria e Invenzione Futurista.* Edited by Luciano De Maria. Milan: Arnoldo Mondadori Editore, 1968.

Martin, Marianne W. *Futurist Art and Theory 1909–1915.* Oxford: Clarendon Press, 1968.

New York, The Solomon R. Guggenheim Museum. *Futurism: A Modern Focus: The Lydia and Harry Lewis Winston Collection, Dr. and Mrs. Barnett Malbin.* November 16, 1973–February 3, 1974. Catalogue essays by Linda Shearer and Marianne W. Martin.

New York, The Museum of Modern Art. *Futurism.* May 31–September 5, 1961. Catalogue by Joshua C. Taylor.

Pacini, Piero, ed. *Esposizioni Futuriste.* Vol. 1, *1912–1918.* Florence: Edizioni Scelte, 1977. Facsimiles of 26 Futurist exhibition catalogues.

Paris, Musée National d'Art Moderne. *Le Futurisme 1909–1916.* September 19–November 19, 1973. Catalogue essays by Guido Ballo, Françoise Cachin-Nora, Jean Leymarie, and Franco Russoli.

Severini, Gino. *Tutta la Vita di un Pittore.* Milan: Garzanti, 1946.

Tisdall, Caroline, and Bozzolla, Angelo. *Futurism.* New York and Toronto: Oxford University Press, 1978.

THE INTERNATIONAL AVANT-GARDE

Apollinaire, Guillaume. *Apollinaire on Art: Essays and Reviews 1902–1918.* Edited by LeRoy C. Breunig; translated by Susan Suleiman. New York: Viking Press, 1972.

Bowlt, John E., ed. and trans. *Russian Art of the Avant-Garde: Theory and Criticism 1902–1934.* New York: Viking Press, 1976.

Cabanne, Pierre. *Dialogues with Marcel Duchamp.* Translated by Ron Padgett. New York: Viking Press, 1971.

Cambridge, Mass., Harvard University, Fogg Art Museum. *Jacques Villon.* January 17–February 29, 1976. Catalogue edited by Daniel Robbins.

Compton, Susan P. *The World Backwards: Russian Futurist Books 1912–16.* London: The British Library, 1978.

Cork, Richard. *Vorticism and Abstract Art in the First Machine Age.* 2 vols. Berkeley and Los Angeles: University of California Press, 1976.

Daix, Pierre, and Rosselet, Joan. *Picasso: The Cubist Years 1907–1916. A Catalogue Raisonné of the Paintings and Related Works.* Translated by Dorothy S. Blair. Boston: New York Graphic Society, 1979.

Delaunay, Robert. *Du Cubisme à l'Art Abstrait.* Edited by Pierre Francastel. Paris: S.E.V.P.E.N., 1957.

Douglas, Charlotte. *Swans of Other Worlds: Kazimir Malevich and the Origins of Abstraction in Russia.* Ann Arbor, Mich.: UMI Research Press, 1980.

Eddy, Arthur Jerome. *Cubists and Post-Impressionism.* Chicago: A. C. McClurg & Co., 1914.

Elsen, Albert E. *Origins of Modern Sculpture: Pioneers and Premises.* New York: George Braziller, 1974.

Fry, Edward F., ed. *Cubism.* New York and Toronto: McGraw-Hill Book Company, 1966.

Golding, John. *Cubism: A History and an Analysis 1907–1914.* 2d ed. Boston: Boston Book and Art Shop, 1968.

Gray, Camilla. *The Great Experiment: Russian Art 1863–1922.* New York: Harry N. Abrams, 1962.

Green, Christopher. *Léger and the Avant-Garde.* New Haven and London: Yale University Press, 1976.

Hamilton, George Heard. *Painting and Sculpture in Europe 1880 to 1940.* Baltimore: Penguin Books, 1967.

Homer, William Innes. *Alfred Stieglitz and the American Avant-Garde.* Boston: New York Graphic Society, 1977.

Lewis, Wyndham. *Wyndham Lewis on Art: Collected Writings 1913–1956.* Edited by Walter Michel and C. J. Fox. New York: Funk & Wagnalls, 1969.

Livshits, Benedikt. *The One and a Half-Eyed Archer.* Edited and translated by John E. Bowlt. Newtonville, Mass.: Oriental Research Partners, 1977.

Los Angeles, Los Angeles County Museum of Art. *The Cubist Epoch.* December 15, 1970–February 21, 1971. Catalogue by Douglas Cooper.

Los Angeles, Los Angeles County Museum of Art. *The Avant-Garde in Russia, 1910–1930: New Perspectives.* July 8–September 28, 1980. Catalogue edited by Stephanie Barron and Maurice Tuchman.

Malévitch, Kasimir. *Ecrits.* Edited by Andrei B. Nakov; translated by Andrée Robel-Chicurel. Paris: Editions Champ Libre, 1975.

New York, The Solomon R. Guggenheim Museum. *Albert Gleizes 1881–1953: A Retrospective Exhibition.* September 15–November 1, 1964. Catalogue by Daniel Robbins.

New York, The Solomon R. Guggenheim Museum. *Frantisek Kupka 1871–1957: A Retrospective.* October 10–December 7, 1975. Catalogue by Margit Rowell.

New York, The Whitney Museum of American Art. *Synchromism and American Color Abstraction 1910–1925.* January 24–March 26, 1978. Catalogue by Gail Levin.

Rosenblum, Robert. *Cubism and Twentieth-Century Art.* 2d rev. ed. New York: Harry N. Abrams, 1976.

Selz, Peter. *German Expressionist Painting.* Berkeley and Los Angeles: University of California Press, 1957.

Spate, Virginia. *Orphism: The Evolution of Non-Figurative Painting in Paris 1910–1914.* Oxford: Clarendon Press, 1979.

Tashjian, Dickran. *Skyscraper Primitives: Dada and the American Avant-Garde 1910–1925.* Middletown, Conn.: Wesleyan University Press, 1975.

Wilmington, Delaware Art Museum. *Avant-Garde Painting & Sculpture in America 1910–25.* April 4–May 18, 1975.

ITALY

Giacomo Balla (nos. 1–14)

Umberto Boccioni (nos. 15–53)

Carlo Carrà (nos. 54–58)

Leonardo Dudreville (nos. 59–60)

Luigi Russolo (nos. 61–63)

Gino Severini (nos. 64–75)

ENGLAND

David Bomberg (nos. 76–77)

Jacob Epstein (nos. 78–79)

Percy Wyndham Lewis (no. 80)

Christopher R. W. Nevinson (nos. 81–82)

FRANCE

Alexander Archipenko (no. 83)

Robert Delaunay (nos. 84–86)

Sonia Delaunay-Terk (no. 87)

Félix Del Marle (no. 88)

Marcel Duchamp (nos. 89–93)

Raymond Duchamp-Villon (nos. 94–99)

Albert Gleizes (no. 100)

Juan Gris (no. 101)

Frantisek Kupka (nos. 102–3)

Fernand Léger (no. 104)

Henri Matisse (no. 105)

Jean Metzinger (no. 106)

Piet Mondrian (no. 107)

Francis Picabia (no. 108)

Pablo Picasso (nos. 109–11)

Jacques Villon (nos. 112–14)

GERMANY

Lyonel Feininger (no. 115)

Wassily Kandinsky (no. 116)

Franz Marc (no. 117)

RUSSIA

Natalia Gontcharova (nos. 118–19)

Mikhail Larionov (nos. 120–21)

Kasimir Malevich (no. 122)

UNITED STATES

James R. Daugherty (no. 123)

Stanton MacDonald-Wright (no. 124)

John Marin (nos. 125–26)

Morgan Russell (no. 127)

Joseph Stella (nos. 128–30)

Frances Simpson Stevens (no. 131)

Max Weber (nos. 132–34)

NOTES FOR USE OF THE CATALOGUE

Date:
The date given for a work is that proposed by current scholarship. It is not always identical to that inscribed on the work itself. Artists often signed and dated their works years after they were actually executed, and may have misdated them inadvertently or with the hope of substantiating a claim to have been the first to introduce a particular innovation.

Dimensions:
Sizes are given in inches and in centimeters, height precedes width precedes depth.

Exhibitions:
When possible, the first exhibition in which a work was shown has been cited. Additional important early exhibitions that exposed the work to a wider audience have been given when known. Several of the exhibitions frequently cited had exposure in other cities after their first showing.

Paris, Galerie Bernheim-Jeune, *Les Peintres Futuristes Italiens,* February 5–24, 1912

Works included in this important exhibition are assumed to have traveled to the following stops: London, Sackville Gallery (March 1912); Berlin, Der Sturm (April–May 1912); Brussels, Galerie Georges Giroux (May–June 1912). A subsequent tour included The Hague, Amsterdam, Cologne, Munich, and Budapest.

New York, Armory of the 69th Regiment, *International Exhibition of Modern Art,* February 17–March 15, 1913

"The Armory Show" also traveled to The Art Institute of Chicago (March 24–April 16, 1913) and to Boston, Copley Hall (April 28–May 19, 1913).

San Francisco, *The Panama-Pacific International Exposition,* Department of Fine Arts, February 20, 1915 –May 1, 1916

The Futurist works were not on view for the entirety of this international exposition, although the official opening date was February 20, 1915. The Futurist loans did not arrive in California until April and were stored until a special annex was built to house them and other late arrivals. They were actually on view from September 1915 to May 1,1916.

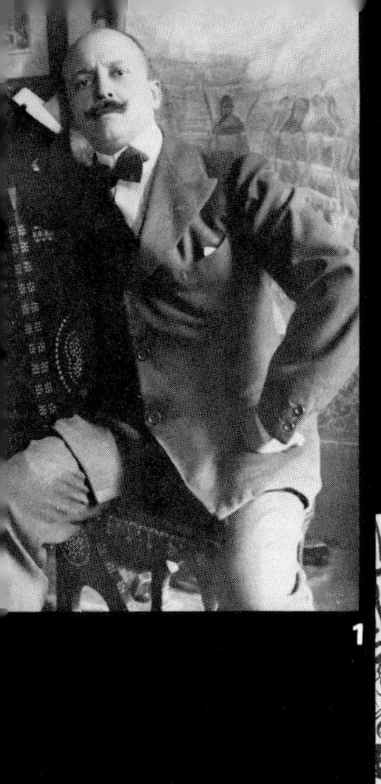

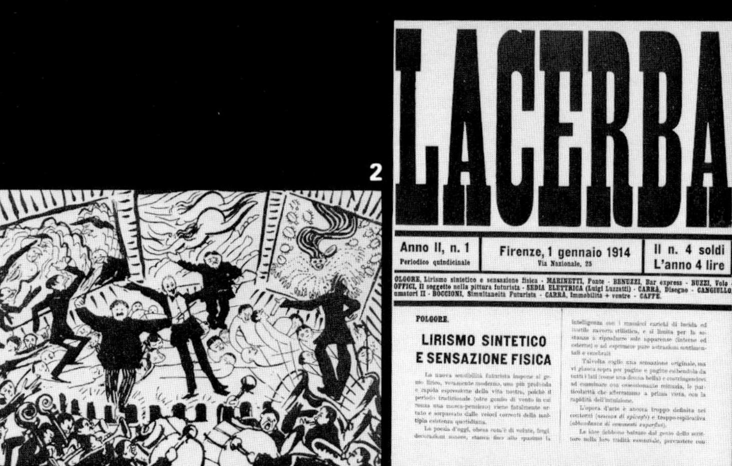

LACERBA

Anno II, n. 1
Periodico quindicinale

Firenze, 1 gennaio 1914
Via Nazionale, 25

Il n. 4 soldi
L'anno 4 lire

FOLGORE.

LIRISMO SINTETICO
E SENSAZIONE FISICA

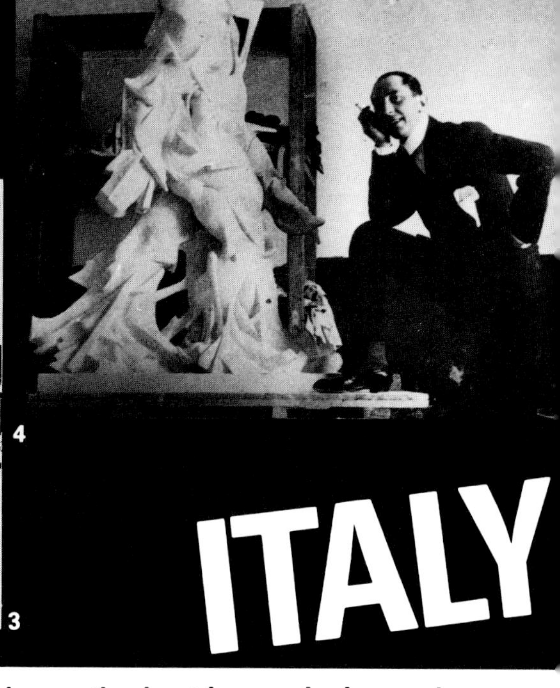

ITALY

Futurism was officially announced in Paris on February 20, 1909, when Filippo Tommaso Marinetti's founding Manifesto of Futurism appeared on the front page of *Le Figaro,* but at that time there were no Futurist painters in Italy or in any other country; the fateful meetings of Marinetti with Umberto Boccioni, Carlo Carrà, and Luigi Russolo occurred in Milan early in 1910. Delighted with the prospect of a phalanx of visual artists to join what had begun as a literary movement, Marinetti welcomed a small band of painters who were to invent a variety of Futurist theories and styles over the next five years. Two early adherents to the movement, Romolo Romani and Aroldo Bonzagni, whose names appear on the first edition of the Manifesto of Futurist Painters (February 11, 1910), were to withdraw rapidly. Other candidates, including Leonardo Dudreville, were considered by Marinetti and Boccioni and rejected. (In 1914 Dudreville was to launch Nuove Tendenze, a second major wave of avant-garde activity in Milan.) The inner circle of Futurist painters, as it emerged in the spring of 1910 and continued (not without considerable internal dissension) until World War I, brought together five men of remarkably diverse personalities and talents, each of whom made a highly individual contribution to the movement and hence to the history of modern art. The brilliant and erratic Boccioni was born in Calabria and had relatively little academic training before plunging into the urban life of Milan. Carrà, on the contrary, had begun as an apprentice in mural decoration and had a certificate from the Brera Academy. Gino Severini had settled in Paris in 1906 and was to serve as the vital contact with the French art world for his friends in Milan. Boccioni and Severini had been fellow students of the Divisionist painter Giacomo Balla, who was eventually invited to join the Futurist brotherhood. Some ten years older than the others, with a studio and a wife and two daughters in Rome, Balla remained remote from the frenzied theorizing and polemics of the Milan group, moving from a rather eccentric version of Divisionism to an equally idiosyncratic abstraction based on color theory and studies of motion. The fifth and least celebrated member of the group, Russolo, was part of the Milanese circle but divided his interest between painting and new forms of music, to which his "noise intoners" *(intonarumori)* were a daring contribution.

Although the Futurist painters were preoccupied with the French art world, Marinetti promoted events, lectures, and exhibitions throughout Italy in a highly successful effort to shock "the land of the dead" out of its pleasant dreams of the past. Magazines and publications played a vital role in his program; manifestos were printed by the thousands and flung from theater balconies, church towers, and speeding taxis. Marinetti's literary journal *Poesia* (1905–9) revealed his early interest in mixing Italian contributions with poems and articles by a distinguished array of international figures. Several editors of the Florentine journal *La Voce* (1908–16), initially intensely critical of the Futurists, eventually joined forces in a new publication and *Lacerba* (1913–15) became the energetic voice of the movement, often responding to Marinetti's inspired sense of timing for the appearance of a provocative article or innovations in poetic form. Ardengo Soffici, a critic for *La Voce* and *Lacerba* who wrote eloquently about Impressionism and Cubism, joined the ranks of the Futurist painters between 1912 and 1914; few of his paintings, which combined Cubist style with Futurist nuances, appear to have survived.

The first of many tumultuous Futurist "evenings" was presented in Trieste on January 12, 1910, and audiences in Turin, Milan, Naples, Venice, and Padua were soon subjected to barrages of new poetry and manifestos, often followed by fisticuffs and even riots. Marinetti continued to enlist poets, musicians, cinematographers in the cause, and in 1914 succeeded in representing architecture in the person of Antonio Sant'Elia. Only the outbreak of war, eagerly awaited as the final Futurist explosion of energy, curtailed his own extraordinary travels, which sent him rushing to London, Berlin, Paris, Brussels, Moscow, as well as the length of the Italian peninsula: Marinetti's stimulating and ubiquitous presence earned him the sobriquet "the Caffeine of Europe."

Futurism itself faded from European consciousness after 1915, except in Italy, where it took an increasingly political turn. The brotherhood of five was sadly dispersed: Boccioni died tragically after a fall from a horse (August 17, 1916); Carrà joined Giorgio de Chirico in a new and more serene school of Metaphysical painting; Severini began to explore a return to classicism in Paris; and Russolo, badly wounded in the war, turned increasingly to music. Of the original group, Balla alone maintained a proudly Futurist stance until his death in 1958.

1. Filippo Tommaso Marinetti, c. 1913, in front of Luigi Russolo's *Solidity of Fog;* 2. Umberto Boccioni, *Cartoon of a Futurist Evening* (from *Uno, Due e . . . Tre,* June 17, 1911); 3. Cover of *Lacerba*, January 1, 1914; 4. Umberto Boccioni in his studio with *Synthesis of Human Dynamism*, 1913

Giacomo Balla

1 8 7 1 – 1 9 5 8

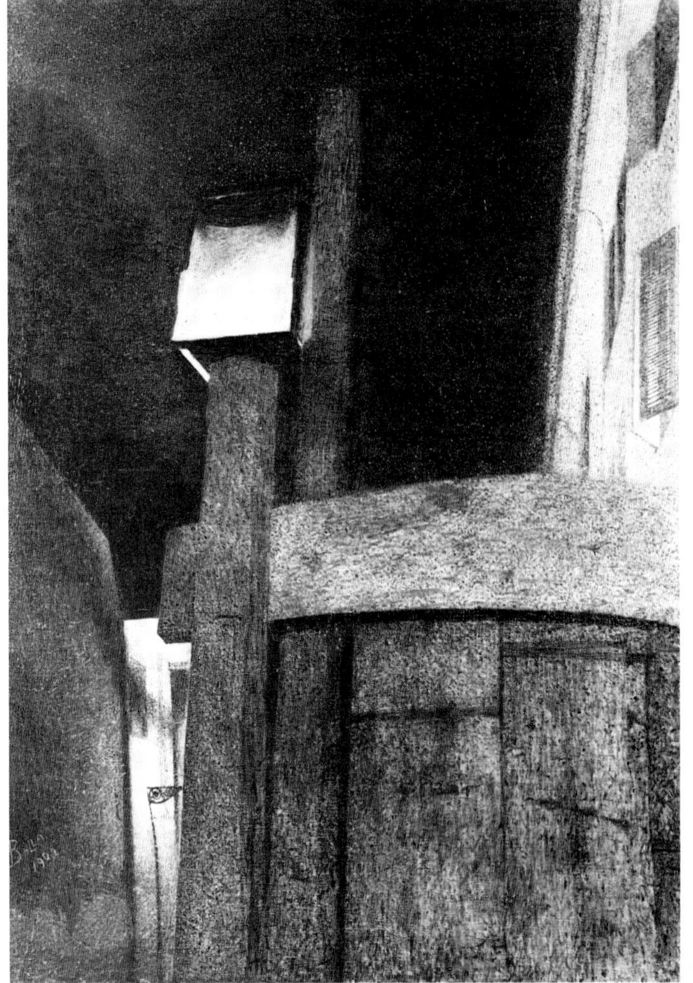

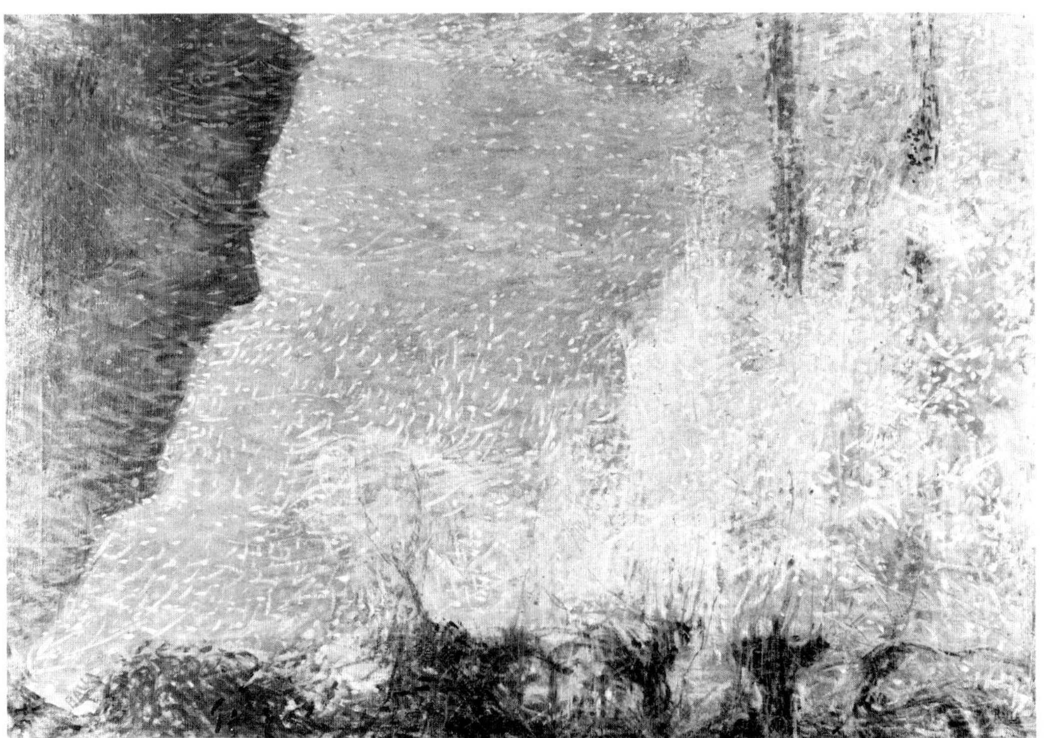

1. Work, 1902
Oil on canvas, 68 x 48½" (172.7 x 123.2 cm)
The Lydia and Harry Lewis Winston Collection
(Dr. and Mrs. Barnett Malbin, New York)
Exhibition: Rome, Societa degli Amatori e Cultori, *LXXVI Esposizione Internazionale di Belle Arti,* 1904, no. 1057

2. Spring Buds, c. 1906
Oil on canvas, 19¼ x 29¼" (48.9 x 74.3 cm)
The Lydia and Harry Lewis Winston Collection
(Dr. and Mrs. Barnett Malbin, New York)

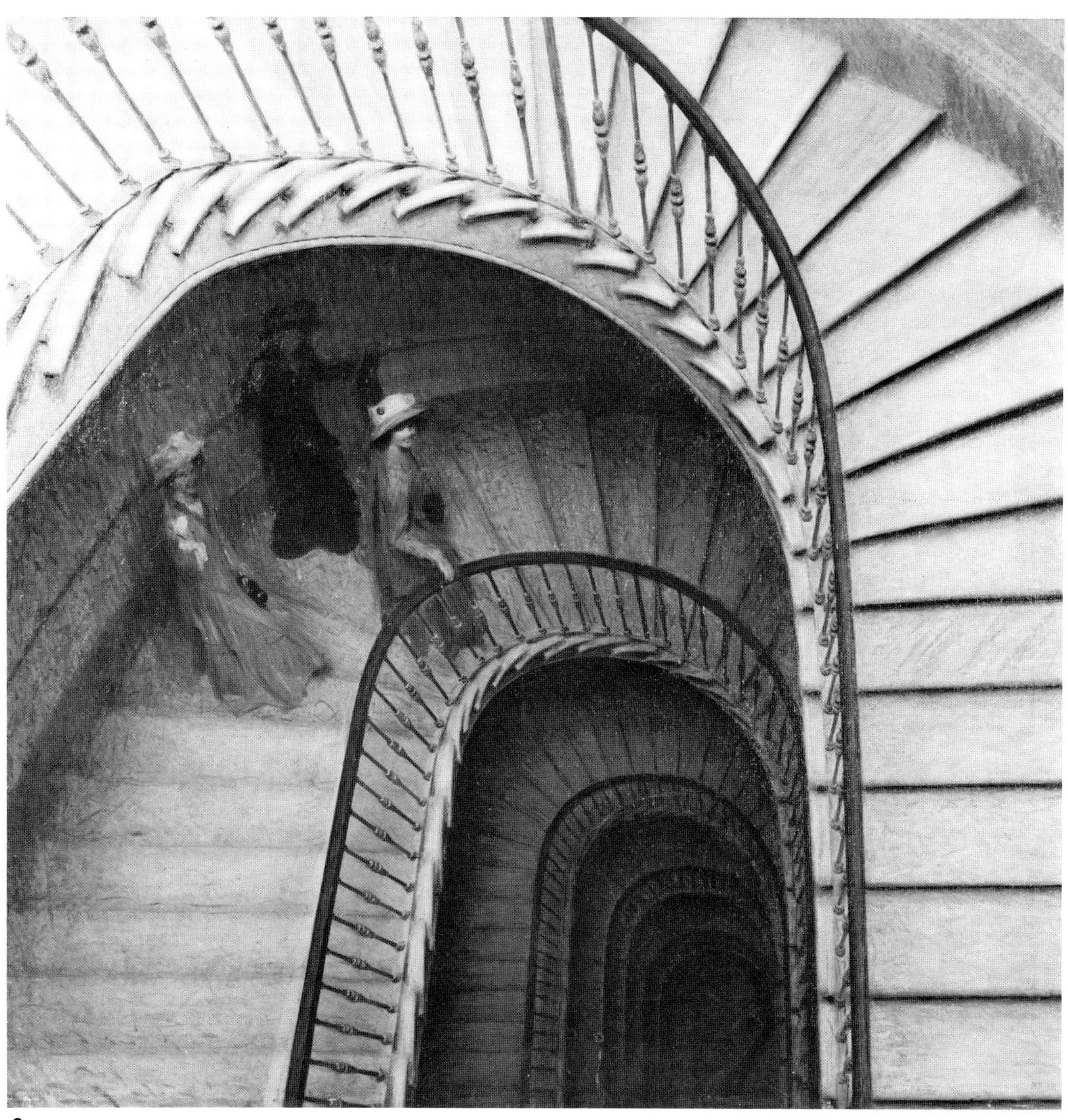

3

3. The Stairway of Farewells, c. 1908
Oil on canvas, 40¾ x 41" (103.5 x 104.1 cm)
The Lydia and Harry Lewis Winston Collection
(Dr. and Mrs. Barnett Malbin, New York)
Exhibition: Rome, Societa degli Amatori e Cultori, *LXXX Esposizione Internazionale di Belle Arti,* 1910, no. 194, pl. VI

Giacomo Balla

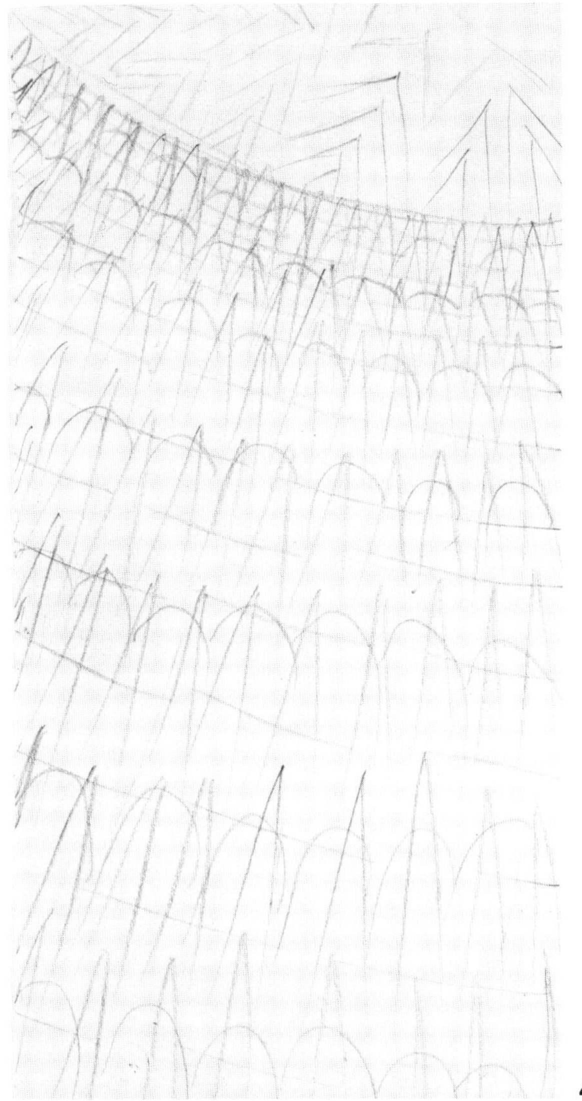

4

5

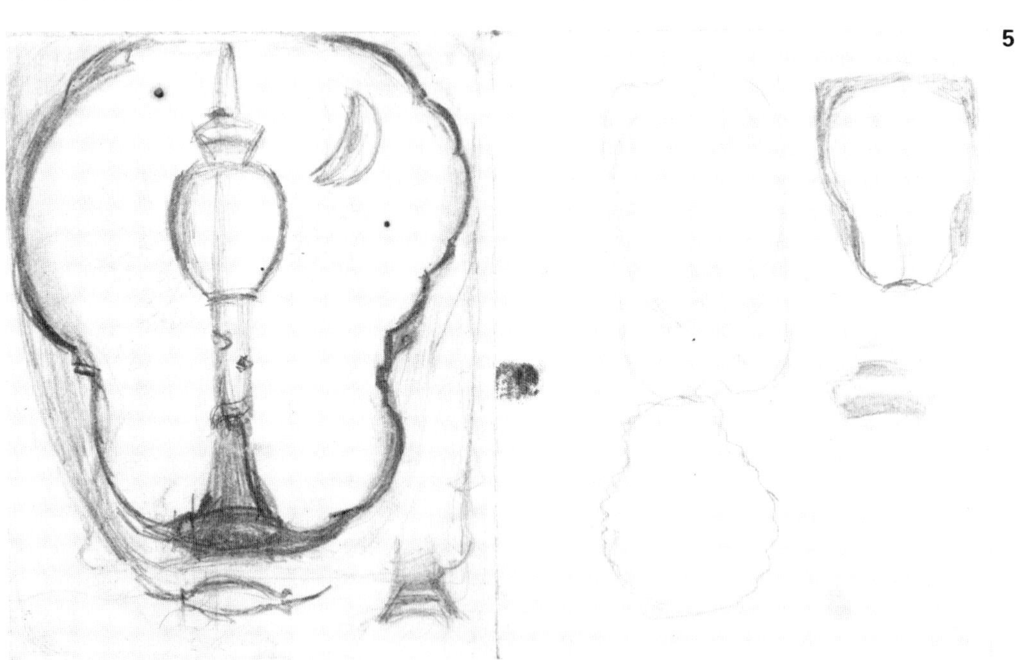

4. Study for "Street Light (Electric Light)," c. 1909
Pencil on paper, 10⅞ x 5⅝" (27.7 x 14.2 cm)
The Museum of Modern Art, New York
Christopher Tietze Fund, 1967

5. Study for "Street Light (Electric Light)," c. 1909
Pencil on paper, 4⅜ x 7⅛" (11.1 x 18 cm)
The Museum of Modern Art, New York
Mrs. Bertram Smith Fund, 1967

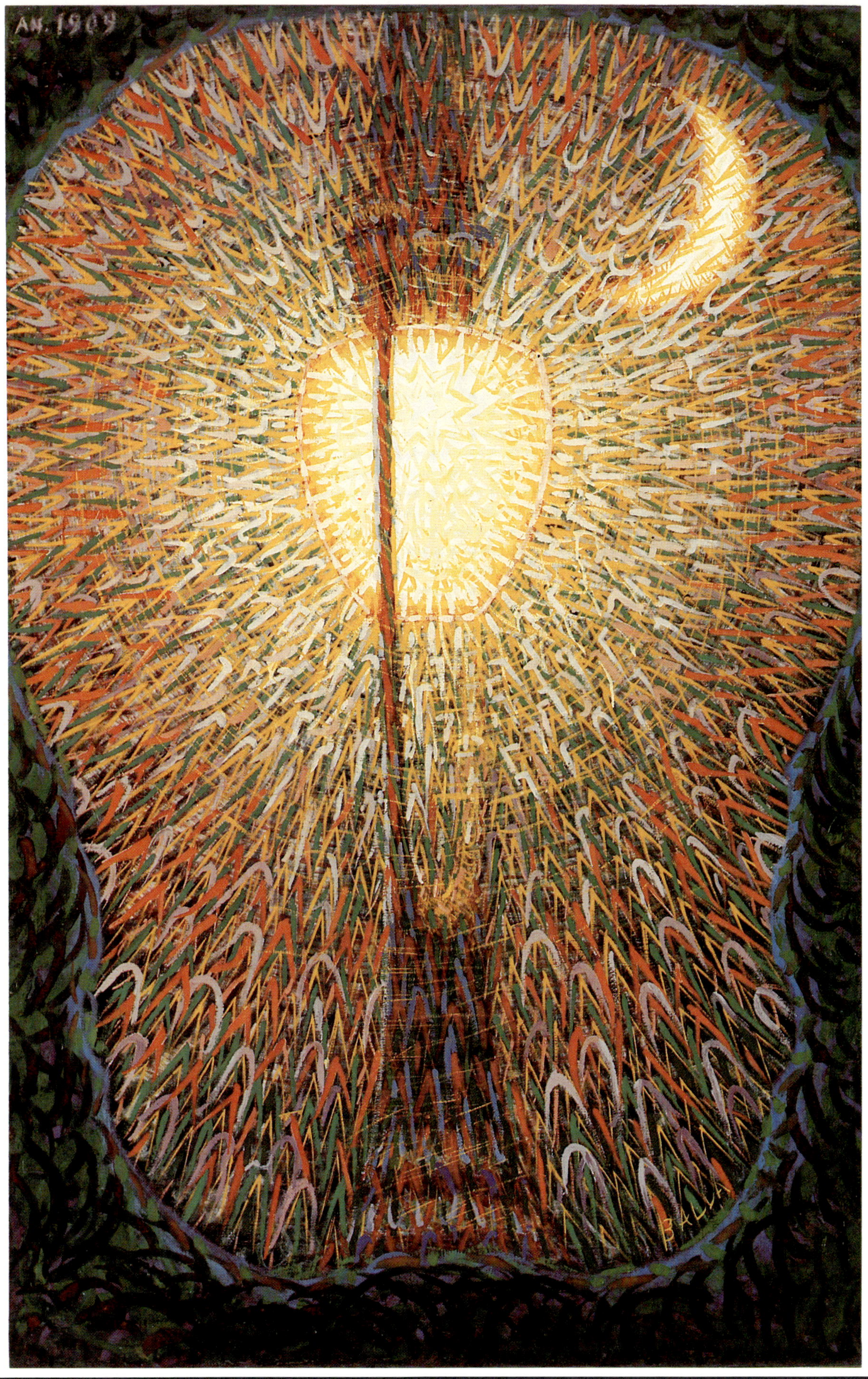

6

6. Street Light (Electric Light), c. 1909
Oil on canvas, 68¾ x 45⅛″ (174.7 x 114.7 cm)
The Museum of Modern Art, New York
Hillman Periodicals Fund, 1954
Exhibition: Rome, Galleria G. Giosi, *Prima Esposizione Pittura Futurista,* from February 11, 1913, no. 3

Giacomo Balla

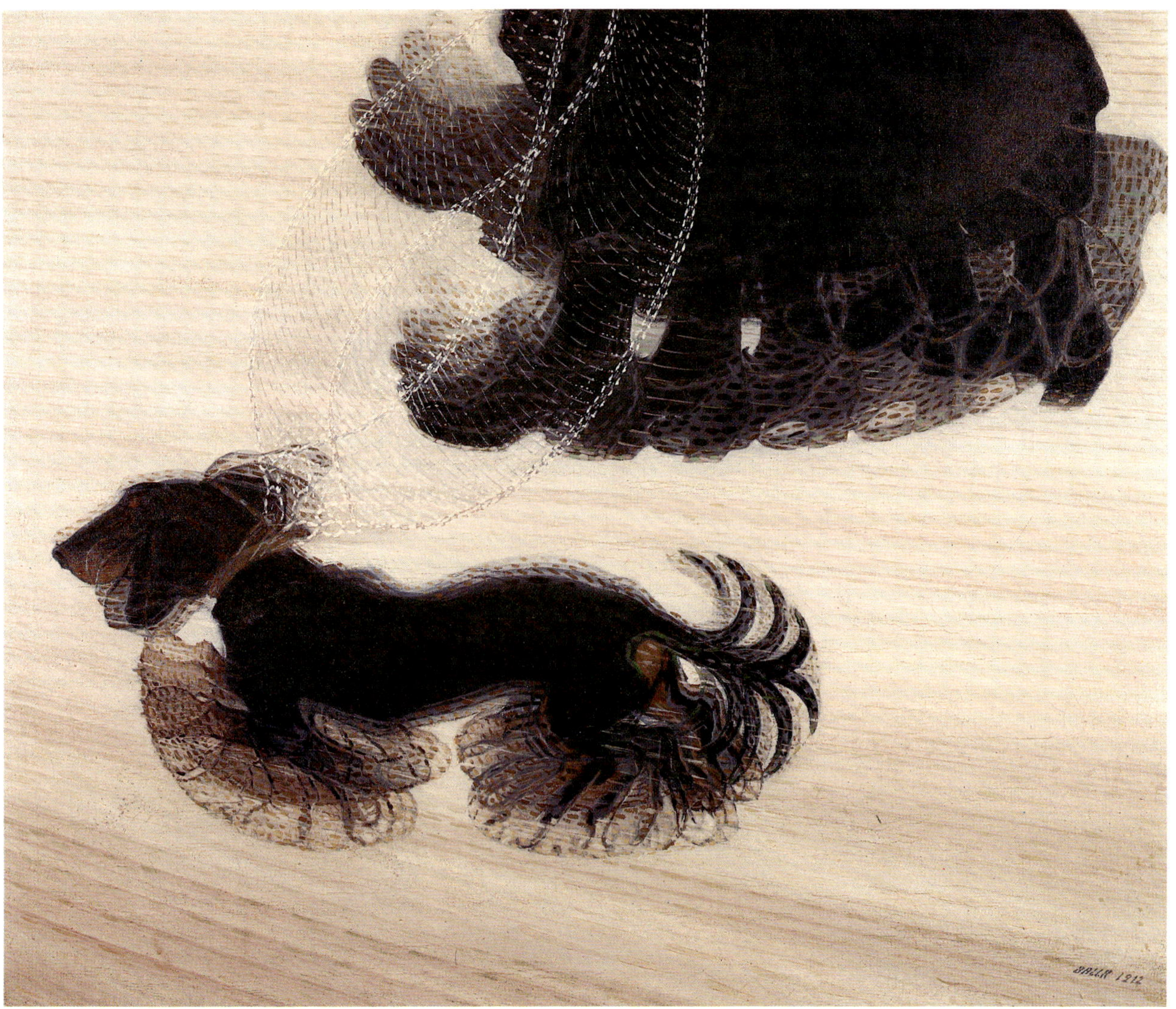

7

7. Dynamism of a Dog on a Leash (Leash in Motion), 1912
Oil on canvas, 35¾ x 43⅜" (90.8 x 110.2 cm)
Albright-Knox Art Gallery, Buffalo
Bequest of A. Conger Goodyear to George F. Goodyear, life interest, and Albright-Knox Art Gallery, 1964
Exhibitions: Rome, Galleria G. Giosi, *Prima Esposizione Pittura Futurista,* from February 11, 1913, no. 1; Rotterdam, Rotterdamsche Kunstkring, *Les Peintres et les Sculpteurs Futuristes Italiens,* May 18–June 15, 1913, no. 26, repro.; Berlin, Der Sturm, *Erster Deutscher Herbstsalon,* September 20–December 1, 1913, no. 32, repro.

Giacomo Balla

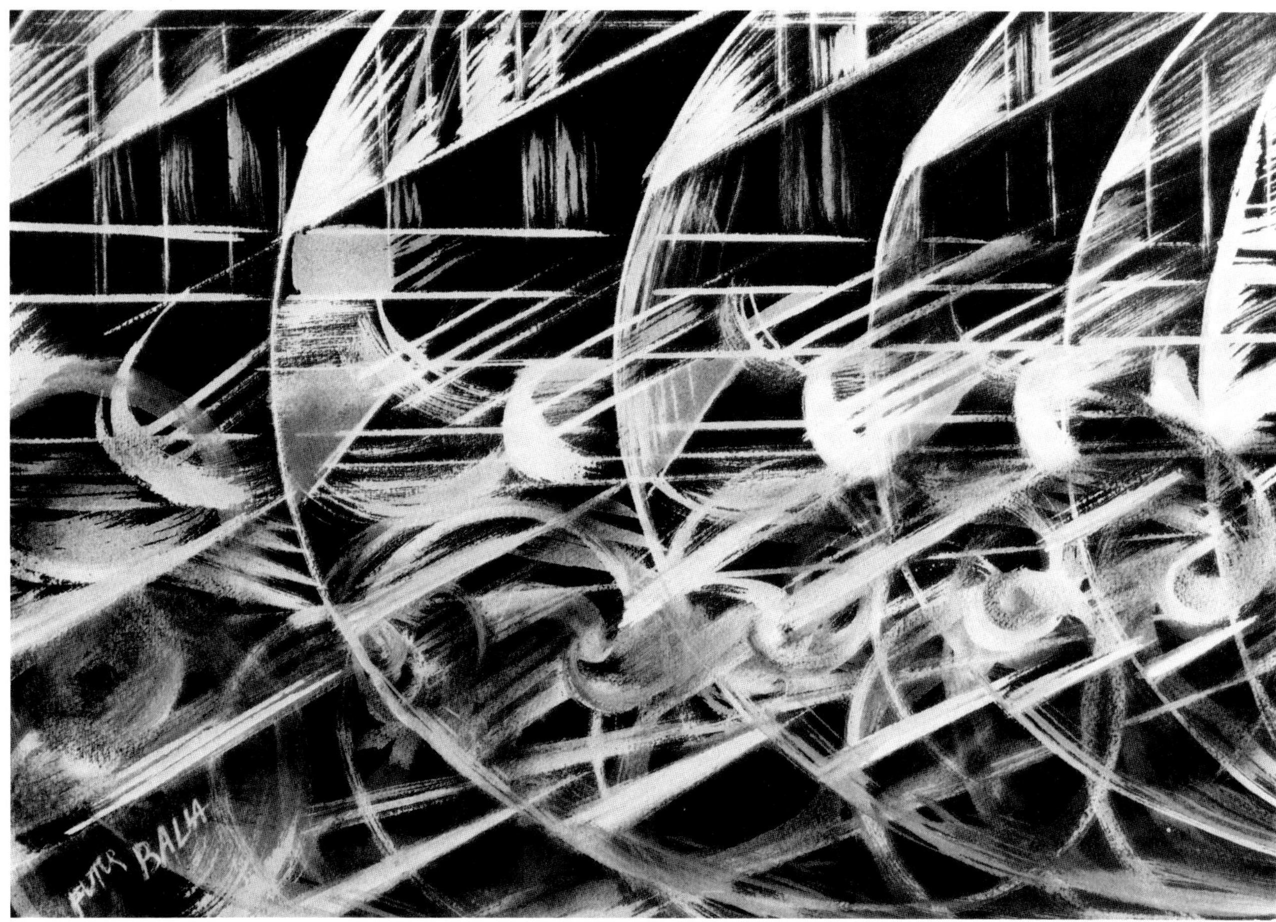

8

8. Study Related to "Abstract Velocity," c. 1913
Gouache on paper, 11¾ x 17" (29.8 x 43.2 cm)
The Lydia and Harry Lewis Winston Collection
(Dr. and Mrs. Barnett Malbin, New York)

Giacomo Balla

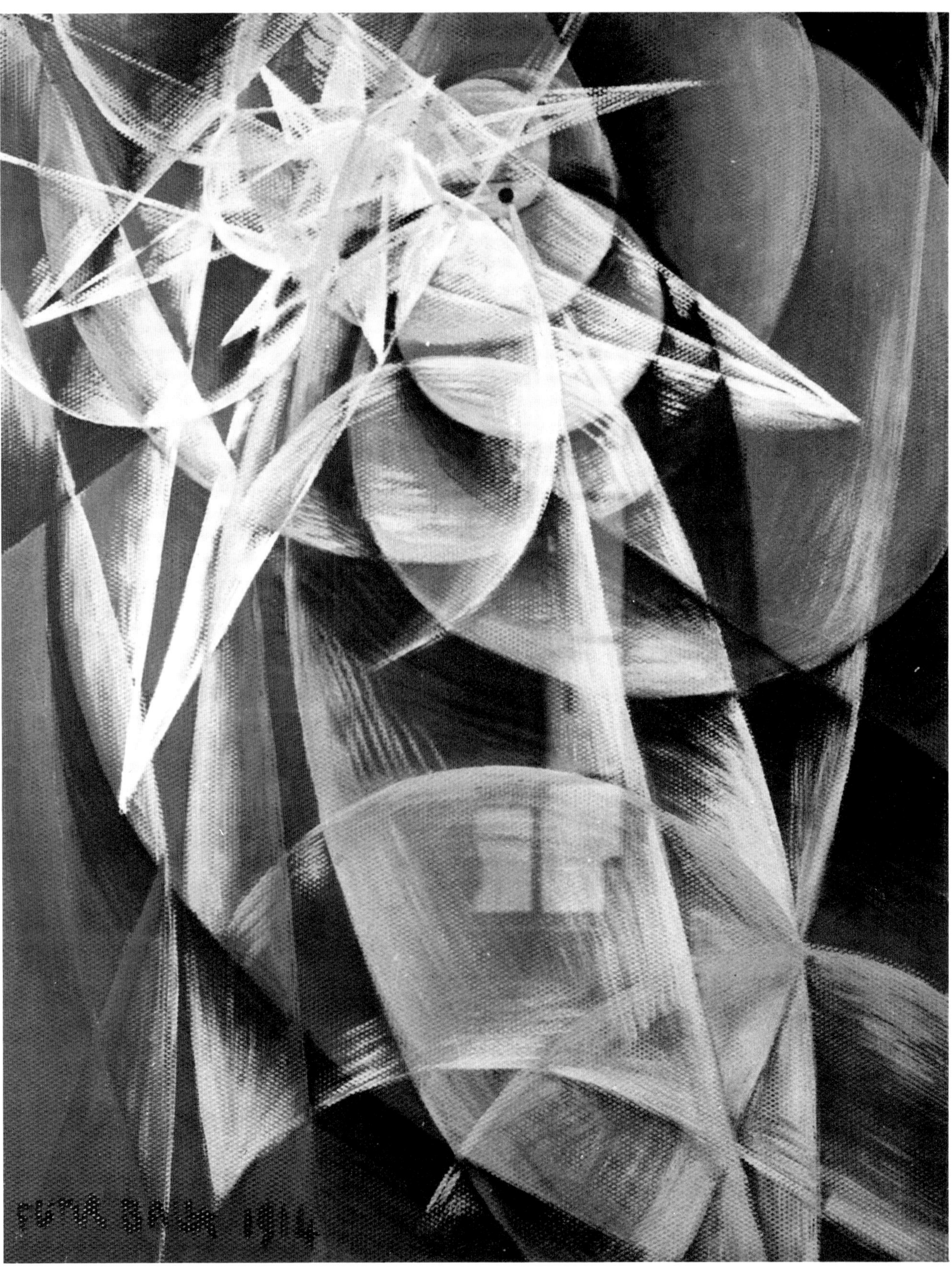

9

9. Study for "Mercury Passing Before the Sun," 1914
Gouache on paper, 25¾ x 19¾" (65.4 x 50.2 cm)
The Lydia and Harry Lewis Winston Collection
(Dr. and Mrs. Barnett Malbin, New York)

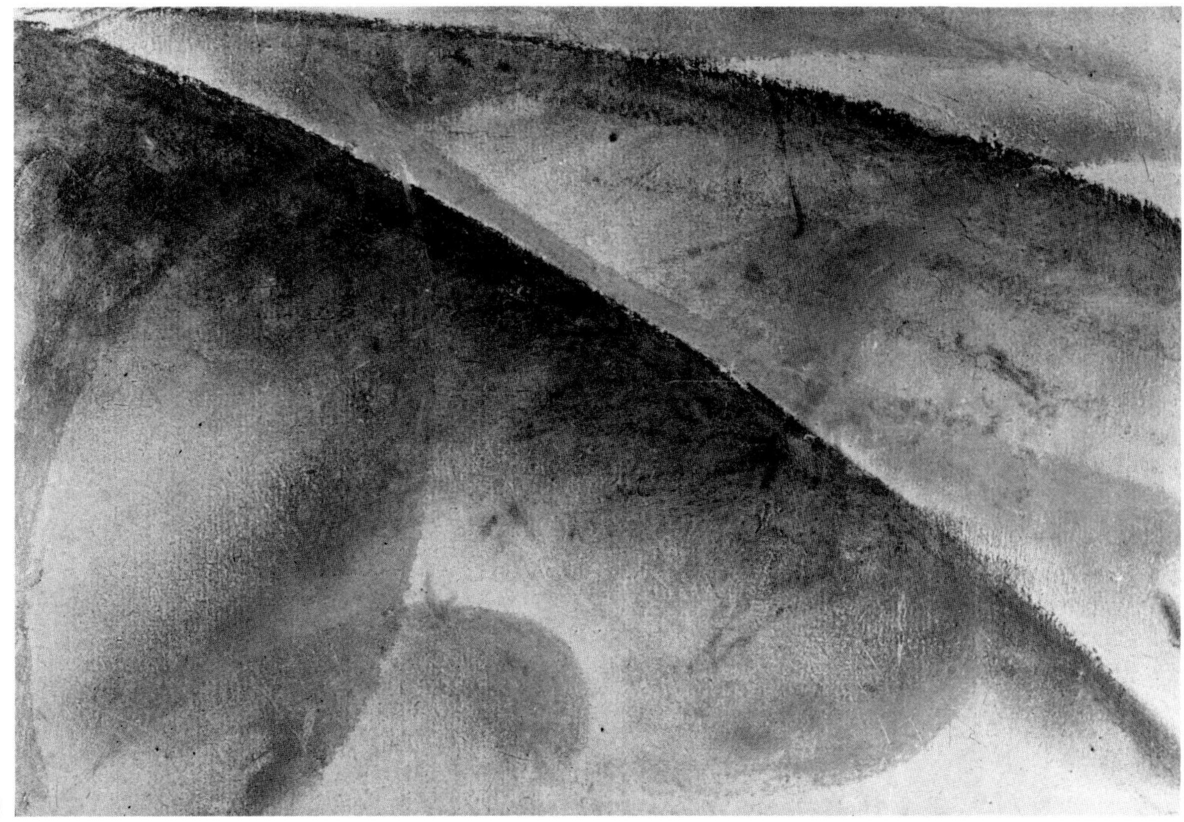

10

11

10. Goldfish, c. 1914
Pastel on paper, 9¼ x 14¼″ (23.5 x 36.2 cm)
The Lydia and Harry Lewis Winston Collection
(Dr. and Mrs. Barnett Malbin, New York)

11. Vortex + Line of Velocity, c. 1914–15
Pencil on paper, 16¾ x 25″ (42.5 x 63.5 cm)
The Lydia and Harry Lewis Winston Collection
(Dr. and Mrs. Barnett Malbin, New York)

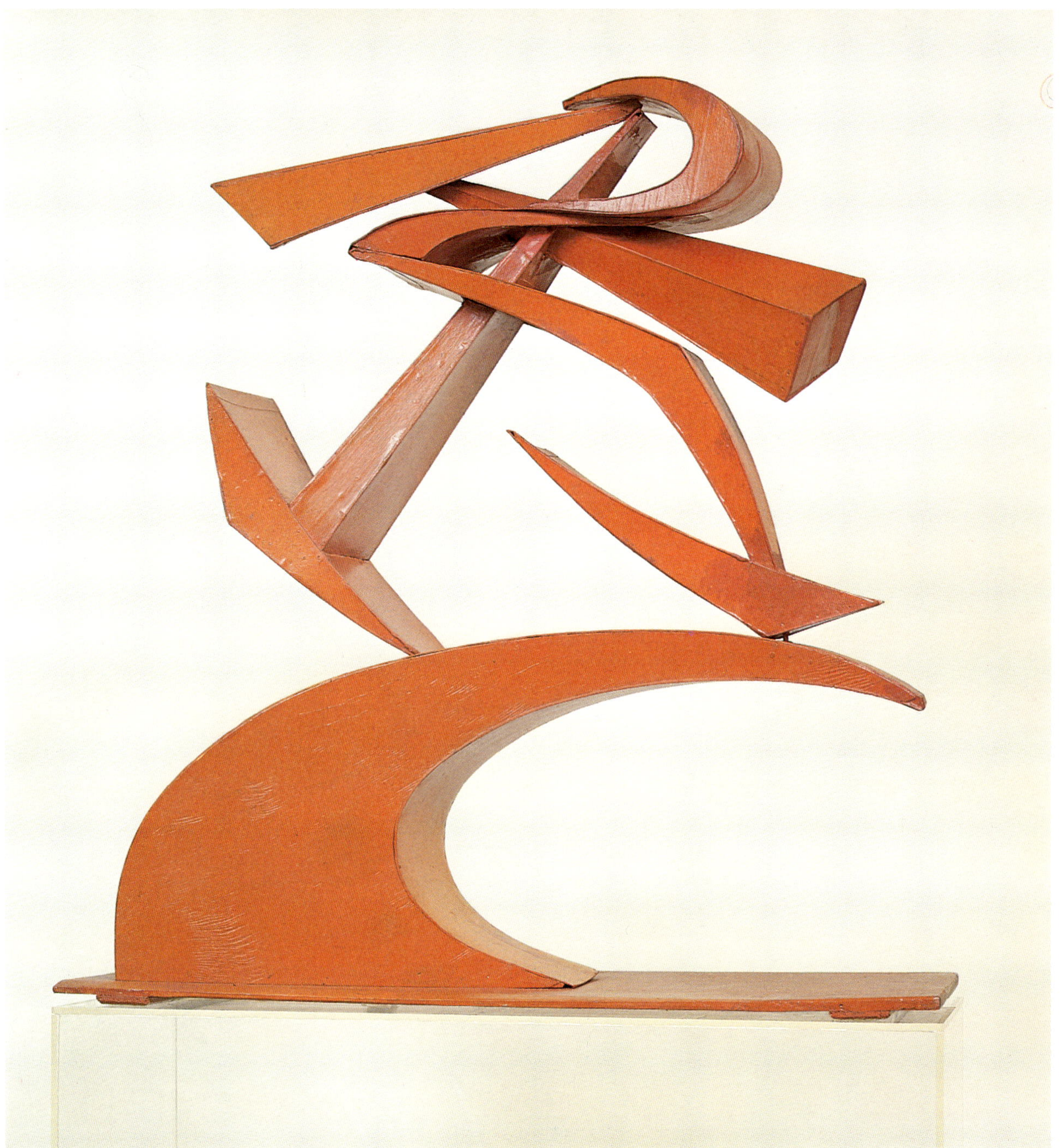

12

12. Fist of Boccioni (Force-Lines of the Fist of Boccioni), c. 1915
Painted wood and cardboard, 33 x 31 x 12½"
(83.8 x 78.7 x 31.8 cm)
The Lydia and Harry Lewis Winston Collection
(Dr. and Mrs. Barnett Malbin, New York)

13

13. Crowd and Landscape, c. 1915 (?)
Collage on paper, 60 x 26¼″ (152.4 x 66.7 cm)
The Lydia and Harry Lewis Winston Collection
(Dr. and Mrs. Barnett Malbin, New York)

Giacomo Balla

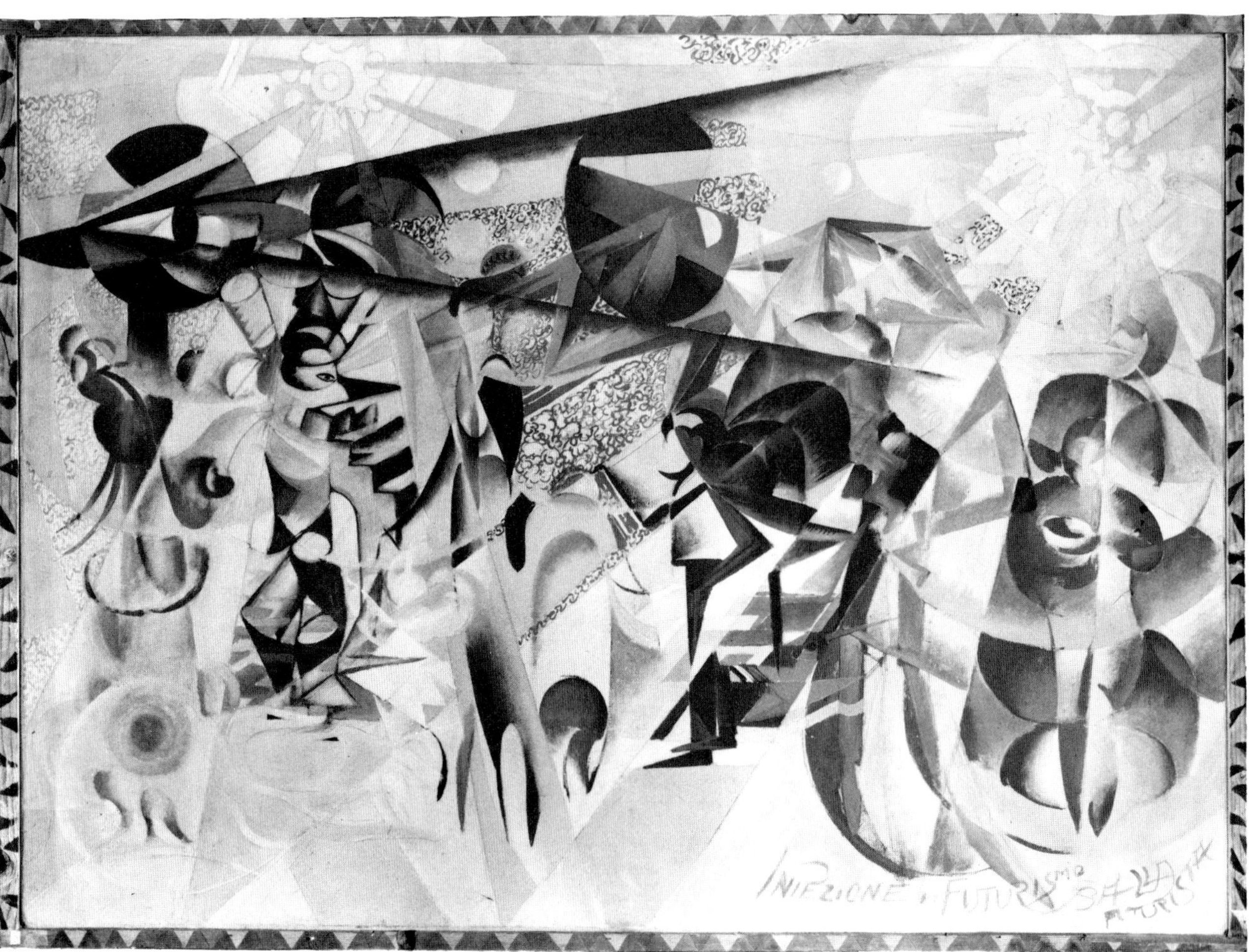

14

14. The Injection of Futurism, c. 1918
Oil on canvas, 31¾ x 45¼″ (80.6 x 114.9 cm)
The Lydia and Harry Lewis Winston Collection
(Dr. and Mrs. Barnett Malbin, New York)

Umberto Boccioni

1 8 8 2 – 1 9 1 6

15

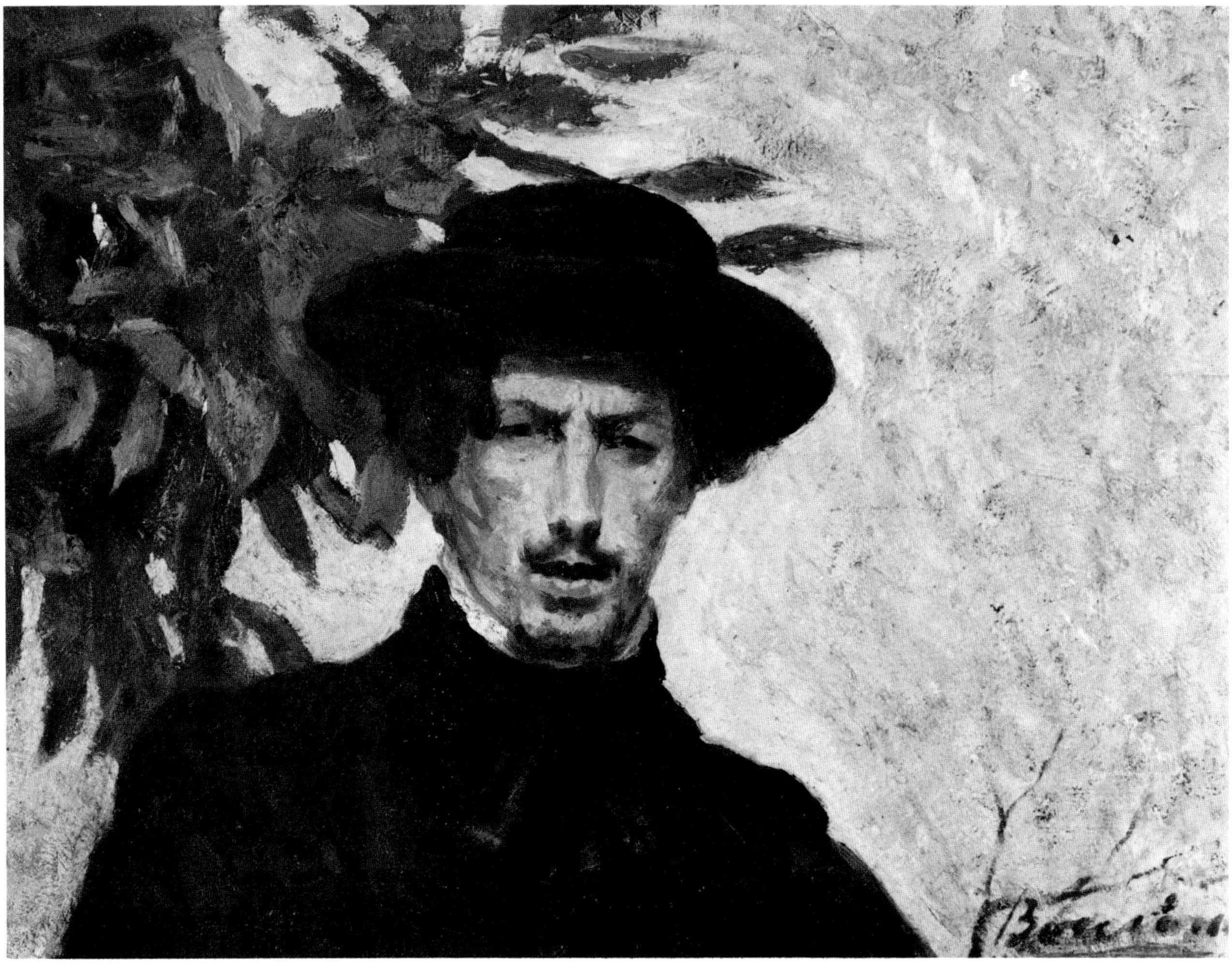

16

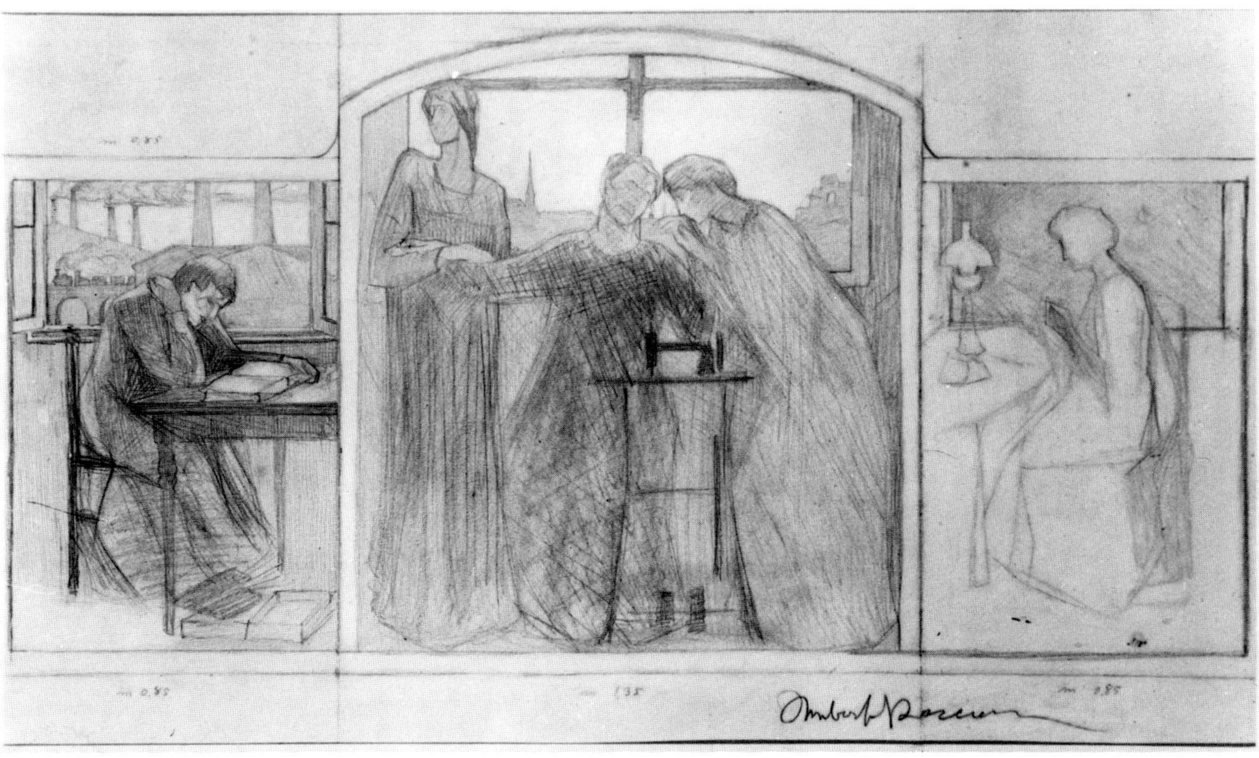

15. Self-Portrait, c. 1905
Oil on canvas, 20¼ x 27″ (51.4 x 68.6 cm)
The Lydia and Harry Lewis Winston Collection
(Dr. and Mrs. Barnett Malbin, New York)
Exhibition: Rome, Societa degli Amatori e Cultori, *LXXVII Esposizione Internazionale di Belle Arti,* 1905

16. Homage to Mother, 1907
Pencil on paper, 15⅜ x 22¾″ (39.1 x 57.8 cm)
The Lydia and Harry Lewis Winston Collection
(Dr. and Mrs. Barnett Malbin, New York)

Umberto Boccioni

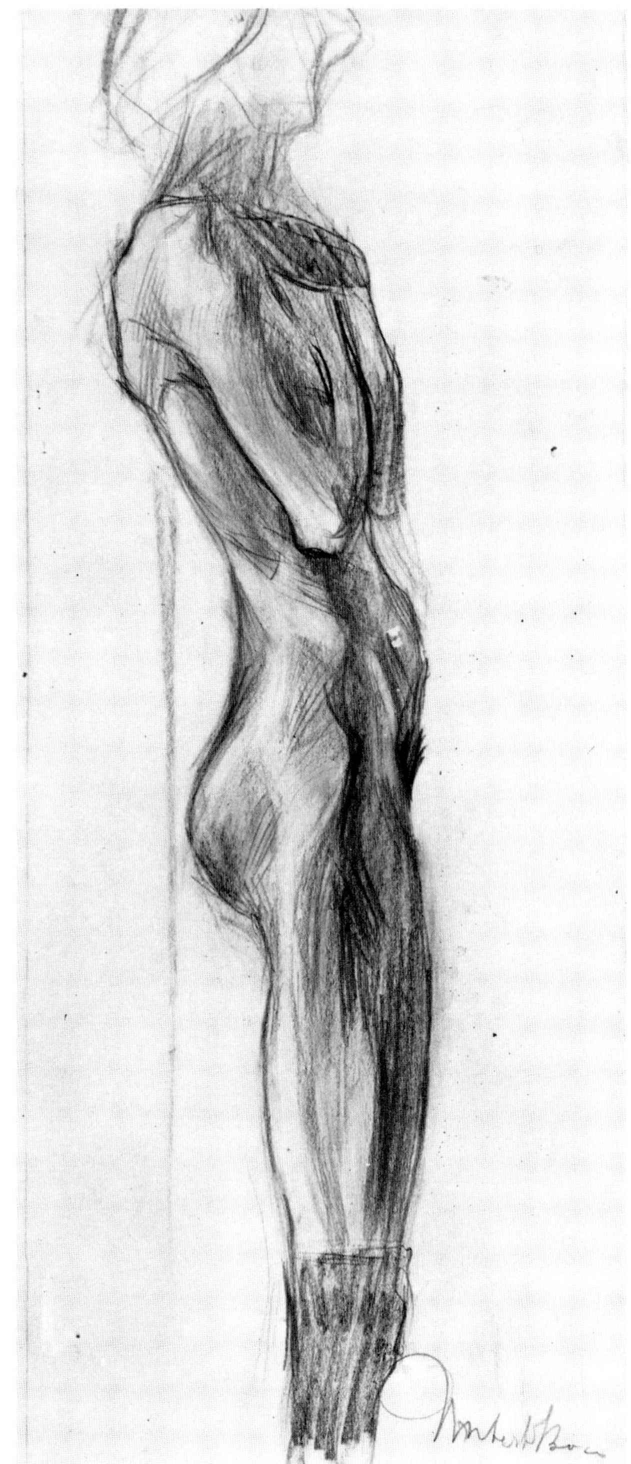

17

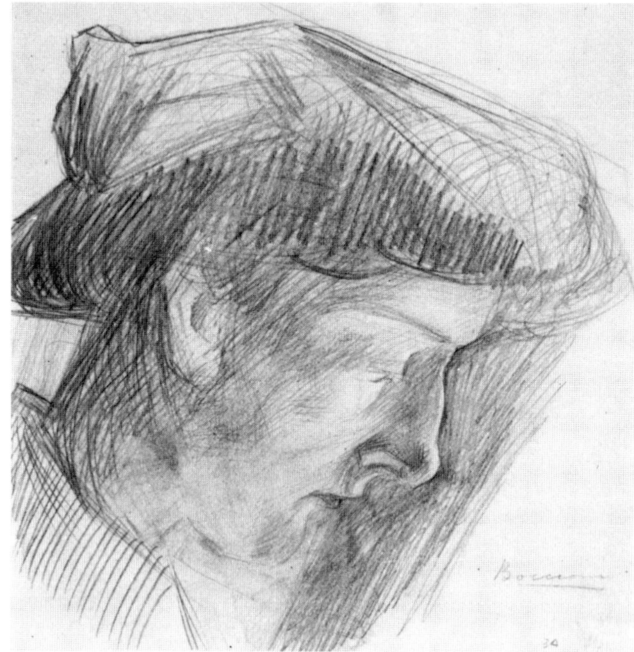

18

17. Standing Nude Girl, 1907
Pencil on board, 16⅝ x 7" (42.2 x 17.8 cm)
The Lydia and Harry Lewis Winston Collection
(Dr. and Mrs. Barnett Malbin, New York)

18. Head of a Young Woman (Study for "The Story of a Seamstress"), 1908
Pencil on paper, 6½ x 6½" (16.5 x 16.5 cm)
The Lydia and Harry Lewis Winston Collection
(Dr. and Mrs. Barnett Malbin, New York)

19

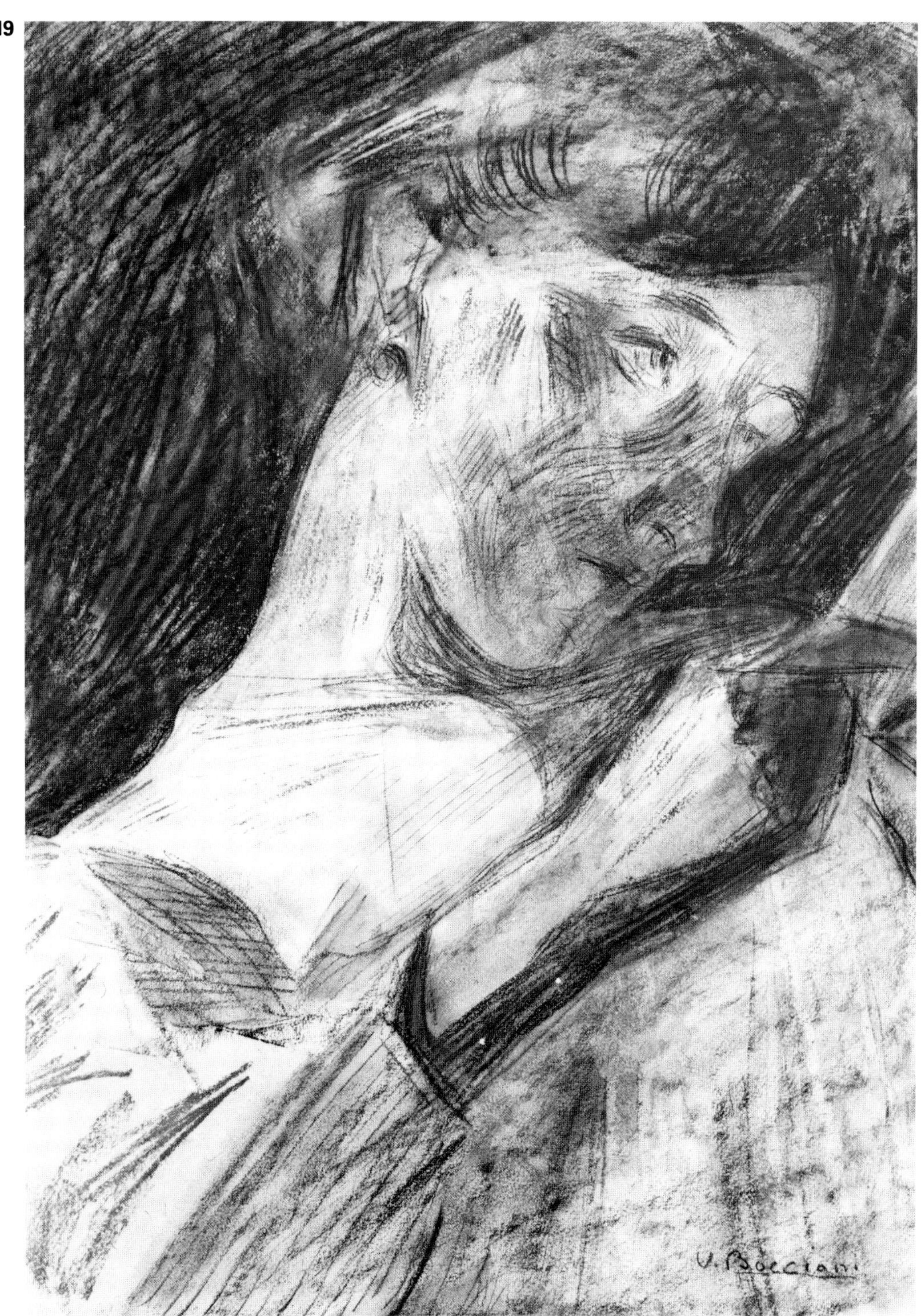

19. Young Woman Reading (Ines), 1910
Charcoal and wash on paper, 18$\frac{3}{8}$ x 13$\frac{1}{8}$" (46.7 x 33.3 cm)
The Lydia and Harry Lewis Winston Collection
(Dr. and Mrs. Barnett Malbin, New York)

Umberto Boccioni

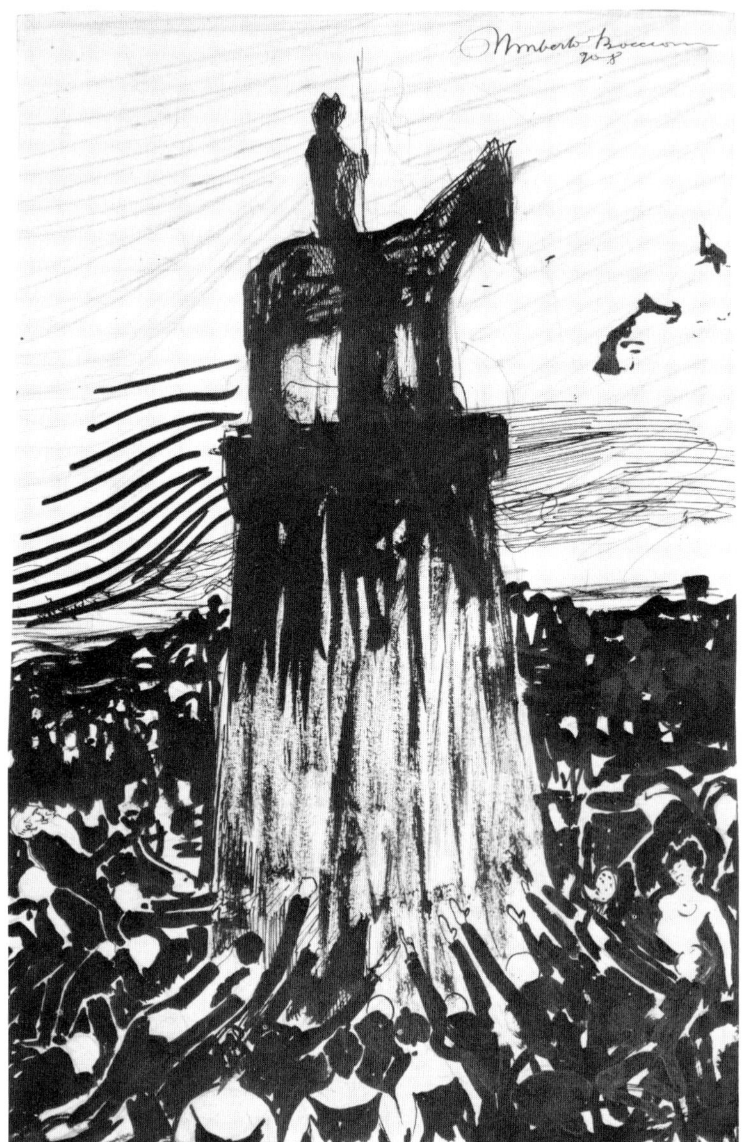
20

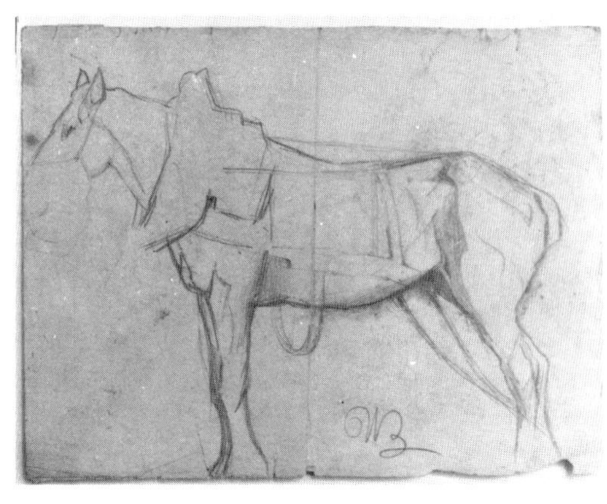
21

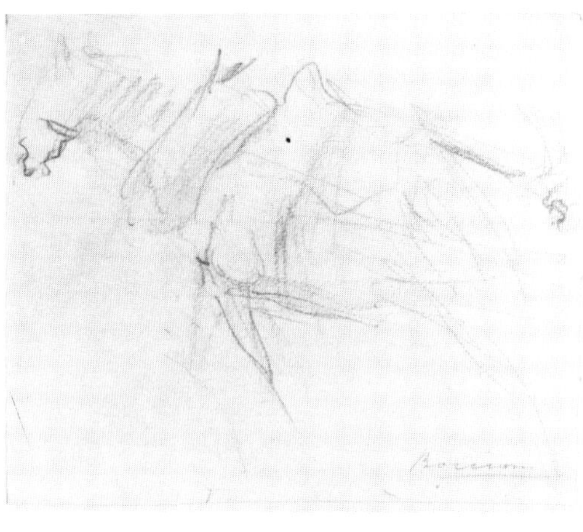
22

23
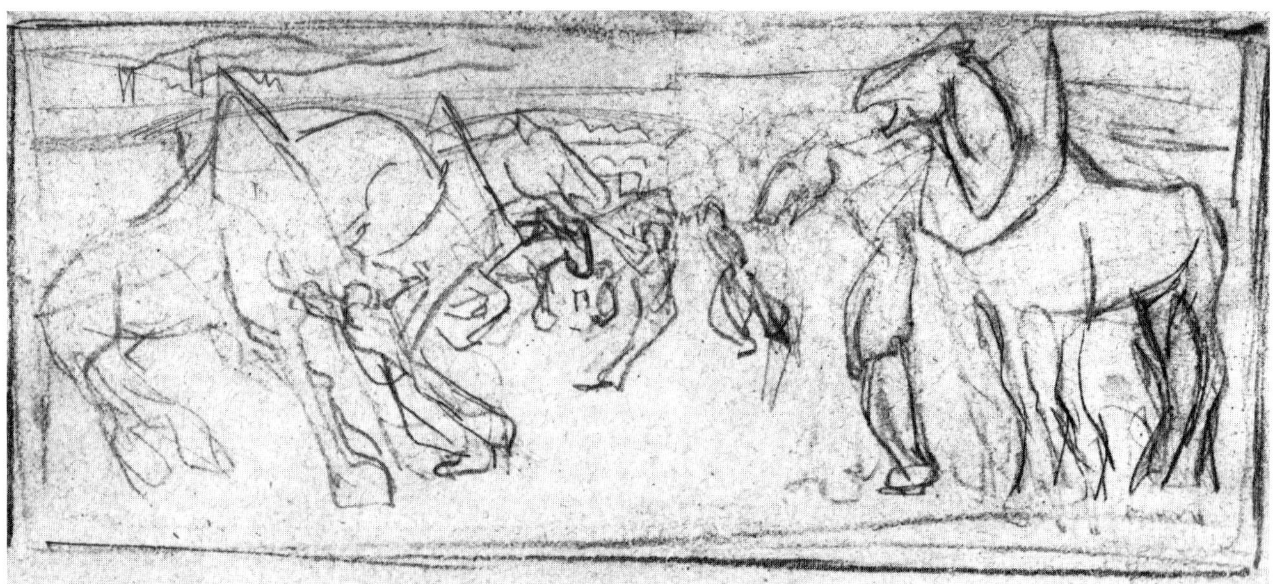

20. Agitated Crowd Surrounding a High Equestrian Monument, 1908
Pencil and india ink on paper, 14¼ x 9½″ (36.2 x 24.1 cm)
The Lydia and Harry Lewis Winston Collection (Dr. and Mrs. Barnett Malbin, New York)

21. Harnessed Horse with Feedbag, c. 1909–10
Pencil on paper, 7 x 9⅛″ (17.8 x 23.2 cm)
The Lydia and Harry Lewis Winston Collection (Dr. and Mrs. Barnett Malbin, New York)

22. Harnessed Horse, 1910
Pencil on paper, 4⅞ x 5⅞″ (12.4 x 14.9 cm)
The Lydia and Harry Lewis Winston Collection (Dr. and Mrs. Barnett Malbin, New York)

23. Study for "The City Rises," 1910
Pencil on paper, 3⅞ x 6″ (9.8 x 15.2 cm)
The Lydia and Harry Lewis Winston Collection (Dr. and Mrs. Barnett Malbin, New York)

24

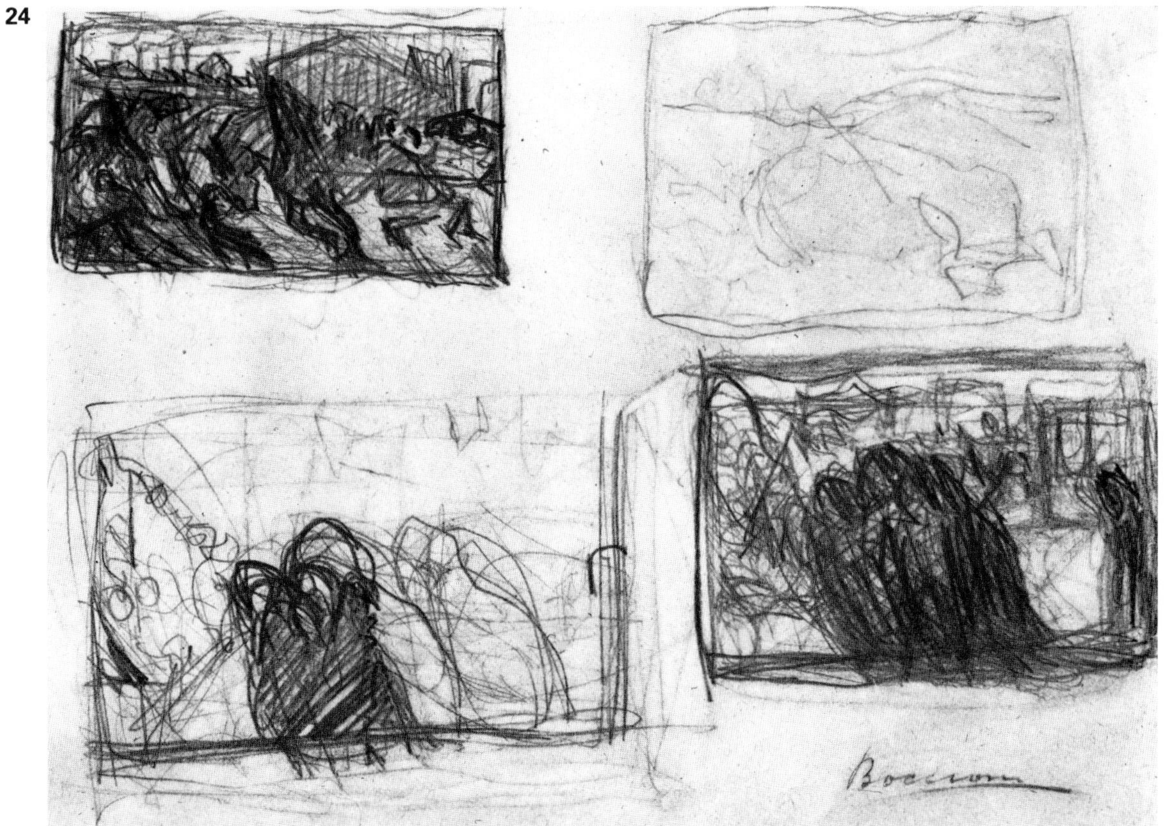

25

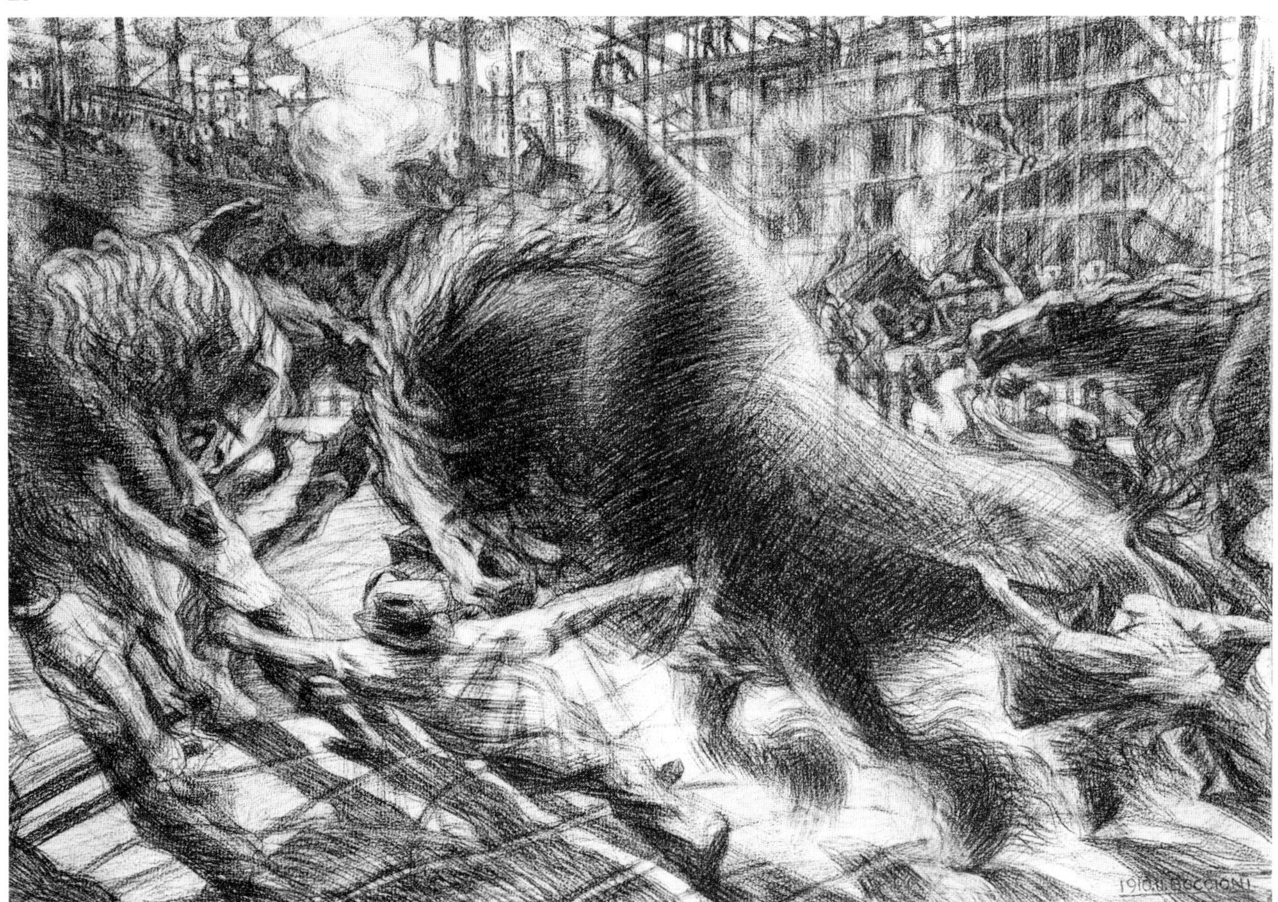

24. Studies for "The City Rises" and "Scene of an Urban Crowd," 1910
Pencil on paper, 5½ x 7⅛" (14 x 18.1 cm)
The Lydia and Harry Lewis Winston Collection
(Dr. and Mrs. Barnett Malbin, New York)

25. Study for "The City Rises," 1910
Crayon, chalk, and charcoal on paper,
23⅛ x 34⅛" (58.8 x 86.7 cm)
The Museum of Modern Art, New York
Mrs. Simon Guggenheim Fund, 1961

Umberto Boccioni

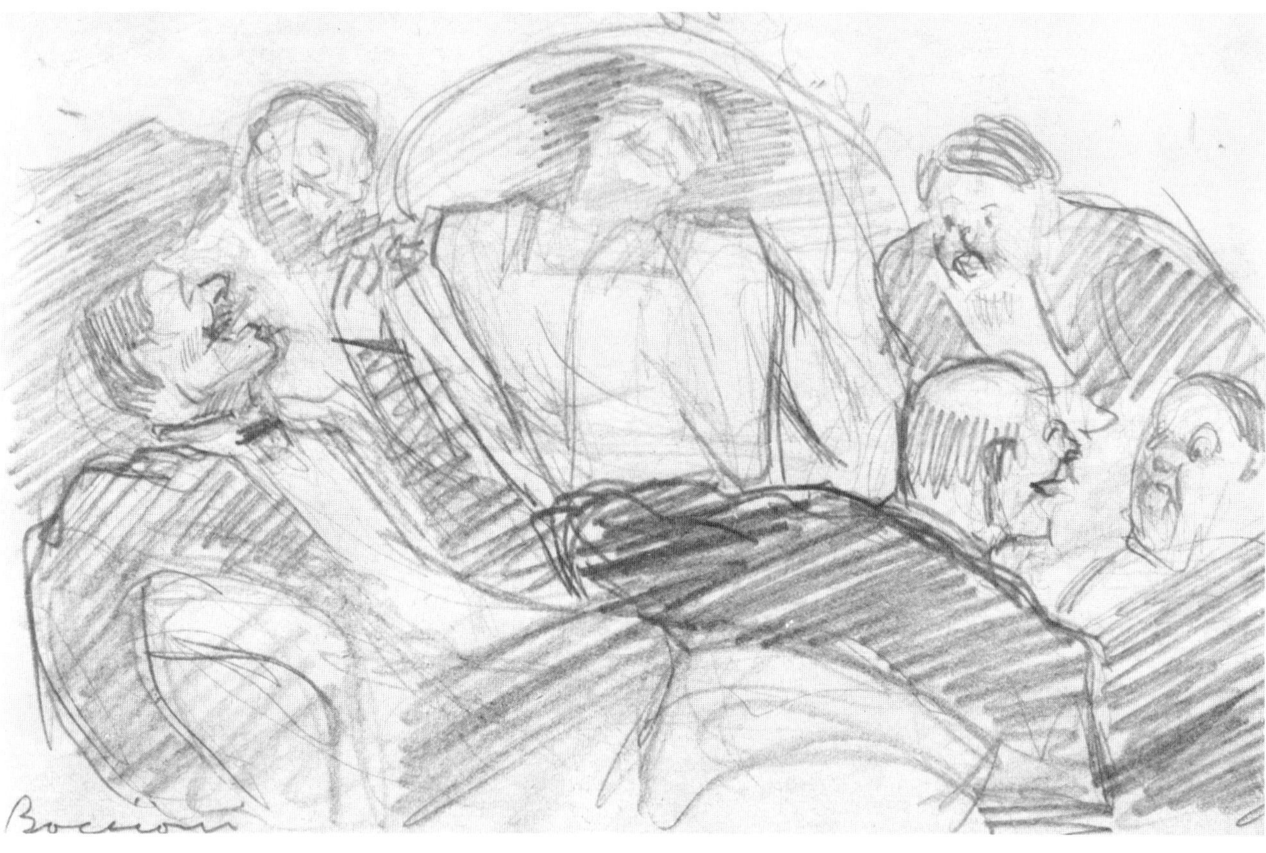

26

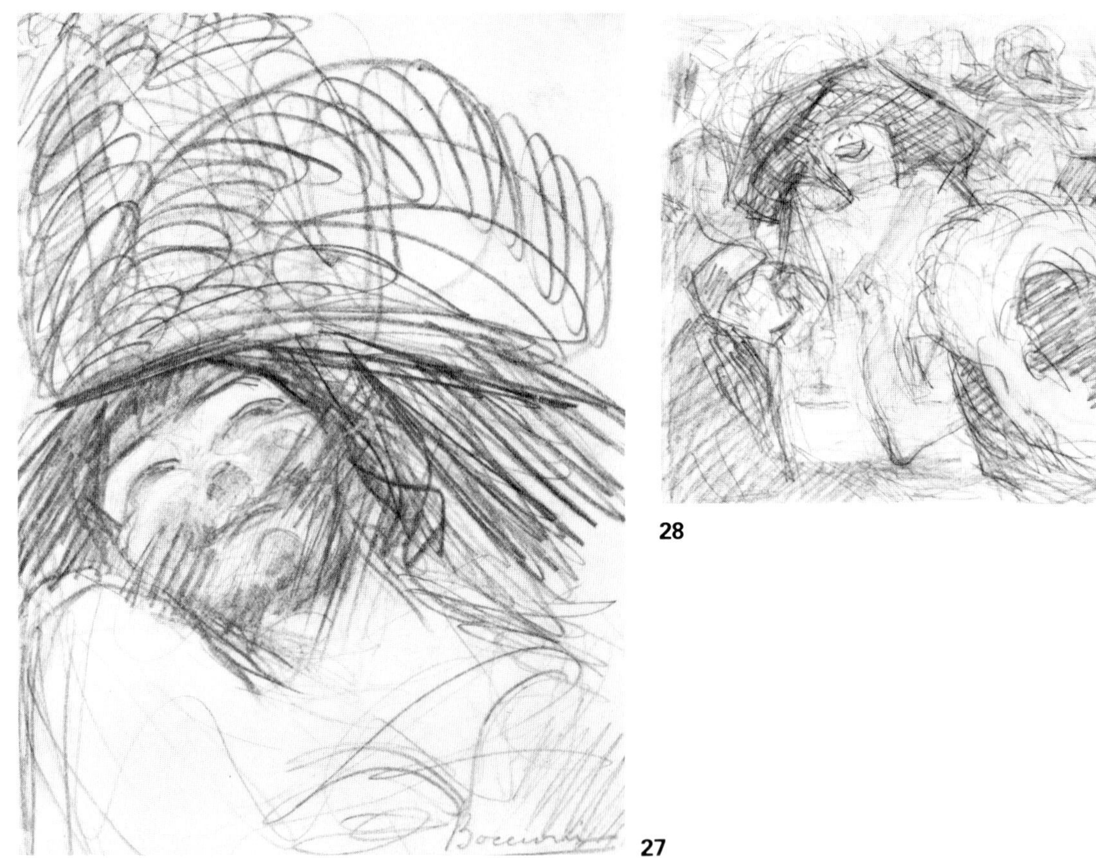

28

27

26. Study for "The Laugh (Laughter)," 1910
Pencil on paper, 5 x 8⅛" (12.7 x 20.6 cm)
The Museum of Modern Art, New York
Gift of Herbert and Nannette Rothschild, 1962

27. Study for "The Laugh (Laughter)," 1910–11
Pencil on paper, 6⅛ x 4½" (15.4 x 11.4 cm)
The Museum of Modern Art, New York
Gift of Herbert and Nannette Rothschild, 1967

28. Study for "The Laugh (Laughter)," 1910–11
Pencil on paper, 4½ x 6" (11.4 x 15.2 cm)
The Museum of Modern Art, New York
Gift of Herbert and Nannette Rothschild, 1967

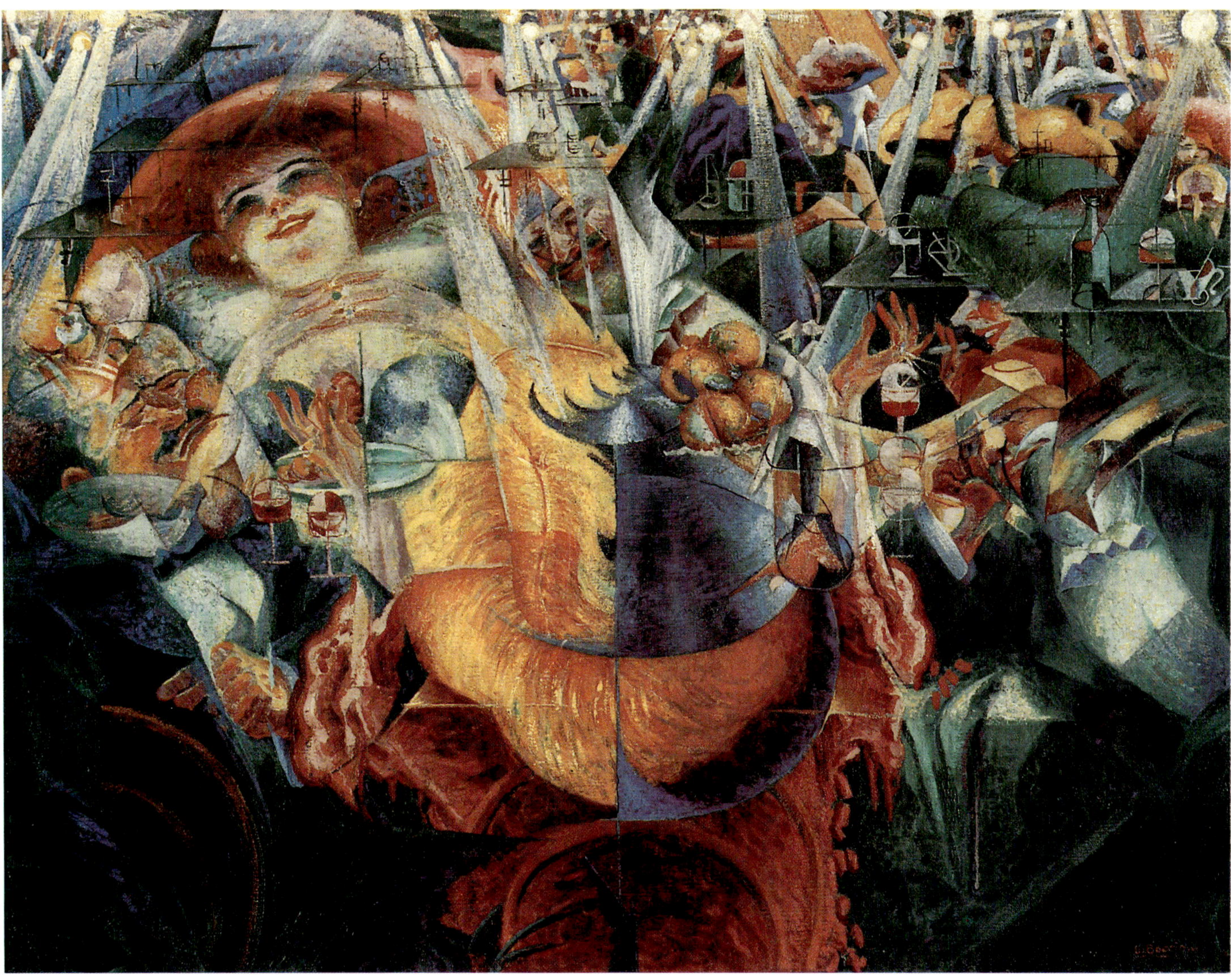

29

29. The Laugh (Laughter), 1911
Oil on canvas, 43⅜ x 57¼" (110.2 x 145.4 cm)
The Museum of Modern Art, New York
Gift of Herbert and Nannette Rothschild, 1959
Exhibitions: Milan, Padiglione Ricordi, *Esposizione d'Arte Libera,* from April 30, 1911; Paris, Galerie Bernheim-Jeune, *Les Peintres Futuristes Italiens,* February 5–24, 1912, no. 5, repro. p. 26

Umberto Boccioni

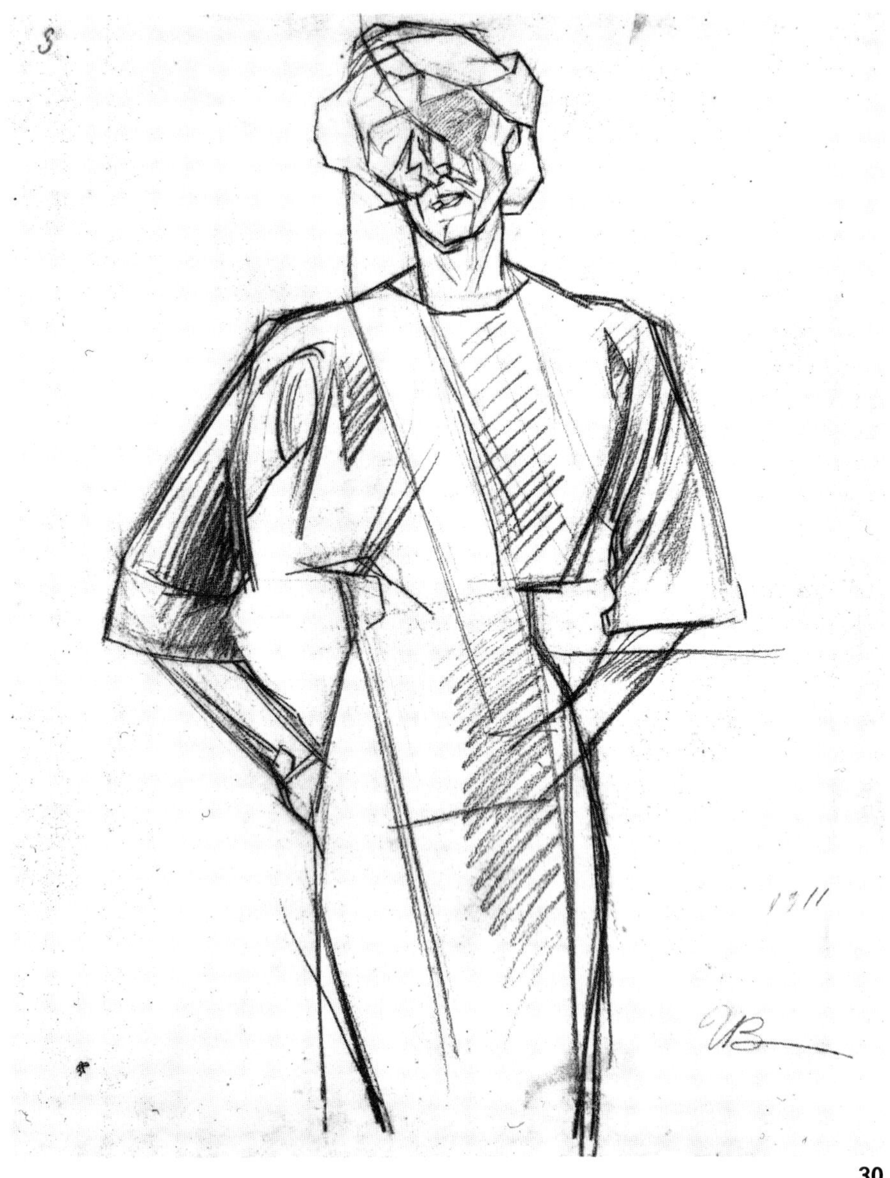

30

30. Study for "Woman Surrounded by Houses (Ines))," 1911
Verso: Study for "States of Mind: The Farewells," 1911
Pencil on paper, 24 x 19⅛" (61 x 48.6 cm)
The Lydia and Harry Lewis Winston Collection
(Dr. and Mrs. Barnett Malbin, New York)

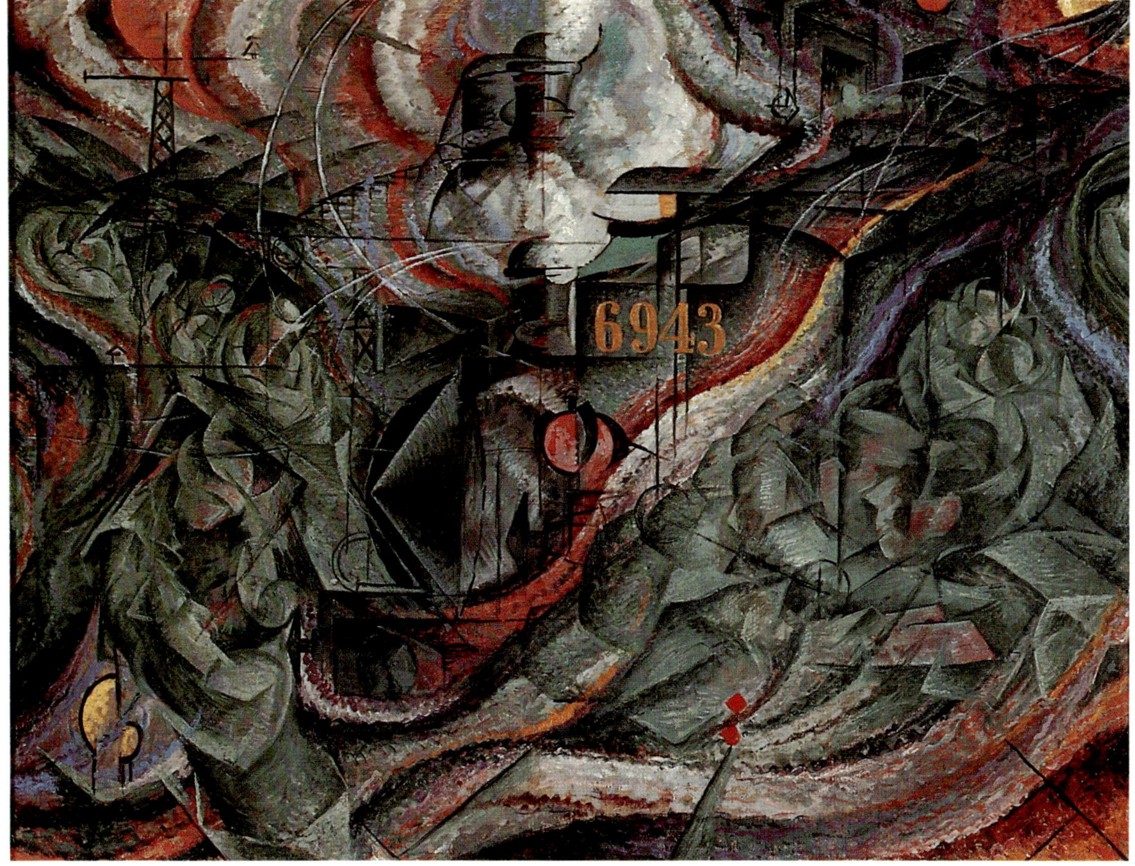

31

32

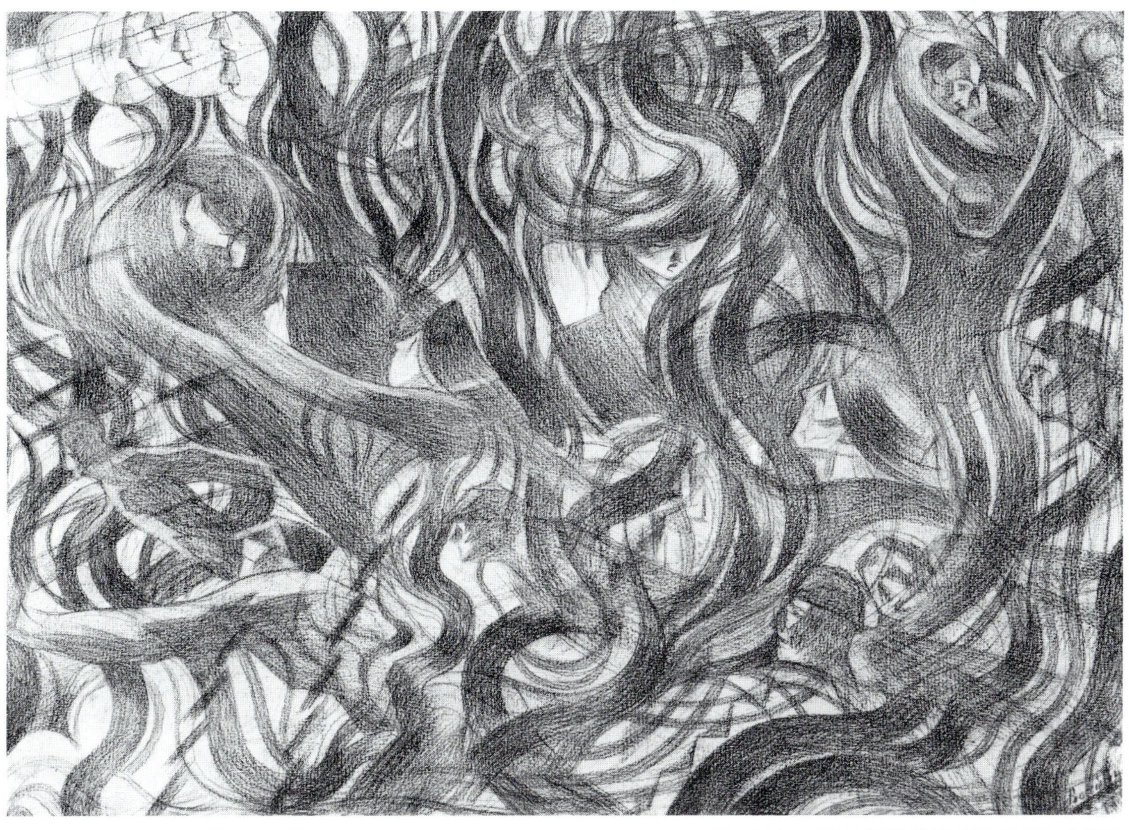

31. States of Mind: The Farewells, 1911
Oil on canvas, 27¾ x 37⅞" (70.5 x 96.2 cm)
The Museum of Modern Art, New York
Gift of Nelson A. Rockefeller, 1979
Exhibition: Paris, Galerie Bernheim-Jeune, *Les Peintres Futuristes Italiens,* February 5–24, 1912, no. 1, repro. p. 25

32. States of Mind: The Farewells, 1911
Charcoal and chalk on paper, 23 x 34" (58.4 x 86.3 cm)
The Museum of Modern Art, New York
Gift of Vico Baer, 1941

Umberto Boccioni

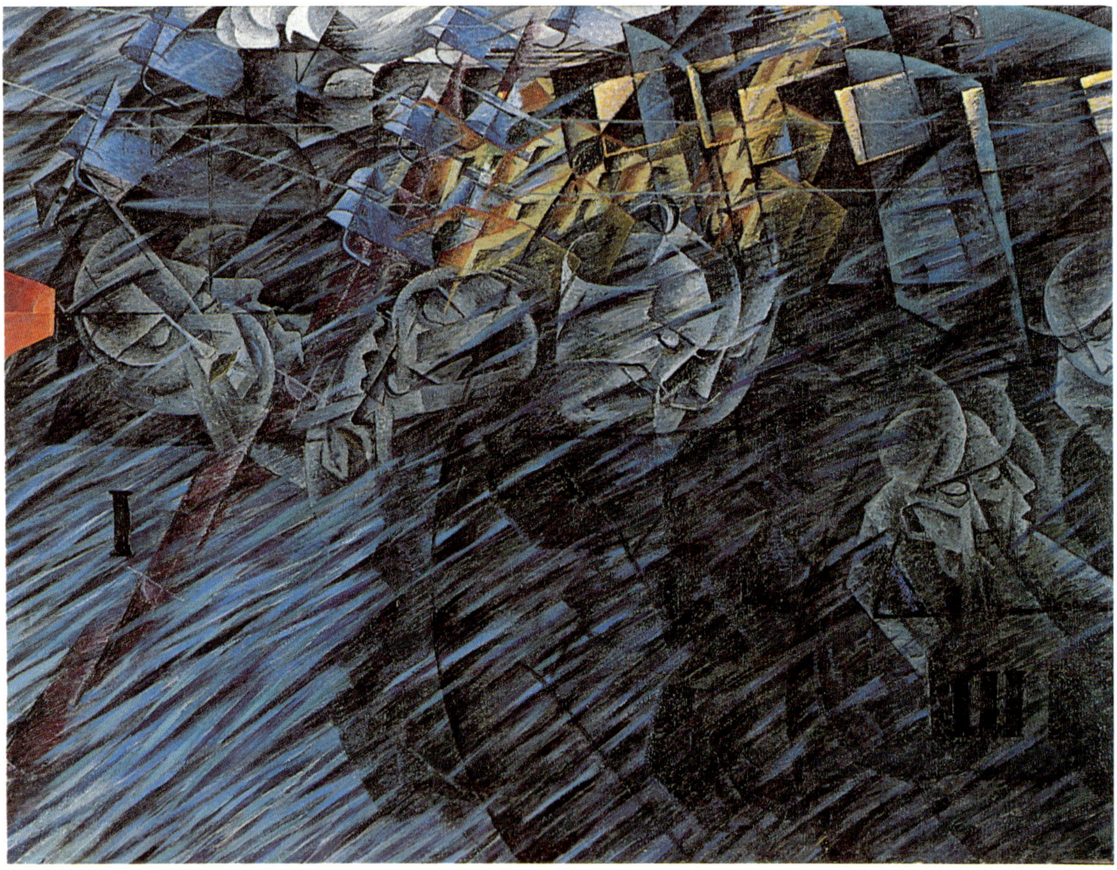

33

34

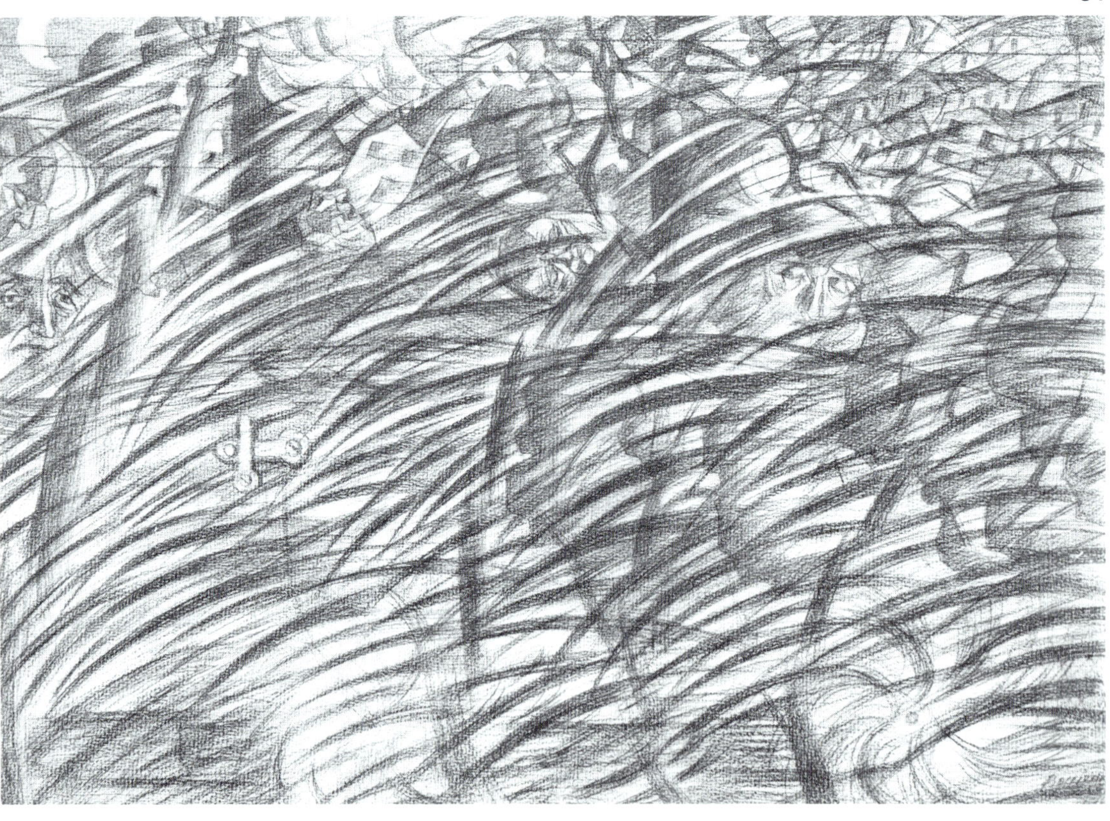

33. States of Mind: Those Who Go, 1911
Oil on canvas, 27⅞ x 37¾" (70.8 x 95.9 cm)
The Museum of Modern Art, New York
Gift of Nelson A. Rockefeller, 1979
Exhibition: Paris, Galerie Bernheim-Jeune, *Les Peintres Futuristes Italiens,* February 5–24, 1912, no. 2

34. States of Mind: Those Who Go, 1911
Charcoal and chalk on paper, 23 x 34" (58.4 x 86.3 cm)
The Museum of Modern Art, New York
Gift of Vico Baer, 1941

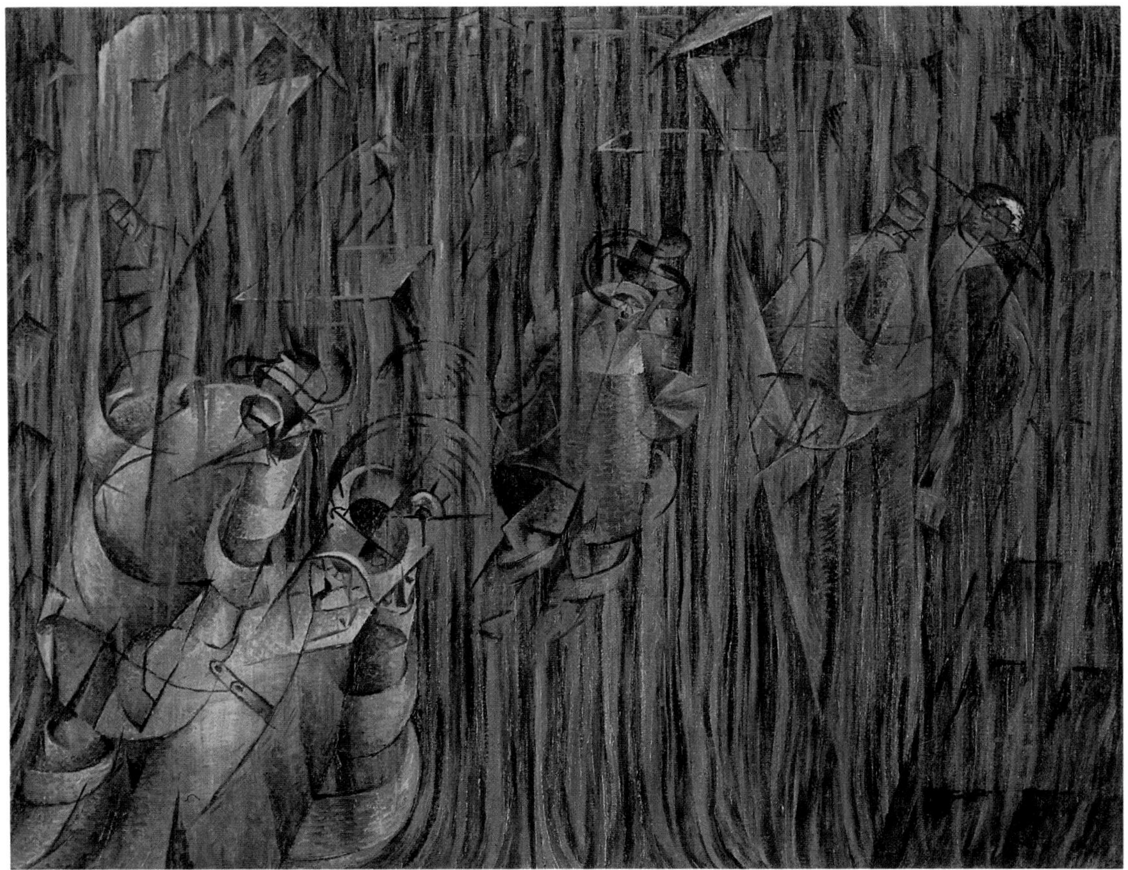

35

36

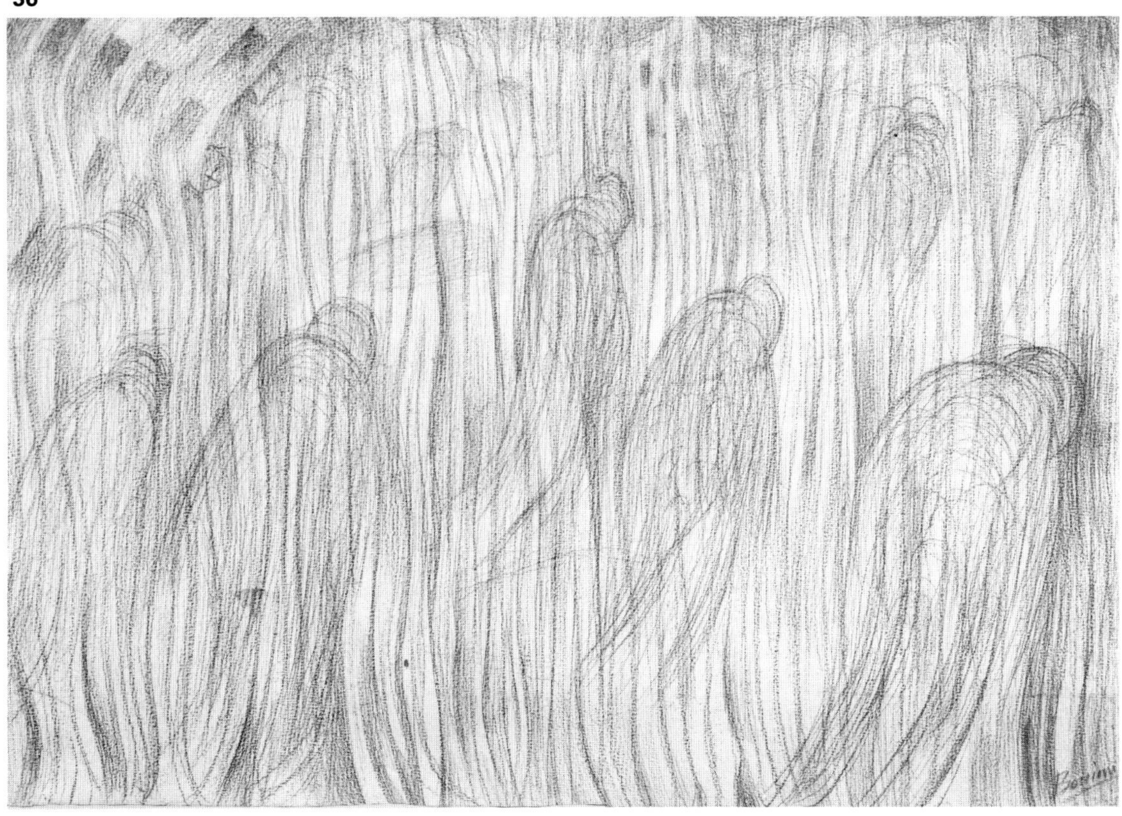

35. States of Mind: Those Who Stay, 1911
Oil on canvas, 27⅞ x 37¾" (70.8 x 95.9 cm)
The Museum of Modern Art, New York
Gift of Nelson A. Rockefeller, 1979
Exhibition: Paris, Galerie Bernheim-Jeune, *Les Peintres Futuristes Italiens,* February 5–24, 1912, no. 3

36. States of Mind: Those Who Stay, 1911
Charcoal and chalk on paper, 23 x 34" (58.4 x 86.3 cm)
The Museum of Modern Art, New York
Gift of Vico Baer, 1941

Umberto Boccioni

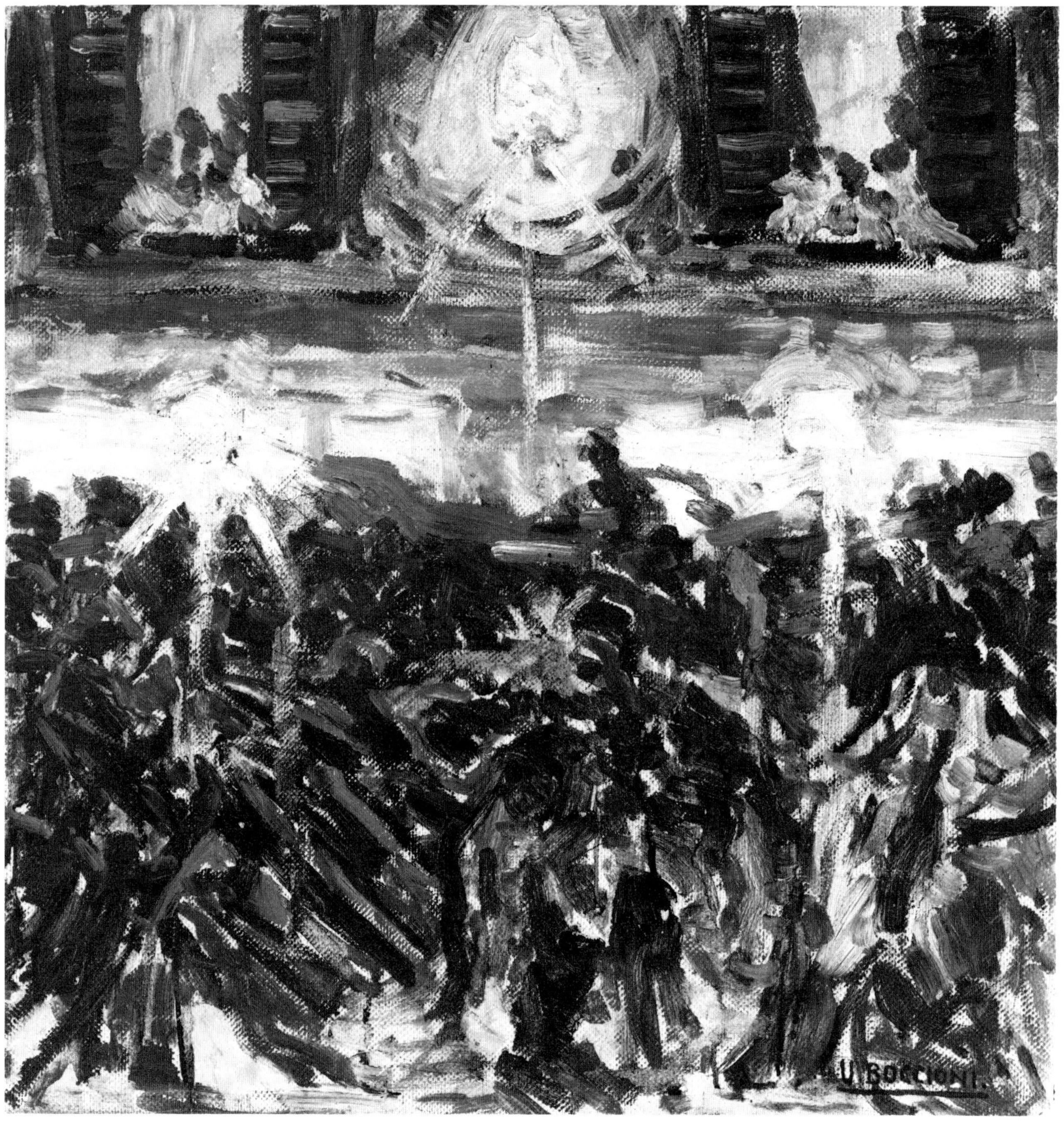

37

37. The Riot, c. 1911
Oil on canvas, 19⅞ x 19⅞" (50.5 x 50.5 cm)
The Museum of Modern Art, New York
Gift of Herbert and Nannette Rothschild, 1957

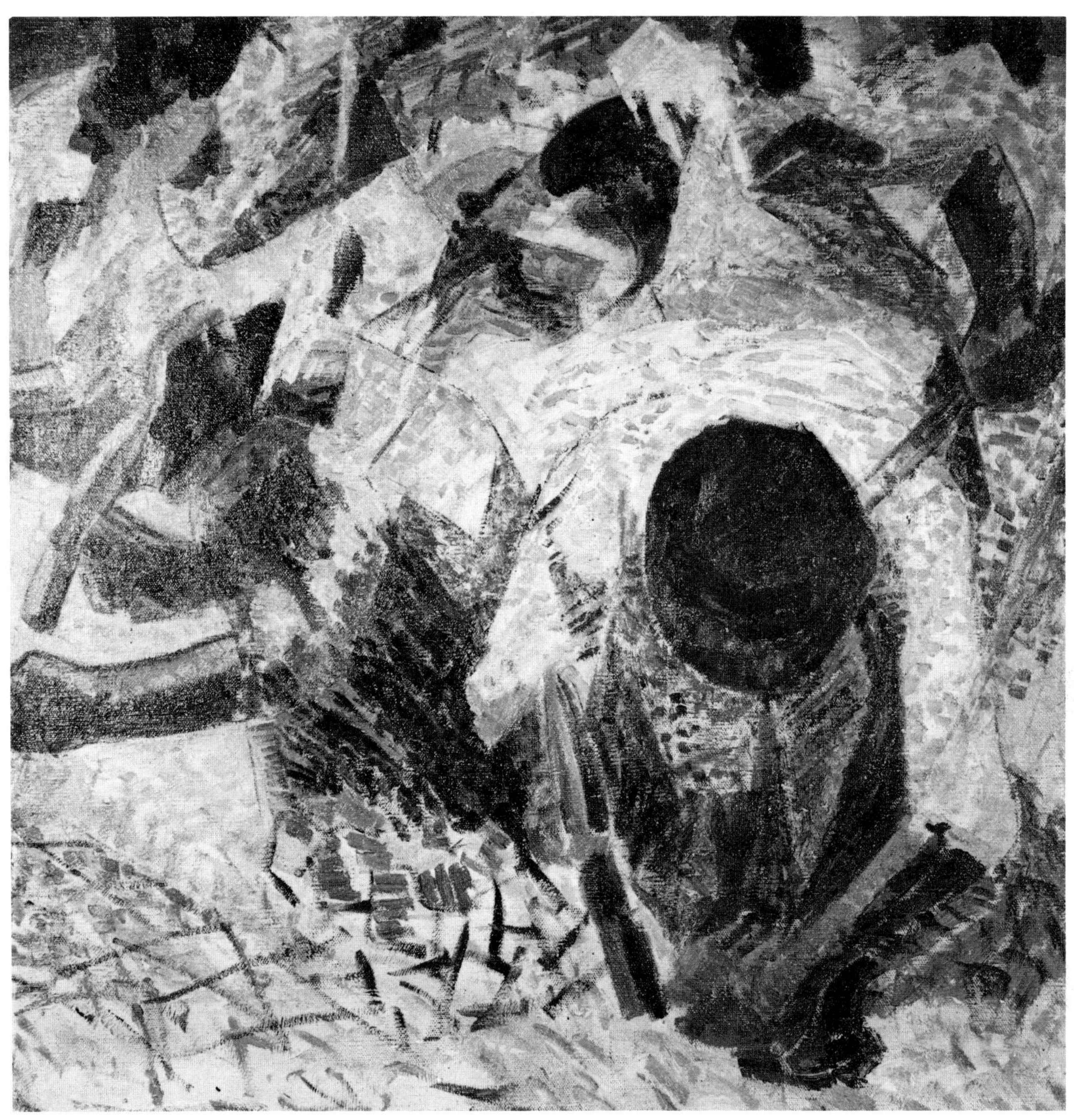

38

38. The Street Pavers, c. 1911
Oil on canvas, 39⅜ x 39⅜" (100 x 100 cm)
The Lydia and Harry Lewis Winston Collection
(Dr. and Mrs. Barnett Malbin, New York)
Exhibition: Milan, Galleria Centrale d'Arte (Palazzo Cova), *Grande Esposizione Boccioni, Pittore e Scultore Futurista,* December 28, 1916–January 14, 1917, no. 10

Umberto Boccioni

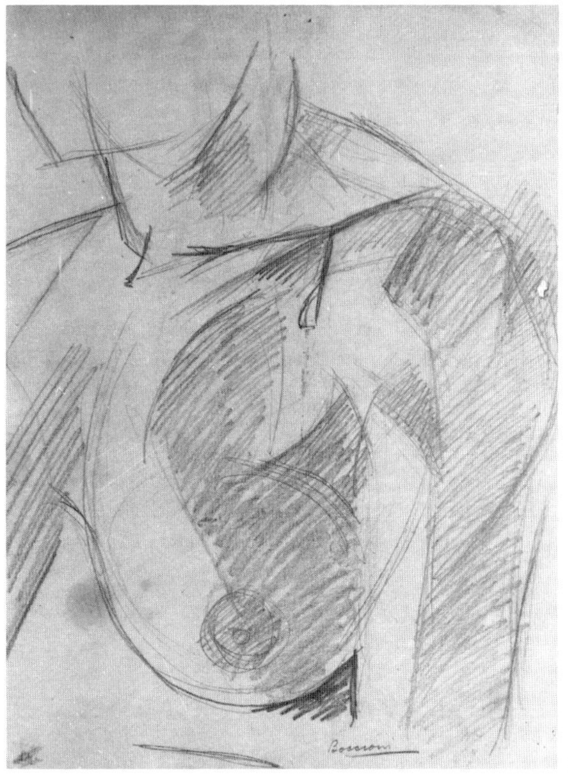

39

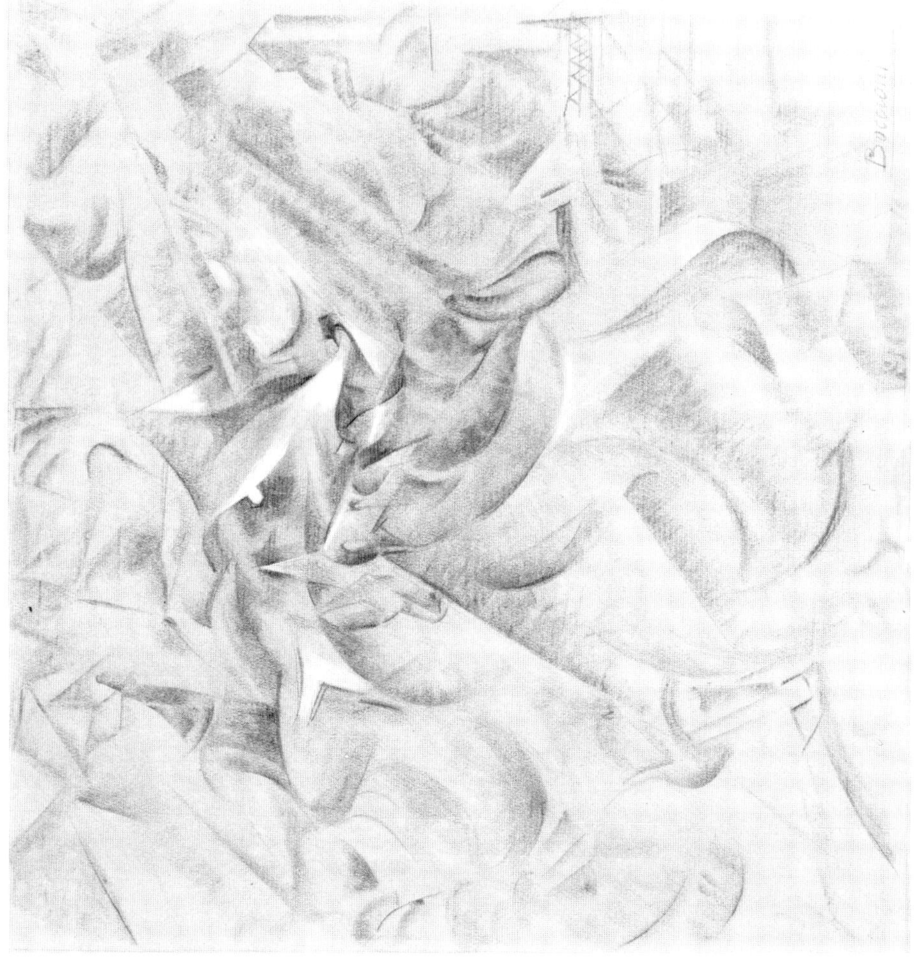

40

39. Analytical Study of the Shoulder and Breast of a Woman, 1912
Pencil on paper, 13 x 9½" (33 x 24.1 cm)
The Lydia and Harry Lewis Winston Collection
(Dr. and Mrs. Barnett Malbin, New York)

40. Study for "Elasticity," 1912
Pencil and gouache on paper, 18¾ x 24¼" (47.6 x 61.6 cm)
The Museum of Modern Art, New York
Purchase, 1949

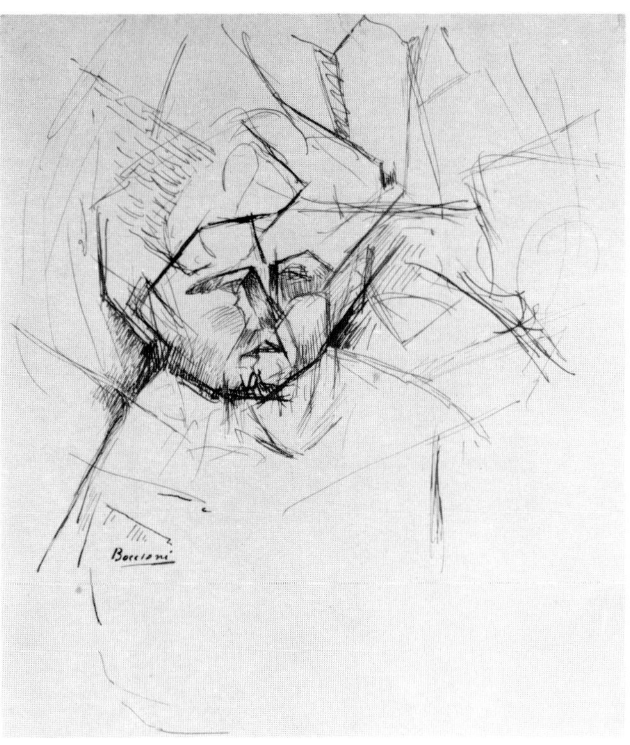

41

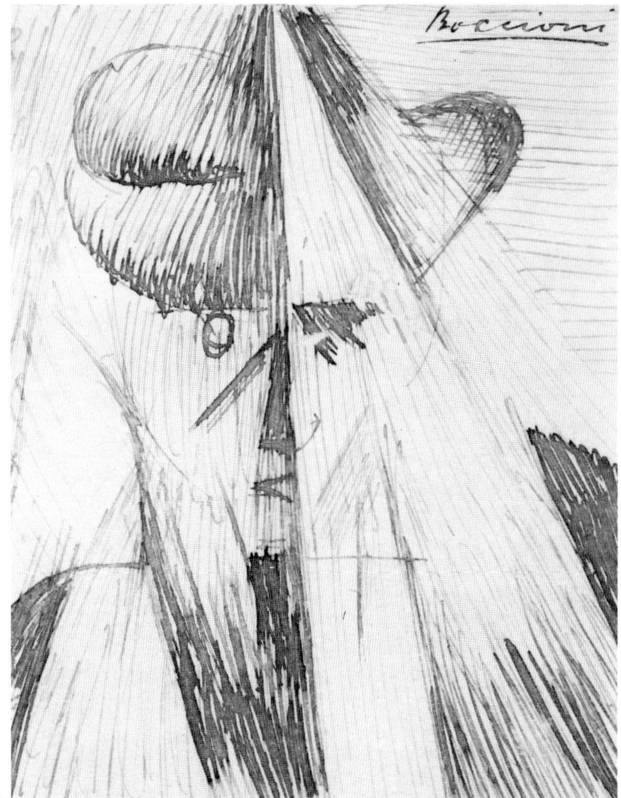

42

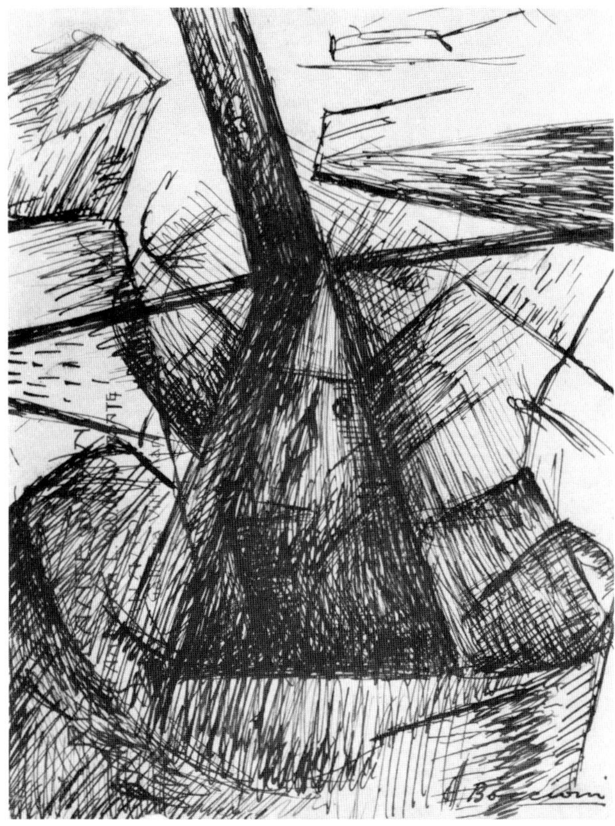

43

41. Analytical Study of a Woman's Head Against Buildings, 1911–12
Ink on paper, 11⅞ x 8½" (30.2 x 21.6 cm)
The Lydia and Harry Lewis Winston Collection
(Dr. and Mrs. Barnett Malbin, New York)

42. Head Against the Light (Boccioni's Sister), 1912
Ink on paper, 5 x 4" (12.7 x 10.2 cm)
The Lydia and Harry Lewis Winston Collection
(Dr. and Mrs. Barnett Malbin, New York)

43. Study for the Sculpture "Fusion of a Head and Window," 1912
Ink on paper, 5¾ x 4⅜" (14.6 x 11.1 cm)
The Lydia and Harry Lewis Winston Collection
(Dr. and Mrs. Barnett Malbin, New York)

Umberto Boccioni

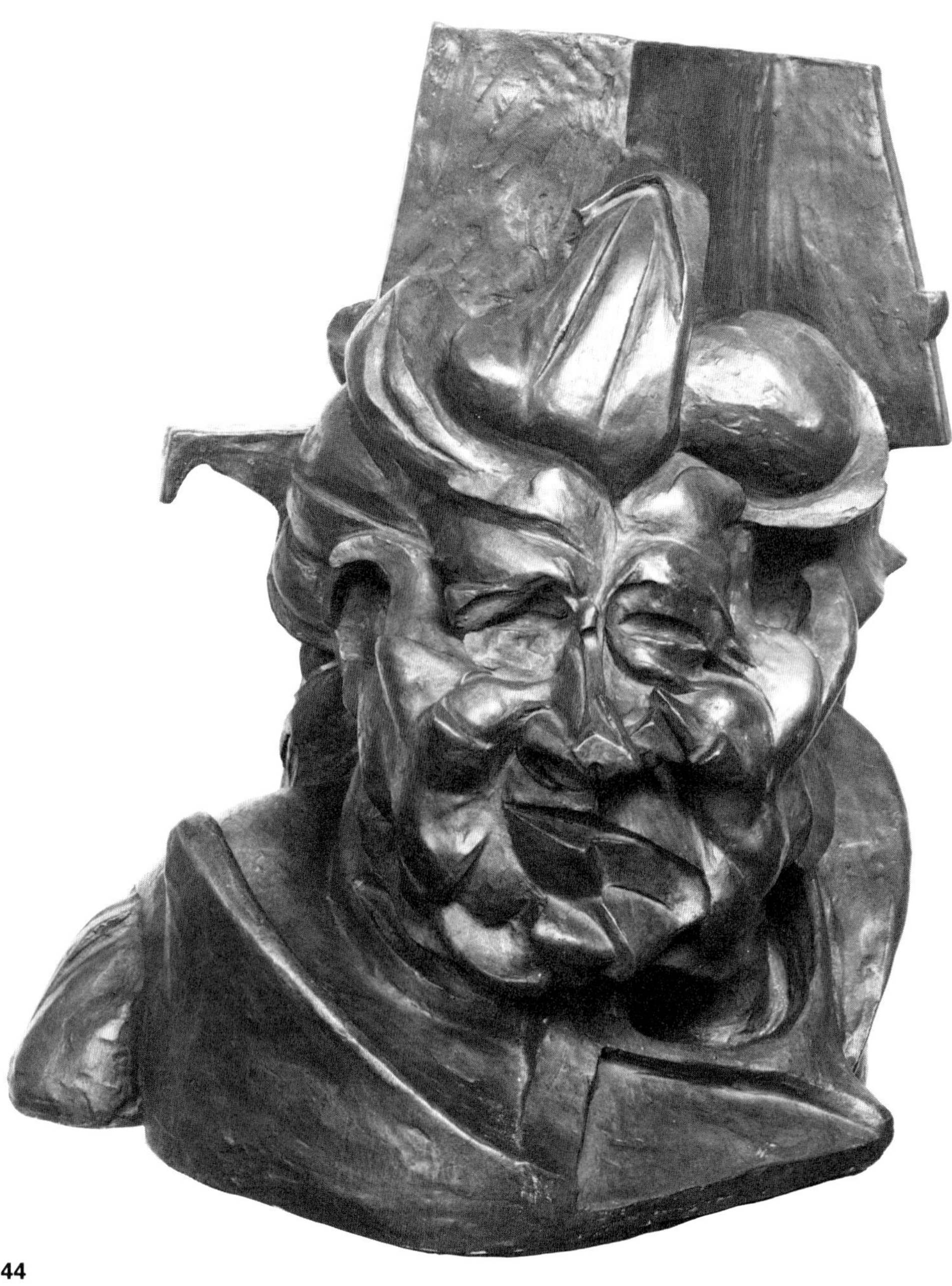

44

44. Anti-Graceful; The Mother (Portrait of the Artist's Mother), 1912 (cast 1950–51)
Bronze, 23½ x 20½ x 16" (59.7 x 52.1 x 40.6 cm)
The Lydia and Harry Lewis Winston Collection
(Dr. and Mrs. Barnett Malbin, New York)
Exhibition: Paris, Galerie La Boëtie, *1re Exposition de Sculpture Futuriste du Peintre et Sculpteur Futuriste Boccioni,* June 20–July 16, 1913, no. 9 (plaster version)

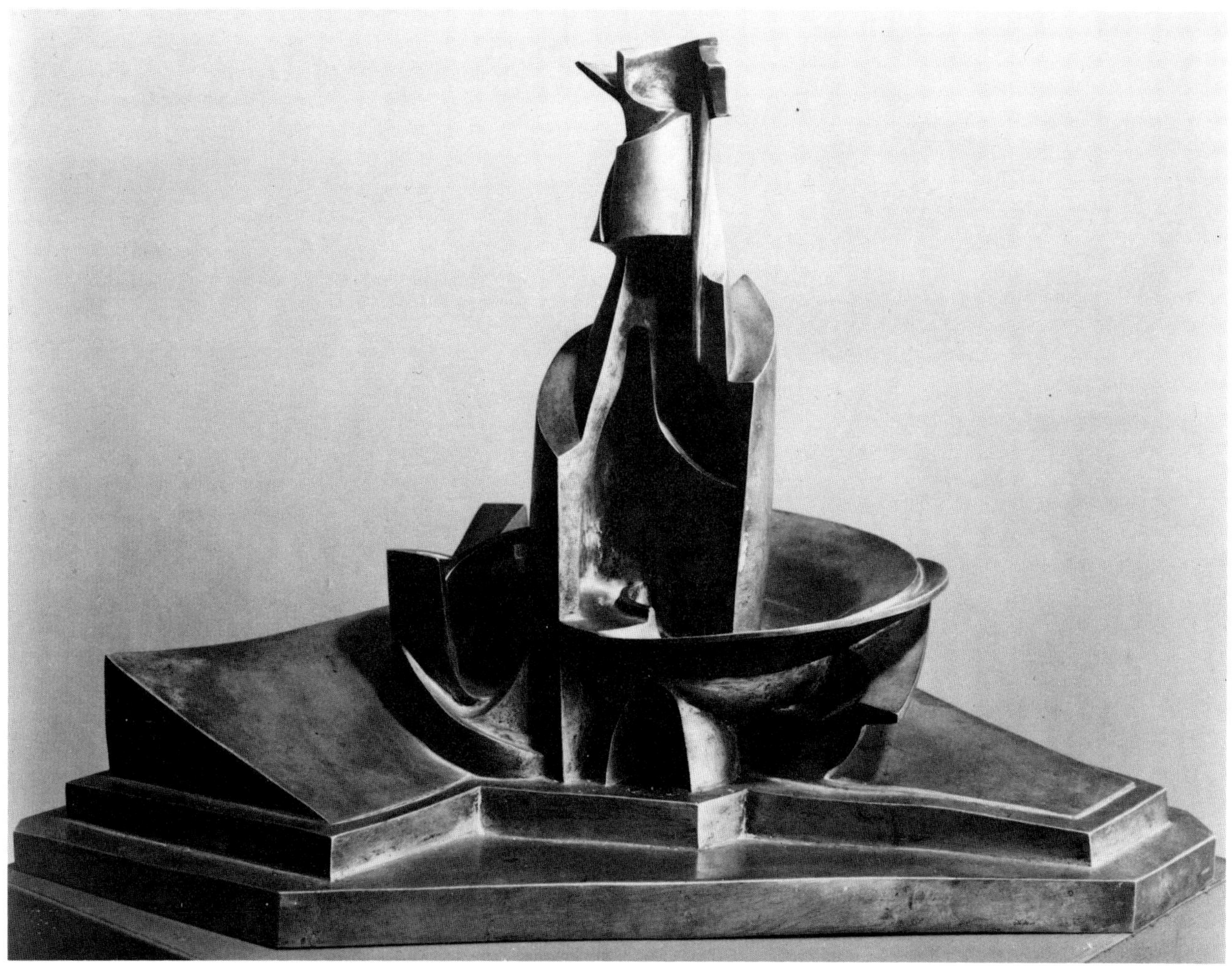

45

45. Development of a Bottle in Space (Still Life),
1912 (cast 1931)
Silvered bronze, 15 x 12⅞ x 23¾" (38.1 x 32.7 x 60.3 cm)
The Museum of Modern Art, New York
Aristide Maillol Fund, 1948
Exhibitions (plaster version): Paris, Galerie La Boëtie, *1re Exposition de Sculpture Futuriste du Peintre et Sculpteur Futuriste Boccioni,* June 20–July 16, 1913, no. 6; London, Doré Galleries, *Exhibition of the Works of the Italian Futurist Painters and Sculptors,* April 23–May 1914, no. 2, repro.; San Francisco, *The Panama-Pacific International Exposition,* Department of Fine Arts, February 20, 1915–May 1, 1916, no. 1178

Umberto Boccioni

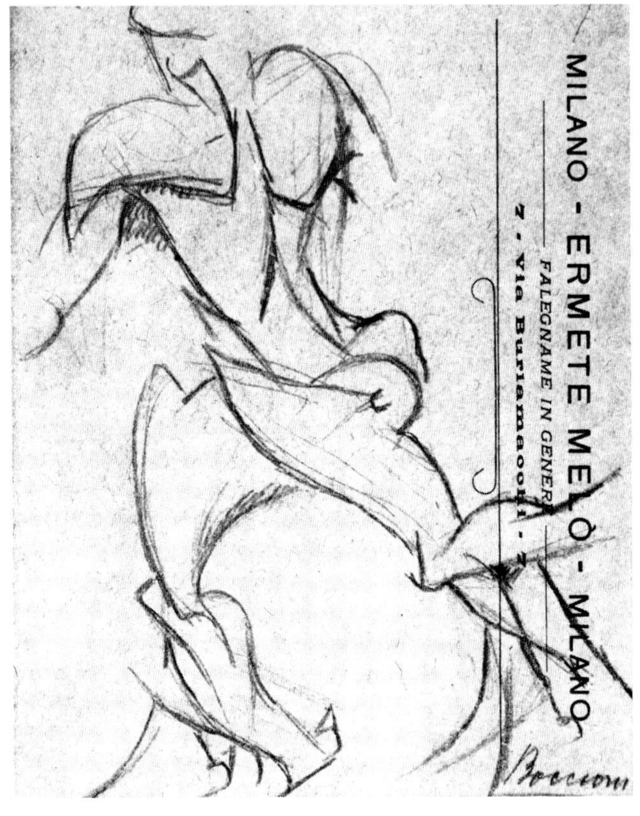

46

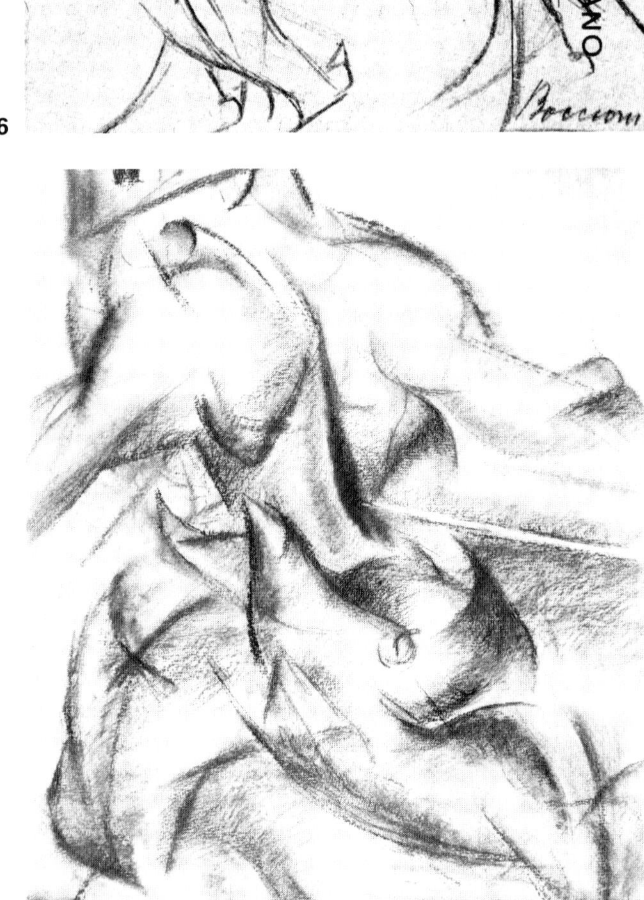

47

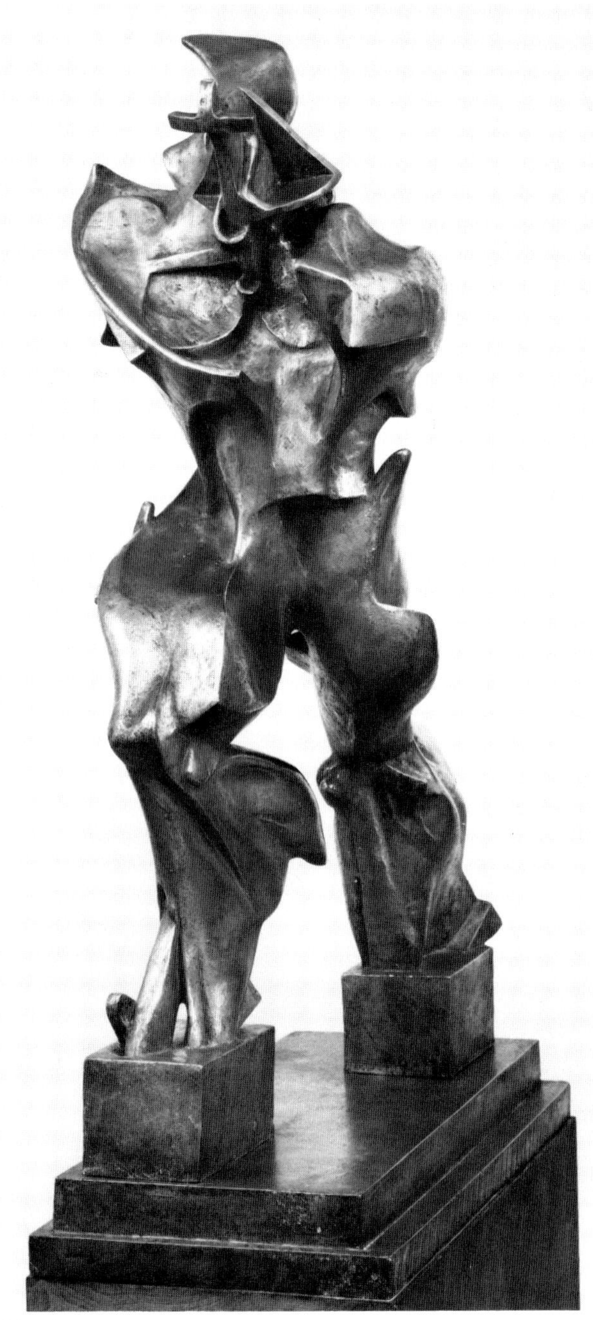

48 **Front view**

46. Study for "Unique Forms of Continuity in Space," c. 1913
Pencil on paper, 6⅛ x 4⅞" (15.5 x 12.4 cm)
The Museum of Modern Art, New York
Gift of René d'Harnoncourt, 1956

47. Muscular Dynamism, 1913
Charcoal and chalk on paper, 34 x 23¼" (86.3 x 59 cm)
The Museum of Modern Art, New York
Purchase, 1949

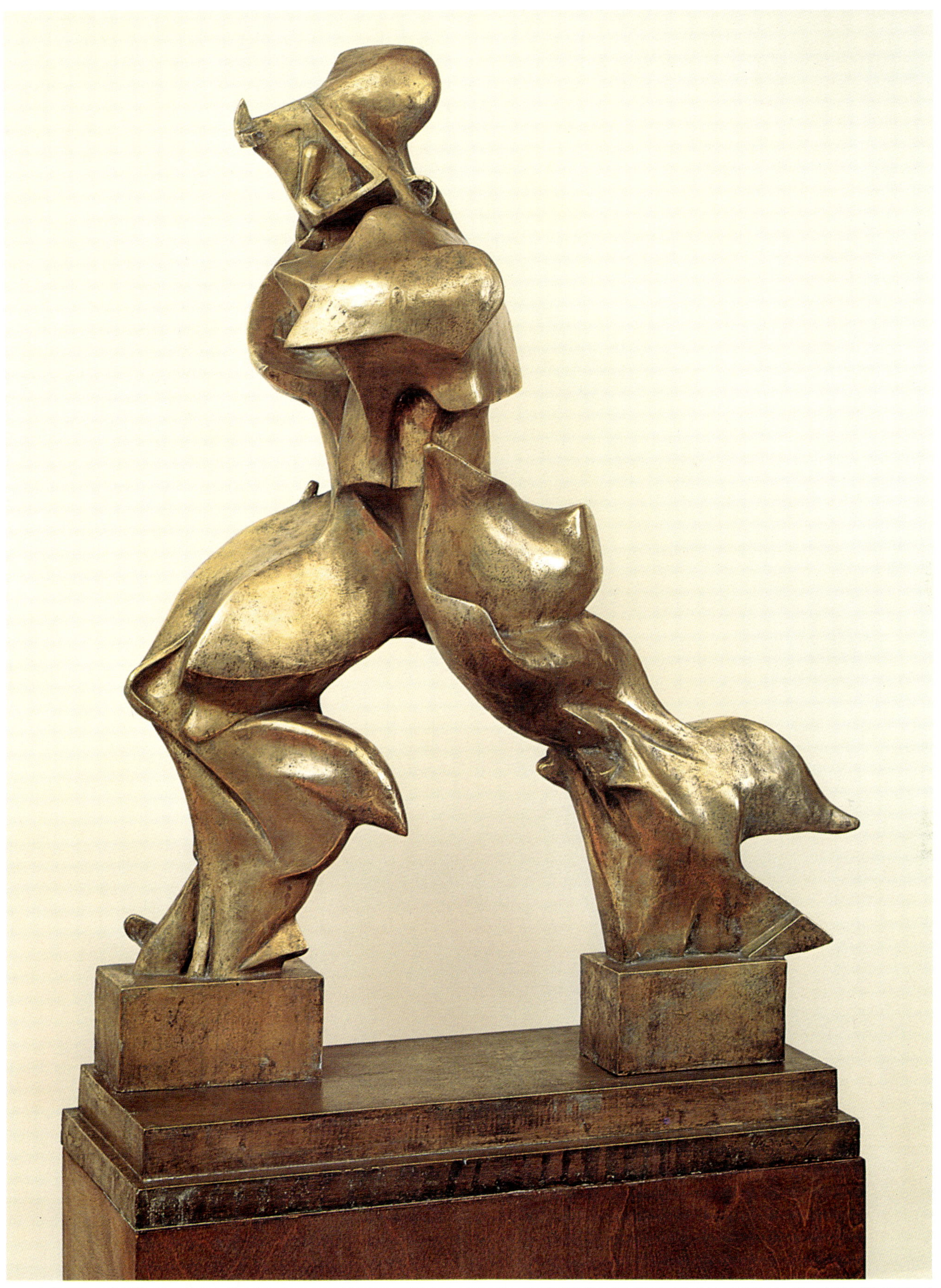

48. Unique Forms of Continuity in Space,
1913 (cast 1949)
Bronze, 48½ x 34" (123.2 x 86.3 cm)
The Lydia and Harry Lewis Winston Collection
(Dr. and Mrs. Barnett Malbin, New York)
Exhibitions (plaster version): Paris, Galerie La Boëtie, *1re Exposition de Sculpture Futuriste du Peintre et Sculpteur Futuriste Boccioni,* June 20–July 16, 1913, no. 10; London, Doré Galleries, *Exhibition of the Works of the Italian Futurist Painters and Sculptors,* April 23–May 1914, no. 3, repro.

Umberto Boccioni

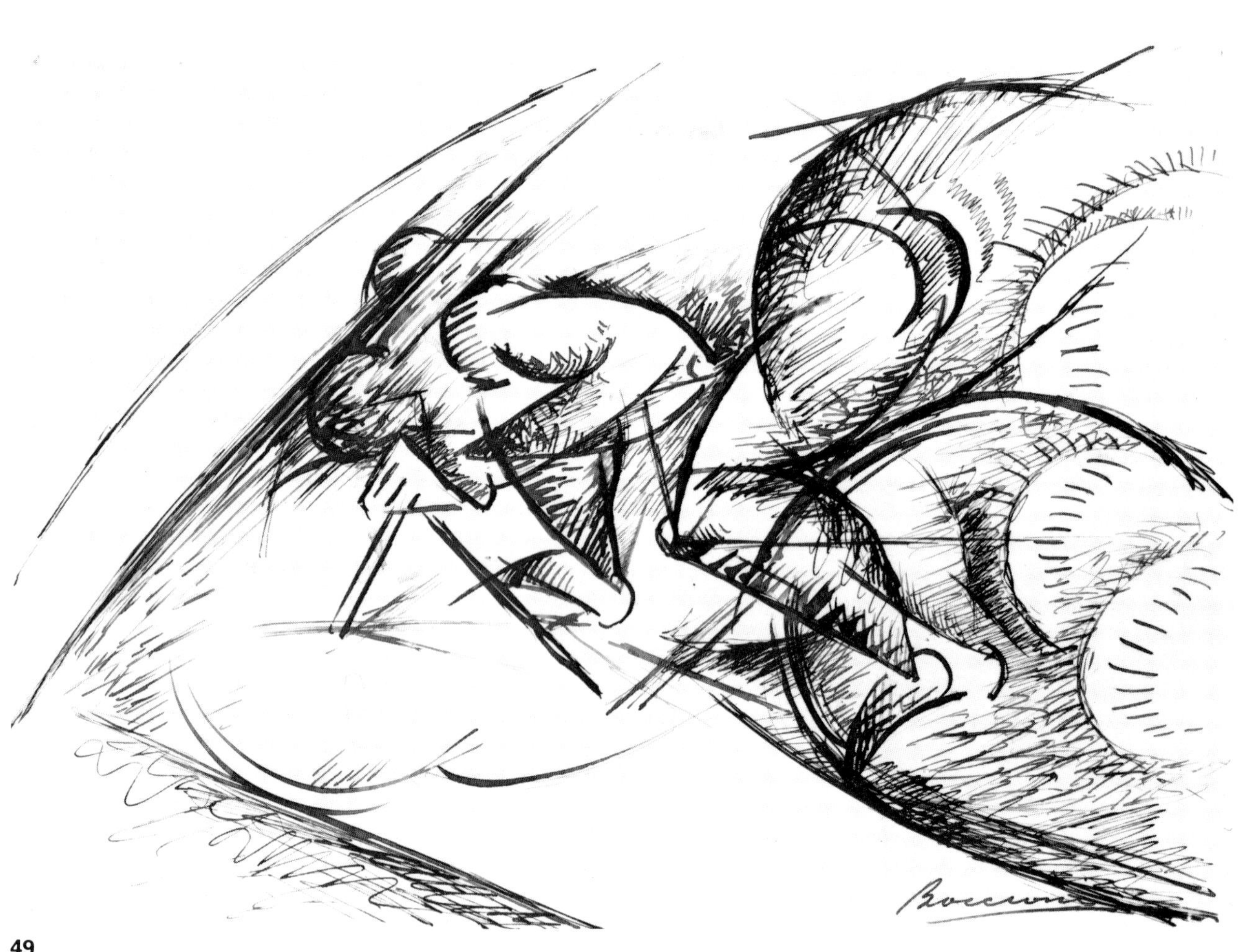

49

49. Study for "Dynamism of a Cyclist" I, 1913
Ink on paper, 8¼ x 12⅜" (21 x 31.4 cm)
Yale University Art Gallery, New Haven
Gift of Collection Société Anonyme

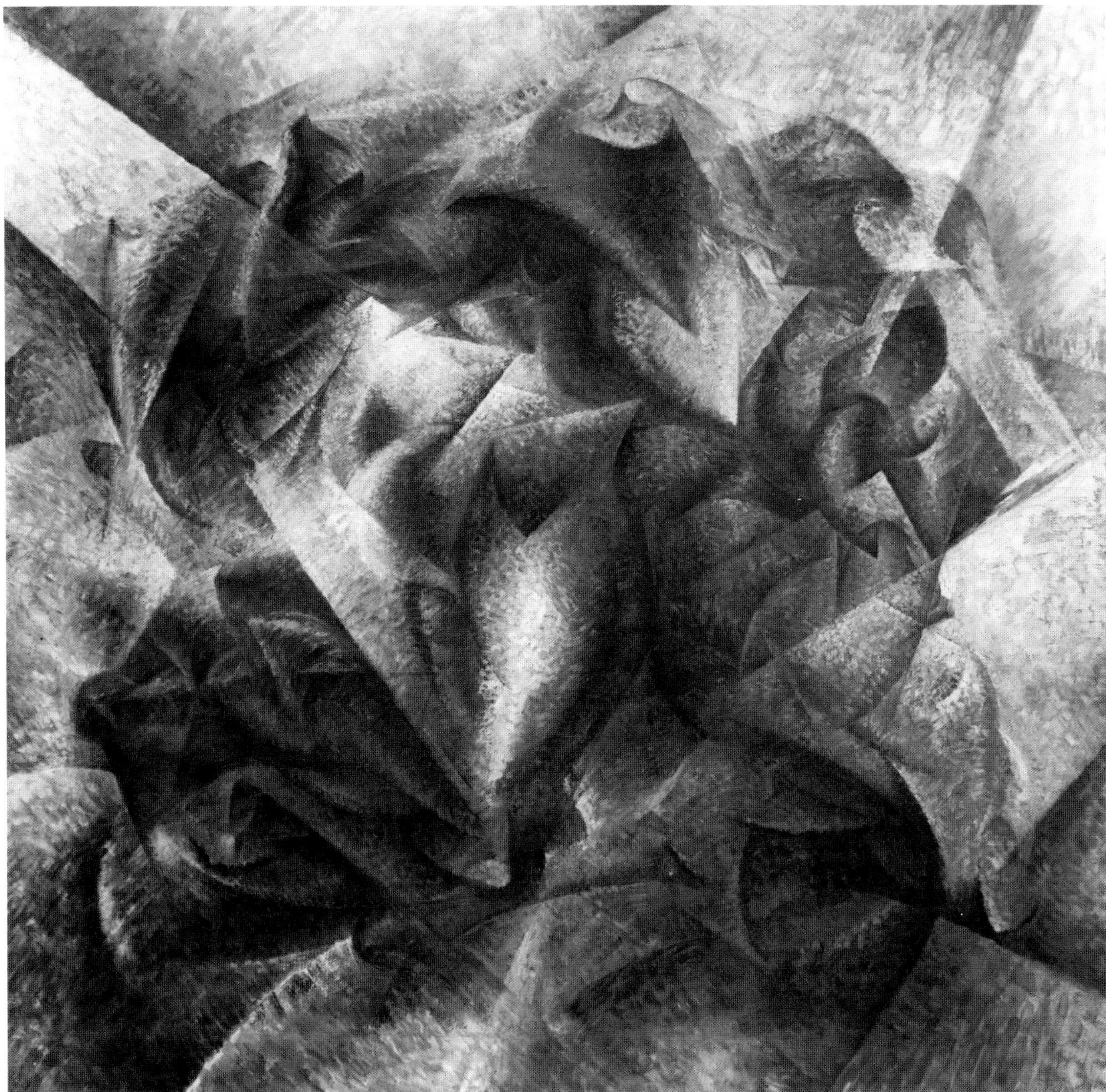

50

50. Dynamism of a Soccer Player, 1913
Oil on canvas, 76⅛ x 79⅛" (193.2 x 201 cm)
The Museum of Modern Art, New York
The Sidney and Harriet Janis Collection, 1967
Exhibitions: London, Doré Galleries, *Exhibition of the Works of the Italian Futurist Painters and Sculptors,* April 23–May 1914, no. 5; San Francisco, *The Panama-Pacific International Exposition,* Department of Fine Arts, February 20, 1915–May 1, 1916, no. 1143

Umberto Boccioni

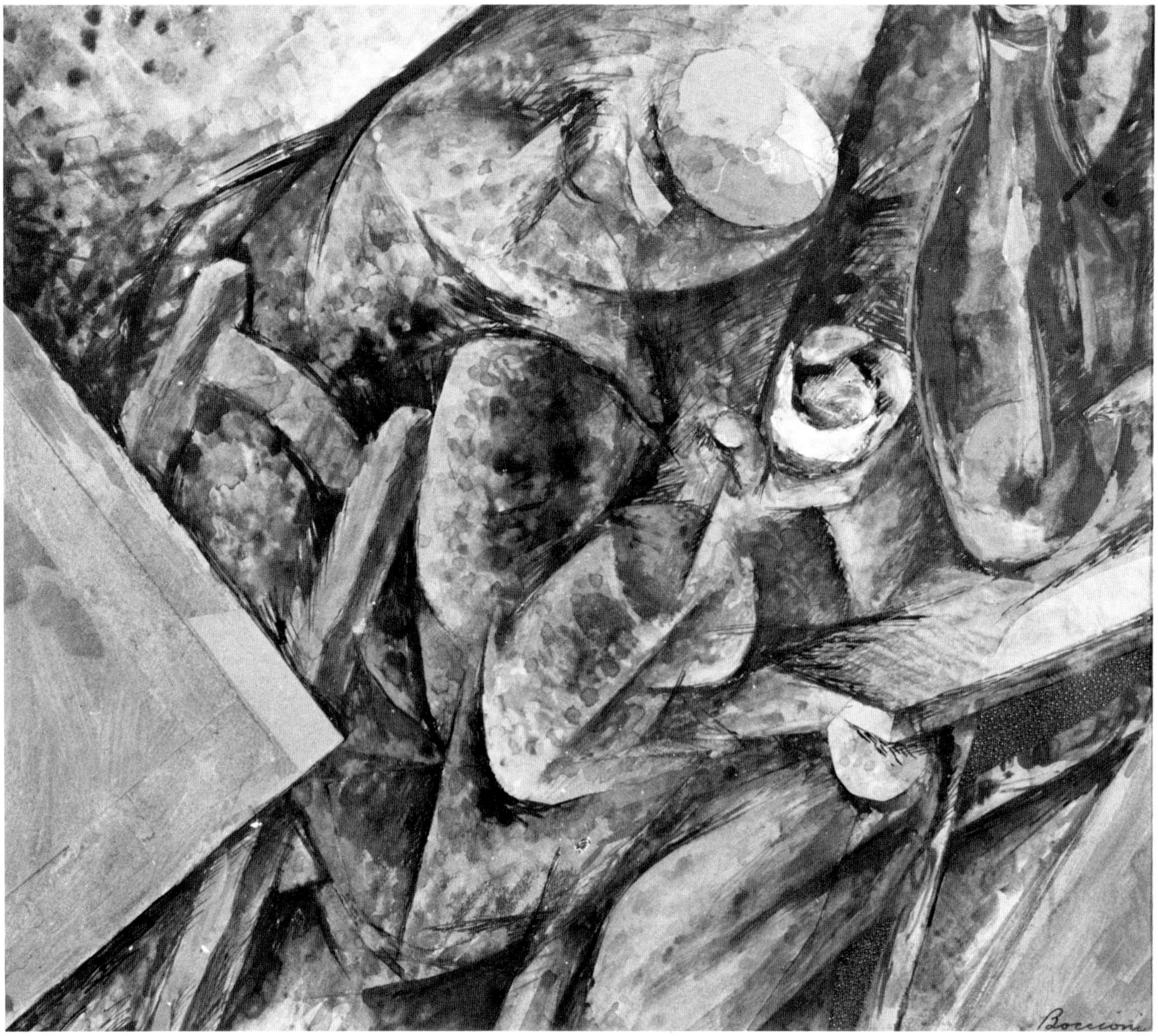

51

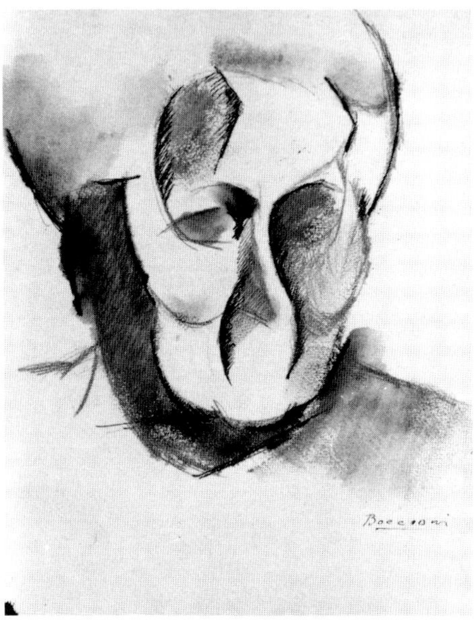

52

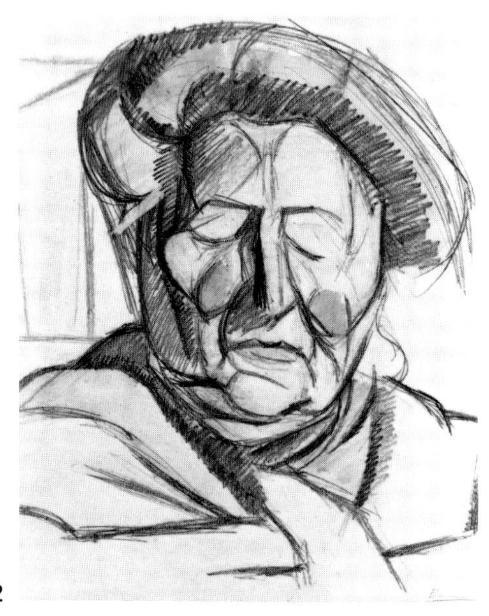

53

51. Study for "The Drinker," 1914
Oil, gouache, and collage on paper,
11½ x 14½" (29.2 x 36.8 cm)
The Lydia and Harry Lewis Winston Collection
(Dr. and Mrs. Barnett Malbin, New York)

52. Head of Boccioni's Mother, 1914–15
Pencil, wash, and india ink on paper,
12¼ x 9½" (31.1 x 24.1 cm)
The Lydia and Harry Lewis Winston Collection
(Dr. and Mrs. Barnett Malbin, New York)

53. Portrait of Boccioni's Mother, 1915–16
Chalk and watercolor on paper, 25 x 20¼" (63.5 x 51.4 cm)
The Lydia and Harry Lewis Winston Collection
(Dr. and Mrs. Barnett Malbin, New York)

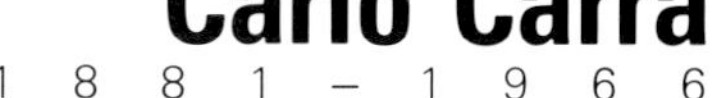

Carlo Carrà

1881–1966

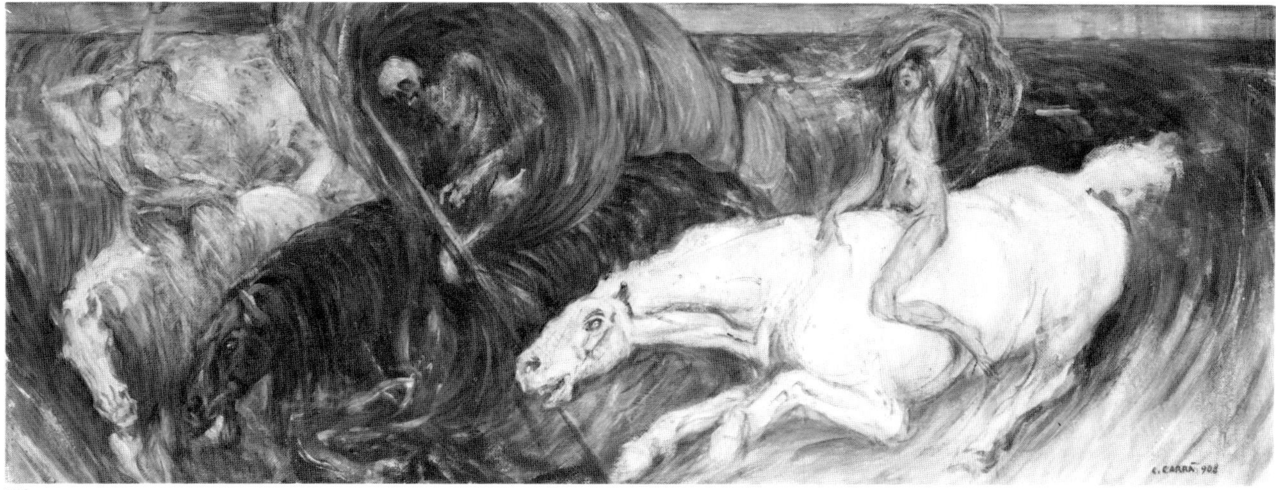

54

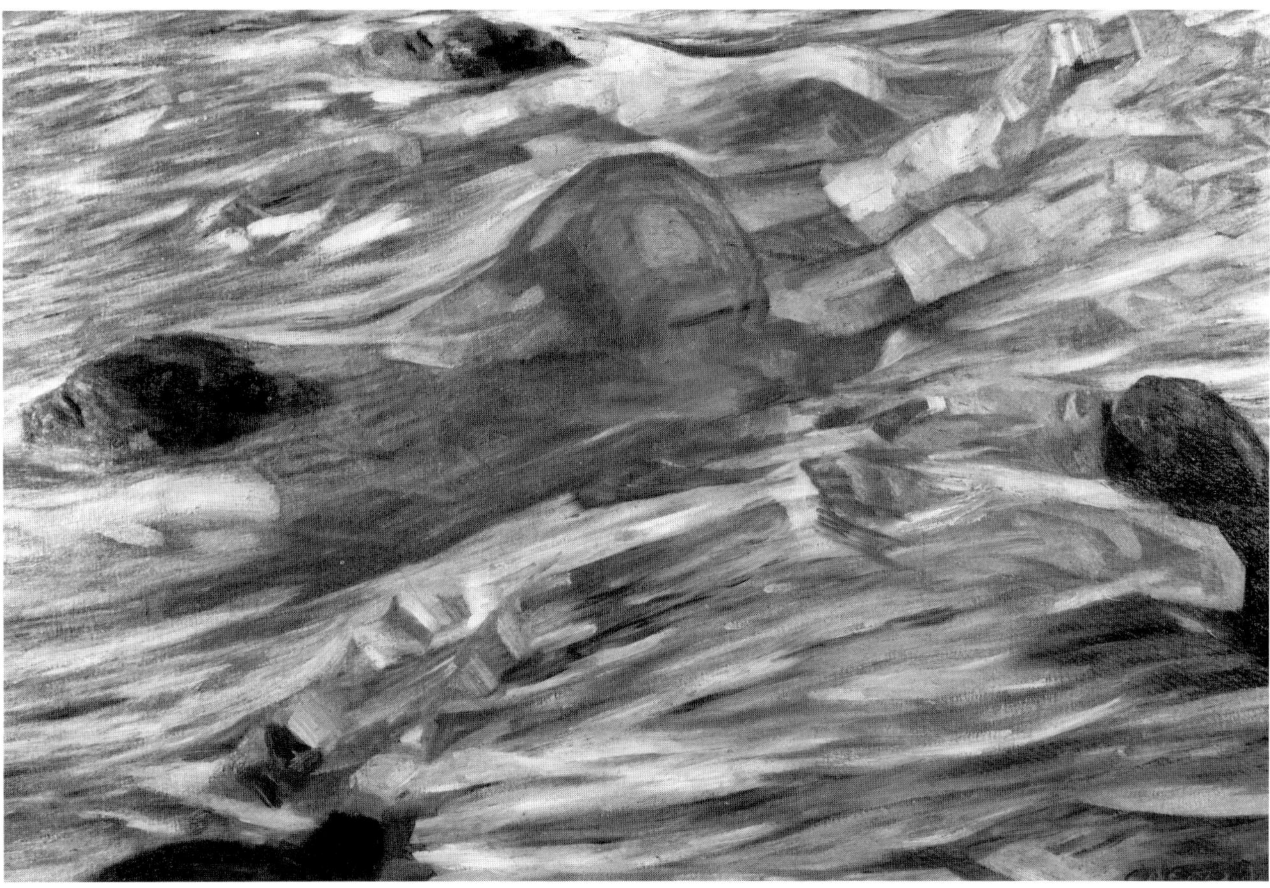

55

54. The Horsemen of the Apocalypse, 1908
Oil on canvas, 14¼ x 37¼" (36.2 x 94.6 cm)
The Art Institute of Chicago
Gift of Mr. and Mrs. Harold X. Weinstein

55. The Swimmers (Swimming), 1910–11
Oil on canvas, 41½ x 62" (105.4 x 157.5 cm)
Museum of Art, Carnegie Institute, Pittsburgh
Gift of G. David Thompson
Exhibitions: Milan, Padiglione Ricordi, *Esposizione d'Arte Libera,* from April 30, 1911; Paris, Galerie Bernheim-Jeune, *Les Peintres Futuristes Italiens,* February 5–24, 1912, no. 17

Carlo Carrà

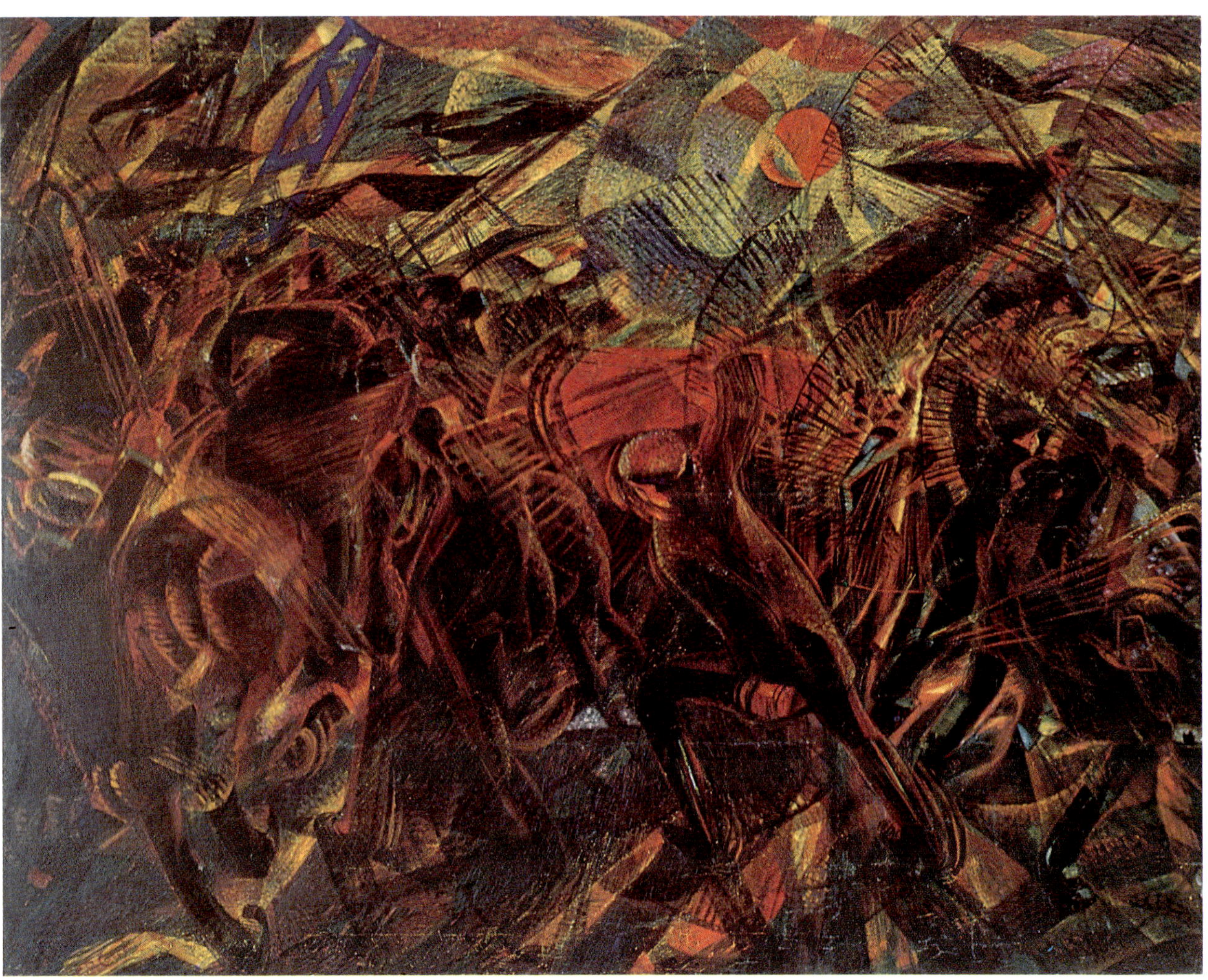

56

56. Funeral of the Anarchist Galli, 1911
Oil on canvas, 78¼ x 102" (198.7 x 259.1 cm)
The Museum of Modern Art, New York
Acquired through the Lillie P. Bliss Bequest, 1948
Exhibitions: Milan, Padiglione Ricordi, *Esposizione d'Arte Libera,* from April 30, 1911; Paris, Galerie Bernheim-Jeune, *Les Peintres Futuristes Italiens,* February 5–24, 1912, no. 11

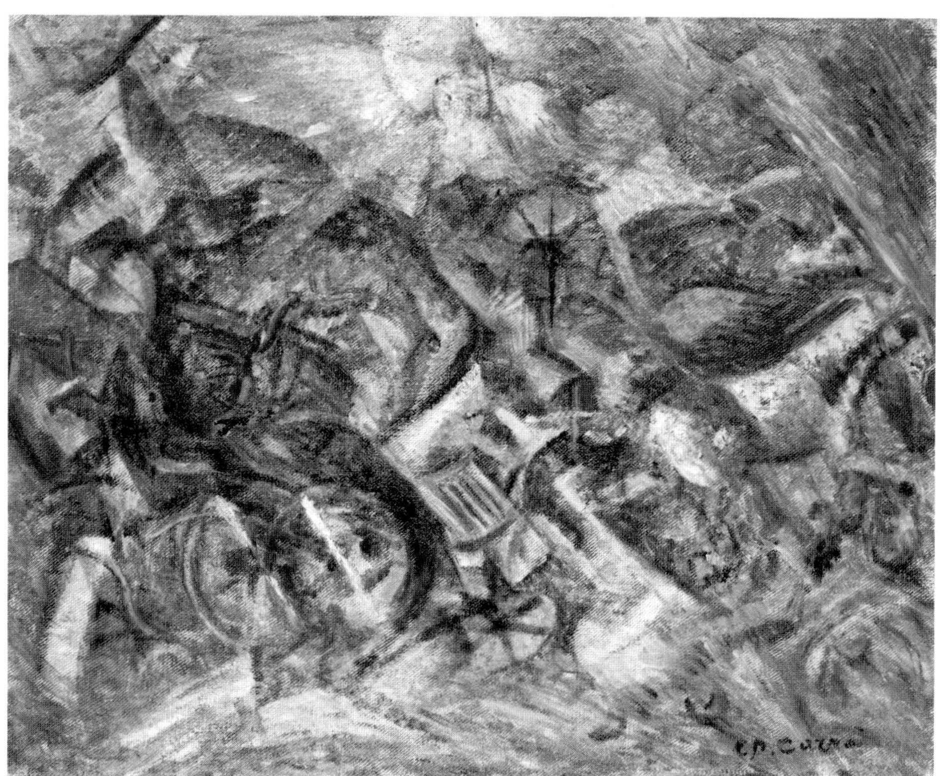
57

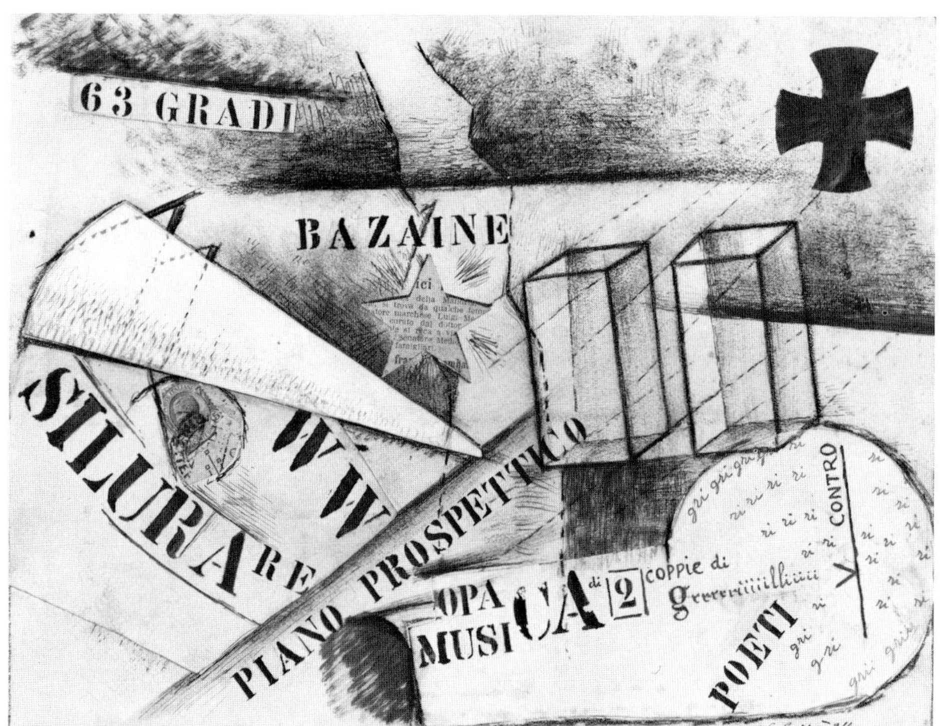

58

57. Jolts of a Cab, 1911
Oil on canvas, 20⅝ x 26½" (52.3 x 67.1 cm)
The Museum of Modern Art, New York
Gift of Herbert and Nannette Rothschild, 1965
Exhibition: Paris, Galerie Bernheim-Jeune, *Les Peintres Futuristes Italiens,* February 5–24, 1912, no. 12, repro. p. 29

58. The Night of January 20, 1915, I Dreamed This Picture (Joffre's Angle of Penetration on the Marne Against the German Cubes), 1915
Collage, gouache, ink, and charcoal on paper, 10 x 13½" (25.4 x 34.3 cm)
The Lydia and Harry Lewis Winston Collection
(Dr. and Mrs. Barnett Malbin, New York)

Leonardo Dudreville

1 8 8 5 – 1 9 7 5

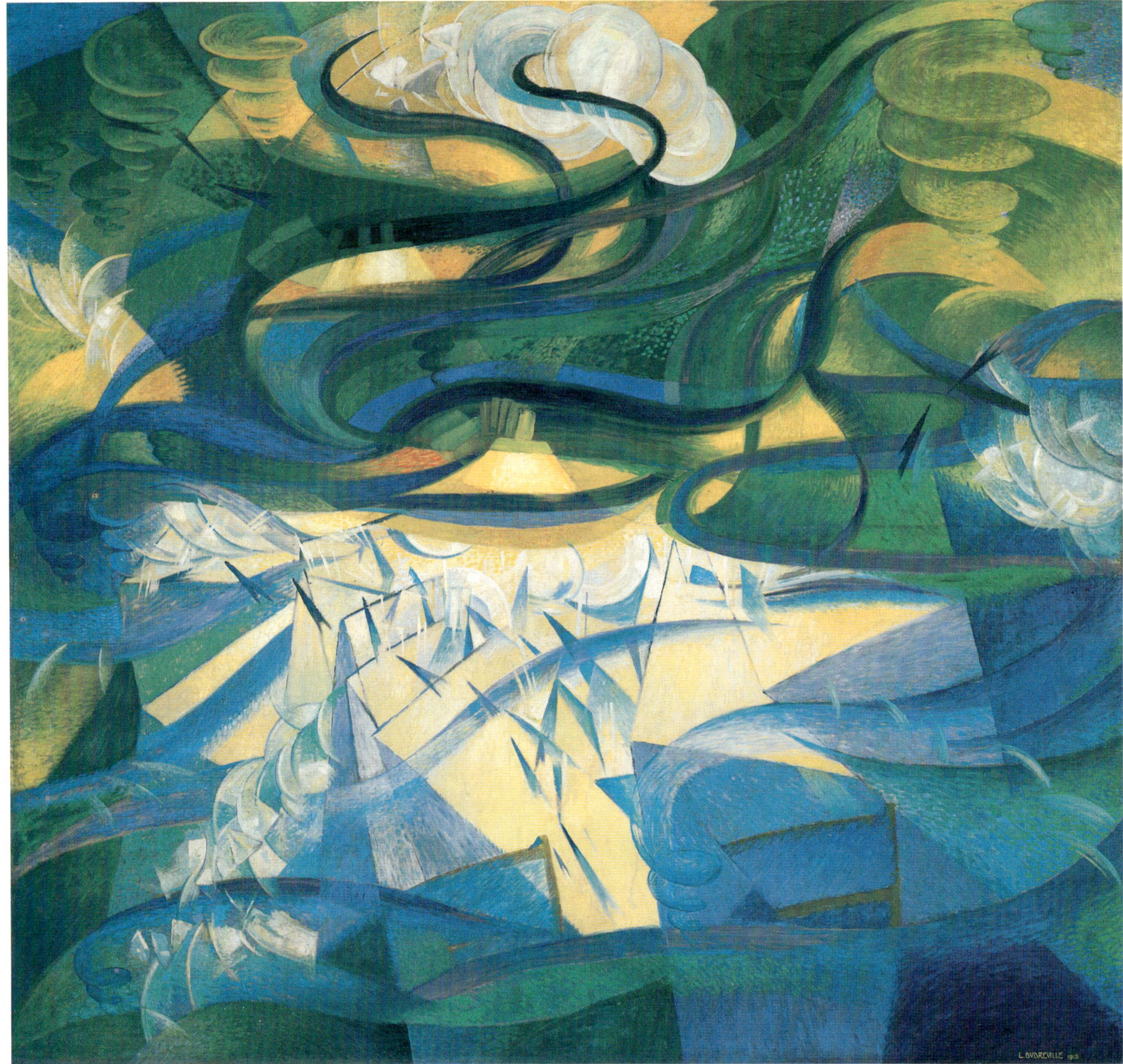

59

59. Daily Domestic Arguments, 1913
Oil on canvas, 98⅞ x 90¾" (251.1 x 230.5 cm)
Philadelphia Museum of Art
Gift of Mr. and Mrs. N. Richard Miller
Exhibition: Milan, Famiglia Artistica, *Prima Esposizione d'Arte del Gruppo Nuove Tendenze,* May 20–June 10, 1914, no. 7, pl. III

60

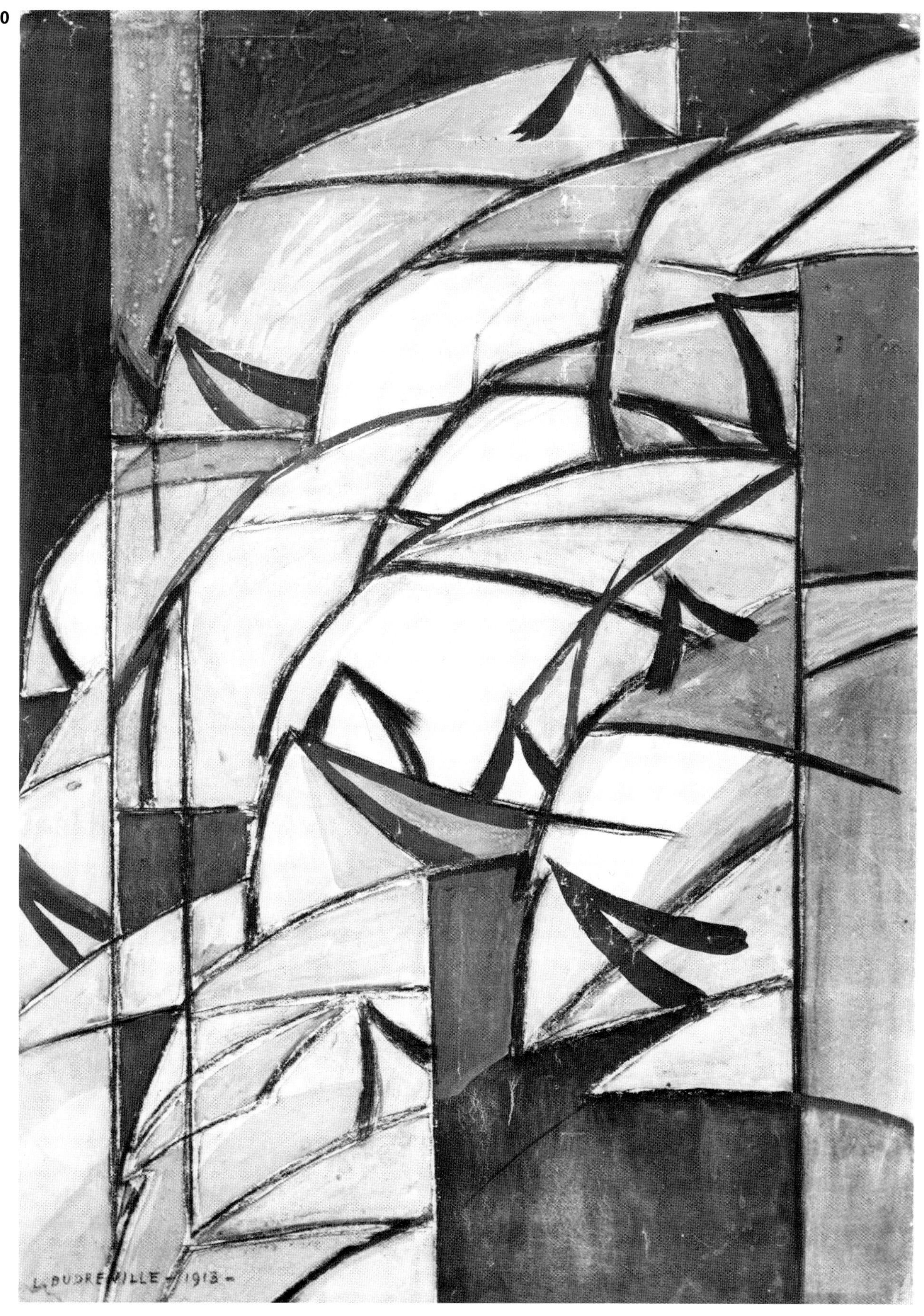

60. Rhythms Emanating from Antonio Sant'Elia, 1913
Gouache and charcoal on paper, 25⅜ x 17¾" (64.5 x 45.1 cm)
Mr. and Mrs. N. Richard Miller, New York
Exhibition: Milan, Famiglia Artistica, *Prima Esposizione d'Arte del Gruppo Nuove Tendenze,* May 20–June 10, 1914, no. 9

Luigi Russolo

1885–1947

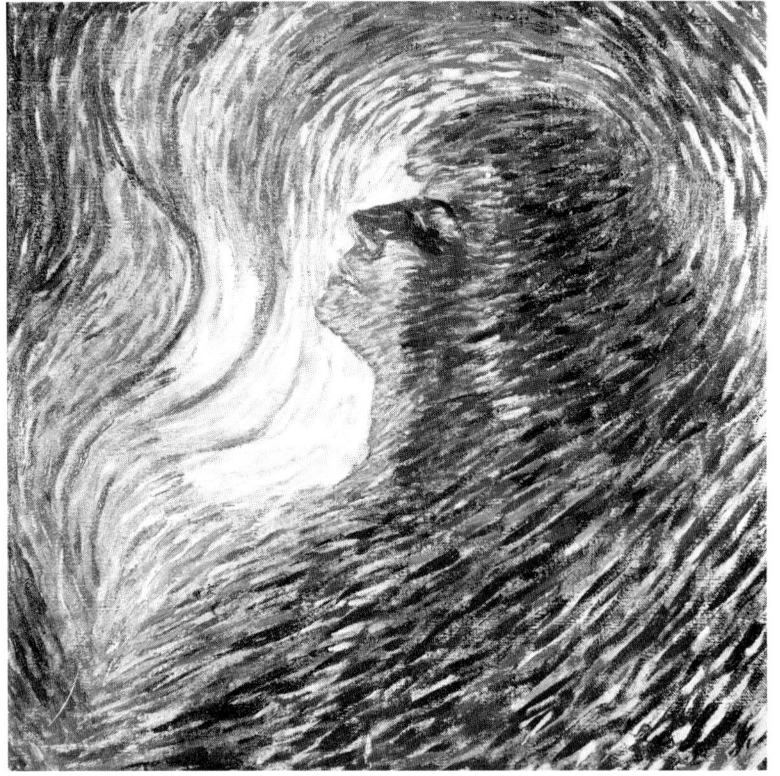

61

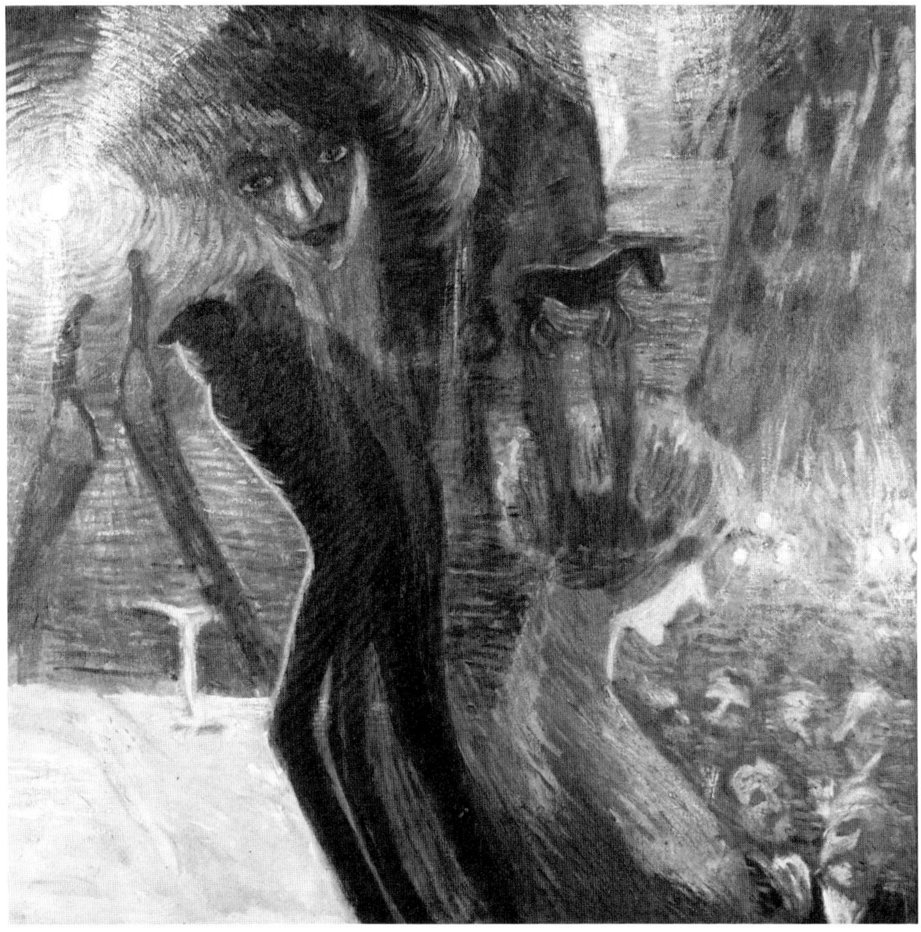

62

61. Perfume, 1909–10
Oil on canvas, 26⅛ x 25¼" (66.4 x 64.1 cm)
The Lydia and Harry Lewis Winston Collection
(Dr. and Mrs. Barnett Malbin, New York)
Exhibitions: Milan, Famiglia Artistica, from December 20, 1910, no. 48; Milan, Padiglione Ricordi, *Esposizione d'Arte Libera,* from April 30, 1911

62. Memories of a Night, 1911
Oil on canvas, 39⅜ x 39⅜" (100 x 100 cm)
Miss Barbara Slifka, New York
Exhibition: Paris, Galerie Bernheim-Jeune, *Les Peintres Futuristes Italiens,* February 5–24, 1912, no. 23, repro. p. 23

Luigi Russolo

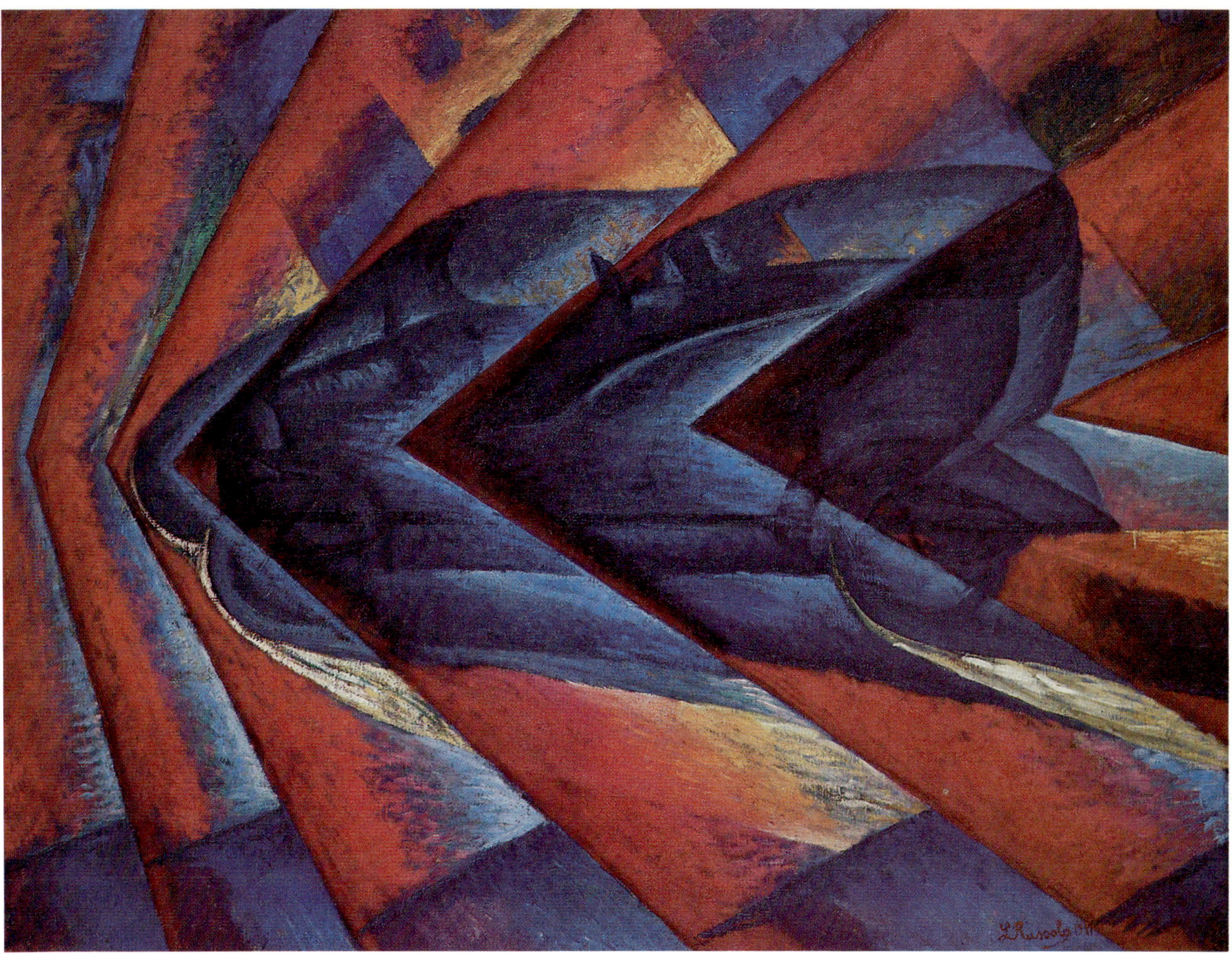

63

63. Dynamism of an Automobile, c. 1912–13
Oil on canvas, 41¾ x 55⅛" (106 x 140 cm)
Musée National d'Art Moderne
Centre Georges Pompidou, Paris
Gift of Mme Sonia Delaunay, 1949
Exhibitions: Florence, Galleria Gonnelli, *Esposizione di Pittura Futurista di "Lacerba,"* November 1913–January 1914, no. 1; London, Doré Galleries, *Exhibition of the Works of the Italian Futurist Painters and Sculptors,* April 23–May 1914, no. 1, repro.; San Francisco, *The Panama-Pacific International Exposition,* Department of Fine Arts, February 20, 1915–May 1, 1916, no. 1159

Gino Severini
1883–1966

64

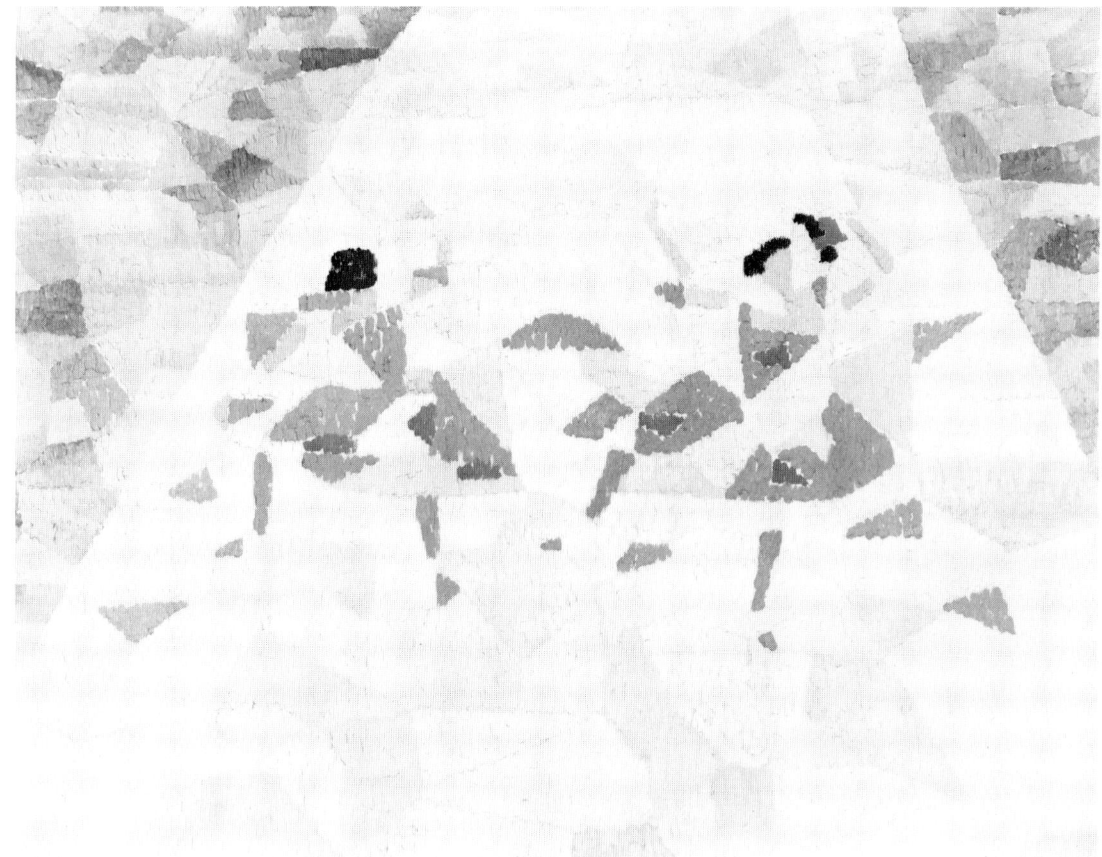

65

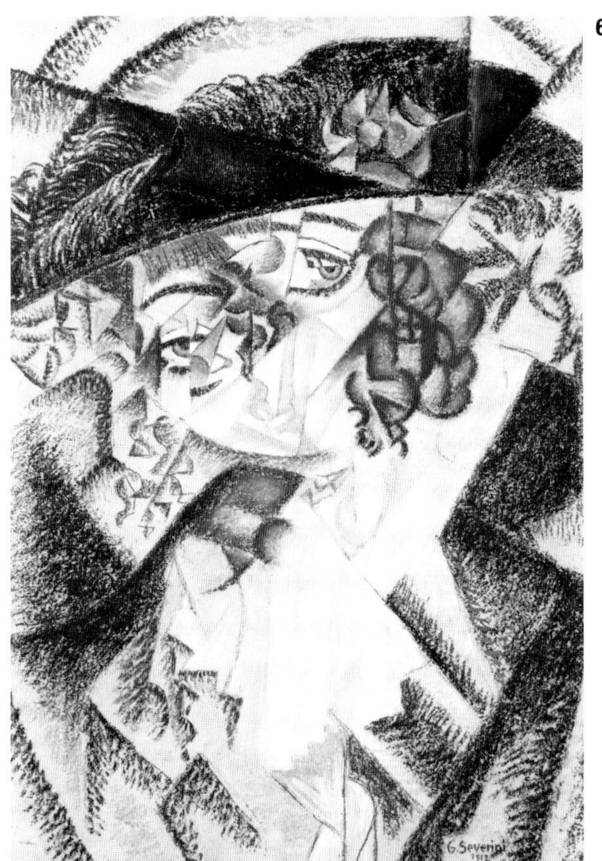

64. Yellow Dancers, 1911
Oil on canvas, 18 x 24" (45.7 x 61 cm)
The Fogg Art Museum, Cambridge, Massachusetts
Gift of Mr. and Mrs. J. H. Hazen
Exhibition: Paris, Galerie Bernheim-Jeune, *Les Peintres Futuristes Italiens,* February 5–24, 1912, no. 32 (?)

65. Study for "Portrait of Madame M. S.," 1912
Pastel and charcoal on paper, 19¼ x 13⅞" (48.9 x 35.2 cm)
The Lydia and Harry Lewis Winston Collection
(Dr. and Mrs. Barnett Malbin, New York)

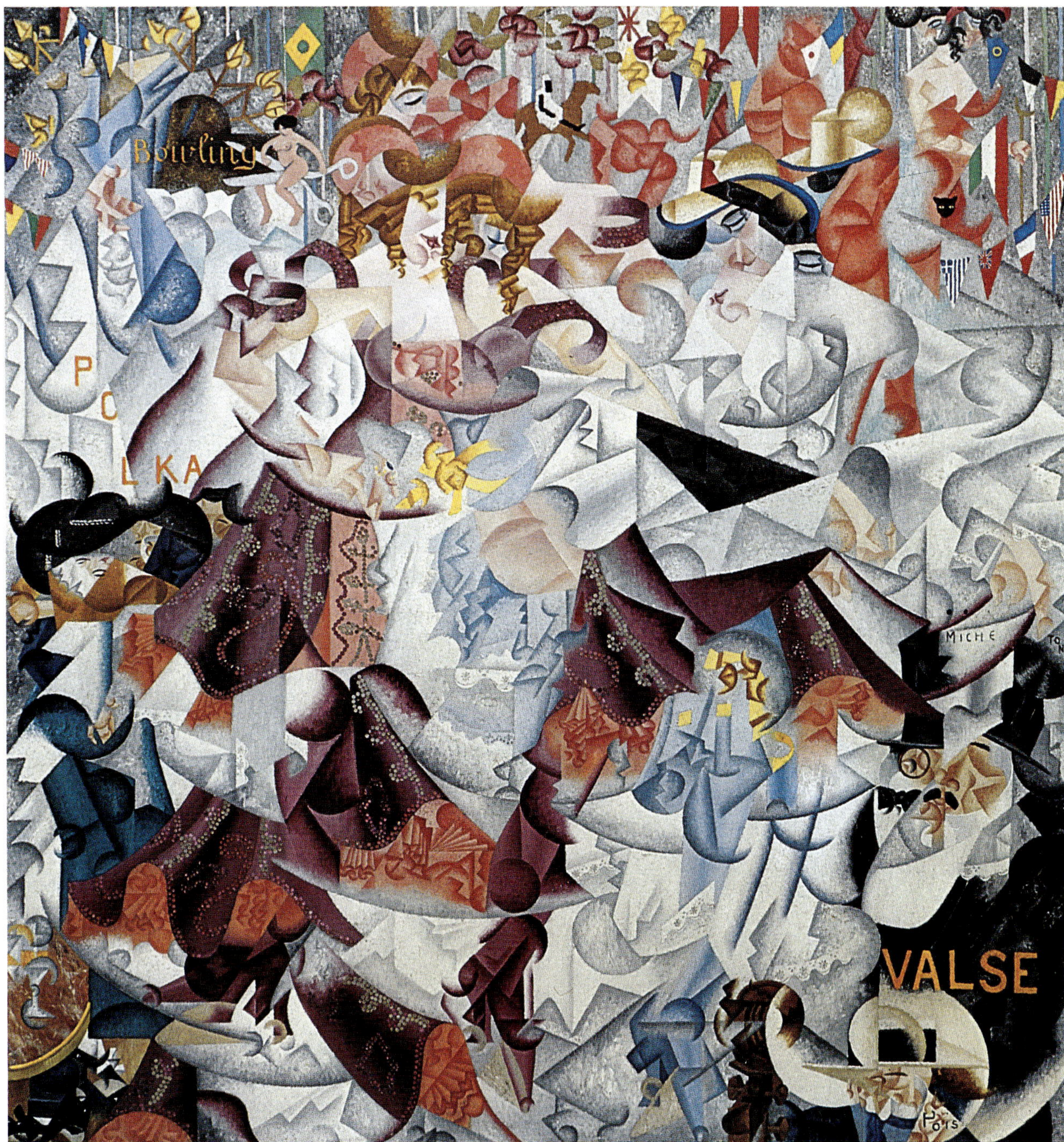

66

66. Dynamic Hieroglyphic of the Bal Tabarin, 1912
Oil on canvas, with sequins, 63⅝ x 61½" (161.6 x 156.2 cm)
The Museum of Modern Art, New York
Acquired through the Lillie P. Bliss Bequest, 1949
Exhibitions: Rome, Galleria G. Giosi, *Prima Esposizione Pittura Futurista,* from February 11, 1913, no. 2; Rotterdam, Rotterdamsche Kunstkring, *Les Peintres et les Sculpteurs Futuristes Italiens,* May 18–June 15, 1913, no. 33, repro. p. 29

Gino Severini

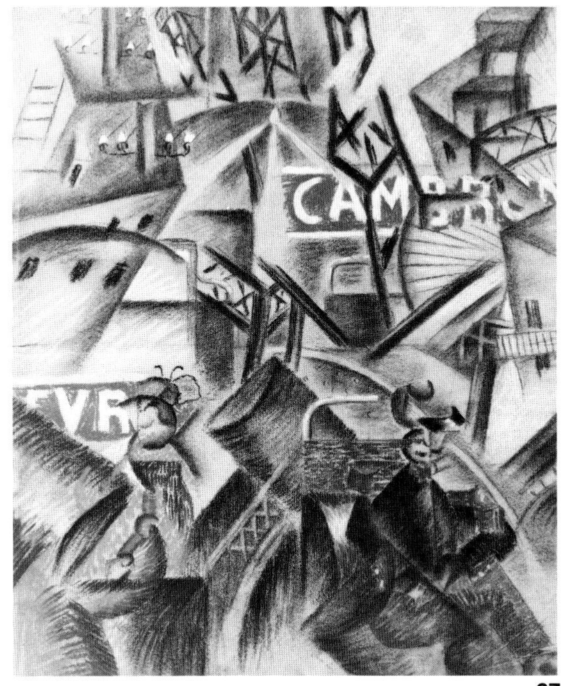

67

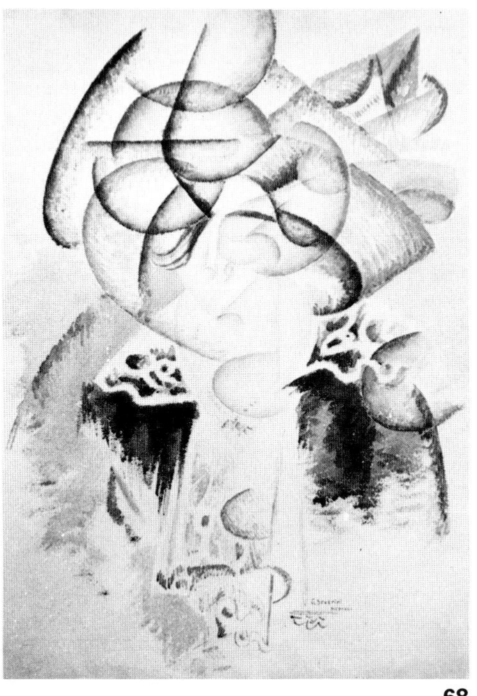

68

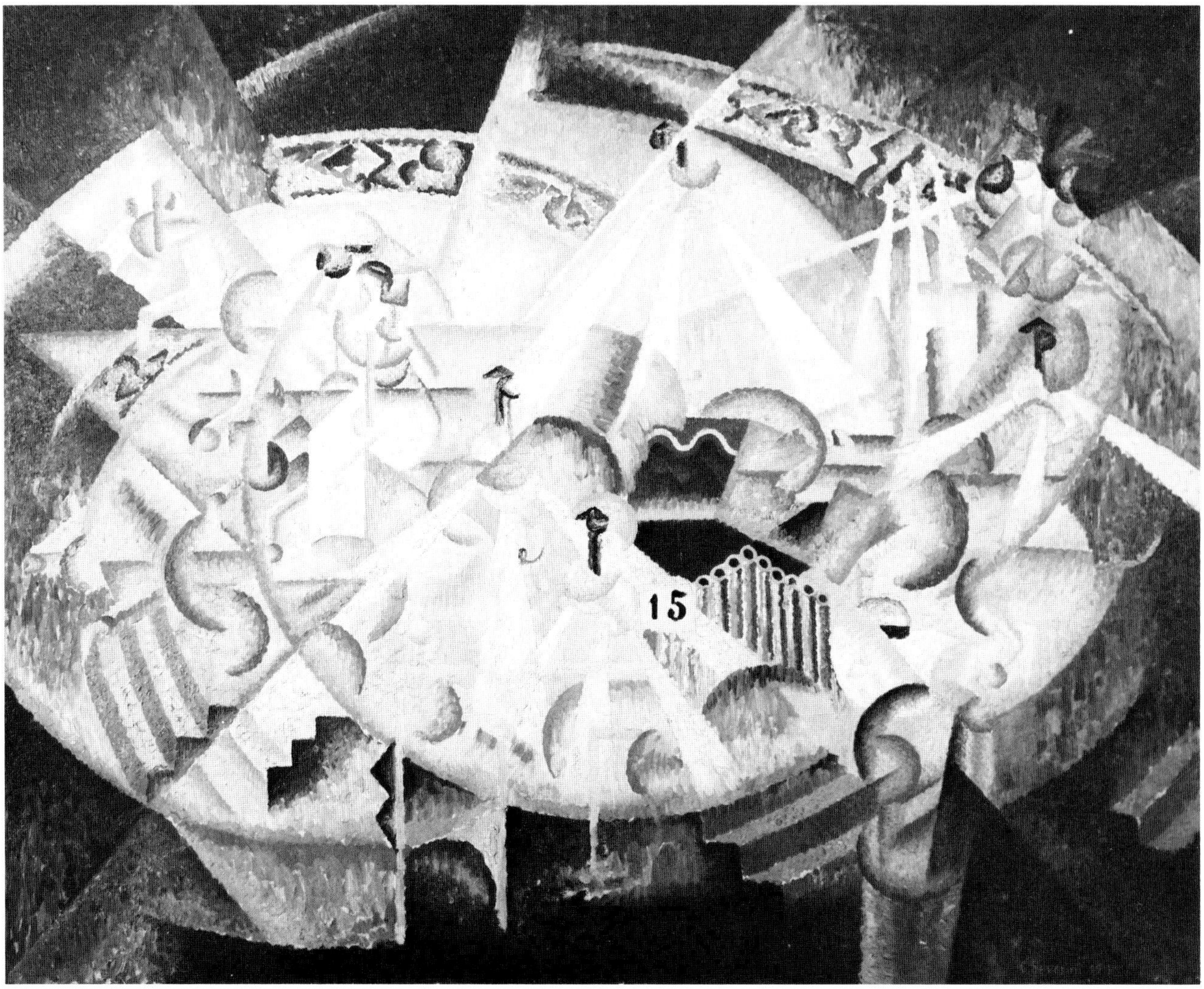

69

67. **Paris Subway—Ferris Wheel—Eiffel Tower,** c. 1912–13
Pastel and charcoal on paper, 23½ x 19" (59.7 x 48.3 cm)
The Cleveland Museum of Art
Gift of Mrs. Malcolm L. McBride
Exhibition: New York, Little Galleries of the Photo-Secession, *Gino Severini,* March 6–17, 1917

68. **Portrait of Madame Severini (Jeanne Paul Fort) (Architecture of a Hat),** 1913
Watercolor on paper, 28¾ x 21¼" (73 x 54 cm)
The Lydia and Harry Lewis Winston Collection
(Dr. and Mrs. Barnett Malbin, New York)
Exhibition: London, Marlborough Gallery, *The Futurist Painter Severini Exhibits His Latest Works,* April 1913, no. 27

69. **Festival in Montmartre (Carousel),** 1913
Oil on canvas, 35 x 45¾" (88.9 x 116.2 cm)
Richard S. Zeisler Collection, New York
Exhibition: London, Marlborough Gallery, *The Futurist Painter Severini Exhibits His Latest Works,* April 1913, no. 6

70. **Spanish Dancer,** c. 1913
Crayon and chalk on paper, 26⅛ x 18⅞" (66.4 x 47.9 cm)
The Museum of Modern Art, New York
Given anonymously, 1949

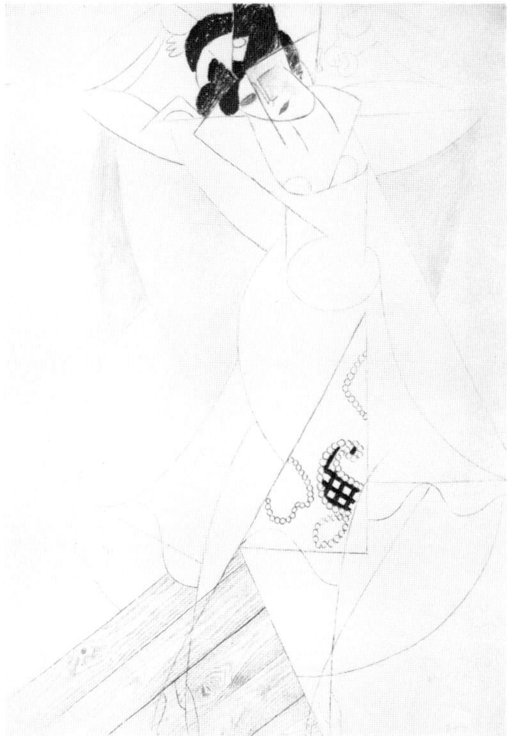

70

72

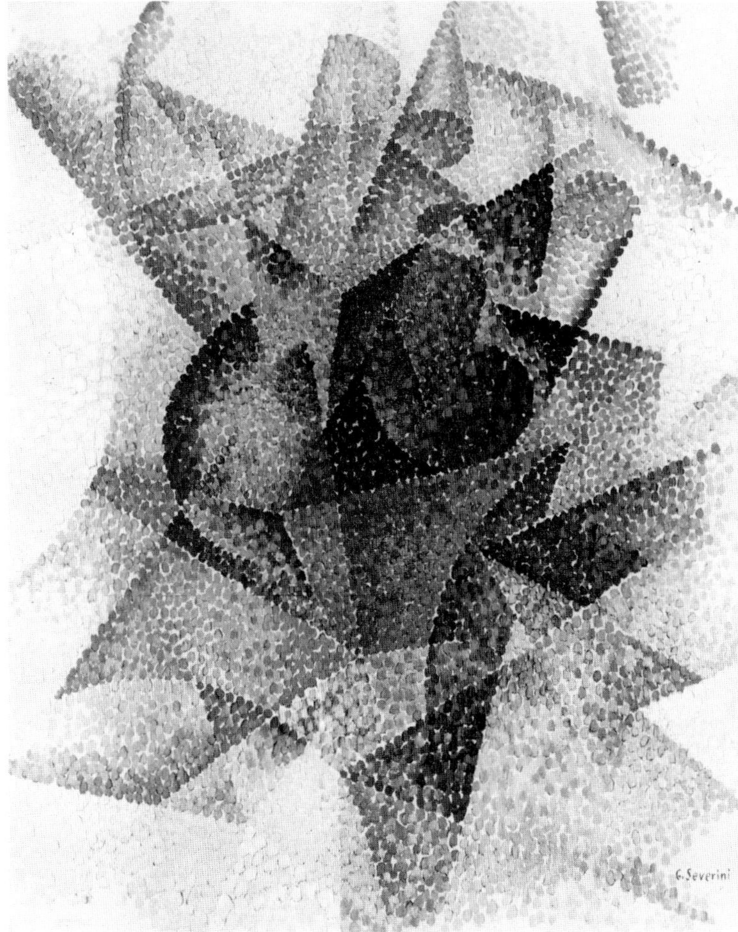

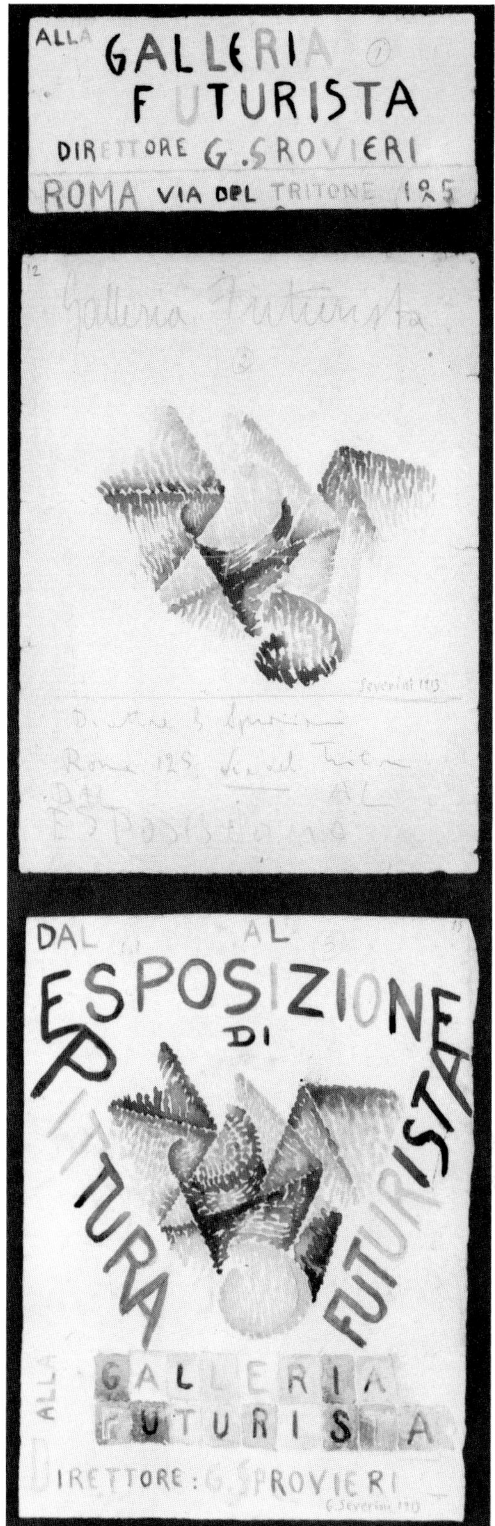

71

Exhibition: New York, Little Galleries of the Photo-Secession, *Gino Severini,* March 6–17, 1917

71. Studies Related to an Exhibition Poster for the Galleria Futurista, Rome, 1913
Pencil and watercolor on three sheets of paper, mounted
Top: 2⅜ x 5½" (6 x 14 cm); center: 7½ x 5¾" (19.1 x 14.6 cm); bottom: 7¼ x 5½" (18.4 x 14 cm)
The Lydia and Harry Lewis Winston Collection (Dr. and Mrs. Barnett Malbin, New York)

72. Spherical Expansion of Light (Centripetal), 1913–14
Oil on canvas, 24 x 19½" (61 x 49.5 cm)
Private collection
Exhibitions: Rome, Galleria Futurista, *Esposizione di Pittura Futurista,* February 11–March 1914, no. 4 (?); London, Doré Galleries, *Exhibition of the Works of the Italian Futurist Painters and Sculptors,* April 23–May 1914, no. 49 (?); San Francisco, *The Panama-Pacific International Exposition,* Department of Fine Arts, February 20, 1915–May 1, 1916, no. 1167 (?)

Gino Severini

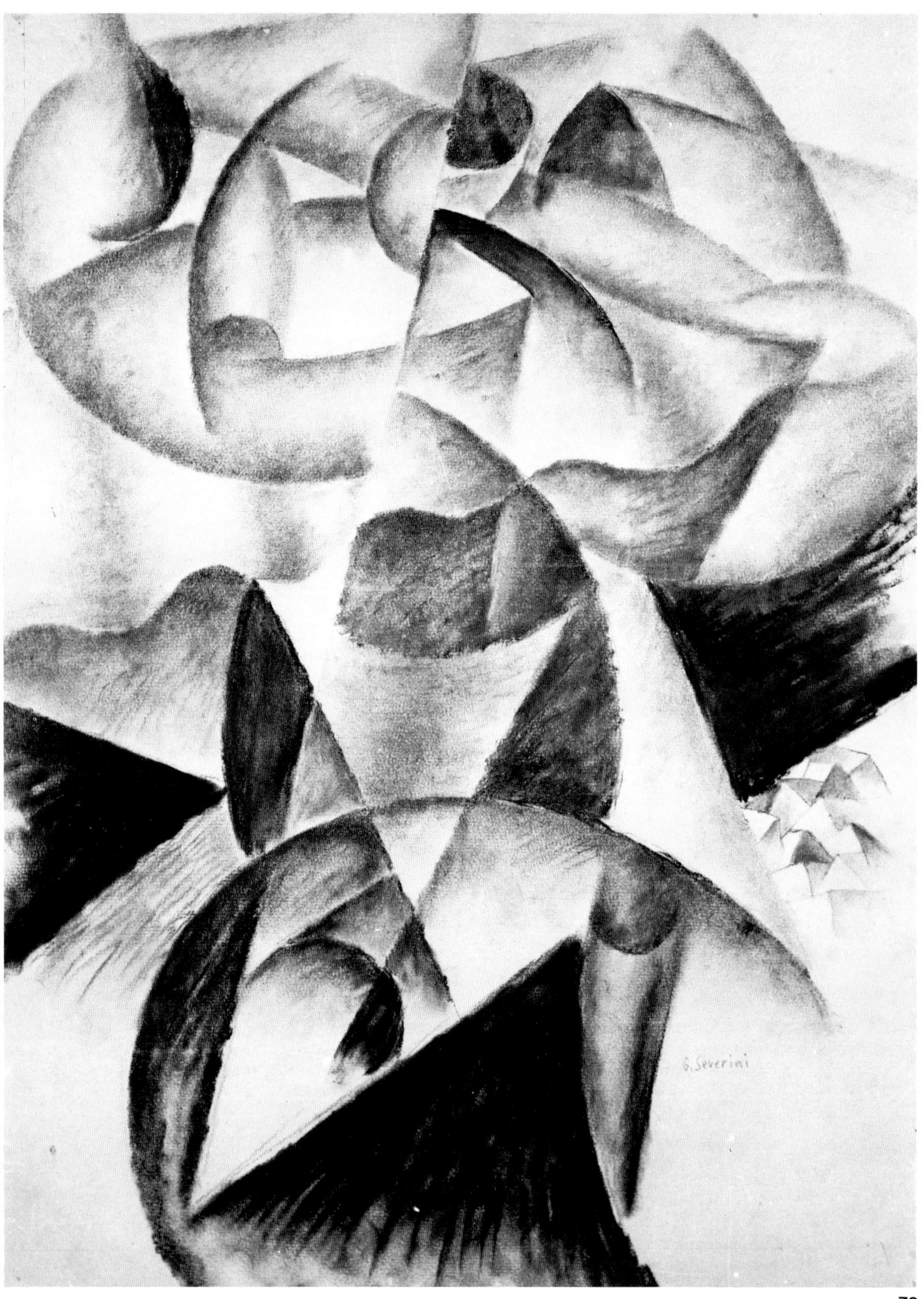

73

73. Study for "Sea = Dancer (Dancer Beside the Sea)."
1913
Charcoal on paper, 27⅞ x 19⅞" (70.8 x 50.5 cm)
The Lydia and Harry Lewis Winston Collection
(Dr. and Mrs. Barnett Malbin, New York)
Exhibitions: Rome, Galleria Futurista, *Esposizione di Pittura Futurista,* February 11–March 1914, no. 11, 16, or 17 (?); London, Doré Galleries, *Exhibition of the Works of the Italian Futurist Painters and Sculptors,* April 23–May 1914, no. 55, 57, or 58 (?); San Francisco, *The Panama-Pacific International Exposition,* Department of Fine Arts, February 20, 1915–May 1, 1916, no. 1174, 1176, or 1177 (?)

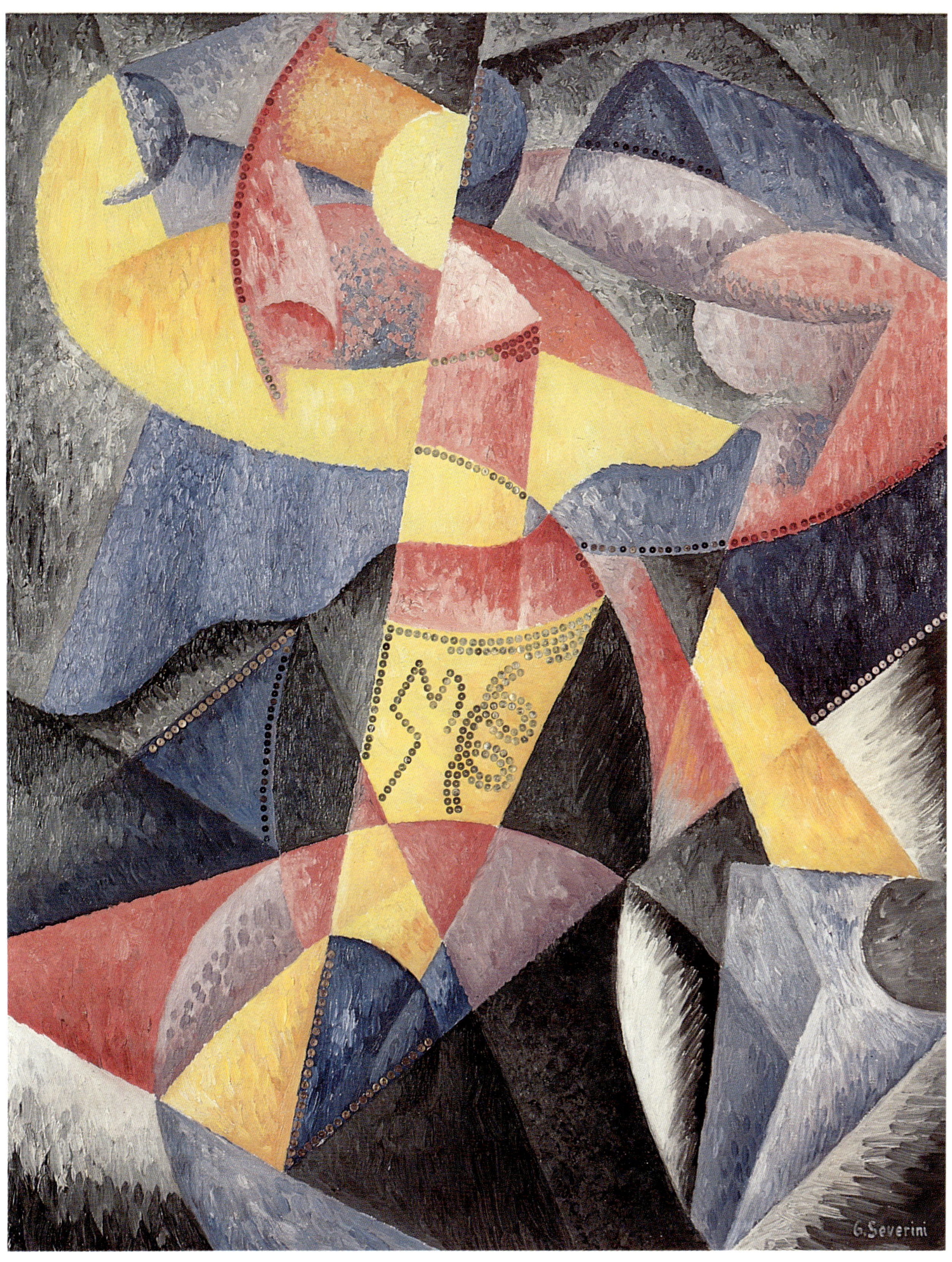

74

74. Sea = Dancer (Dancer Beside the Sea), 1913–14
Oil on canvas, with sequins, 36½ x 28¾" (92.7 x 73 cm)
The Lydia and Harry Lewis Winston Collection
(Dr. and Mrs. Barnett Malbin, New York)
Exhibitions: Rome, Galleria Futurista, *Esposizione di Pittura Futurista,* February 11–March 1914, no. 3 (?); London, Doré Galleries, *Exhibition of the Works of the Italian Futurist Painters and Sculptors,* April 23–May 1914, no. 48 (?); San Francisco, *The Panama-Pacific International Exposition,* Department of Fine Arts, February 20, 1915–May 1, 1916, no. 1166 (?)

Gino Severini

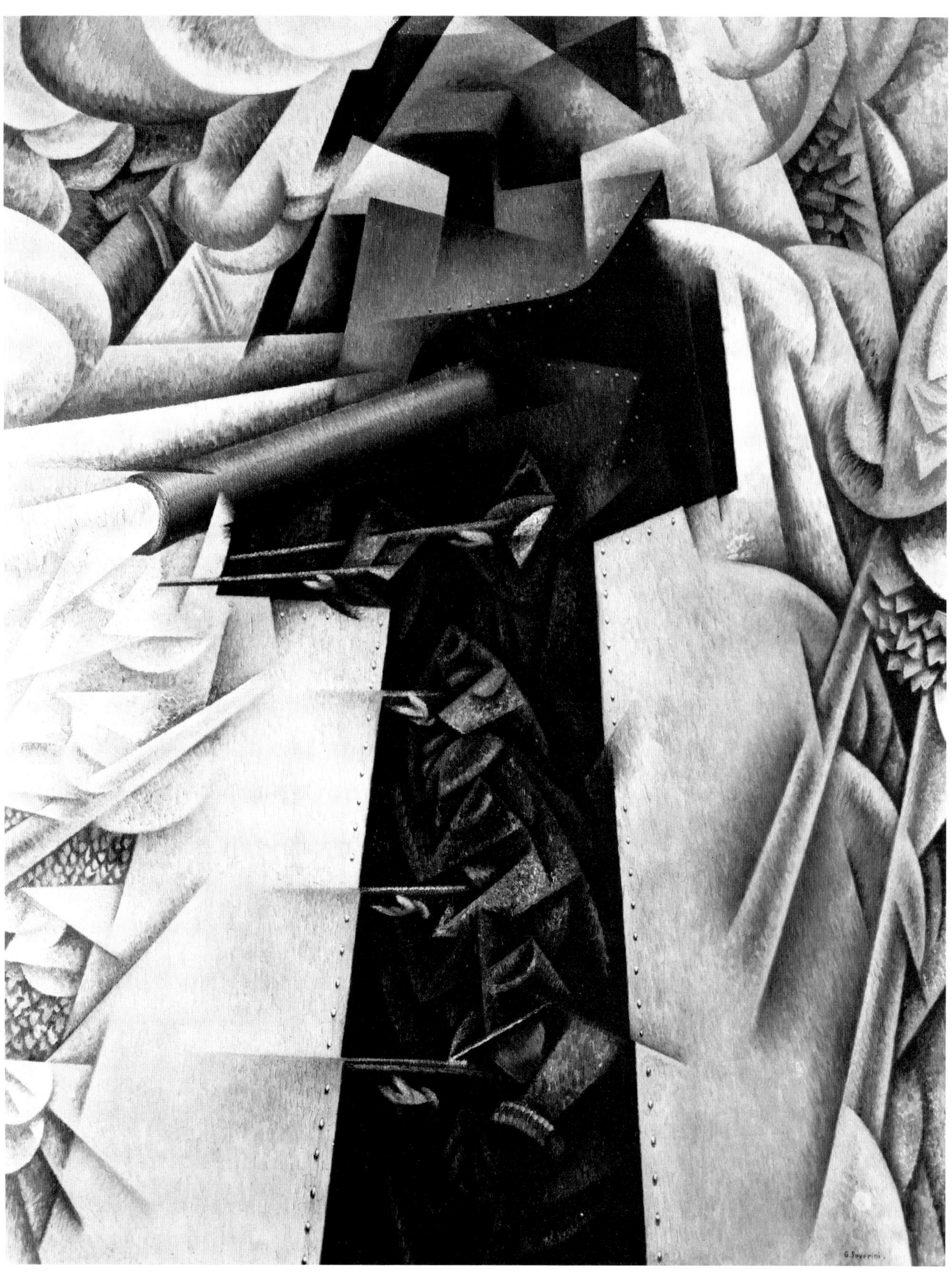

75

75. Armored Train in Action, 1915
Oil on canvas, 46 x 34½" (116.8 x 87.6 cm)
Richard S. Zeisler Collection, New York
Exhibitions: Paris, Galerie Boutet de Monvel, *Première Exposition Futuriste d'Art Plastique de la Guerre et d'Autres Oeuvres Antérieures,* January 15–February 1, 1916, no. 4; New York, Little Galleries of the Photo-Secession, *Gino Severini,* March 6–17, 1917

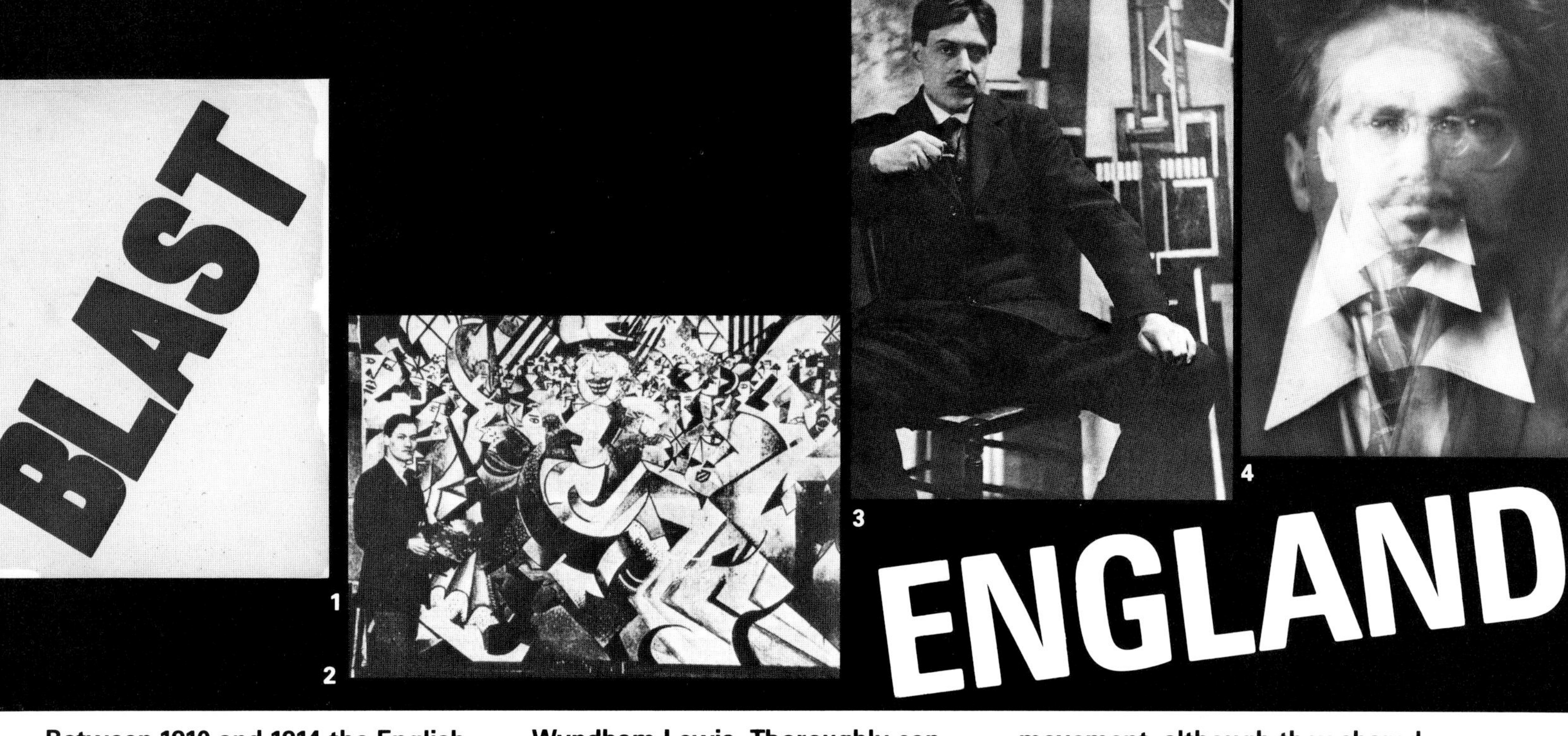

Between 1910 and 1914 the English received the full force of the Futurist campaign. Filippo Tommaso Marinetti lectured at the Lyceum Club for Women in December 1910, offering a violent attack on the "passatist" aesthetics of John Ruskin. The Futurist painters' Paris exhibition traveled to London, where it opened at the Sackville Gallery in March 1912. The Paris catalogue was translated and notes on the individual paintings were added, apparently by the gallery director, R. Meyer-See.

The Futurists were fascinated by London, a modern metropolis which took them to its heart with a warmth that Paris never displayed. British newspapers were filled with stories and photographs, and Harold Monro later devoted the September 1913 issue of his magazine *Poetry and Drama* to the movement. D. H. Lawrence admired the Futurists' rebellious attitude toward the past, and a number of poets were influenced by Marinetti's concept of "words in freedom." But English artists were more cautious in their reception of the Italian invasion. Roger Fry's two Post-Impressionist exhibitions (winter 1910 and late fall 1912) constituted the main effort to present international avant-garde art in London and he was particularly eager to include Picasso and Matisse. Fry remained skeptical about Futurism, although friendly to Gino Severini, who had a one-man show at the Marlborough Gallery in London in April 1913.

During 1912 and 1913 a schism gradually widened between two groups of vanguard artists in England: Fry and his Bloomsbury friends, such as Vanessa Bell and Duncan Grant, and the more loosely defined group led by the aggressive Wyndham Lewis. Thoroughly conversant with European modernism after years of living in France, impressed with Marinetti's battle tactics, and increasingly inclined to a sharply geometrized style verging on abstraction, Lewis broke with Fry in the fall of 1913 and founded the Rebel Art Center the following spring. Fellow "rebels" included Edward Wadsworth, Lawrence Atkinson, and Frederick Etchells, as well as Christopher Nevinson, who constituted that rare phenomenon, an outspoken convert to Futurism. In the spring of 1914, when Marinetti recited excerpts from his free-word poem "The Siege of Adrianople," Nevinson dutifully banged away on two drums in the next room. Nevinson's largest Futurist painting, since lost, was *Tum Tiddly Um Tum Pom Pom* of 1914, a picture of holiday revelers, clearly in debt to his friend Severini.

The Italian Futurists held a second major exhibition of their newest works (including Giacomo Balla's studies of speeding automobiles) in London at the Doré Galleries in April 1914. On June 7 Marinetti and Nevinson published the manifesto "Vital English Art" in the *Observer* and infuriated Lewis and other artists of the Rebel Art Center by using their names. In retaliation, Lewis announced the birth of Vorticism with a manifesto in the first issue of his magazine *Blast,* published on July 2, signed by the poet Ezra Pound, the young sculptor Henri Gaudier-Brzeska, and the painters Atkinson and Wadsworth. Other artists such as Jacob Epstein, at work on his menacing man-machine *The Rock Drill,* and the fiercely independent David Bomberg remained outside the movement, although they shared common interests. Although Marinetti's bombast clearly inspired Lewis's polemics, the Vorticists violently denied Italian influence. Lewis denounced Marinetti's "automobilism," claiming that the English had in fact invented modern technology and had no need to fuss about it. In fact, the paintings exhibited by Lewis, Bomberg, and the others during the years 1912 to 1915 exude a cold, mechanical vitality that is quite distinct from the sensuous exuberance of Boccioni's work or the sophisticated gaiety of Severini's.

Vorticism, a short-lived and fragmented movement, produced individual works of great power, many of which have been lost or destroyed. Born a few months before World War I, the movement survived long enough to mount a London exhibition in June 1915, publish a second issue of *Blast,* and make its international debut in New York early in 1917.

1. Cover of *Blast,* July 2, 1914; 2. Christopher Nevinson with *Tum Tiddly Um Tum Pom Pom,* 1914 (from *Western Mail,* May 15, 1914); 3. Alvin Langdon Coburn, *Wyndham Lewis,* photograph, c. 1914, International Museum of Photography, George Eastman House, Rochester; 4. Alvin Langdon Coburn, *Ezra Pound,* vortograph, 1916, International Museum of Photography, George Eastman House, Rochester

David Bomberg

1 8 9 0 – 1 9 5 7

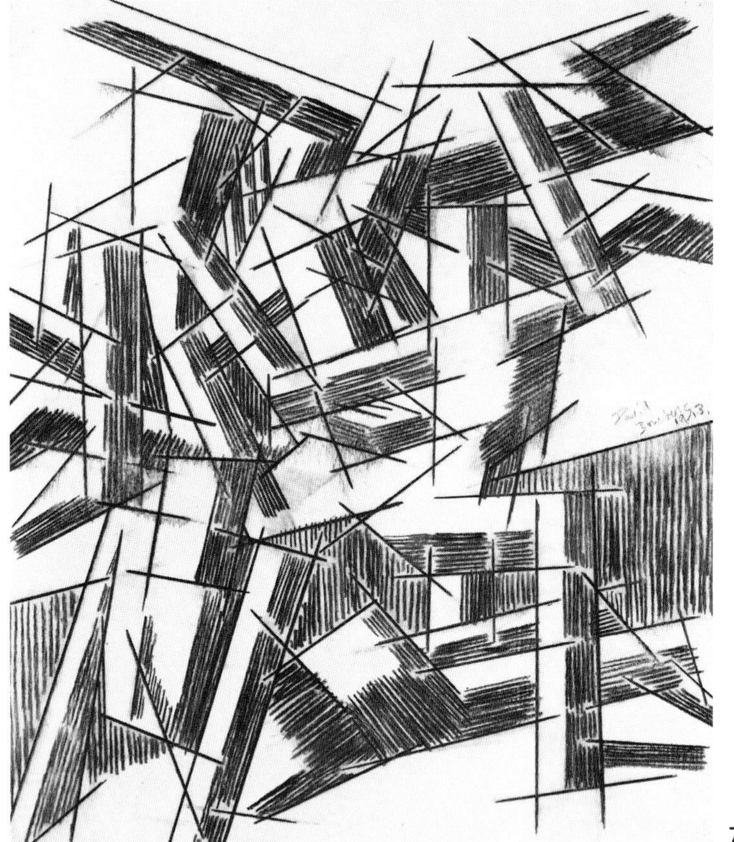

76

77

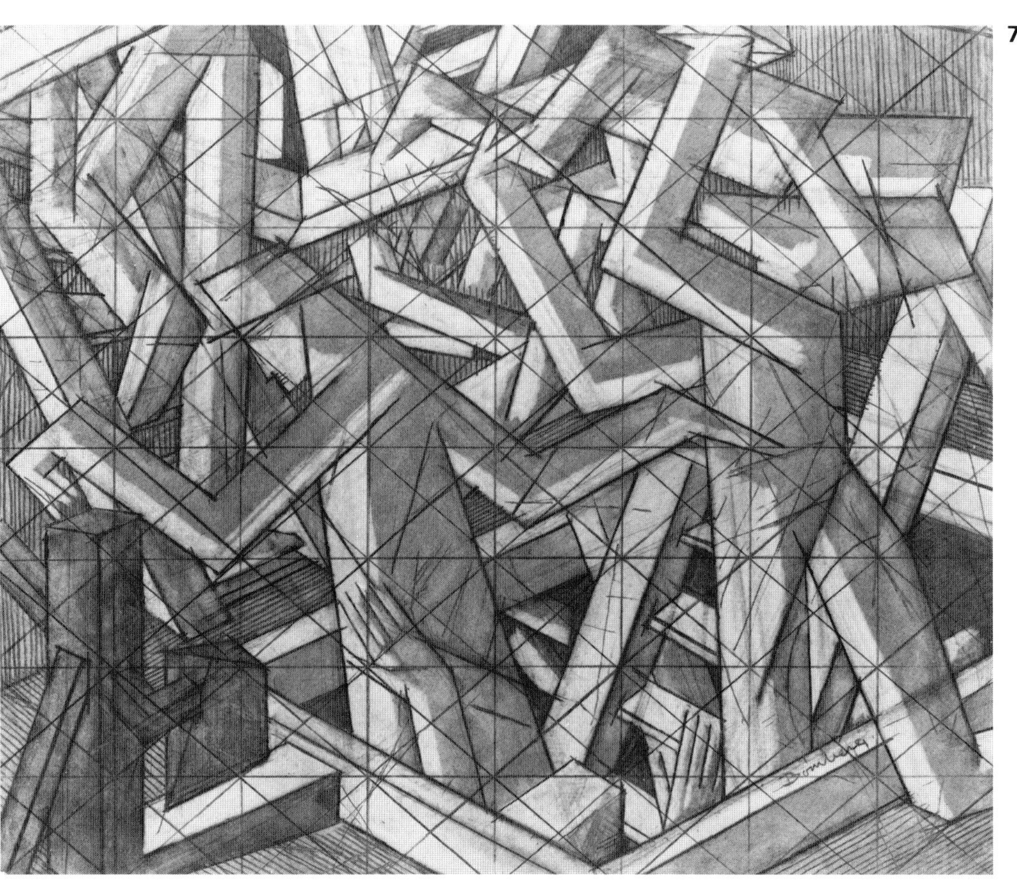

76. Study for "In the Hold," c. 1913
Crayon on paper, 22⅞ x 20" (58.2 x 50.8 cm)
Anthony d'Offay Gallery, London

77. Study for "In the Hold," c. 1914
Chalk and watercolor on paper, 21⅞ x 26" (55.6 x 66 cm)
The Tate Gallery, London
Presented by Friends of the Tate Gallery, 1957

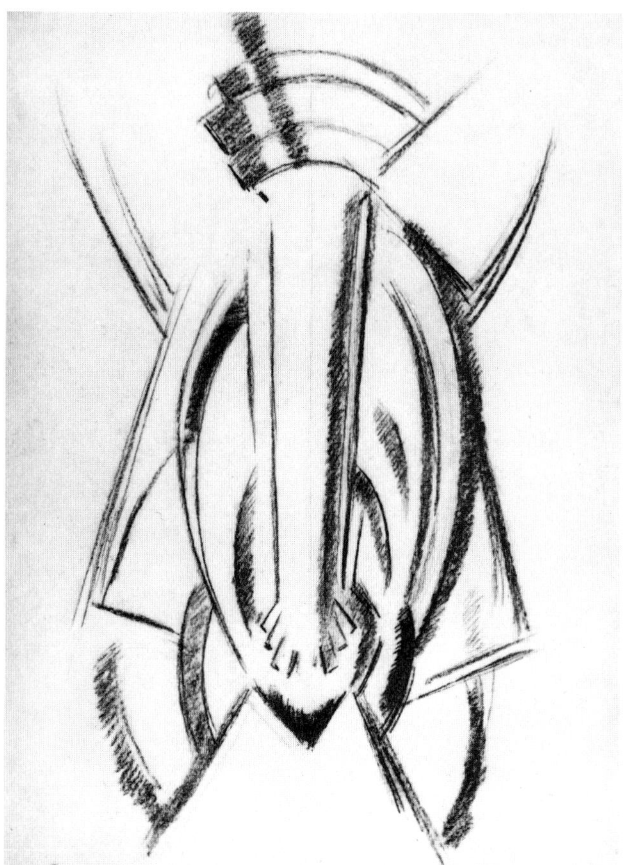

78

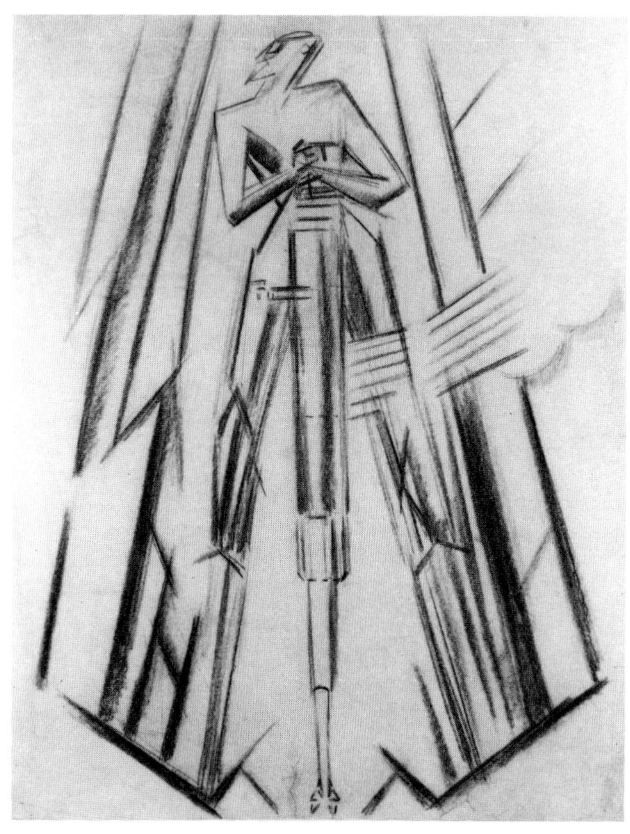

79

78. Study of the Drill's Head for "The Rock Drill," c. 1913
Crayon on paper, 25 x 18½" (63.5 x 47 cm)
Anthony d'Offay Gallery, London

79. Study for "The Rock Drill," c. 1913
Charcoal on paper, 25¼ x 21" (64.1 x 53.3 cm)
The Tate Gallery, London
Purchase, 1960

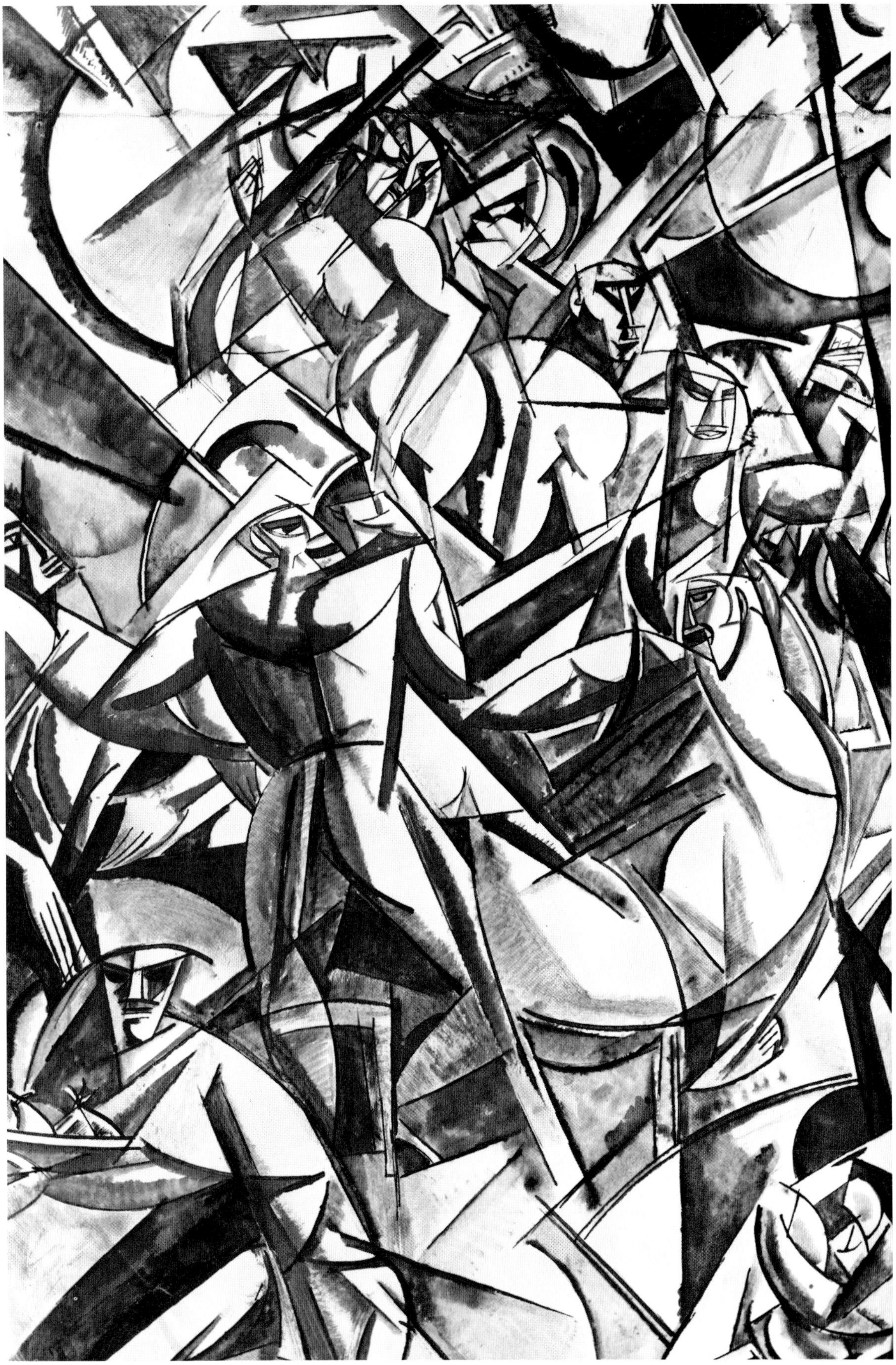

80

80. The Creditors (Study for the Portfolio "Timon of Athens"), 1912–13
Ink, wash, and watercolor on paper,
16½ x 10⅞" (41.9 x 27.7 cm)
Wadsworth Atheneum, Hartford
The Ella Gallup Sumner and Mary Catlin Sumner Collection
Exhibition: London, Grafton Galleries, *Second Post-Impressionist Exhibition,* October 5, 1912–January 31, 1913, no. 194 (?)

Christopher R. W. Nevinson

1 8 8 9 – 1 9 4 6

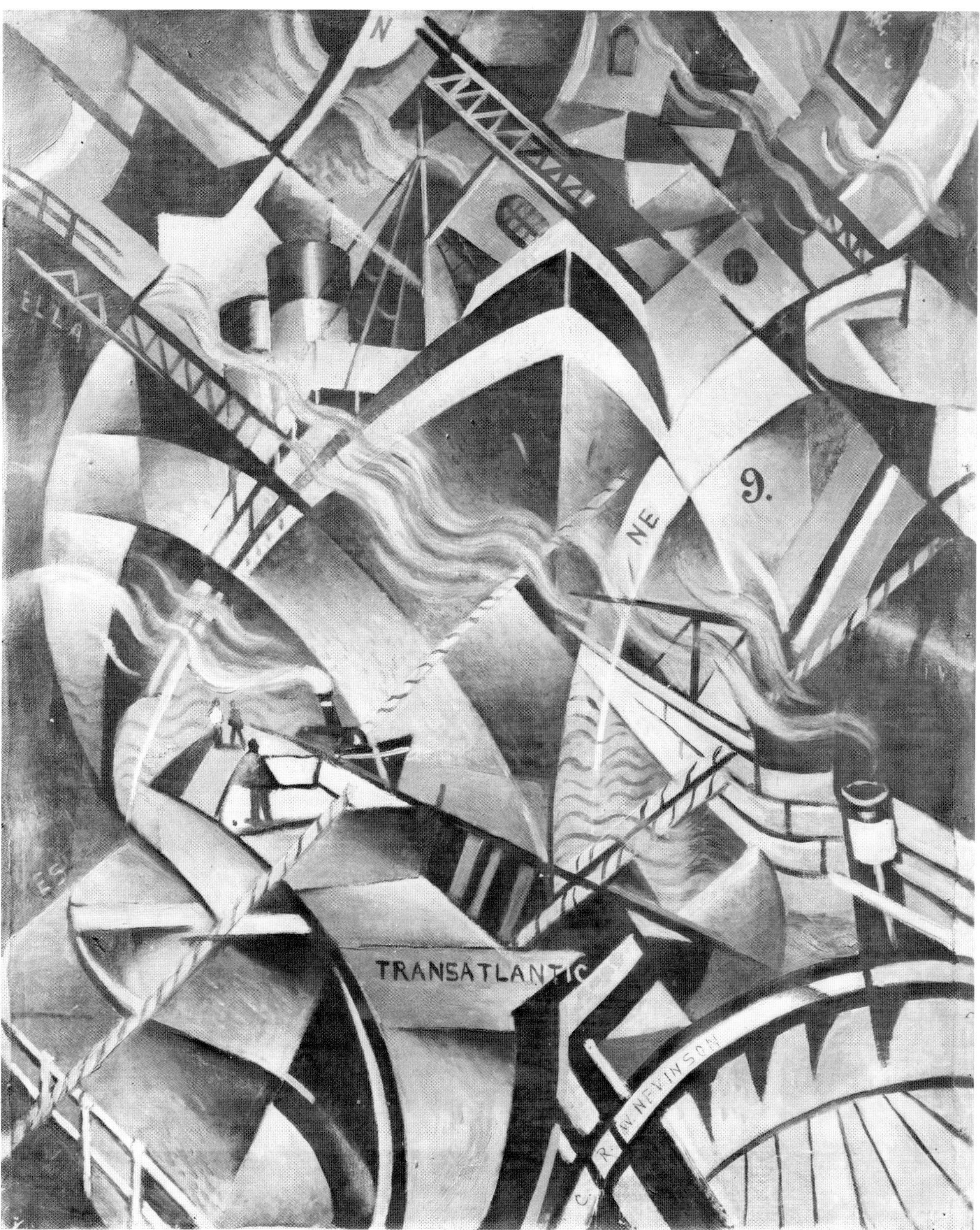

81

81. The Arrival, c. 1913–14
Oil on canvas, 30 x 25″ (76.2 x 63.5 cm)
The Tate Gallery, London
Gift of Mrs. Christopher R. W. Nevinson, 1956
Exhibition: London, Goupil Galleries, *First Exhibition of the London Group,* March–April 1914, no. 39

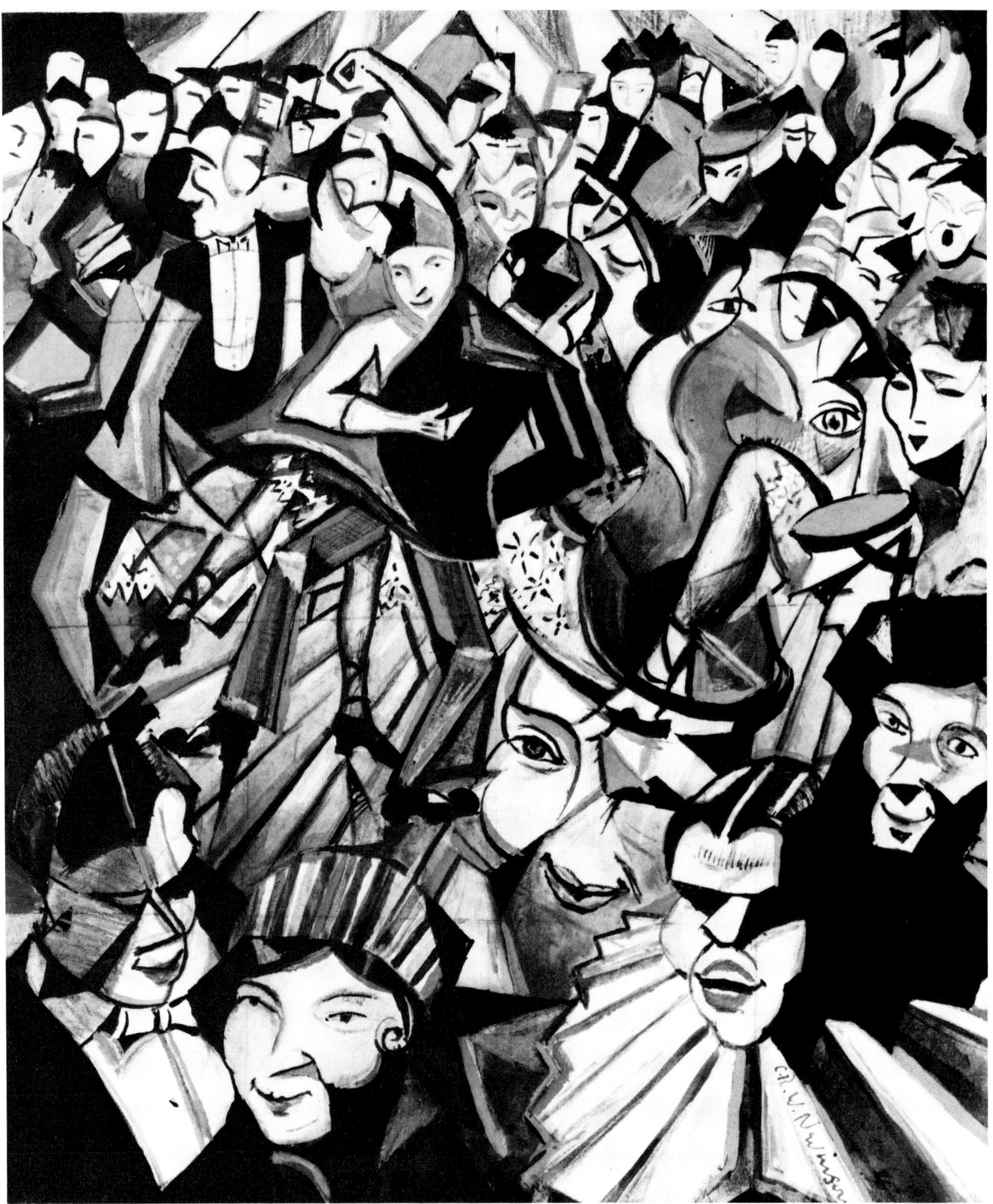

82

82. Dance Hall Scene, c. 1913–14
Gouache on paper, 8¾ x 7¾" (22.2 x 19.7 cm)
The Tate Gallery, London
Purchase, 1974

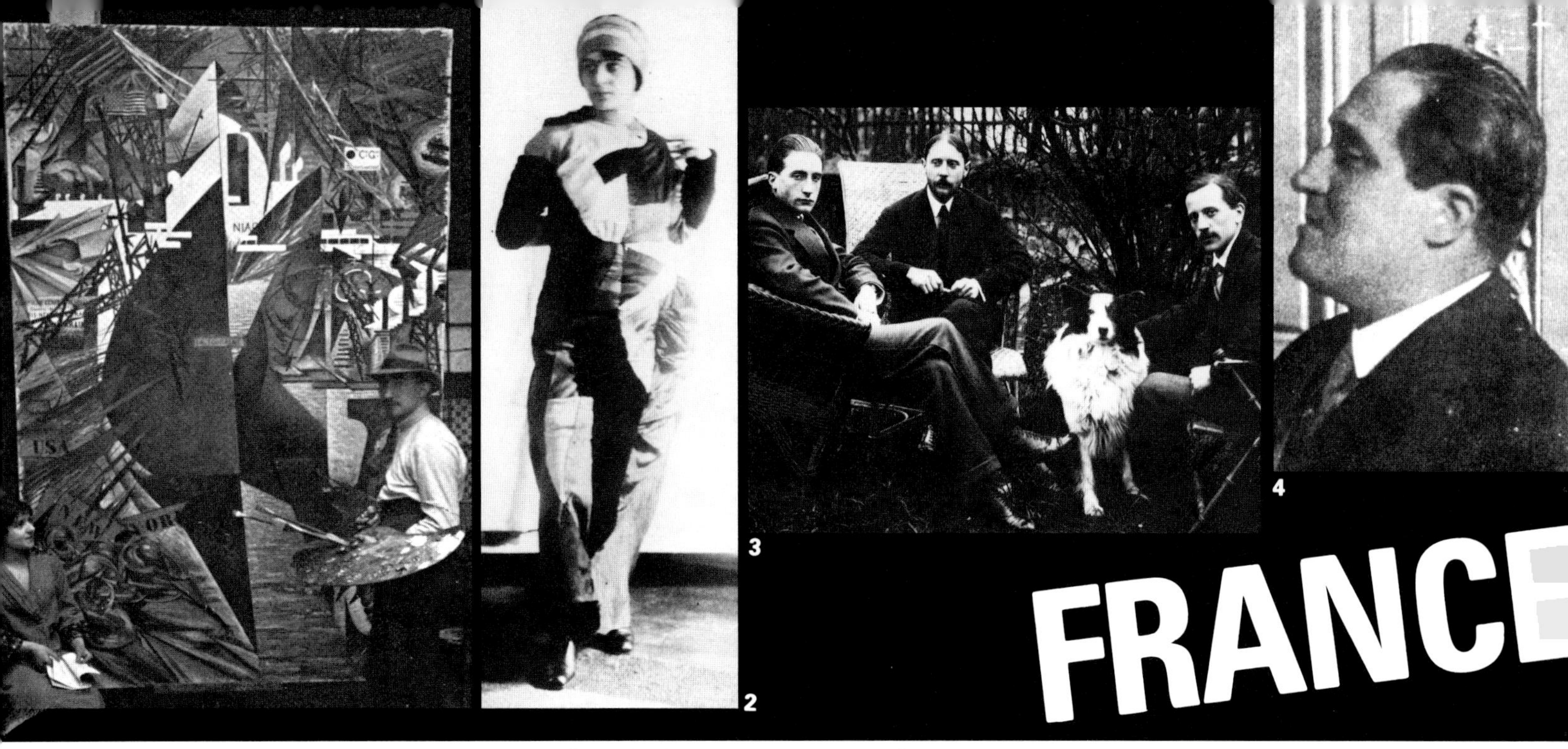

FRANCE

It would be technically true to say that there was only one self-confessed French convert to Futurist painting between 1910 and 1915: the young Félix Del Marle, whom Gino Severini befriended and who concocted his own manifesto attacking Montmartre, dated July 10, 1913. But the poet Guillaume Apollinaire was a far more distinguished catch for Filippo Tommaso Marinetti, and his Futurist Anti-Tradition Manifesto appeared in the Florentine journal *Lacerba* on September 15, 1913. These two cases epitomize the relative success of the Futurists' campaign to conquer France. Their literal follower Del Marle was a capable but derivative painter, whereas Apollinaire, with his inspired ability to detect the contributions of artists of every nationality working in Paris, represented the true intermingling of Futurist ideas with avant-garde French art and thought.

It was also Apollinaire who surveyed the full range of the artistic scene in Paris before the war and noted the simultaneous existence of diverse tendencies: the aged Impressionist Auguste Renoir painting his final series of robust and radiant nudes; the Cubists reconstituting visual reality and "dissecting" the human figure in their paintings; the Futurists vigorously banning the depiction of the nude in favor of "modern" subjects.

The Paris art world between 1910 and 1915 revolved around a steady rhythm of annual exhibitions. The Salon des Indépendants in the spring and the Salon d'Automne revealed the progressive advance of Cubism between 1910 and 1912 and the rise of a marked tendency toward dynamic, color-oriented abstraction (which Apollinaire named Orphism) between 1912 and the end of 1914. The Futurists' Bernheim-Jeune gallery exhibition in February 1912 exerted a strong effect upon this pattern and the impact of Futurism was implicitly countered by the Salon de "La Section d'Or" organized by the Duchamp brothers and their circle for the following October. Although the Futurists never again exhibited as a group in Paris and did not take part in the annual salons, their ideas continued to be circulated and debated in French periodicals devoted to the most advanced art and literature, such as *Les Soirées de Paris* (1912–14), *Poème et Drame* (1912–14), and *Montjoie!* (1913–14), as well as in the daily newspapers. Umberto Boccioni's exhibition of sculpture in Paris in June 1913 (accompanied by "contradictory lectures" by himself and Marinetti) marked a crucial juncture in the intersection of many artists' attitudes to materials and sculptural form. Severini's presence as a Paris resident (with intermittent trips to Italy) surely helped to keep his French colleagues aware of the aims and practices of the Futurist artists and his marriage in August 1913 to the daughter of the poet Paul Fort was a convivial international occasion hailed as the union of France and Italy.

While the Futurists clearly learned from their exposure to the Cubist painting of Braque and Picasso in 1911, the Italians' stress on dynamism, on modern subjects, and on the interpenetration of object and environment was reflected, or at least paralleled, in the development of the Cubist painters Gleizes, Metzinger, Léger, and Gris during the years 1911 to 1914. The three Duchamp brothers shared Marinetti's fascination with the machine and studied the effects of motion, explicit or implied, in their paintings and sculpture. Robert Delaunay and his Russian wife Sonia Delaunay-Terk were interested in painting the movement of light, the swirling energy of crowds, and triumphs of technology, such as the airplane, but carried on the most acrimonious disputes with the Futurists of any artists in Paris. Sonia Delaunay's designs for "simultaneous" clothing seem to have anticipated Giacomo Balla's 1914 manifesto for an Anti-Neutral Suit. Even artists as mature and decidedly independent as Matisse or the Dutch painter Mondrian, who lived in Paris between 1912 and mid-1914, revealed an awareness of the issues emphasized by the Futurists, subsumed into their own pictorial interests.

World War I ended the amazing period of international artistic exchange in Paris. Duchamp and Gleizes went to America, the Delaunays to Spain, the Russian contingent returned home, and Duchamp-Villon and Apollinaire were to be among the casualties. In January 1916 Severini's first one-man show in Paris opened in a deserted city. The exhibition included some of his finest Futurist efforts, but also marked his shift away from Futurist dynamism and disorder toward the search for classical structure and balance which was to preoccupy so many French artists after the war.

1. Félix Del Marle and his wife in his Paris studio with *The Port*, c. 1913; 2. Sonia Delaunay wearing her Simultaneous Dress, c. 1913; 3. Marcel Duchamp, Jacques Villon, and Raymond Duchamp-Villon, Puteaux, 1912; 4. Guillaume Apollinaire, Paris, 1913

Alexander Archipenko
1 8 8 7 – 1 9 6 4

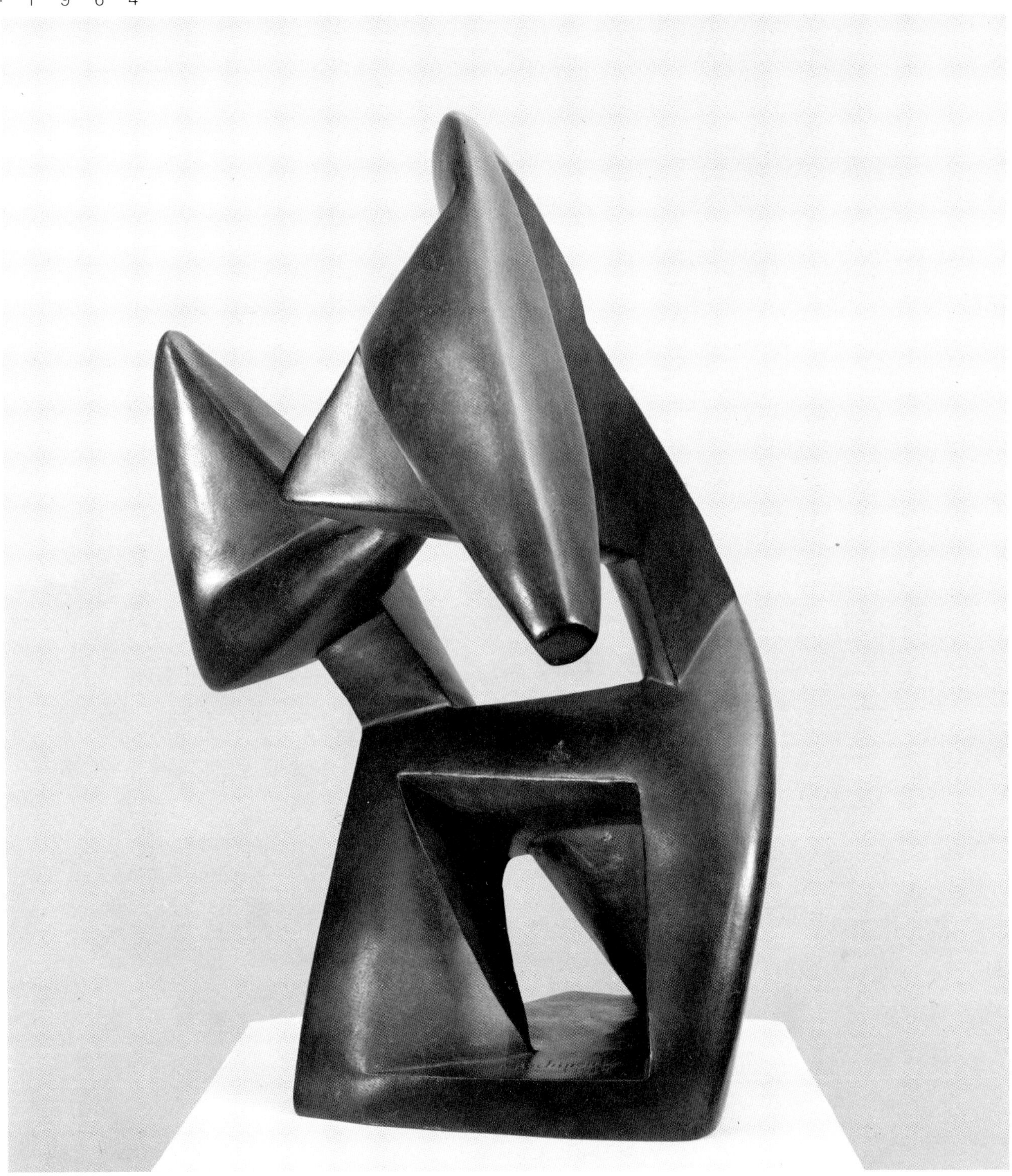

83

83. Boxing (Struggle), 1914 (cast 1966)
Bronze, 23¼ x 18¼ x 15⅞" (59.1 x 46.4 x 40.3 cm)
The Museum of Modern Art, New York
Given anonymously, 1966
Exhibition: Paris, Société des Artistes Indépendants, *30ᵉ Exposition,* March 1–April 30, 1914, no. 85 (plaster version)

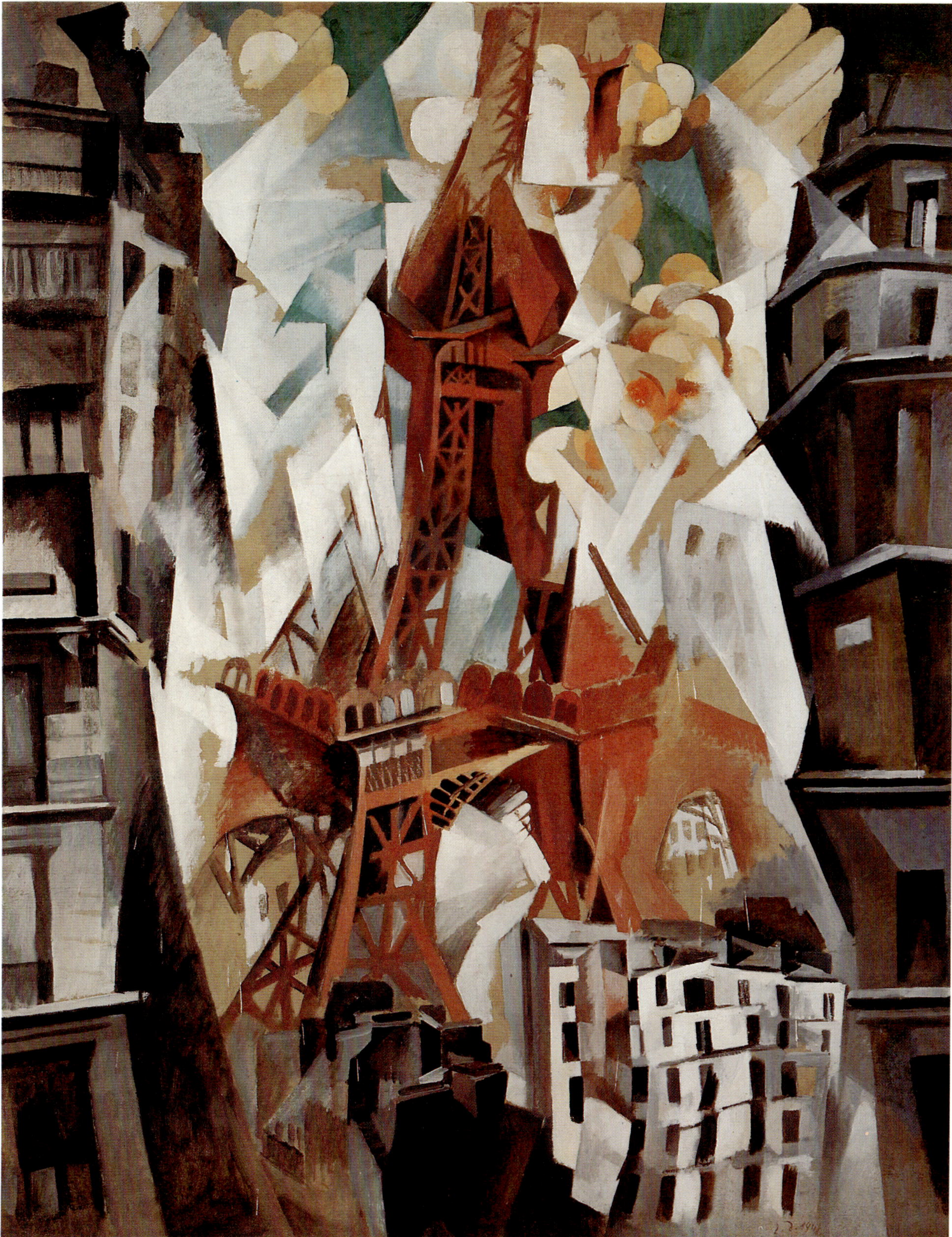

84

84. Champs de Mars, The Red Tower, 1911
Oil on canvas, 64 x 51½" (162.6 x 130.8 cm)
The Art Institute of Chicago
The Joseph Winterbotham Collection
Exhibition: Paris, Galerie Barbazanges, *Les Peintres R. Delaunay, Marie Laurencin,* February 28–March 13, 1912, no. 5, repro. (unfinished state)

Robert Delaunay

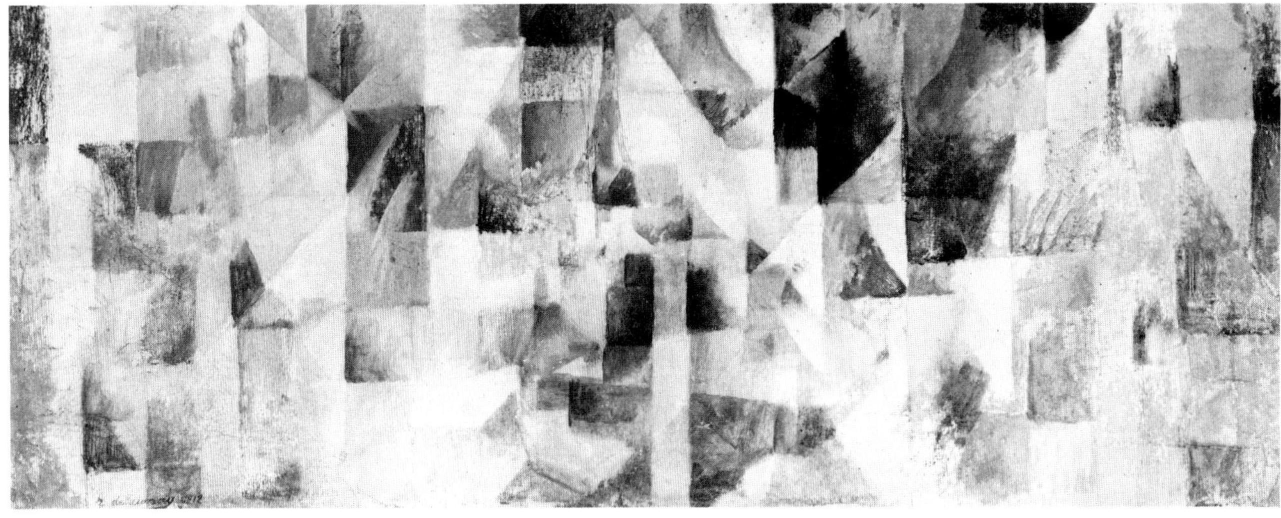

85

86

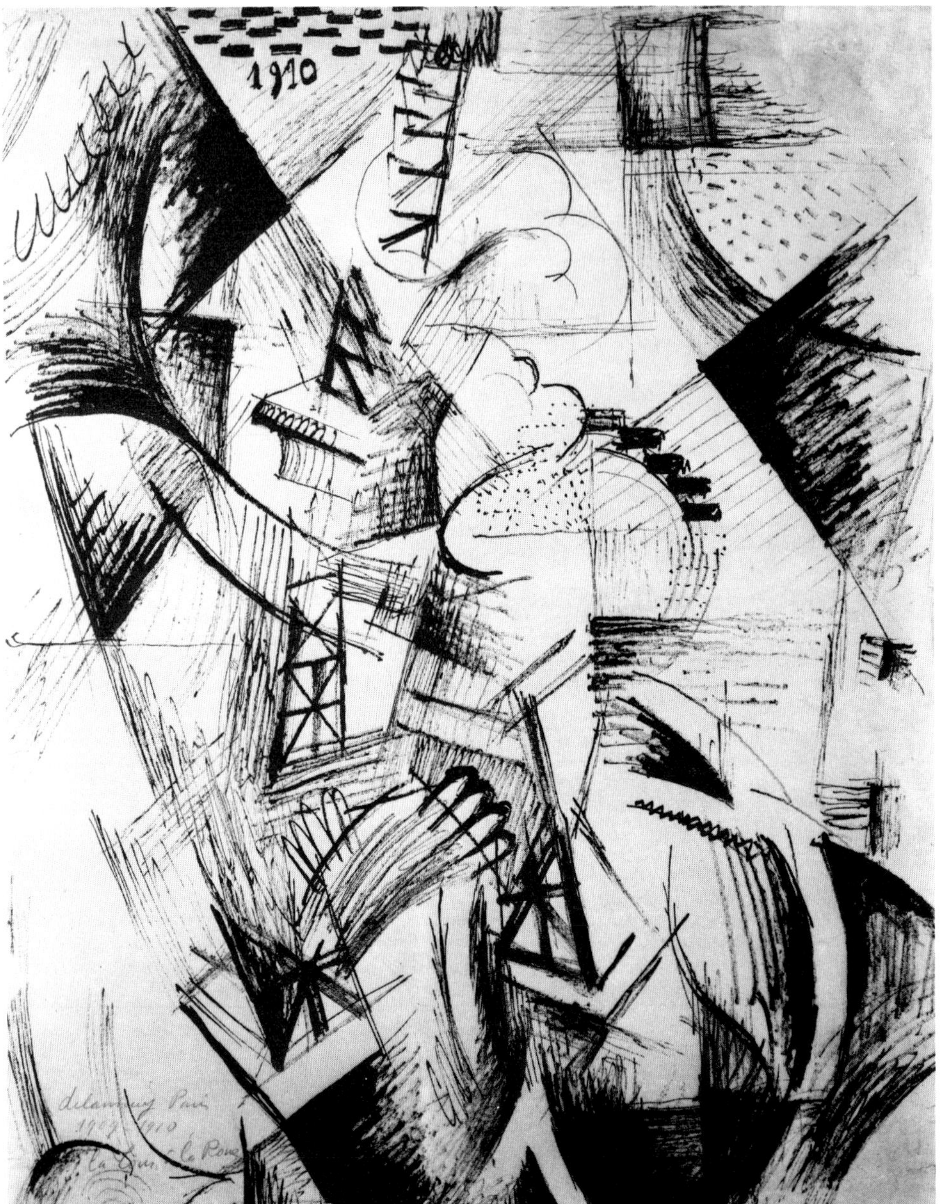

85. 2nd Representation, The Windows Simultaneity City, 1st Part 3 Motifs (Three Part Windows), 1912
Oil on canvas, 13½ x 35" (34.3 x 88.9 cm)
Philadelphia Museum of Art
A. E. Gallatin Collection
Exhibition: Berlin, Der Sturm, *R. Delaunay, Ardengo Soffici, Julie Baum,* February 1913, no. 4

86. The Tower and the Wheel, c. 1912–13
Ink on paper, 25½ x 19½" (64.7 x 49.7 cm)
The Museum of Modern Art, New York
Abby Aldrich Rockefeller Fund, 1935

Sonia Delaunay-Terk

1885–1979

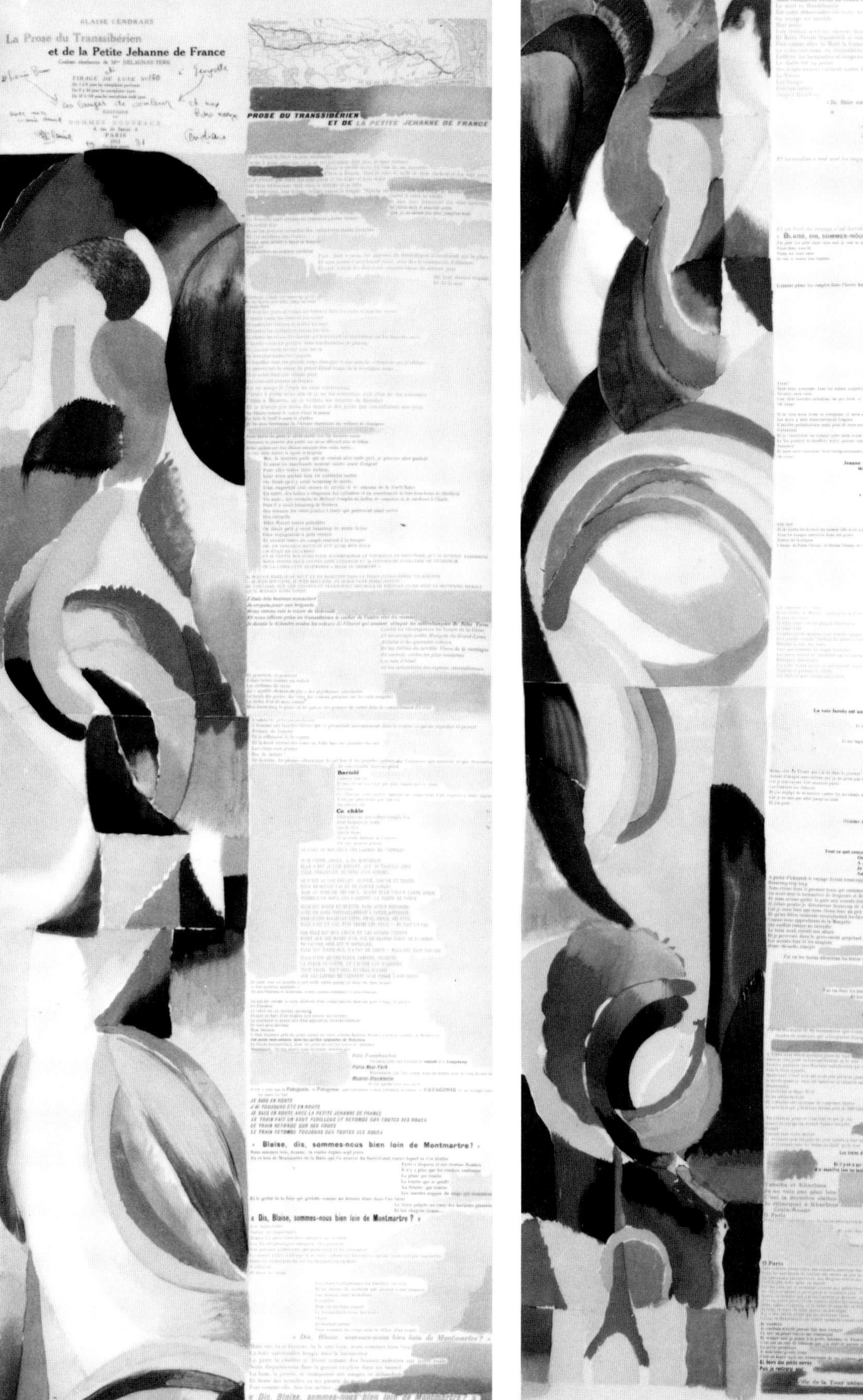

Jpper half

Lower half

87. "La Prose du Transsibérien et de la Petite Jehanne de France," 1913
Text by Blaise Cendrars, Paris, 1913
Pochoir gouache decoration on four sheets of paper (unfolded and unbound) joined into one sheet,
81¾ x 13¾" (207.8 x 34.9 cm)
The Museum of Modern Art, New York
Purchase, 1951
Exhibition: Berlin, Der Sturm, *Erster Deutscher Herbstsalon,* September 20–December 1, 1913, no. 99 (another copy)

Félix Del Marle

1889–1952

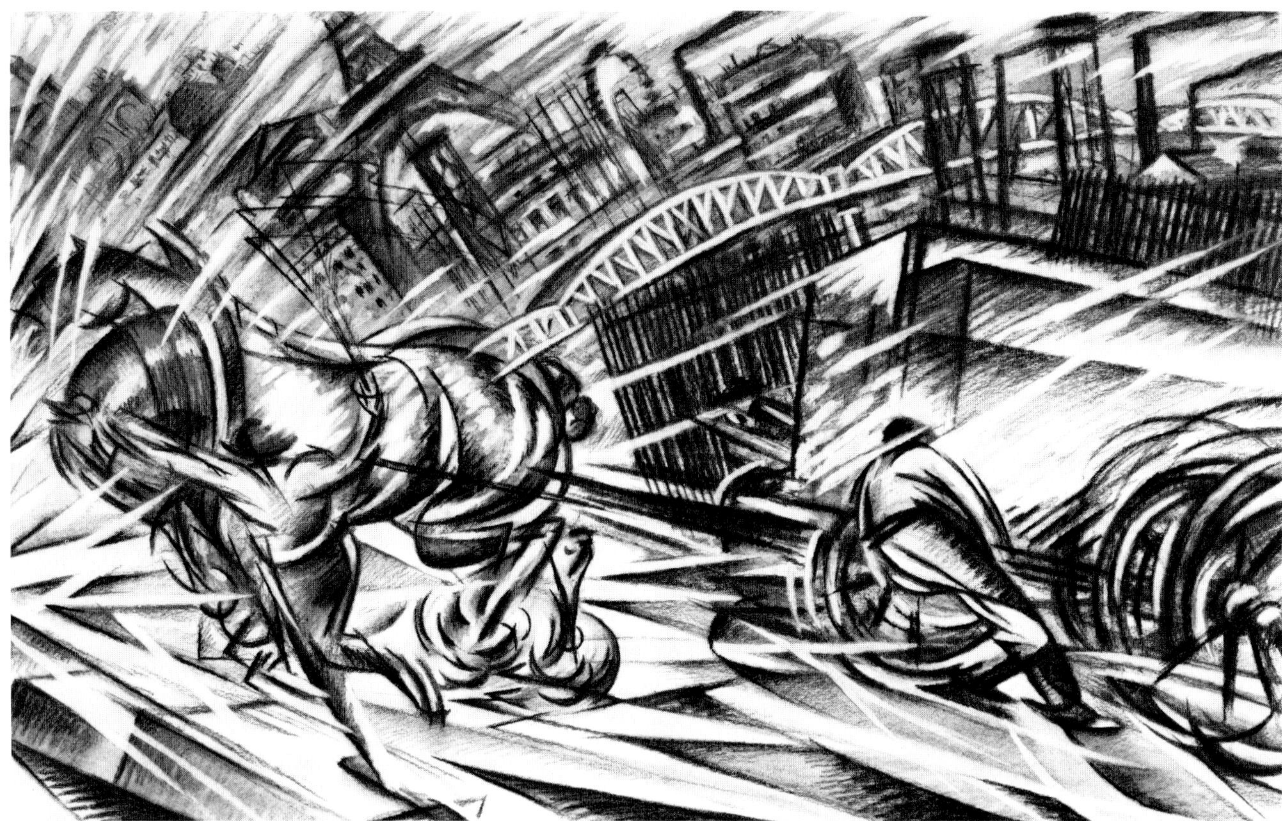

88

88. Endeavor, 1913
Crayon and charcoal on paper, 16⅝ x 27½" (42.2 x 69.8 cm)
The Museum of Modern Art, New York
The J. M. Kaplan Fund, 1973

89

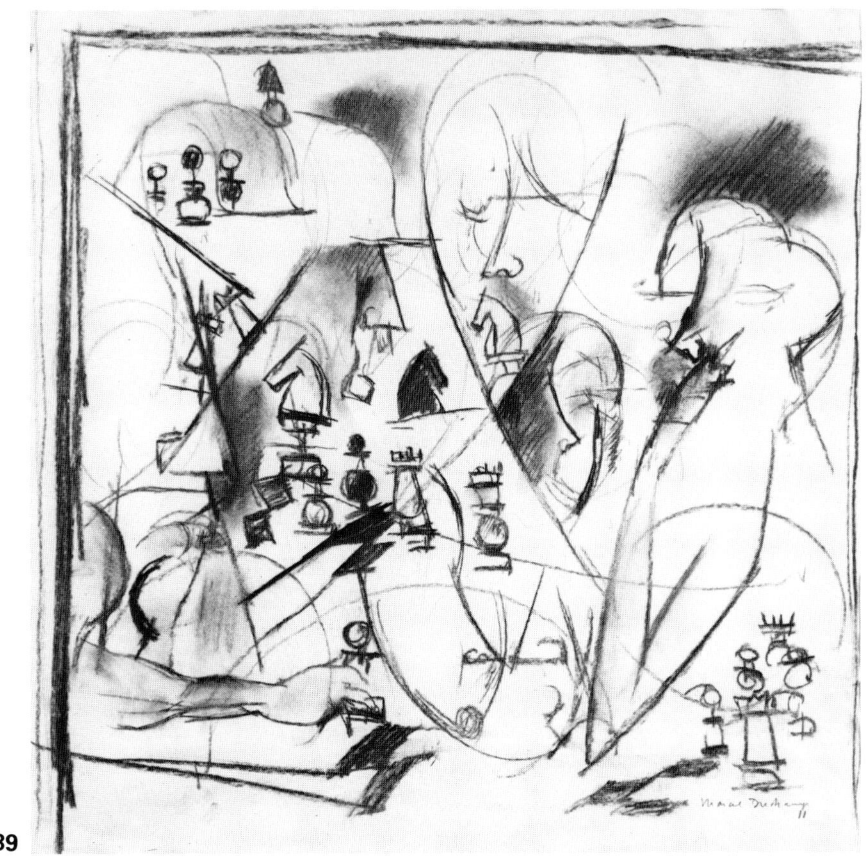

90

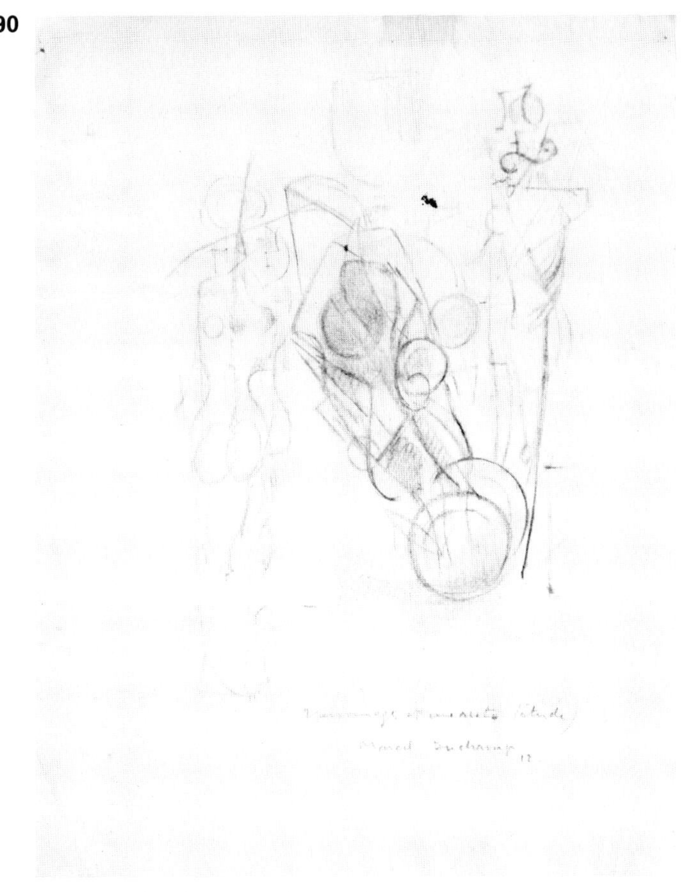

89. Study for "Portrait of Chess Players," 1911
Charcoal on paper, 19½ x 19⅞" (49.5 x 50.5 cm)
Mrs. Louise Varèse, New York

90. Two Personages and a Car (Study), 1912
Charcoal on paper, 13¾ x 11½" (35 x 29.1 cm)
Mme Marcel Duchamp, Villiers-sous-Grez, France

Marcel Duchamp

91

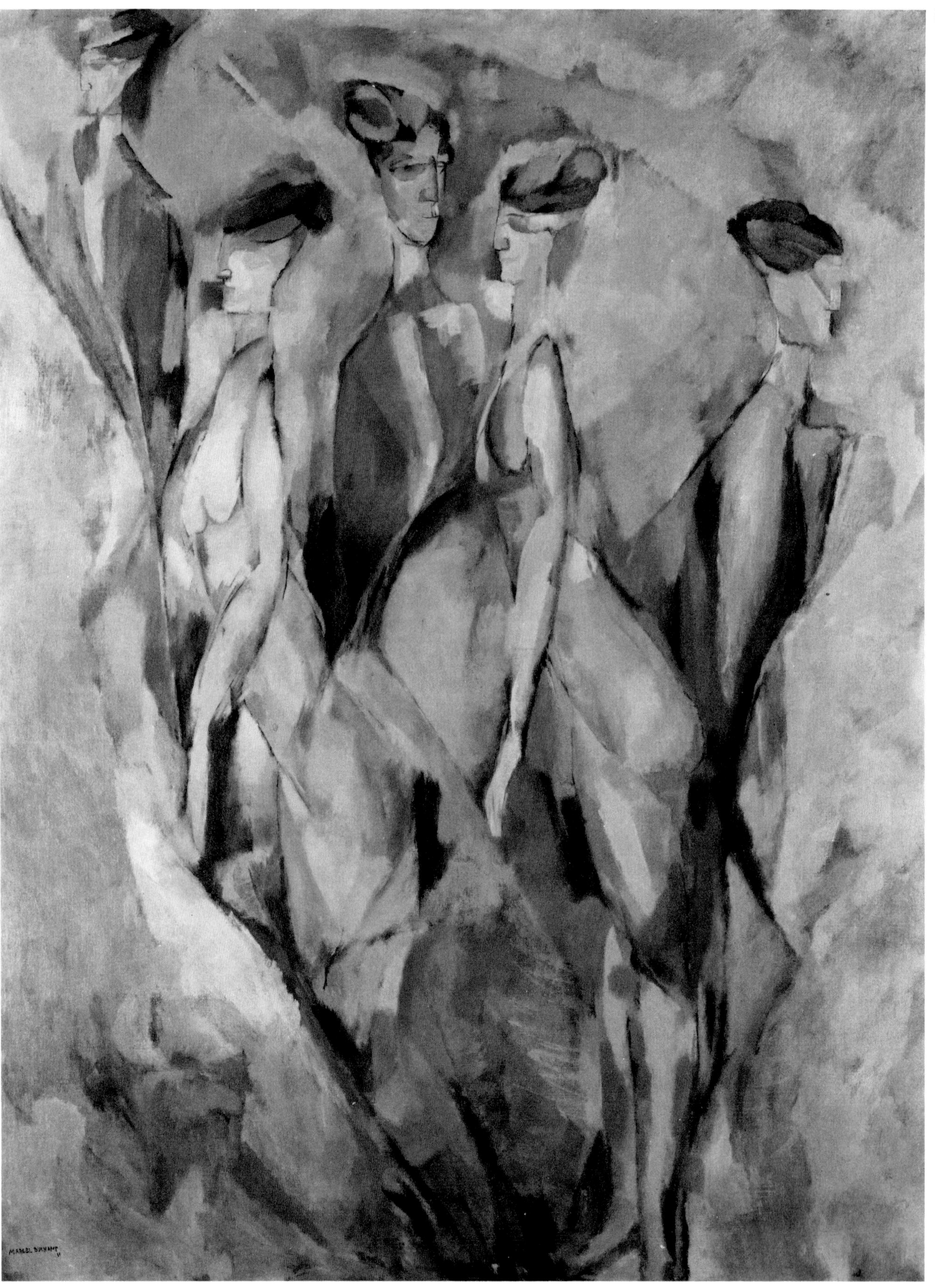

91. Portrait (Dulcinea), 1911
Oil on canvas, 57½ x 44⅞" (146.1 x 114 cm)
Philadelphia Museum of Art
The Louise and Walter Arensberg Collection
Exhibition: Paris, *Salon d'Automne, 9ᵉ Exposition,*
October 1–November 8, 1911, no. 402

Marcel Duchamp

92

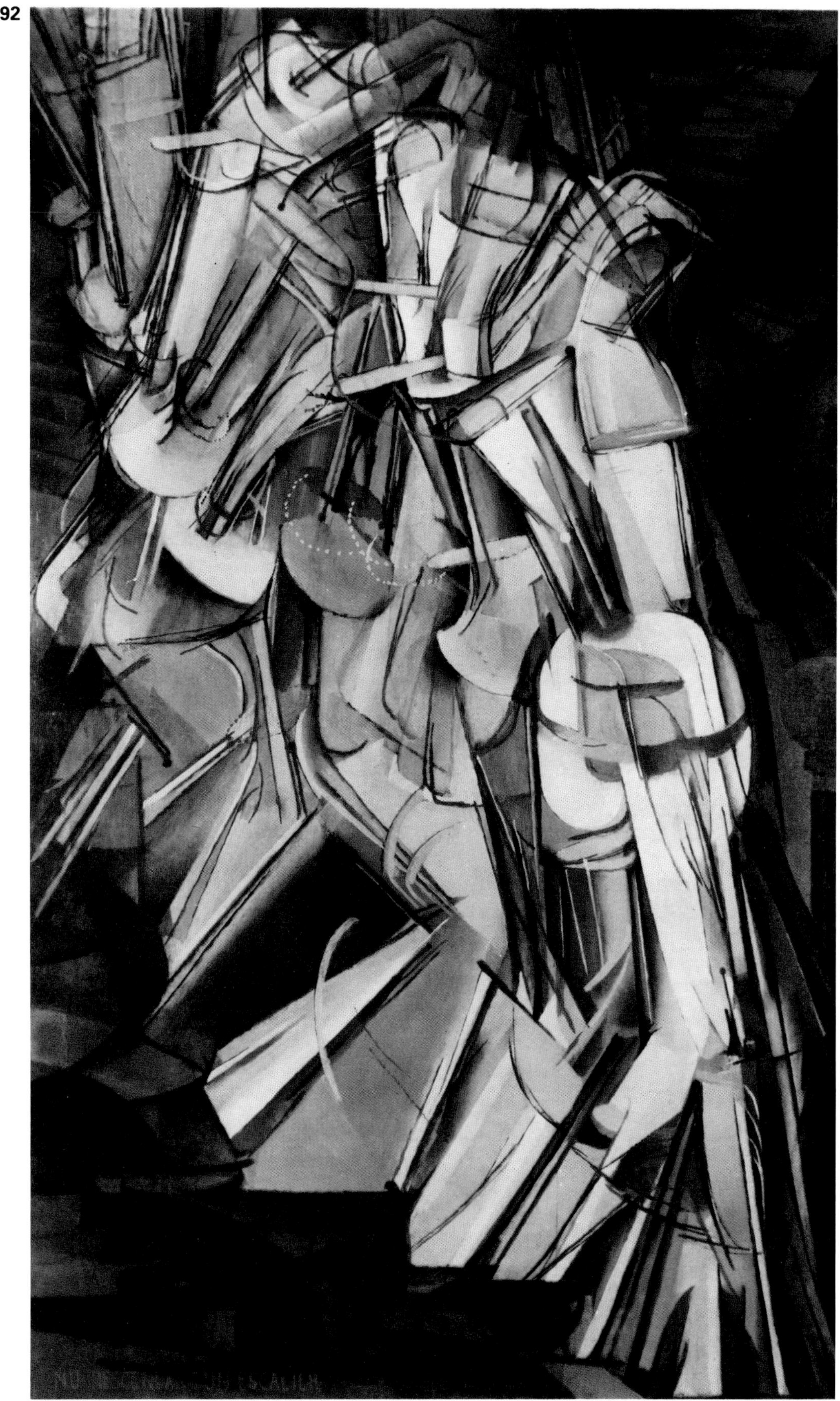

92. Nude Descending a Staircase, No. 2, 1912
Oil on canvas, 57½ x 35" (146.1 x 88.9 cm)
Philadelphia Museum of Art
The Louise and Walter Arensberg Collection
Exhibitions: Paris, Société des Artistes Indépendants, *28*^{e} *Exposition,* March 20–May 16, 1912, no. 1001 (withdrawn); Paris, Galerie La Boëtie, *Salon de "La Section d'Or,"* October 10–30, 1912, no. 19; New York, Armory of the 69th Regiment, *International Exhibition of Modern Art,* February 17–March 15, 1913, no. 241

Marcel Duchamp

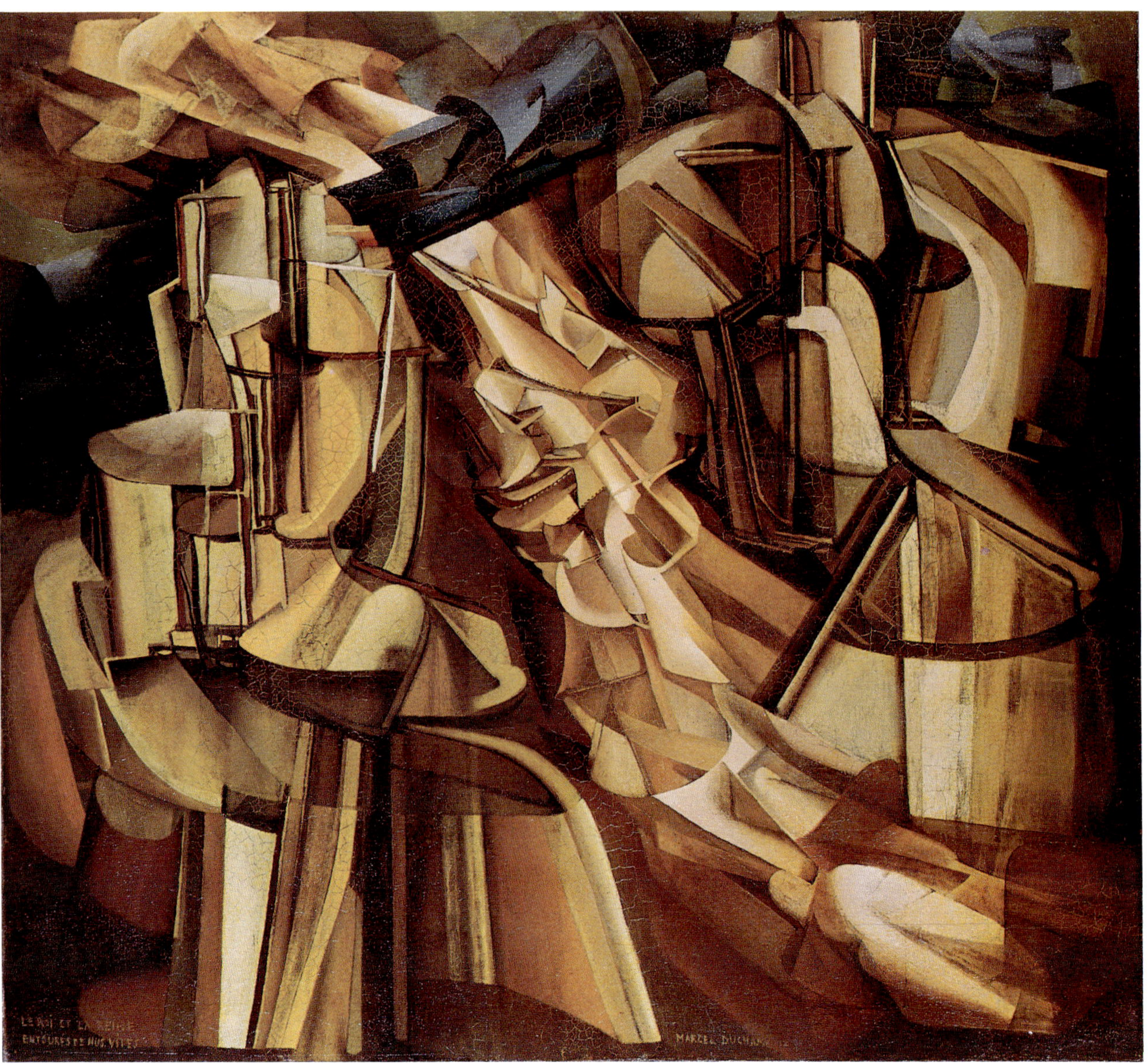

93

93. King and Queen Surrounded by Swift Nudes, 1912
Oil on canvas, 45¼ x 50½" (114.9 x 128.3 cm)
Philadelphia Museum of Art
The Louise and Walter Arensberg Collection
Exhibitions: Paris, Galerie La Boëtie, *Salon de "La Section d'Or,"* October 10–30, 1912, no. 18; New York, Armory of the 69th Regiment, *International Exhibition of Modern Art,* February 17–March 15, 1913, no. 239

Raymond Duchamp-Villon

1876–1918

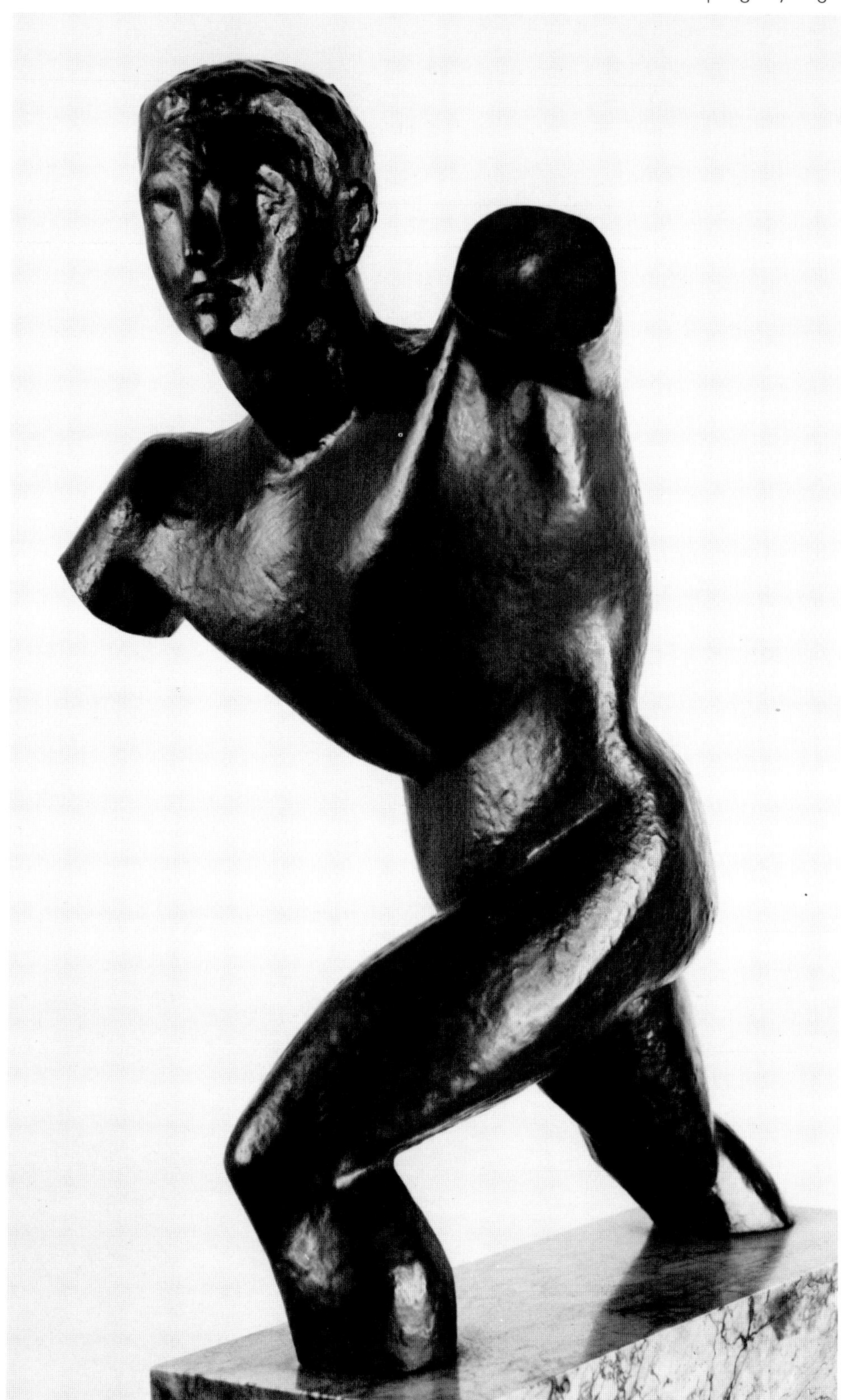

94

94. Torso of a Young Man, 1910 (cast 1913)
Bronze, 23⅞ x 13 x 16" (60.6 x 33 x 40.6 cm)
Dr. and Mrs. James F. Bing, Baltimore
Exhibitions: New York, Armory of the 69th Regiment, *International Exhibition of Modern Art,* February 17–March 15, 1913, no. 610 (plaster version); Paris, Galerie André Groult, *Duchamp-Villon, Gleizes, Metzinger, Villon,* April 6–May 3, 1914, no. 7 (terra cotta version)

Raymond Duchamp-Villon

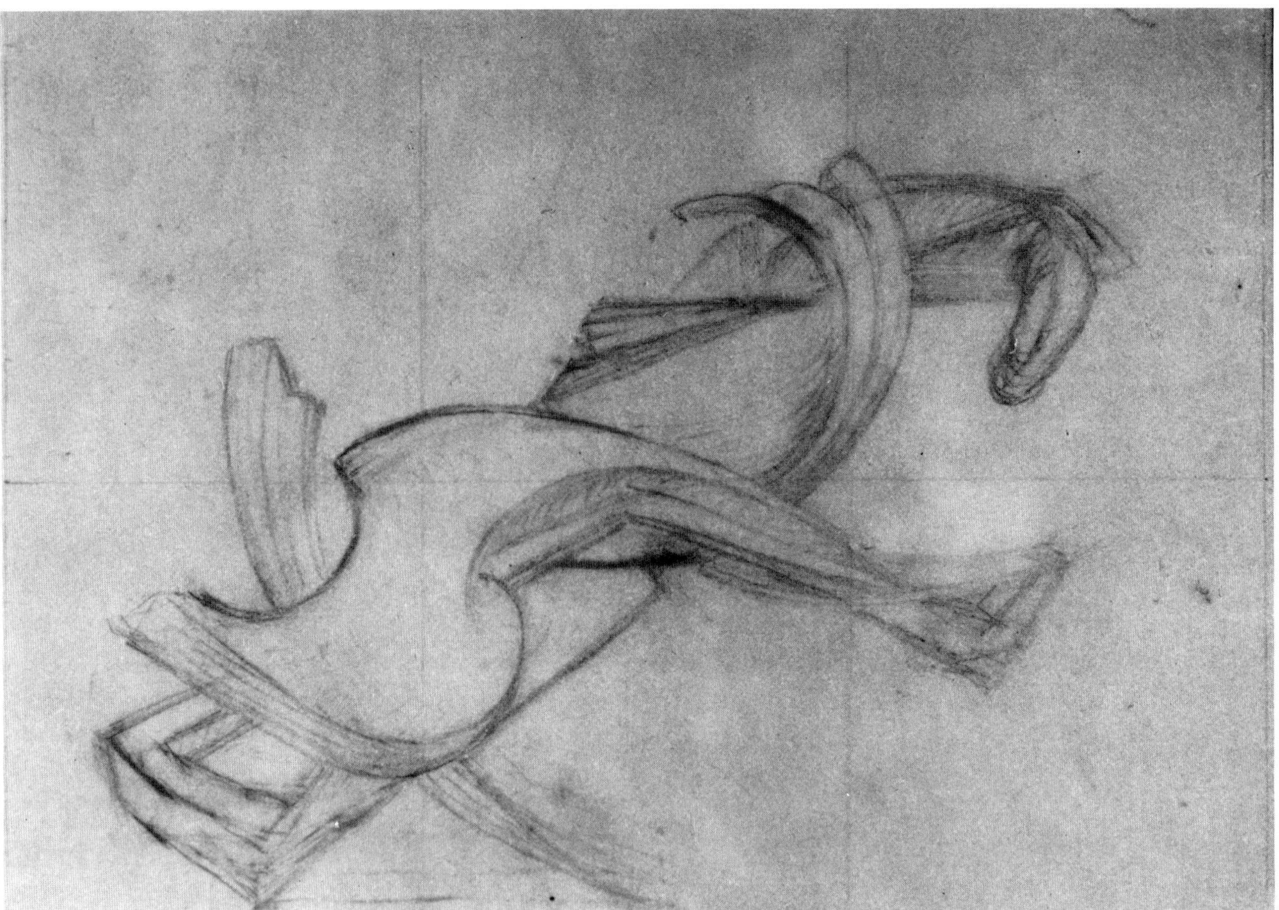

95

97

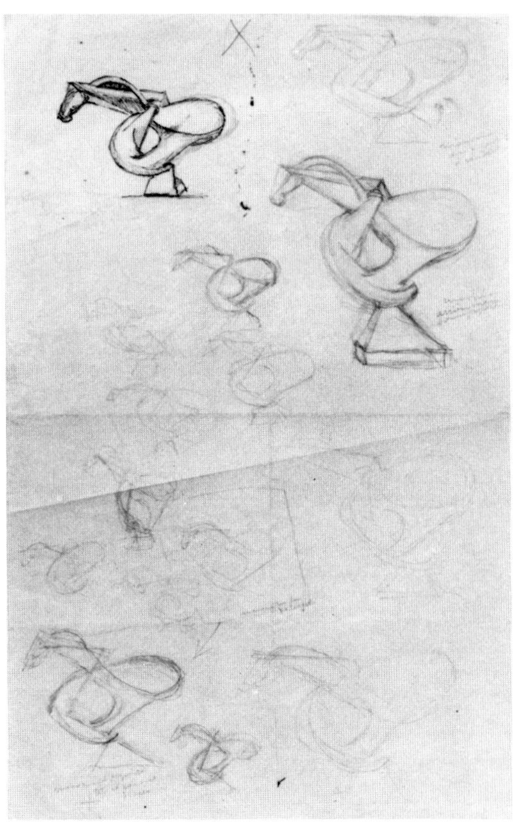

96

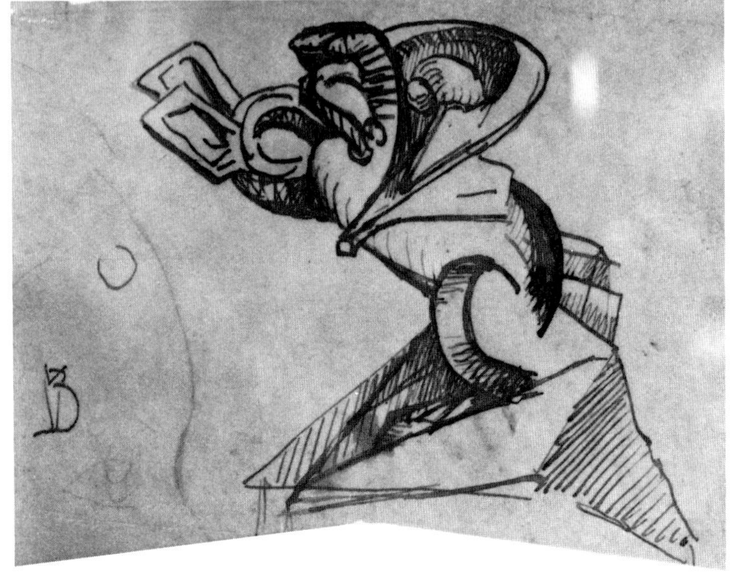

95. Study for "The Horse," c. 1914
Pencil on paper, 7¼ x 10⅝" (18.5 x 27 cm)
Estate of the artist, Paris

96. Study for "The Horse," c. 1914
India ink on paper, 5⅛ x 6¾" (13 x 17 cm)
Estate of the artist, Paris

97. Sketches for "The Horse," c. 1914
Ink and pencil on paper, 12⅛ x 7⅞" (30.9 x 20 cm)
Estate of the artist, Paris

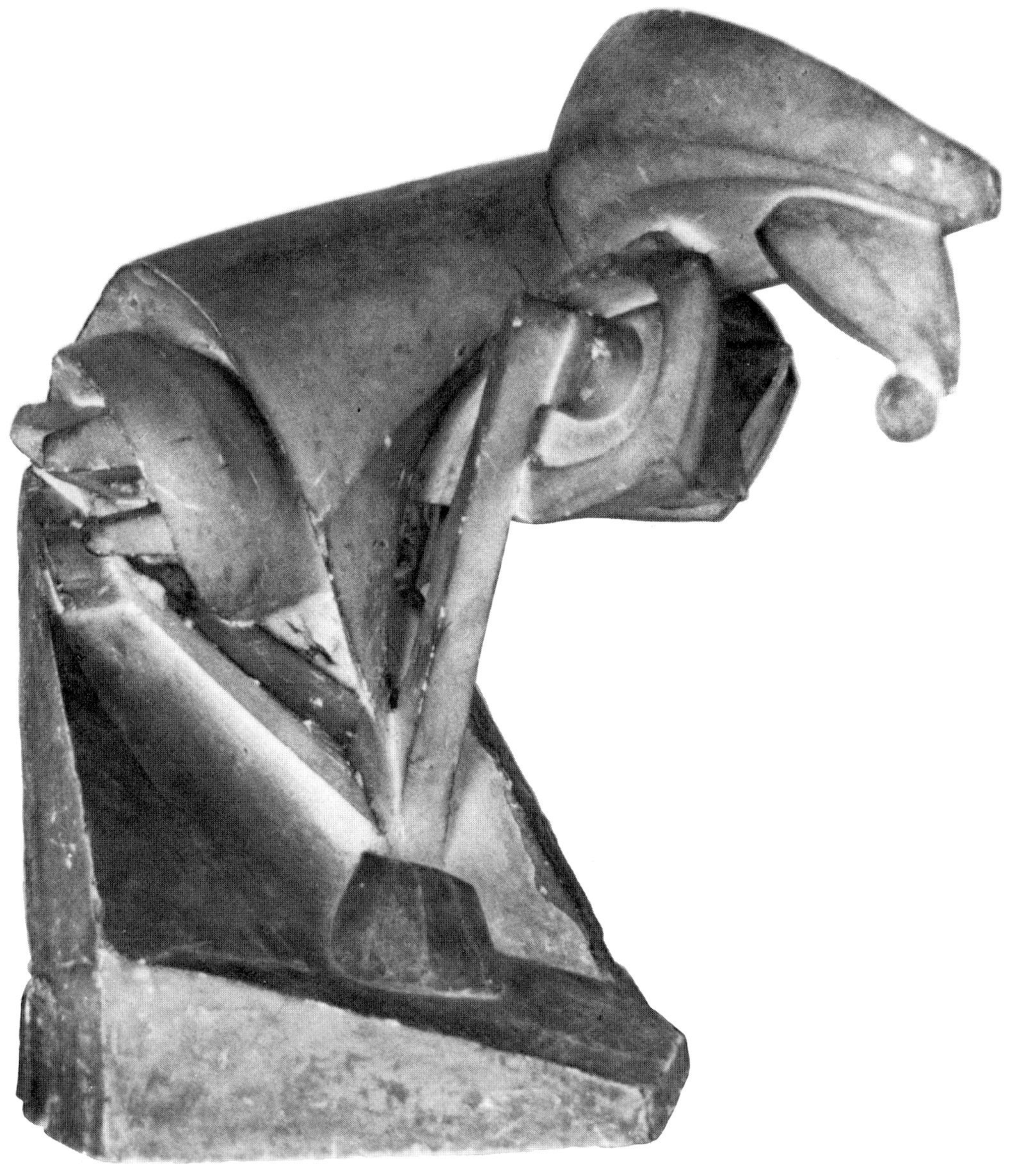

98

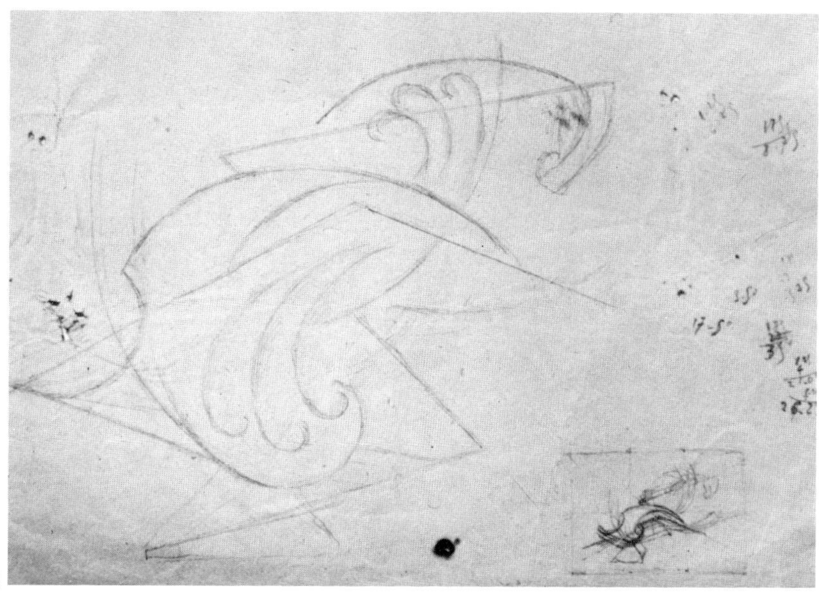

99

98. The Horse, 1914
Plaster, 17½ x 17½ x 8″ (44.5 x 44.5 x 20.3 cm)
Private collection

99. Study for "The Horse," c. 1914
Pencil on paper, 8¼ x 12″ (21 x 30.6 cm)
Estate of the artist, Paris

Albert Gleizes
1 8 8 1 – 1 9 5 3

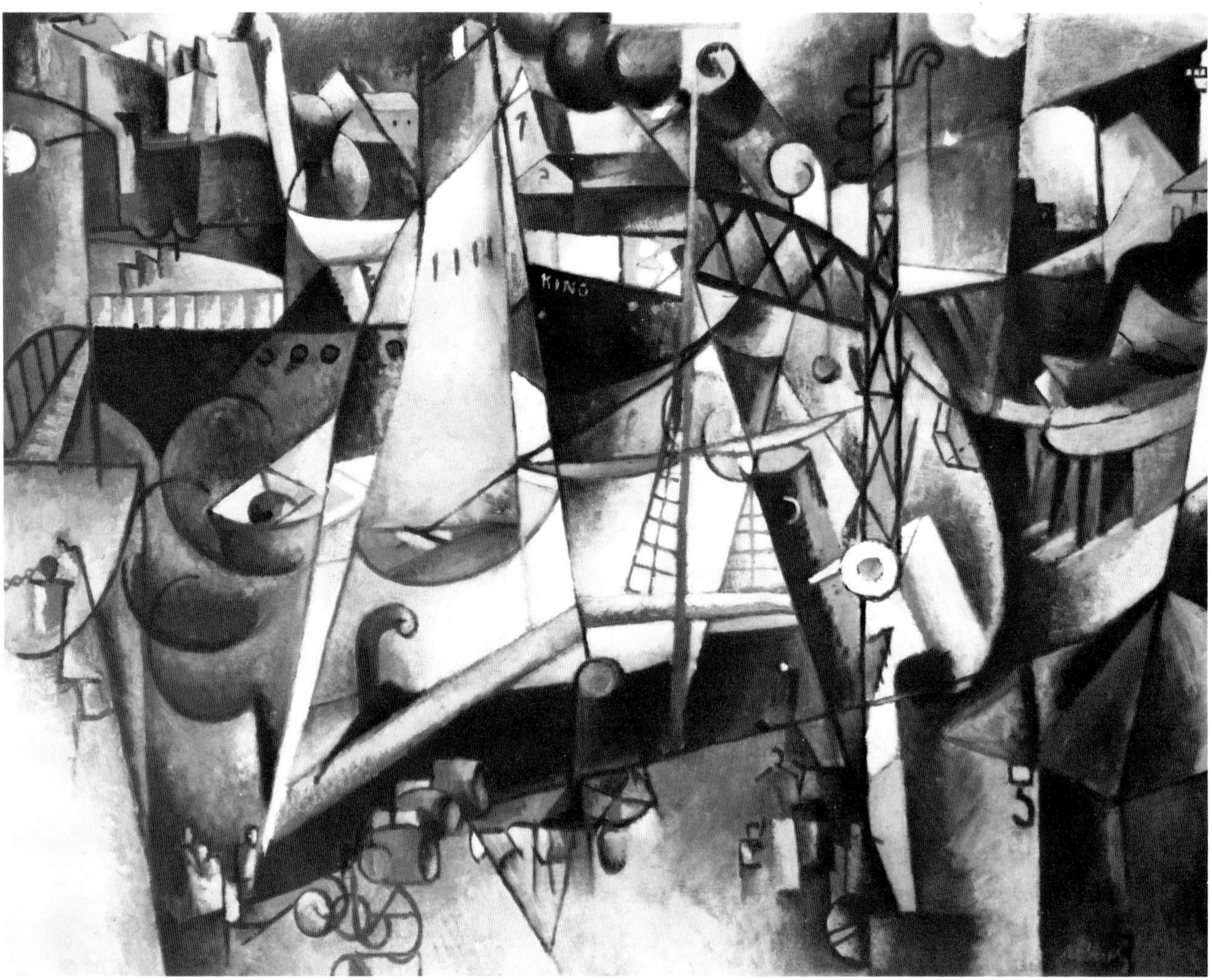

100

100. The Port, 1912
Oil on canvas, $35\frac{1}{2} \times 45\frac{7}{8}$" (90.2 x 116.5 cm)
The Art Gallery of Ontario, Toronto
Gift from the Junior Women's Committee Fund, 1955
Exhibition: Paris, Société des Artistes Indépendants, *29e Exposition,* March 19–May 18, 1913, no. 1294

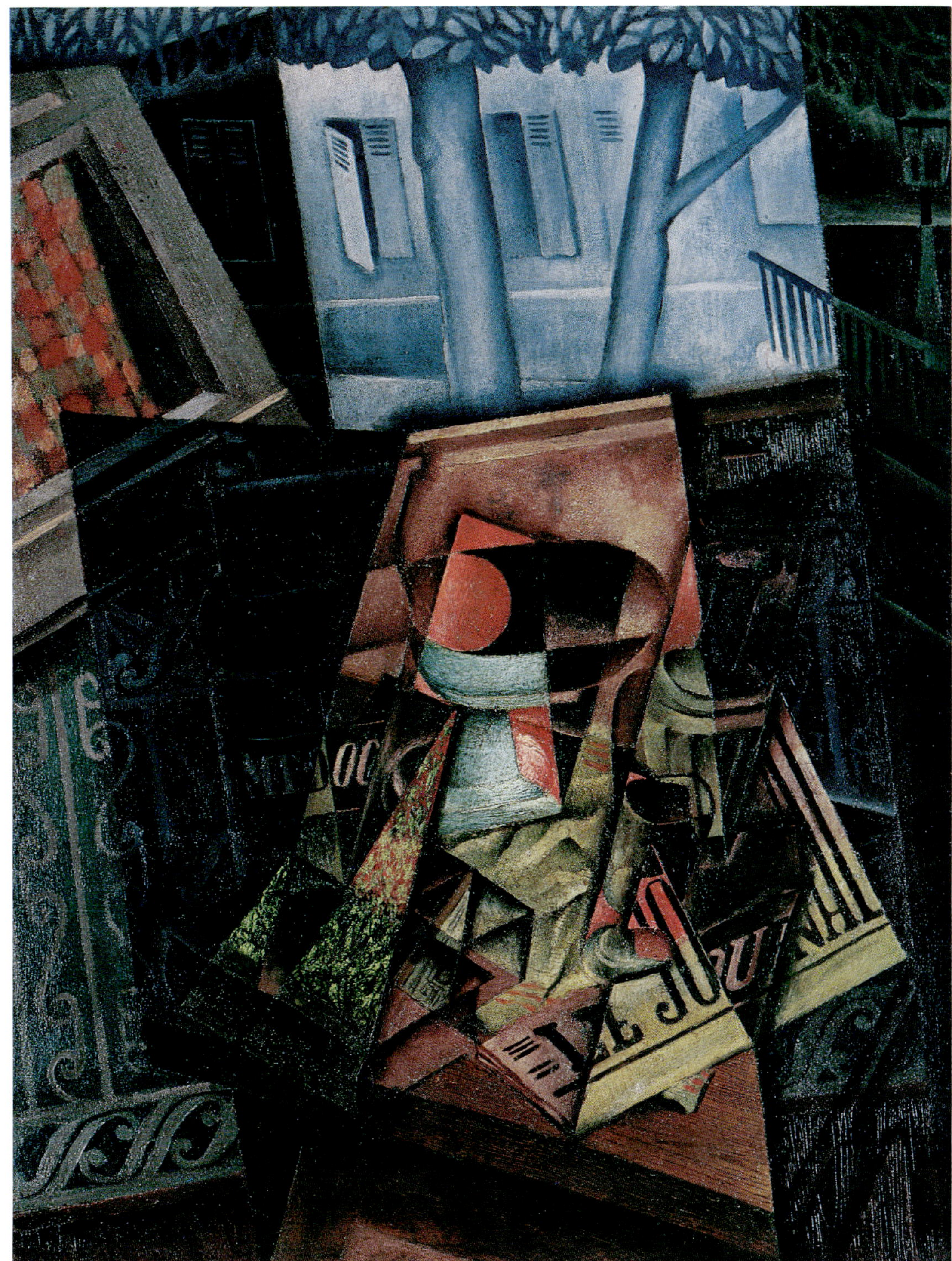

101

101. Still Life Before an Open Window (Place Ravignan), 1915
Oil on canvas, 45⅞ x 35⅛" (116.5 x 89.2 cm)
Philadelphia Museum of Art
The Louise and Walter Arensberg Collection

Frantisek Kupka
1 8 7 1 – 1 9 5 7

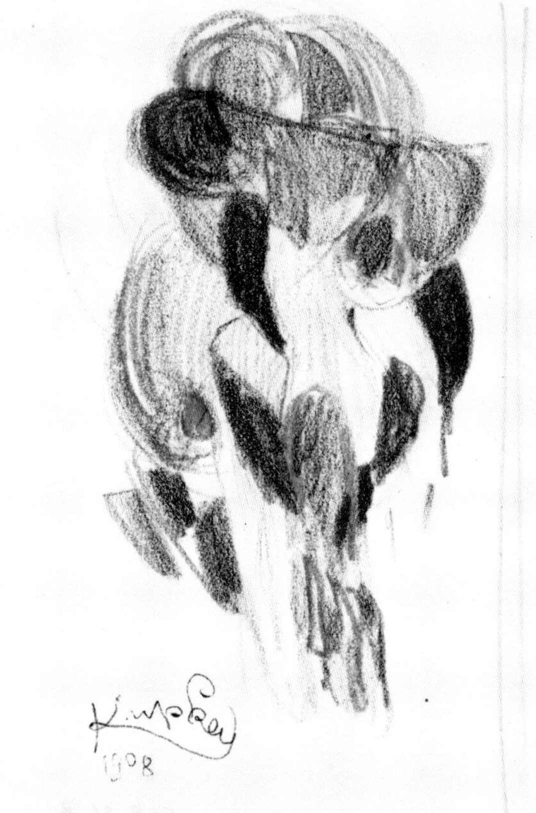

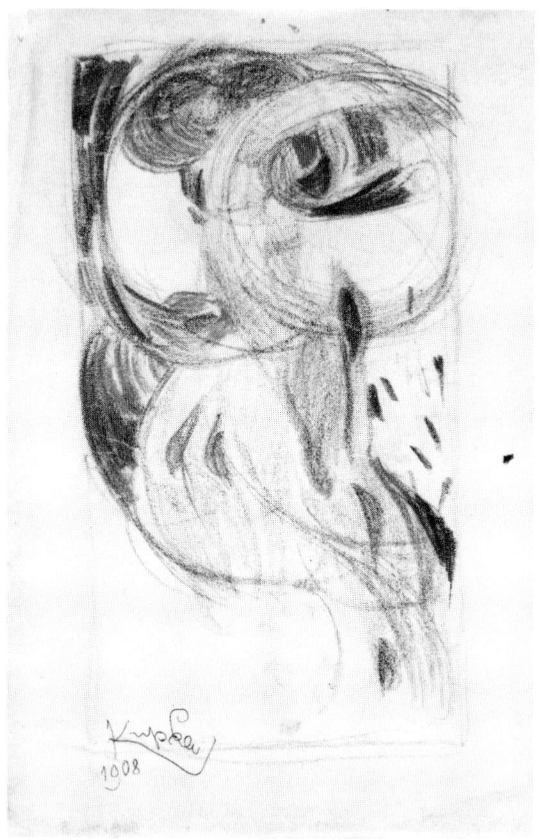

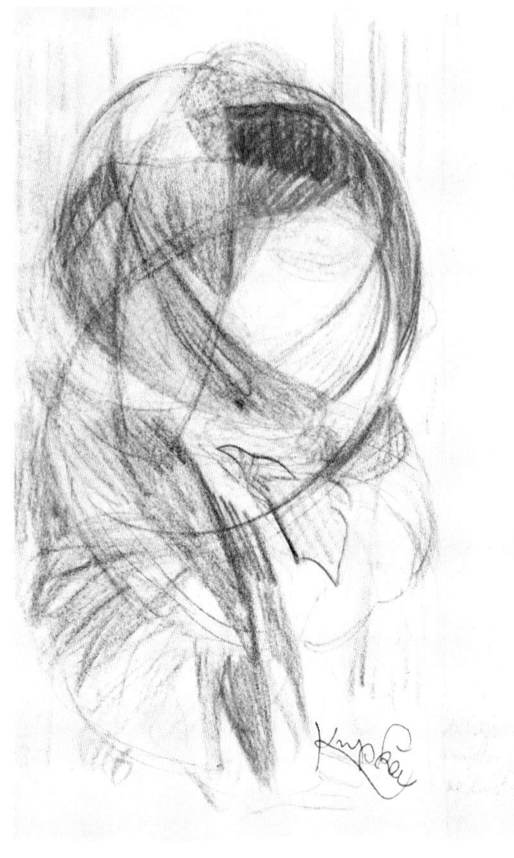

102

102. Studies after "Little Girl with a Ball," 1908–9
Colored pencil and graphite pencil on three sheets of paper, mounted together
Left: 10⅝ x 8¼" (26.9 x 21 cm); right: 8¼ x 7½" (21 x 19 cm); bottom: 6⅝ x 6" (16.8 x 15.2 cm)
The Museum of Modern Art, New York
Gift of Mr. and Mrs. Frantisek Kupka, 1956

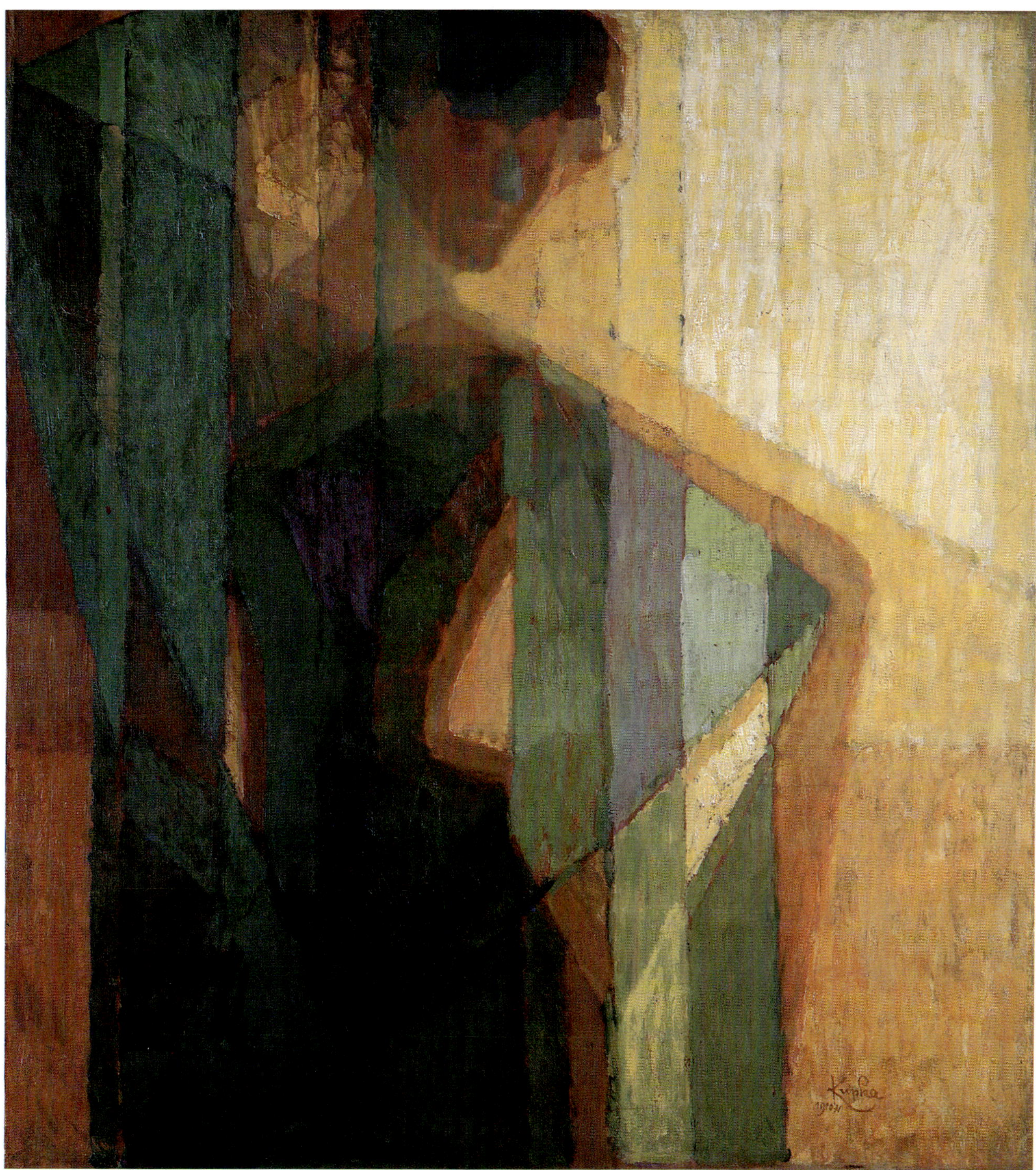

103

103. Planes by Colors, 1910–11
Oil on canvas, 42⅞ x 39¼" (109 x 99.5 cm)
Musée National d'Art Moderne
Centre Georges Pompidou, Paris
Exhibition: Paris, Société des Artistes Indépendants, *28e Exposition,* March 20–May 16, 1912, no. 1833, 1834, or 1835

Fernand Léger

1881–1955

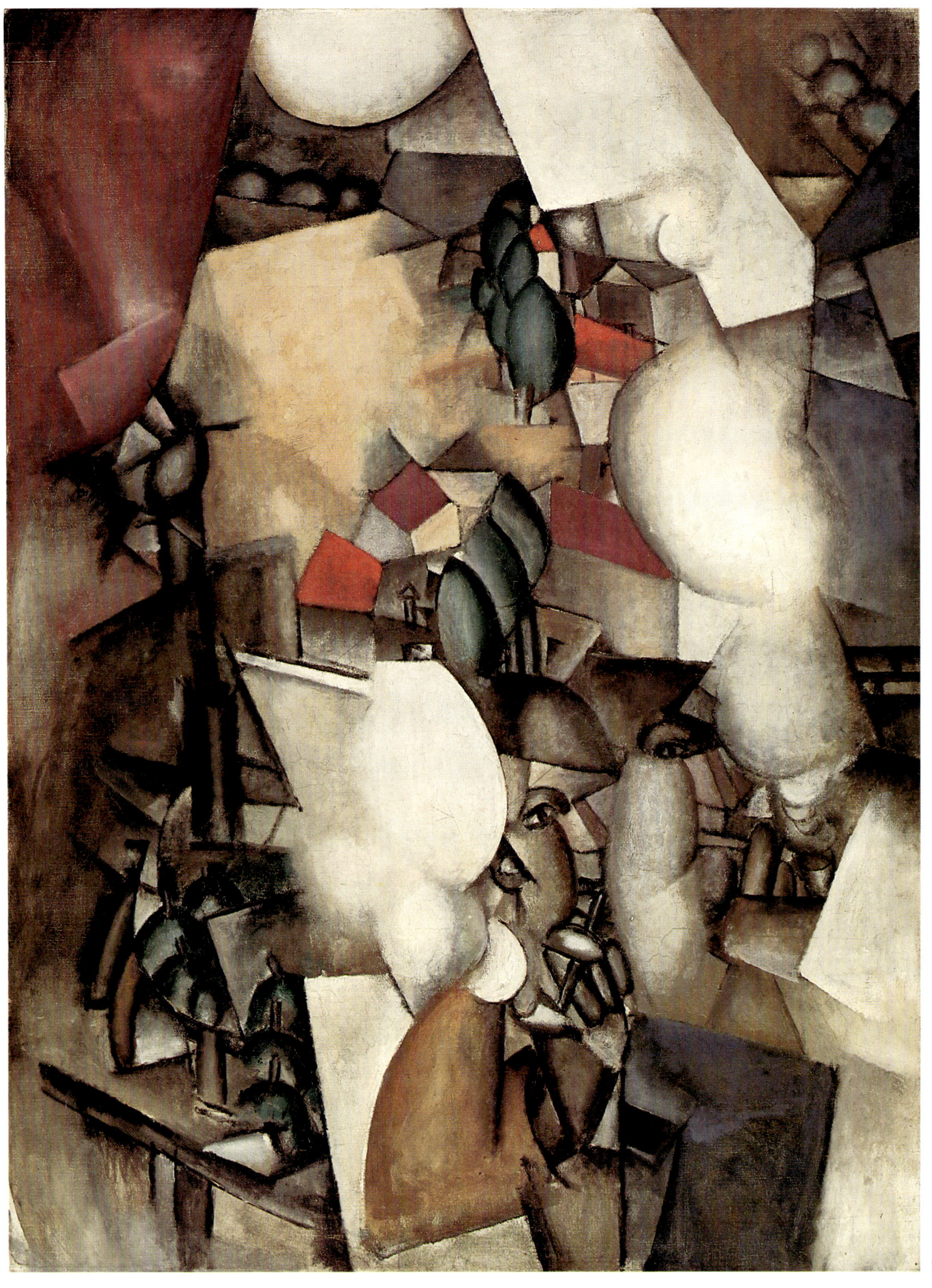

104

104. The Smokers, 1911–12
Oil on canvas, 51 x 38" (129.5 x 96.5 cm)
The Solomon R. Guggenheim Museum, New York
Gift of Solomon R. Guggenheim, 1938

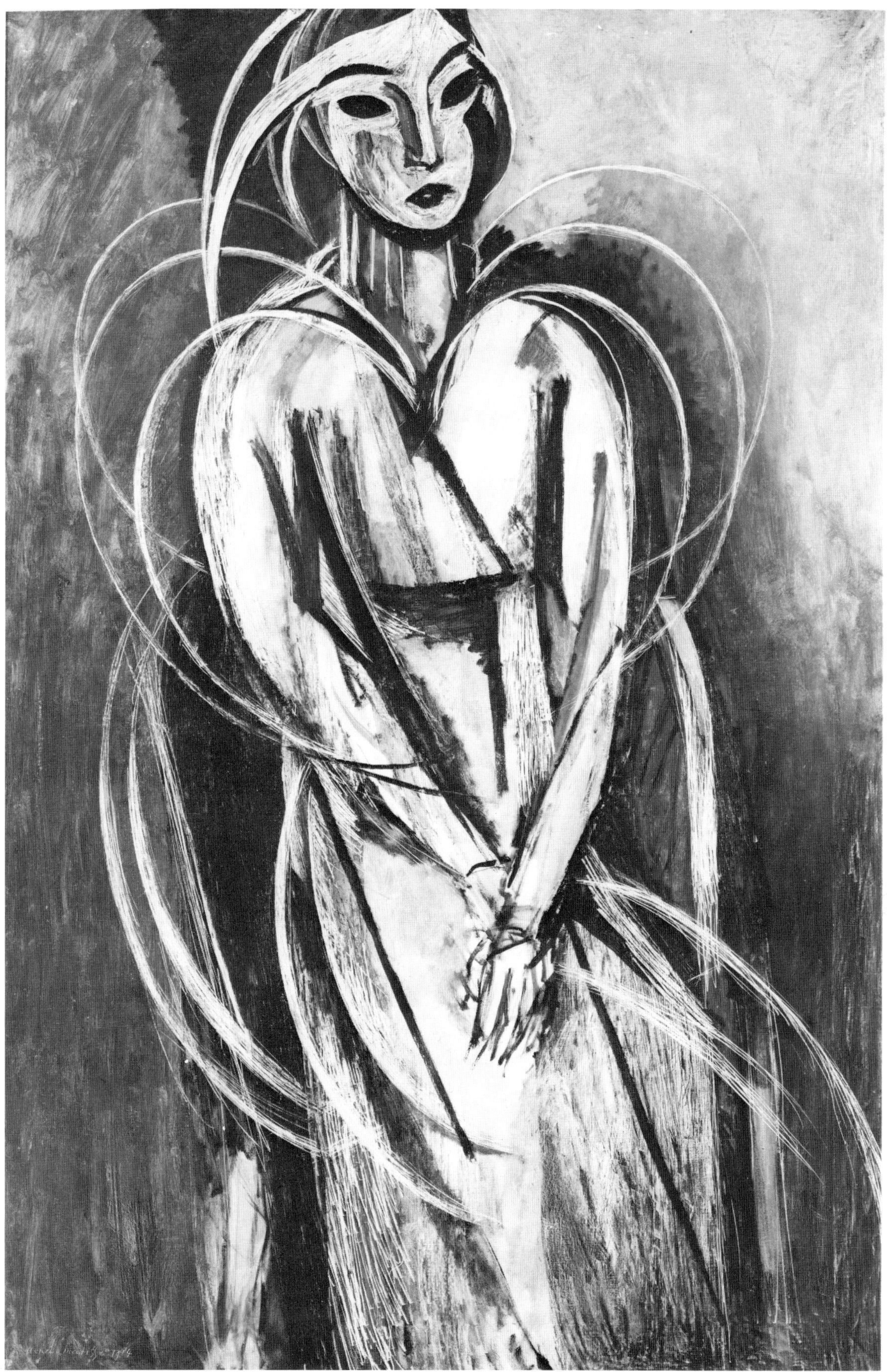

105

105. Mlle Yvonne Landsberg, 1914
Oil on canvas, 58 x 38½" (147.3 x 97.8 cm)
Philadelphia Museum of Art
The Louise and Walter Arensberg Collection
Exhibition: New York, Montross Gallery, *Henri Matisse,*
January 20–February 27, 1915, no. 62, repro.

Jean Metzinger

1 8 8 3 – 1 9 5 6

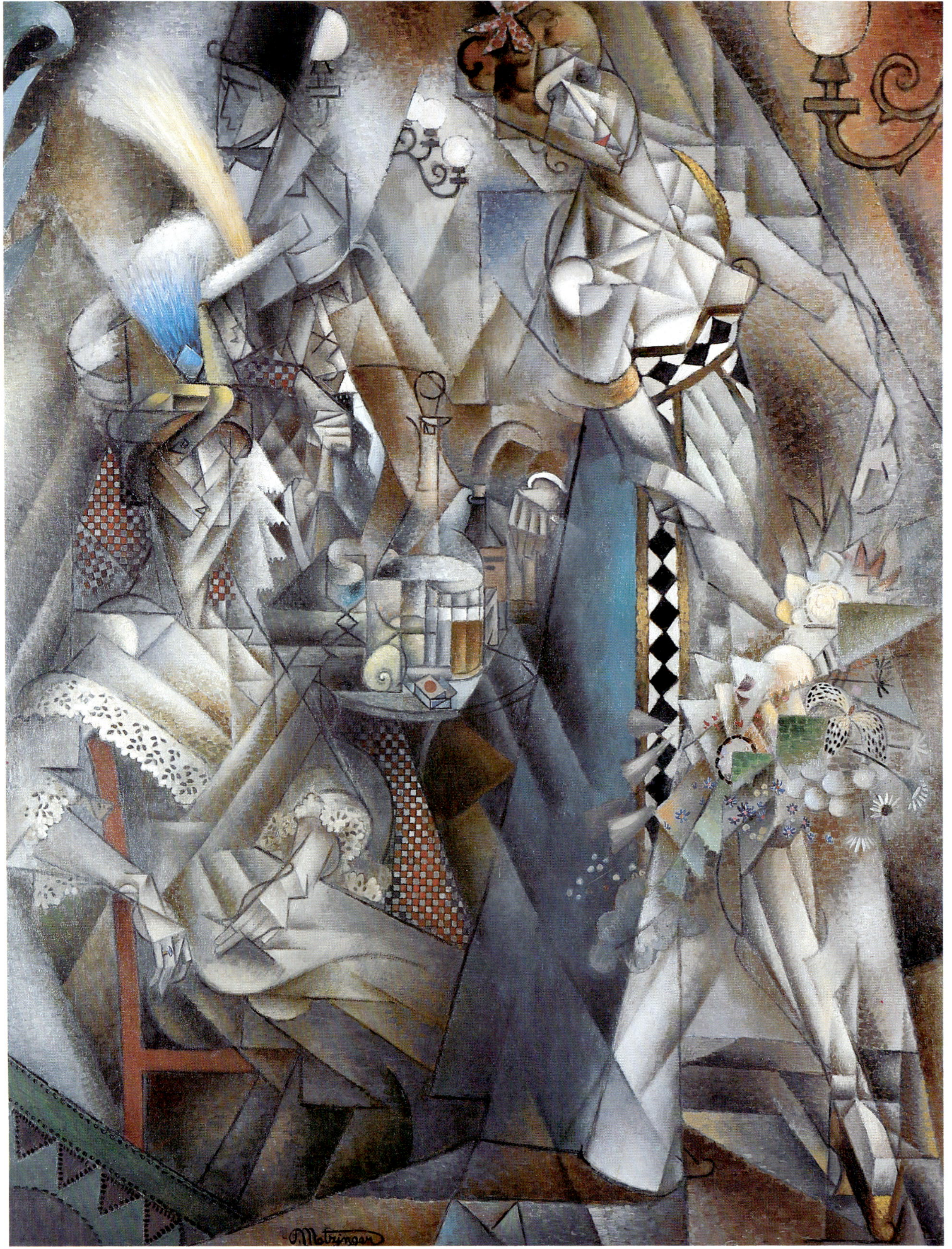

106

106. Dancer in a Café, 1912
Oil on canvas, 57½ x 45″ (146.1 x 114.3 cm)
Albright-Knox Art Gallery, Buffalo
General Purchase Funds, 1957
Exhibition: Paris, *Salon d'Automne, 10ᵉ Exposition,*
October 1–November 8, 1912, no. 1195

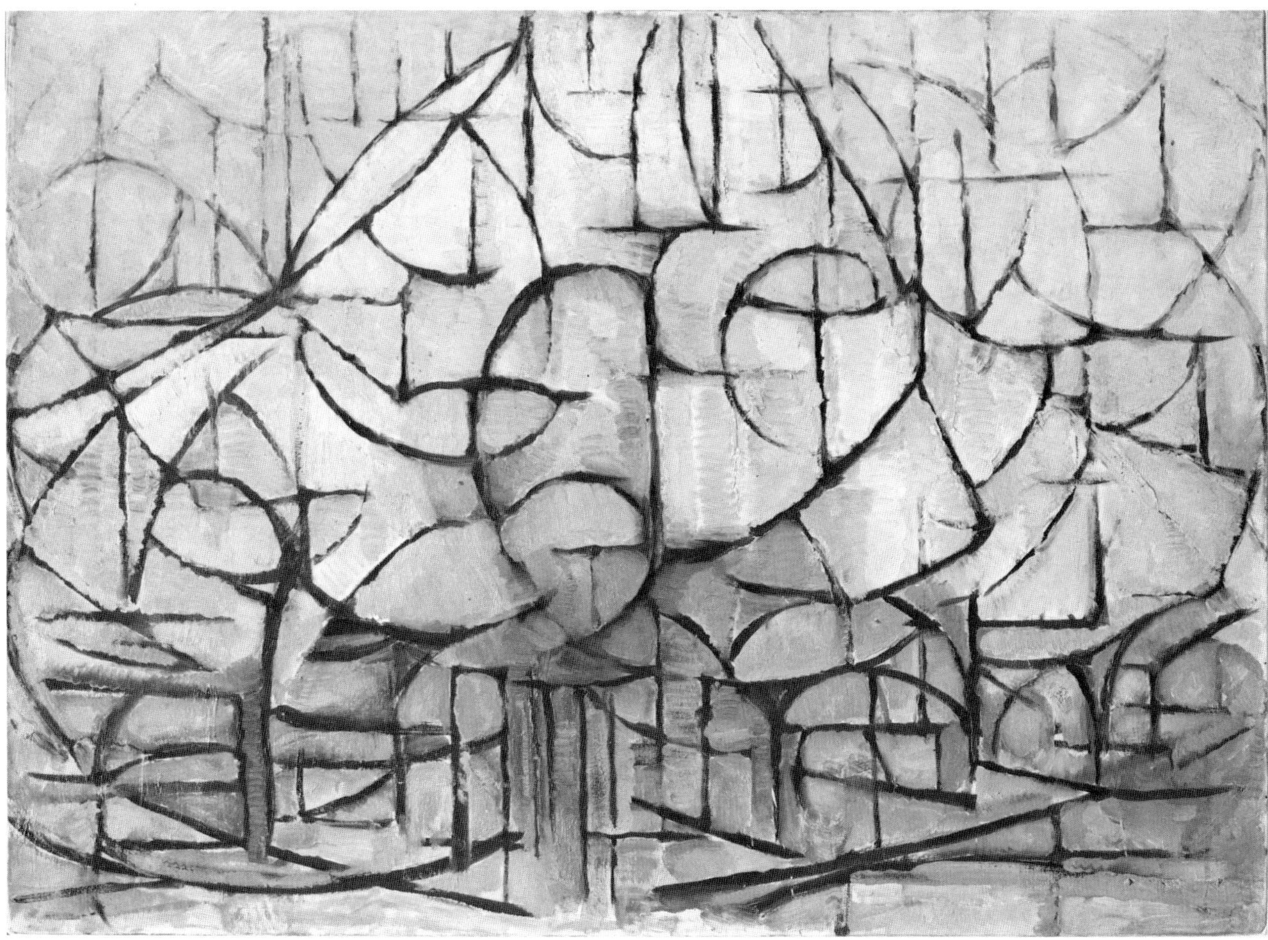

107

107. Trees in Bloom, 1912
Oil on canvas, 23⅝ x 33½" (60 x 85.1 cm)
Private collection
Exhibitions: Amsterdam, Stedelijk Museum, *Moderne Kunst Kring,* October 6–November 7, 1912, no. 159, repro.; Paris, Société des Artistes Indépendants, *29e Exposition,* March 19–May 18, 1913, no. 2136 (?)

Francis Picabia
1 8 7 9 – 1 9 5 3

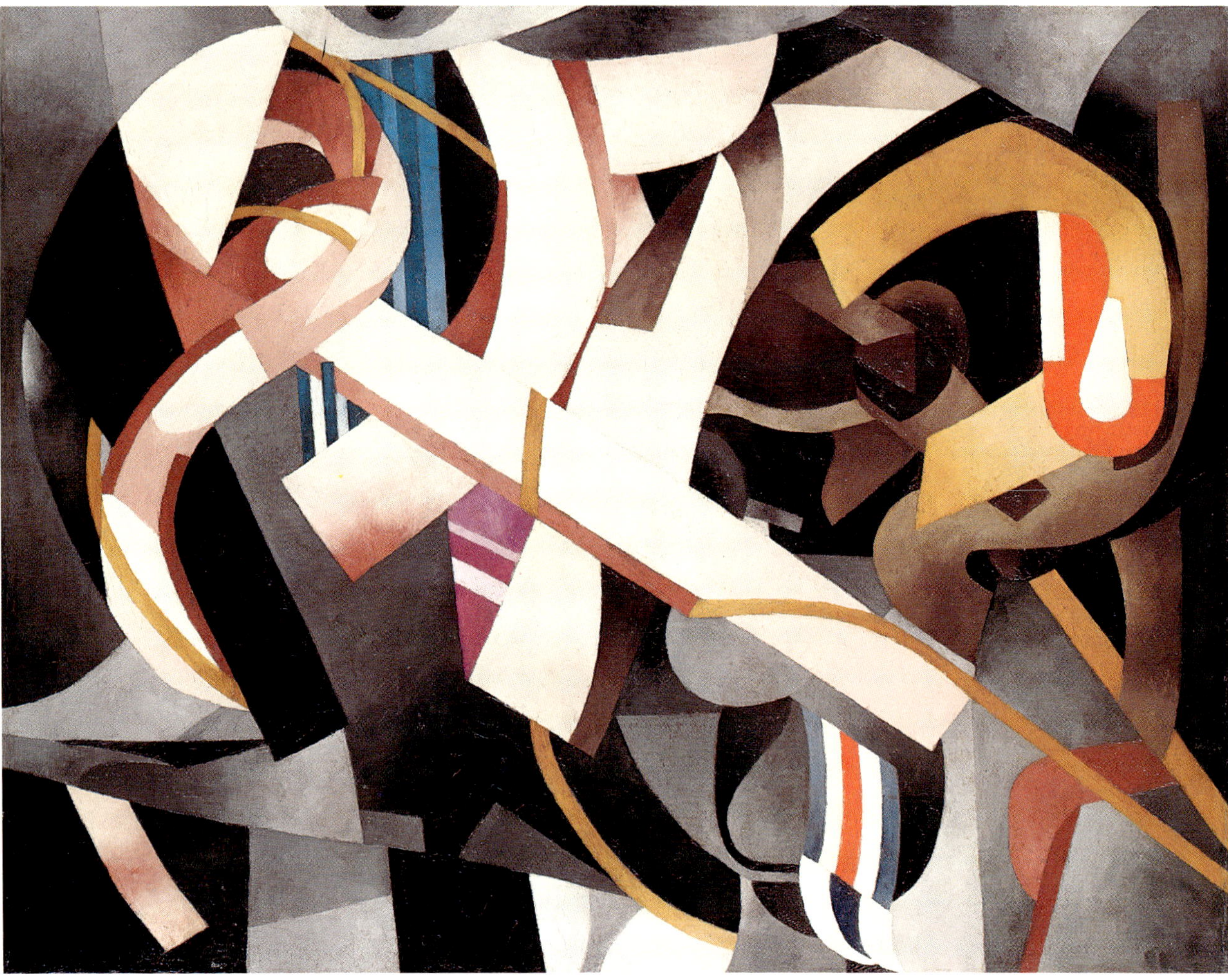

108

108. Physical Culture, 1913
Oil on canvas, 35⅜ x 46" (89.9 x 116.8 cm)
Philadelphia Museum of Art
The Louise and Walter Arensberg Collection
Exhibition: Paris, Société des Artistes Indépendants, *30*ᵉ
Exposition, March 1–April 30, 1914, no. 2619

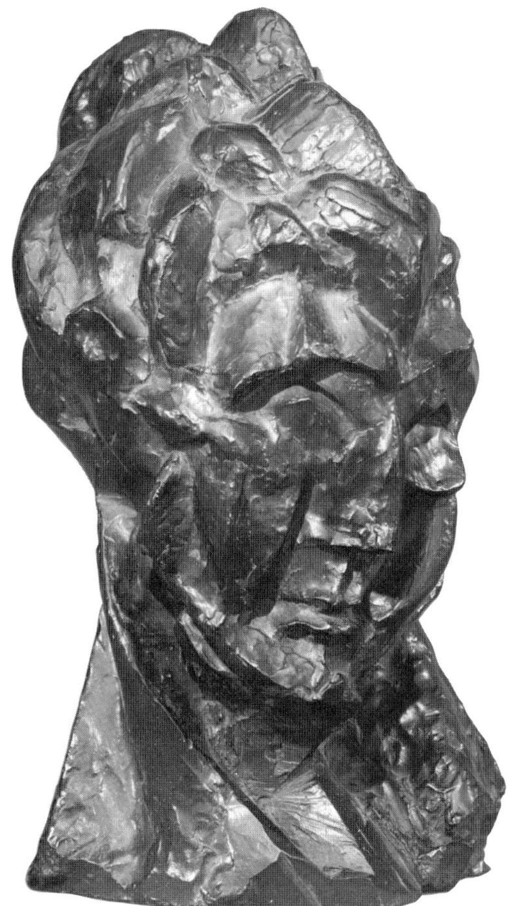

109

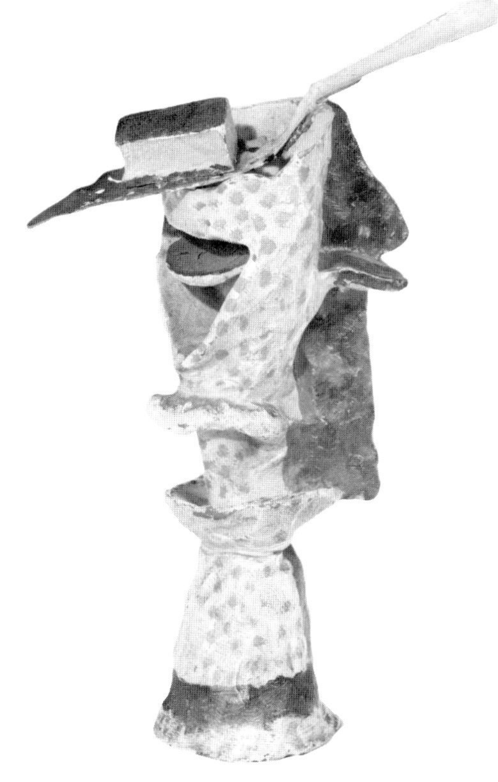

110

109. Head of a Woman (Fernande), 1909 (cast 1960)
Bronze, 16 x 9⅜ x 10⅜" (40.9 x 24 x 26.2 cm)
Hirshhorn Museum and Sculpture Garden,
Smithsonian Institution, Washington, D.C.

110. Glass of Absinthe, 1914
Painted bronze with silver-plated spoon,
8⅞ x 4¾ x 3⅜" (22.5 x 12.1 x 8.6 cm)
Philadelphia Museum of Art
A. E. Gallatin Collection

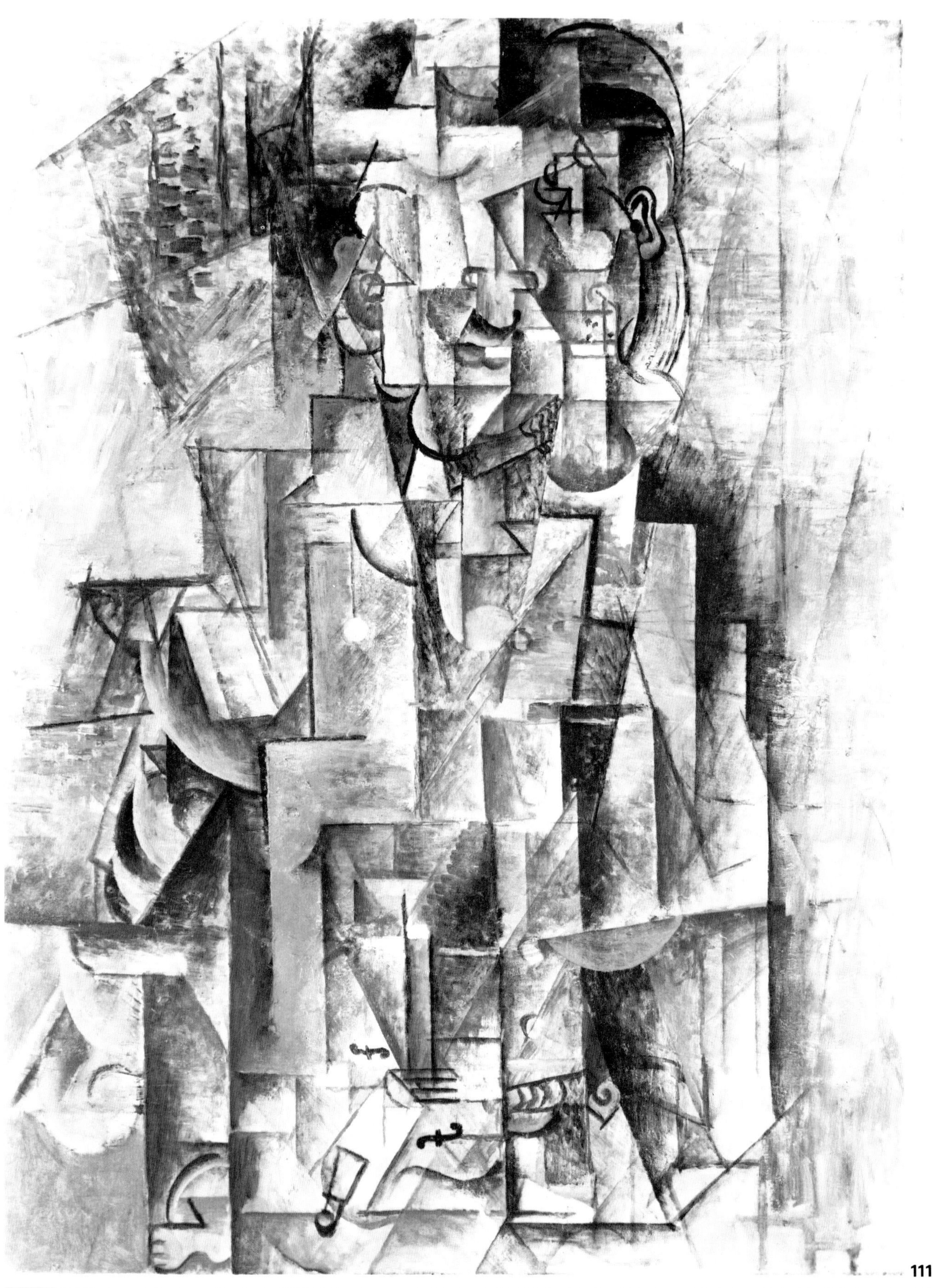

111

111. Man with a Violin, 1912
Oil on canvas, 39⅜ x 28¾" (100 x 73 cm)
Philadelphia Museum of Art
The Louise and Walter Arensberg Collection

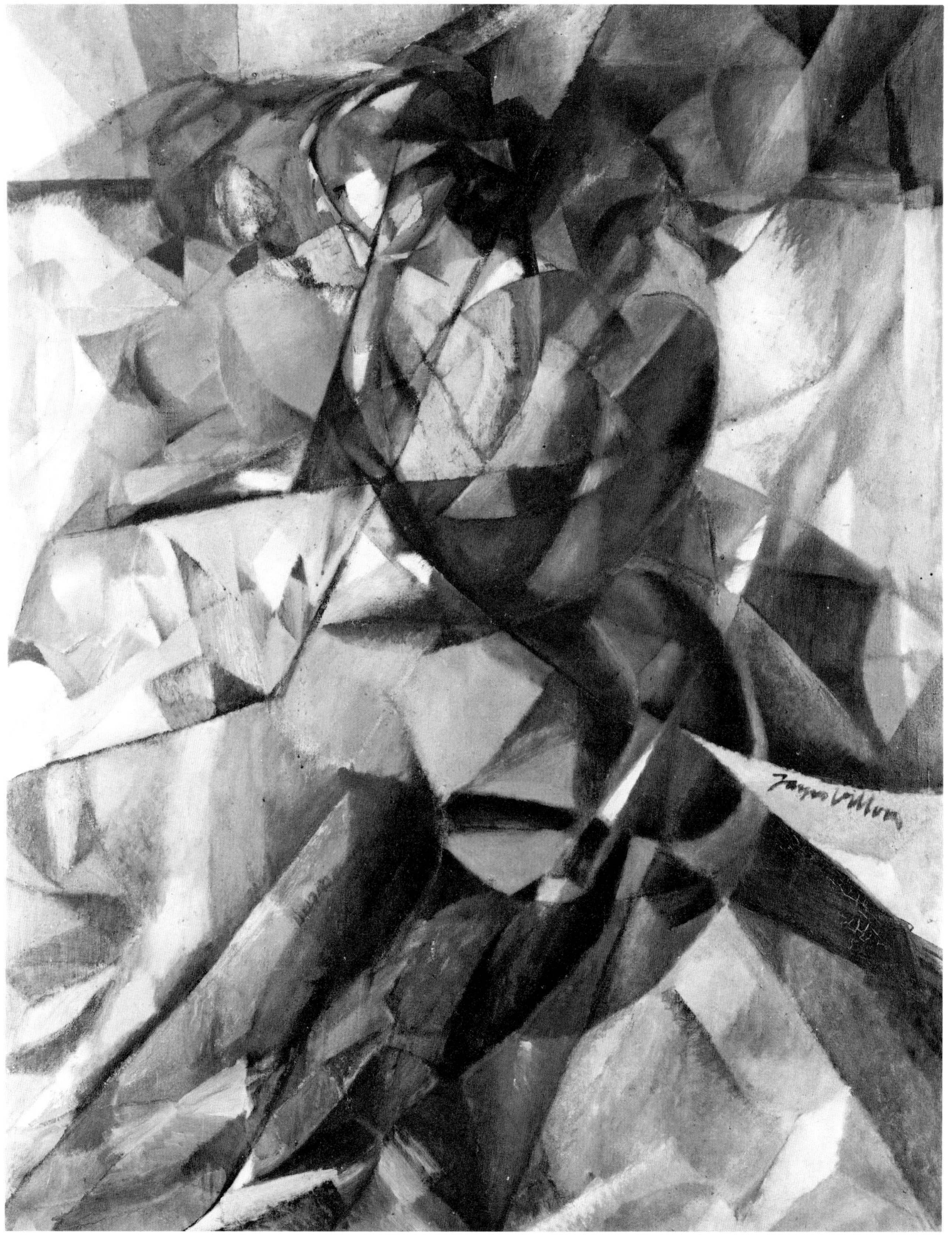

112

112. Young Girl, 1912
Oil on canvas, 57¾ x 45½" (146.7 x 115.6 cm)
Philadelphia Museum of Art
The Louise and Walter Arensberg Collection
Exhibitions: Paris, Galerie La Boëtie, *Salon de "La Section d'Or,"* October 10–30, 1912, no. 166; New York, Armory of the 69th Regiment, *International Exhibition of Modern Art,* February 17–March 15, 1913, no. 452

Jacques Villon

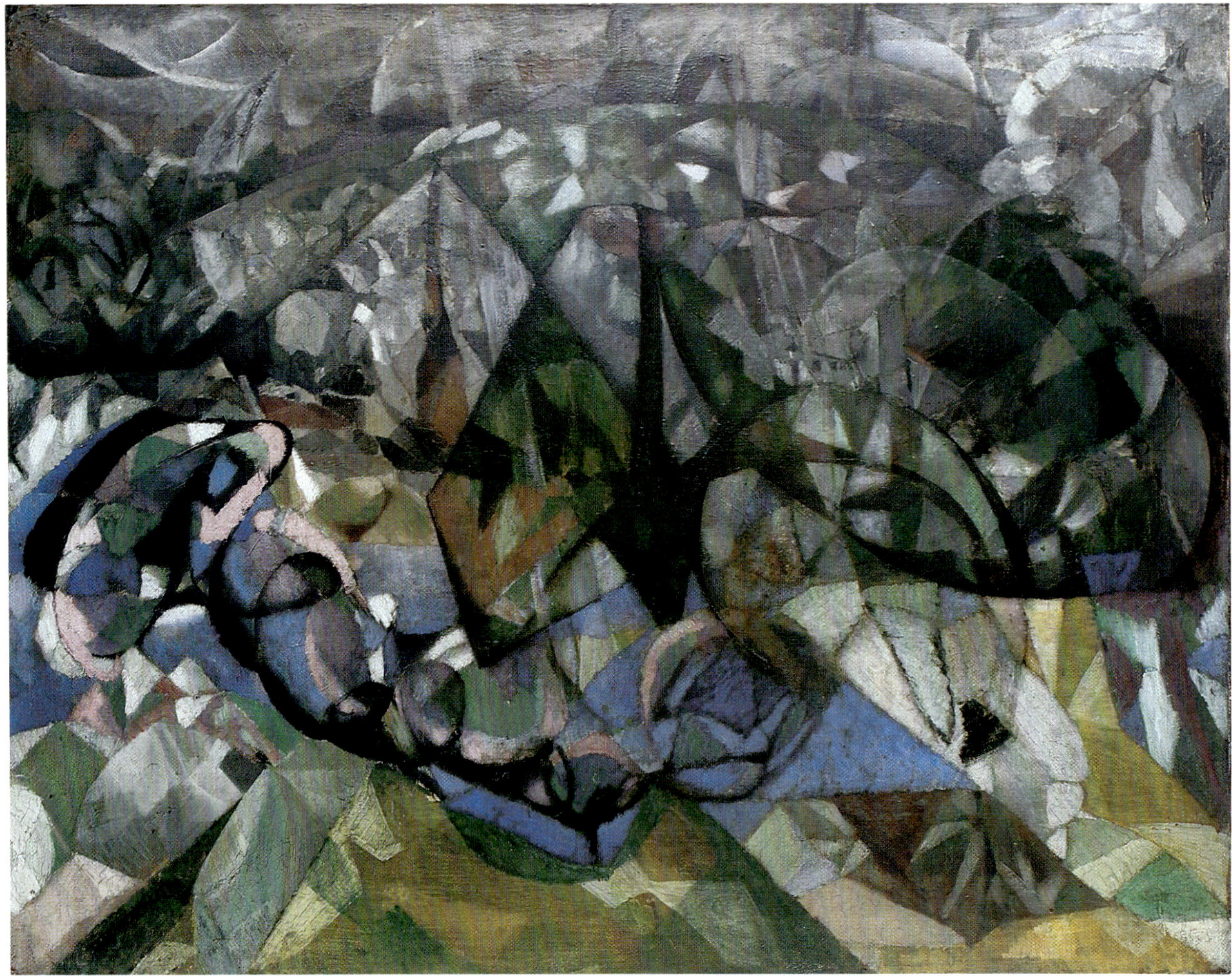

113

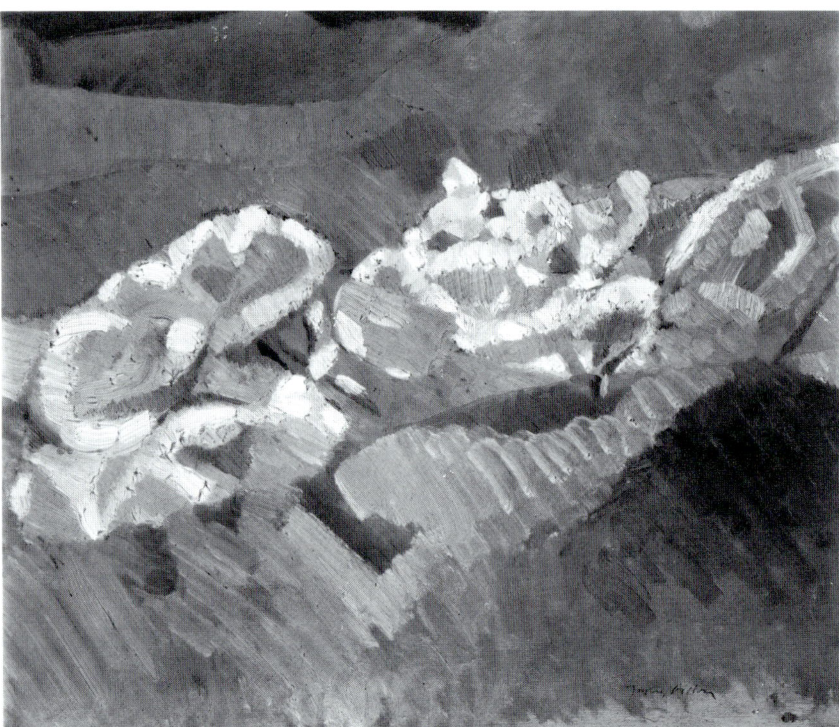

114

113. Puteaux: Smoke and Trees in Bloom, 1912
Oil on canvas, 45¼ x 58½" (114.9 x 148.6 cm)
Mr. and Mrs. Dan Johnson, New York
Exhibitions: Paris, Galerie La Boëtie, *Salon de "La Section d'Or,"* October 10–30, 1912, no. 168; New York, Armory of the 69th Regiment, *International Exhibition of Modern Art,* February 17–March 15, 1913, no. 444

114. Study for "Puteaux: Smoke and Trees in Bloom," No. 2, 1912
Oil on canvas, 18¼ x 21¾" (46.4 x 55.2 cm)
Philadelphia Museum of Art
The Louise and Walter Arensberg Collection
Exhibition: New York, Armory of the 69th Regiment, *International Exhibition of Modern Art,* February 17–March 15, 1913, no. 447

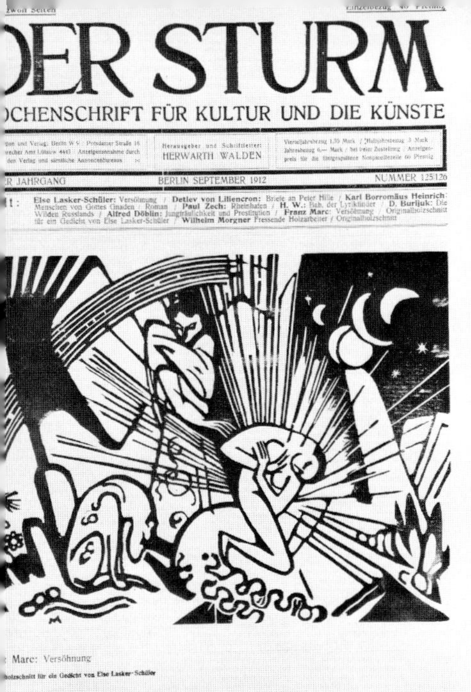

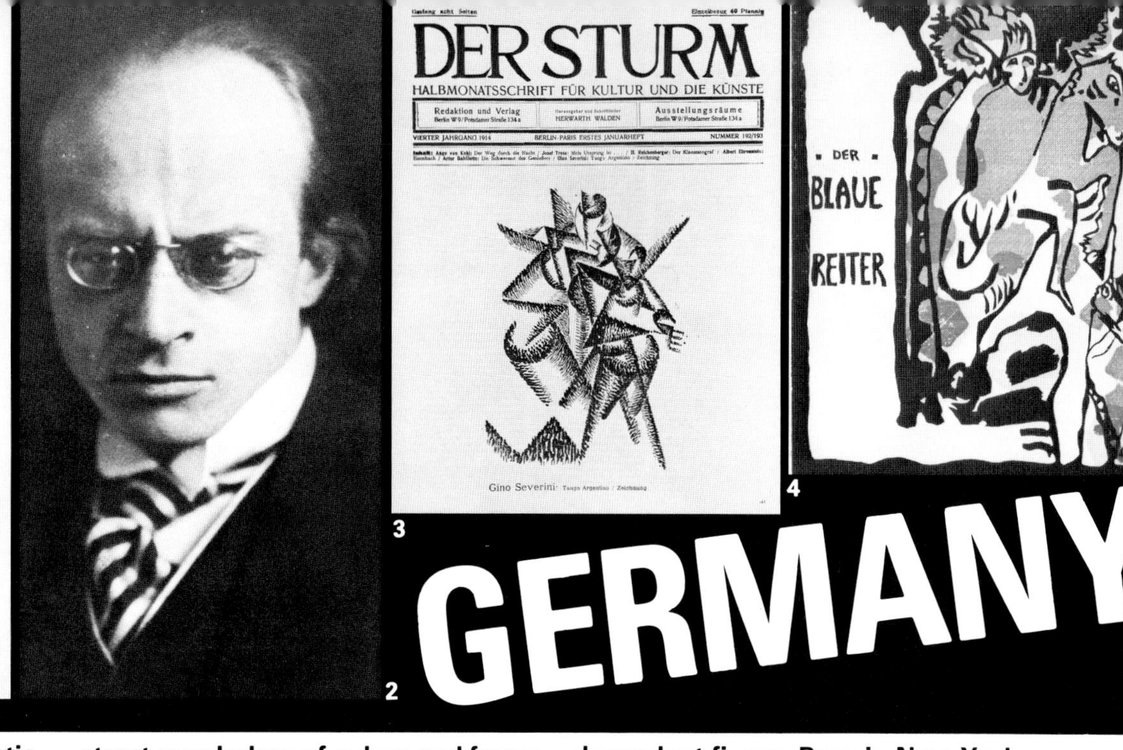

2 3 4

GERMANY

The Futurists received a sympathetic hearing in Germany, thanks to a number of circumstances favorable to the reception of their ideas and their work. Ernst Ludwig Kirchner, Erich Heckel, and other artists of the Brücke group, founded in Dresden in 1905 and transplanted to Berlin by 1911, had formed their own styles before any contact with Futurist paintings. But their anti-academic stance and the vivid colors and expressive crudeness of their pictures had affinities with the Futurists' claim to be the "primitives of a new sensibility." Nor were the sources of German Expressionism in the intensely emotional paintings of Edvard Munch and Vincent Van Gogh and the sinuous line of Jugendstil so far removed from the Italians' own early interests.

It was Herwarth Walden (1878–1941), the Berlin editor, dealer, and impresario who was largely responsible for the dissemination of Futurist art and theory in Germany, a country (like Italy) without a single, powerful cultural center such as Paris. Walden's weekly journal *Der Sturm*, founded in 1910, began to publish the Futurist manifestos early in 1912 and the Futurists' Paris show was booked in April as the second in Walden's program of exhibitions at the new Der Sturm gallery in Berlin. He arranged for its subsequent travel to several cities, including Cologne and Munich, and found a German buyer for many of the Italians' pictures.

The emergence of the Blaue Reiter group in Munich (which Walden also promoted) intersected with the Futurist invasion. Wassily Kandinsky, who had moved to Munich from Russia in 1896 and had developed his own increasingly abstract vocabulary of colors and forms to express inner feelings, was a leader in the Neue Kunstler Vereinigung, which mounted an important international exhibition in the fall of 1910. As the Vereinigung turned increasingly conservative, Kandinsky and Franz Marc organized an exhibition in December 1911 under the name Der Blaue Reiter and later published an almanac of the same name. Marc had been exposed to the avant-garde art in Paris during a trip in 1907, and subsequently made a thorough study of anatomy, which served as preparation for his use of animal subjects to express a pantheistic world view. While Kandinsky kept in touch with avant-garde artists in Russia and corresponded warmly with Robert Delaunay in Paris, he remained little affected by the art or ideas of his colleagues. The sense of speed and turbulent movement in his *Improvisations* and *Compositions* of 1912–14 was certainly not derived from Futurist painting; he was an independent force whose innovations Apollinaire, Marinetti, and even Boccioni acknowledged with admiration. Marc and his young friend August Macke were more deeply touched by their encounters both with contemporary French painting (they visited Delaunay in the fall of 1912) and with Futurism. Marc wrote a brief article defending the Futurists in the October issue of *Der Sturm*, and his apocalyptic paintings of 1913–14 revealed his appropriation of Futurist "force-lines" to evoke the tragic history of the Tyrol or the mysterious workings of nature.

Lyonel Feininger, who lived in Berlin and exhibited with the Blaue Reiter group in the Erster Deutscher Herbstsalon of 1913, was another independent figure. Born in New York, he had moved to Germany in 1887 and visited Paris in 1906–7 and 1911. His familiarity with Cubist faceting of form mingled with Futurist "force-lines" lent dynamic impetus to his compositions of cities and ships.

The Futurists' frequent theme of modern city life, with its frantic pace, garish night life, and potential for mass uprising, appealed to a wide range of German sensibilities. Kirchner expressed a sense of loneliness and fear in his angular crowd scenes, Ludwig Meidner depicted cities burning and exploding in his "Pathetic" compositions of 1912–14, and somewhat later in Berlin, George Grosz painted a series of nightmarish visions of the city trapped within converging rays of depravity and death. Specific Futurist pictures appear to have caught the attention of German artists: Grosz was fascinated by Boccioni's ***The Laugh*** (no. 29), while the Surrealist painter Max Ernst recalled that the large red numerals in Boccioni's ***The Farewells*** (no. 31) had been of profound significance to him.

1. Franz Marc, *The Reconciliation* (cover of *Der Sturm*, September 1912); 2. Herwarth Walden; 3. Gino Severini, *Argentina Tango* (cover of *Der Sturm*, January 1914); 4. Wassily Kandinsky, cover of *Der Blaue Reiter*, 1914 (second edition), The Robert Gore Rifkind Foundation, Beverly Hills

Lyonel Feininger

1871–1956

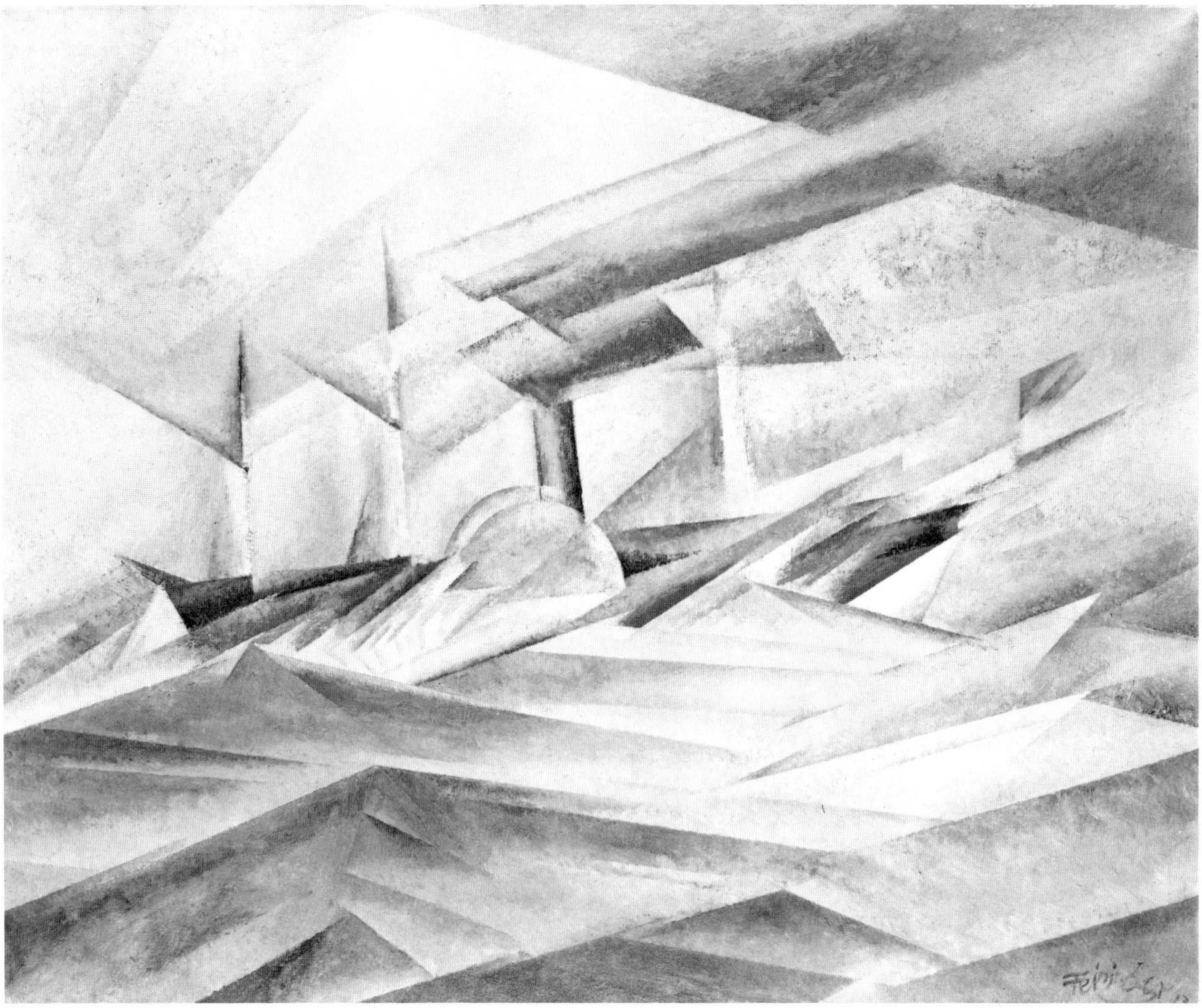

115

115. The Sidewheeler, 1913
Oil on canvas, 31¾ x 39⅝″ (80.6 x 100.6 cm)
The Detroit Institute of Arts
City purchase

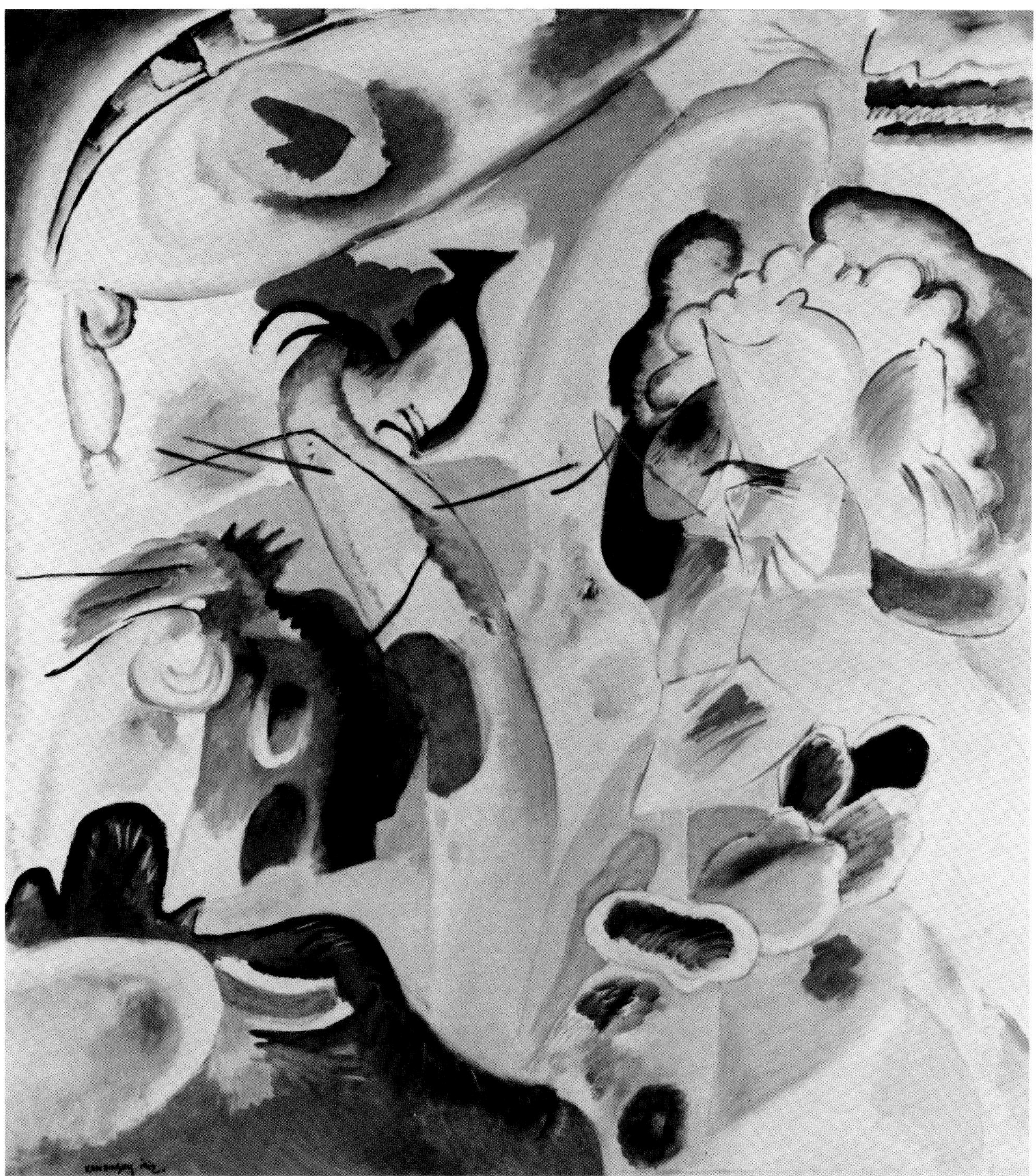

116

116. Improvisation No. 29 (The Swan, No. 160), 1912
Oil on canvas, 41¾ x 38⅛" (106 x 96.8 cm)
Philadelphia Museum of Art
The Louise and Walter Arensberg Collection
Exhibition: London, Royal Albert Hall, *The London Salon of the Allied Artists' Association, Ltd.,* July 1913, no. 285

Franz Marc
1880–1916

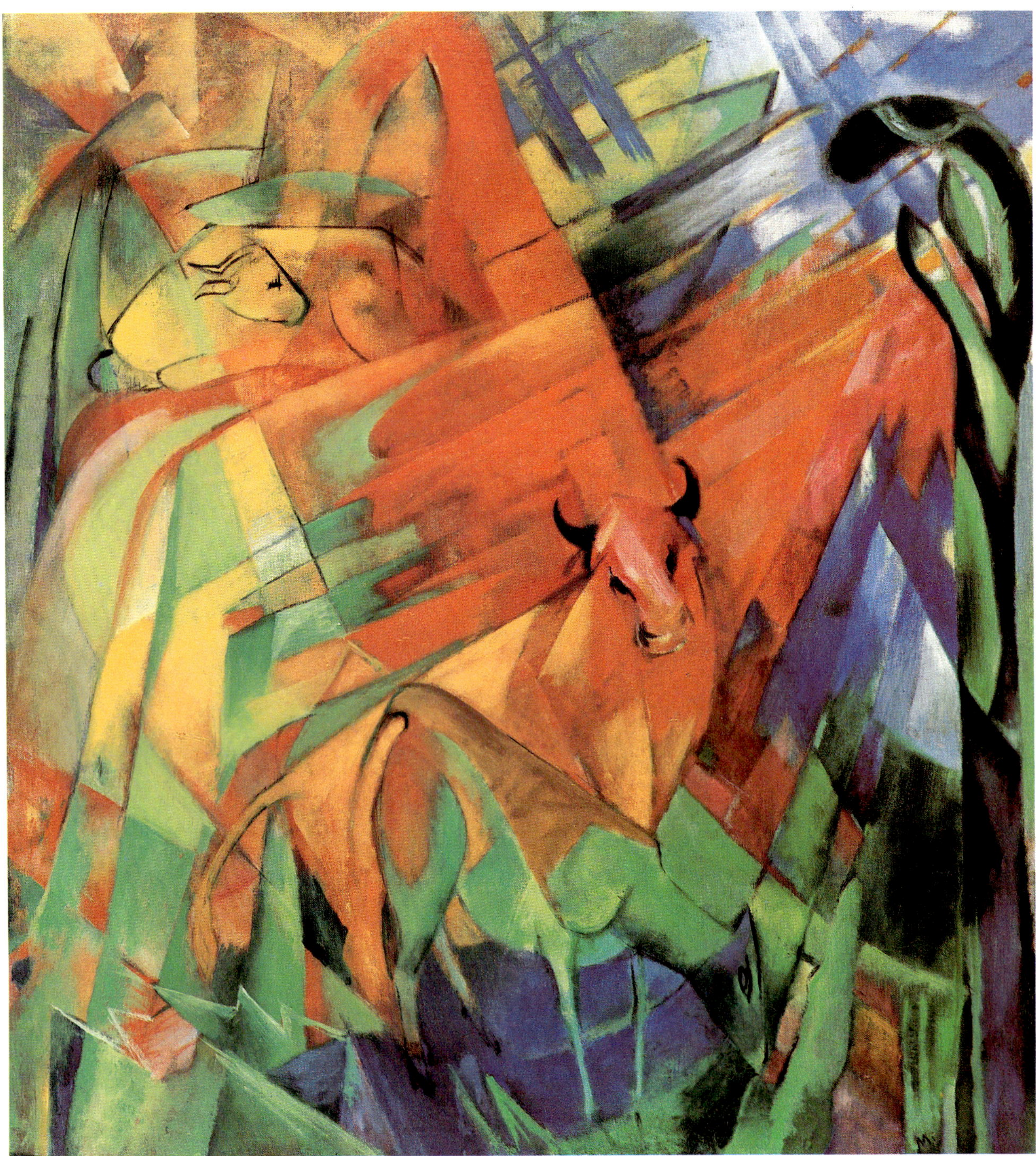

117

117. Painting with Bulls II (Animals in a Landscape), 1914
Oil on canvas, 49⅜ x 39⅛" (125.4 x 99.4 cm)
The Detroit Institute of Arts
Gift of Robert H. Tannahill
Exhibition: Munich, Neue Sezession, *Franz Marc Gedächtnis-Ausstellung,* 1916, no. 145

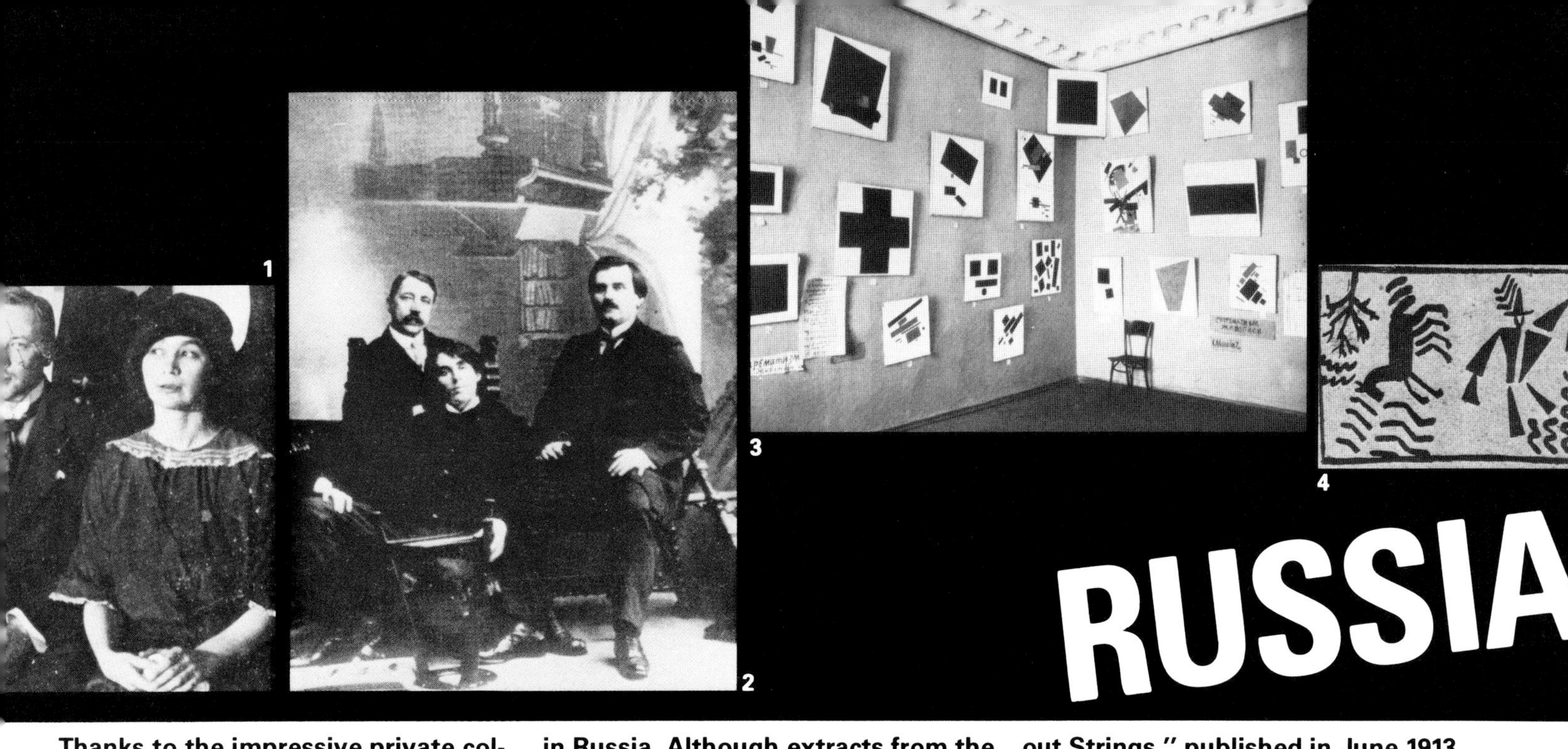

RUSSIA

Thanks to the impressive private collections of modern art in Moscow and to journals and exhibitions sponsored by artists' associations, such as the Golden Fleece, Russian painters were familiar with Post-Impressionism and the work of Matisse and Picasso during the first decade of this century. A liberal climate for art was encouraged by the amateur artist and promoter Dr. Nicolai Kulbin, who urged the exploration of alternative modes of painting and insisted on the necessity of "free art" to respond to the complexity of the human soul. Between 1910 and 1916 alliances of artists and poets formed and reformed, vying with each other in sponsoring radical exhibitions with brash titles such as "Jack of Diamonds," "Donkey's Tail," and "Target."

Extensive but erratic contacts were maintained with contemporary artists in Western Europe. The brothers David and Vladimir Burliuk kept in touch with Wassily Kandinsky and the Blaue Reiter artists in Munich, who were invited to exhibit in Moscow; the painter Alexandra Exter visited Paris frequently, was befriended by Fernand Léger, and returned with photographs and catalogues of the latest French works. Liubov Popova and Nadezhda Udaltzova took studios in Paris during 1912 and 1913 and studied with the Cubist painters Jean Metzinger and Henri Le Fauconnier. But Russian vanguard artists were equally likely to draw upon oriental or folk traditions for inspiration, and a Neo-Primitive movement preceded and overlapped with the European-oriented style of "Cubo-Futurism."

For some reason, no paintings by the Italian Futurists were ever shown in Russia. Although extracts from the Futurist manifestos were translated into Russian as early as 1910, it was not until 1912 that the ideas of Filippo Tommaso Marinetti and the Futurist painters became widely disseminated. David Burliuk traveled to France, Italy, and Germany that spring and returned prepared to deliver slide talks on Futurism. His manifesto "A Slap in the Face of Public Taste," written in December, sounded a defiant Futurist note. Burliuk's crude and vigorous paintings often appropriated Cubist or Futurist elements (such as the running horse with multiple legs) in a Russian context, but the Rayonist paintings and drawings of Mikhail Larionov and Natalia Gontcharova revealed a more sophisticated absorption and expansion of European ideas. A large group of their Rayonist works were shown in the Moscow "Target" exhibition (April 1913), which also included Kasimir Malevich's *Knife Grinder* (no. 122). The year 1913 was crucial for Russian Futurism—a much broader and more variegated movement than its Italian counterpart. Larionov published several essays and a manifesto for Rayonism (which remained a two-person movement), while Malevich explored several Futurist subjects (such as *Simultaneous Death in an Airplane and on the Railway*) and moved gradually toward an alogical juxtaposition of images in a collage style. The poets Alexei Kruchenych and Velimir Khlebnikov evolved versions of *zaum*, a transrational language in which words and sounds soared to dizzy heights of freedom from grammar and logic, even beyond those proposed by Marinetti in his manifesto "Imagination without Strings," published in June 1913.

The Russians not only matched or surpassed the Italian Futurists in their poetry of non-sense and in the proliferation of brilliantly innovative illustrated books, but they moved boldly into the field of performance. In the fall of 1913 Larionov and his friends paraded Moscow streets with Rayonist designs painted on their faces; an uproarious evening of lectures ended with hot tea poured into the first row of the audience. The opera *Victory over the Sun*, produced in Saint Petersburg in December 1913, with sets and lighting by Malevich, music by Mikhail Matiushin, and an alogical libretto by Kruchenych, depicted the transition to a future world beyond cause and effect.

Marinetti's celebrated visit to Russia began on January 26, 1914, and disappointed the Russian avant-garde. Supported by the tolerant Kulbin, politely greeted by Malevich, and heckled by Larionov, his lectures were warmly welcomed by Russian audiences less interested in his theories than captivated by his style and charm. As a result of his trip, two collections of Futurist manifestos were published in translation, and three Russian artists contributed to the Free Exhibition of International Futurists in Rome that April.

Two Saint Petersburg exhibitions in 1915 marked the decline of Russian Futurism and the birth of a new non-objective art. Vladimir Tatlin showed his relief constructions in "Tramway 5" in March and in December, "0–10, The Last Futurist Exhibition" introduced Malevich's fully abstract Suprematist paintings.

1. Mikhail Larionov and Natalia Gontcharova, c. 1913; 2. Mikhail Matiushin, Alexei Kruchenych, and Kasimir Malevich, with upside-down backdrop and furniture, 1913; 3. Installation of Malevich's works in "0-10, The Last Futurist Exhibition," Saint Petersburg, 1915; 4. Back cover (detail) of libretto for *Victory over the Sun,* 1913, with design by David Burliuk, British Library, London

Natalia Gontcharova
1 8 8 1 – 1 9 6 2

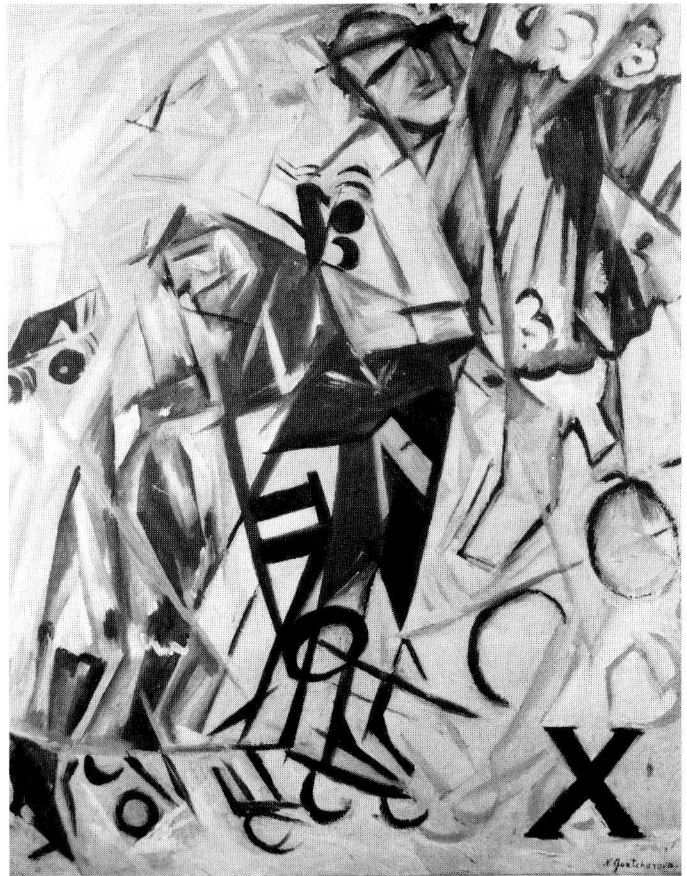

118

119

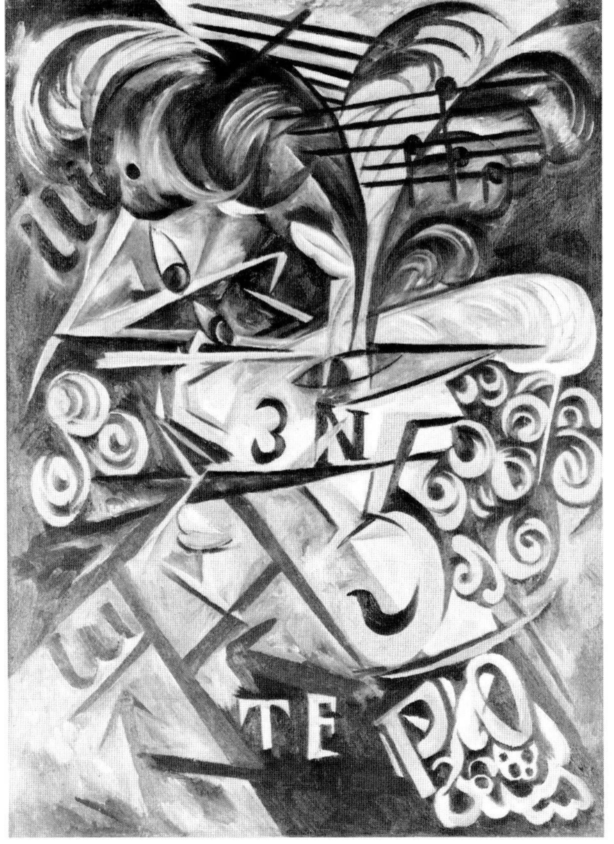

118. Skating Rink (Skating), 1912
Oil on canvas, 36½ x 29¾" (92.7 x 75.6 cm)
Private collection
Exhibitions: Moscow, *Natalia Gontcharova 1900–1913,* 1913, no. 628; Paris, Galerie Paul Guillaume, *Exposition Natalie de Gontcharowa et Michel Larionov,* June 17–30, 1914, no. 30

119. Lady with a Hat, 1912
Oil on canvas, 35½ x 26" (90 x 66 cm)
Musée National d'Art Moderne
Centre Georges Pompidou, Paris
Gift of M. J. Cassou, 1960
Exhibitions: Berlin, Der Sturm, *Erster Deutscher Herbstsalon,* September 20–December 1, 1913, no. 150; Paris, Galerie Paul Guillaume, *Exposition Natalie de Gontcharowa et Michel Larionov,* June 17–30, 1914, no. 31

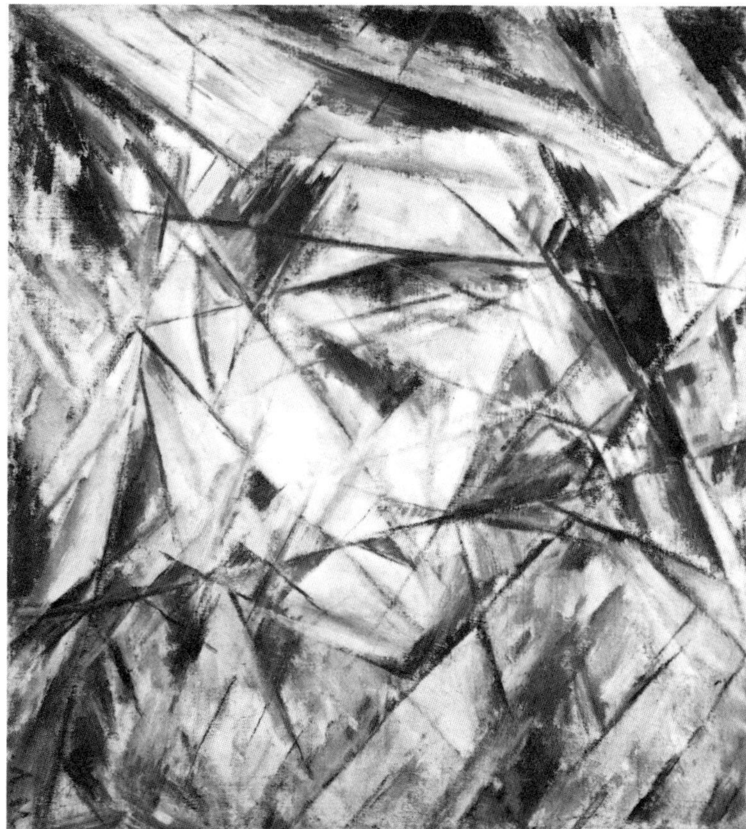

120

121

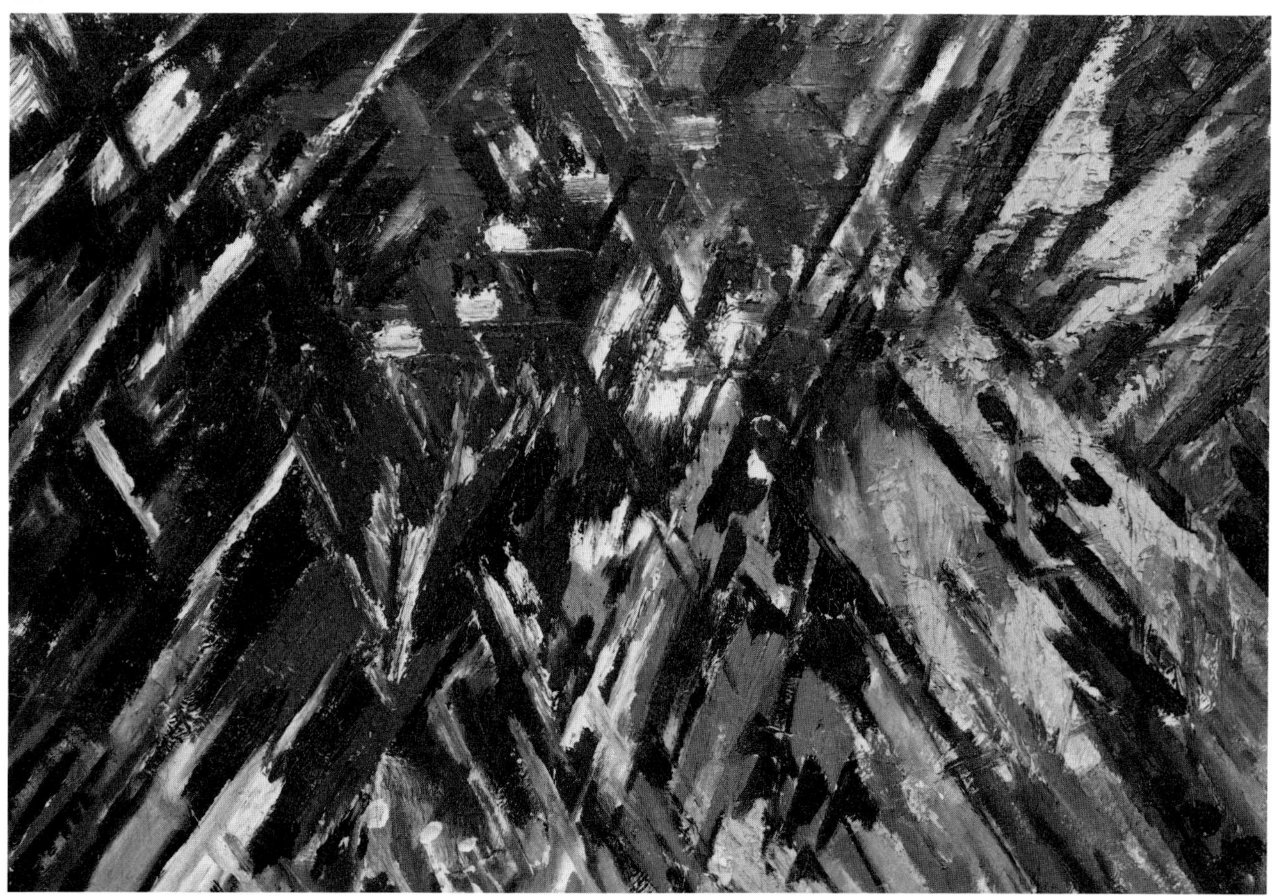

120. Blue Rayonism (Portrait of a Fool), 1912
Oil on canvas, 27½ x 25⅝" (69.9 x 65.1 cm)
Private collection
Exhibition: Moscow, *Target,* April 6–20, 1913, no. 78 (?)

121. Rayonist Composition—Domination of Red, 1913–14
Oil on canvas, 20¾ x 28½" (52.7 x 72.4 cm)
The Museum of Modern Art, New York
Gift of the artist, 1936

Kasimir Malevich

1878–1935

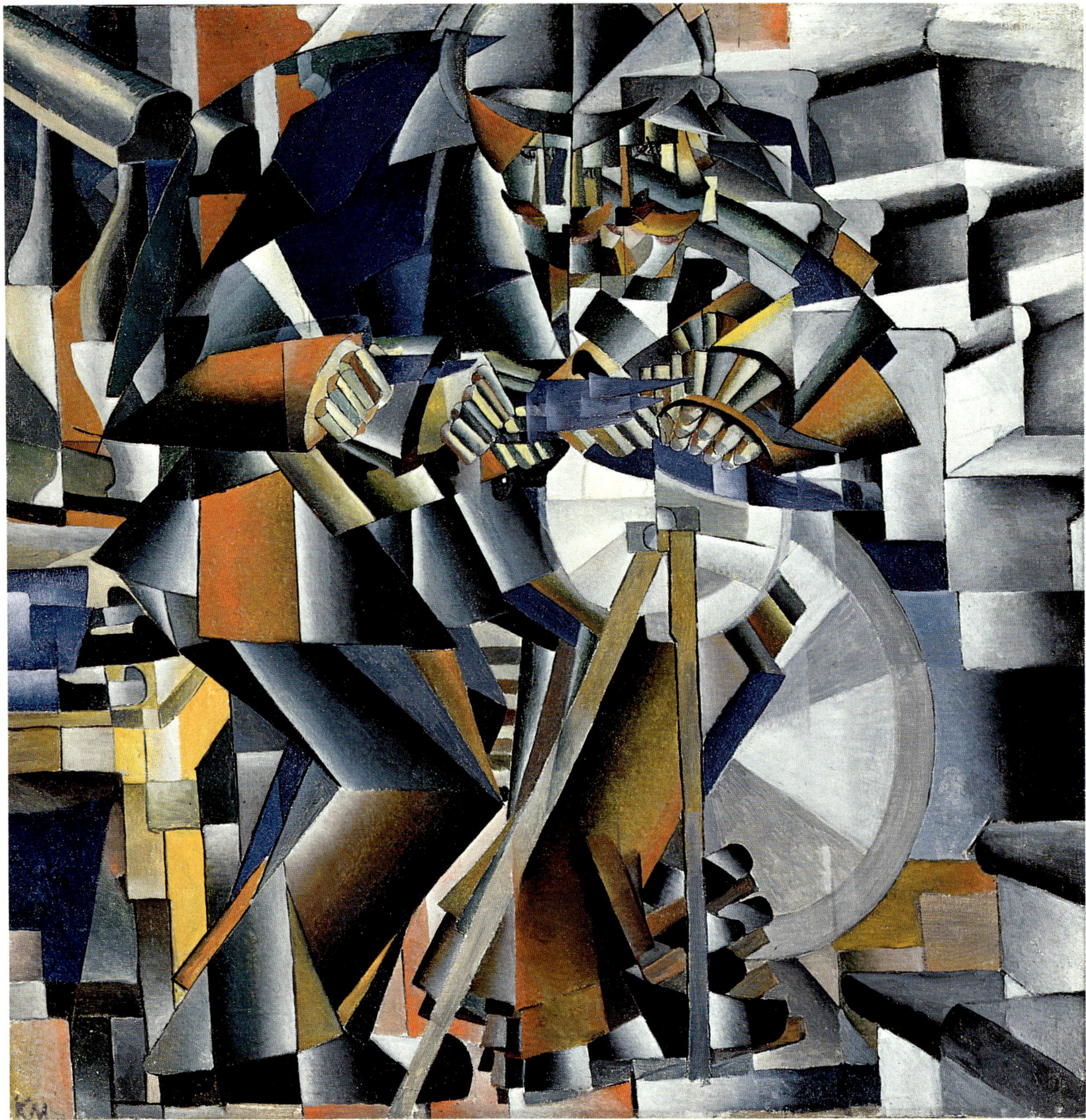

122

122. The Knife Grinder (Principle of Glittering), 1912
Oil on canvas, 31⅜ x 31⅜" (79.7 x 79.7 cm)
Yale University Art Gallery, New Haven
Gift of Collection Société Anonyme
Exhibition: Moscow, *Target,* April 6–20, 1913, no. 95

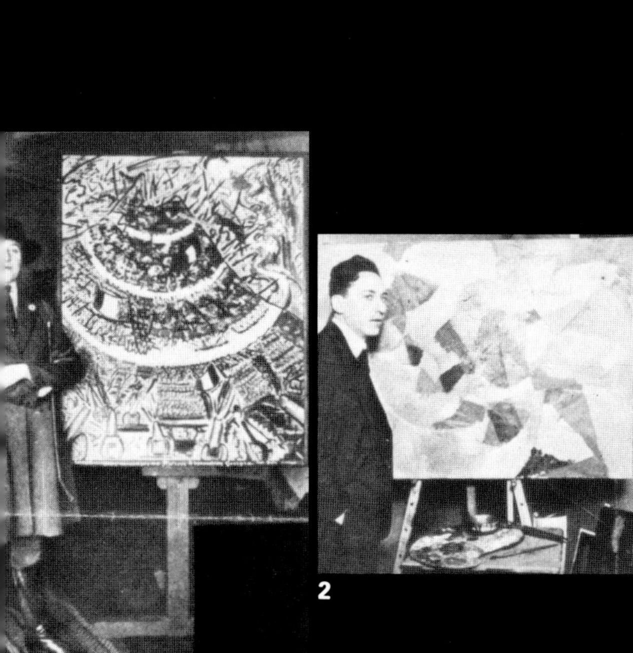

2

1

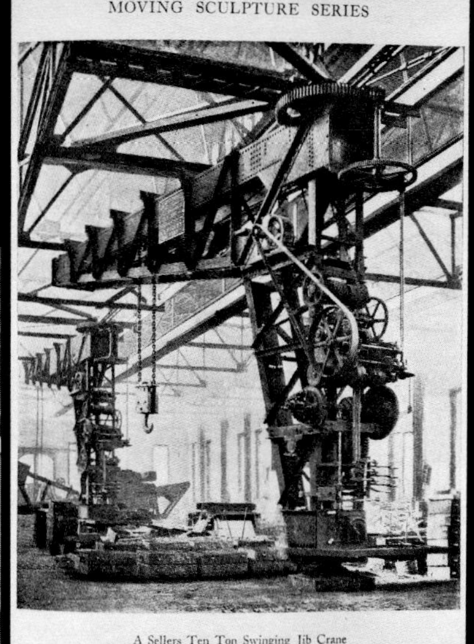

3

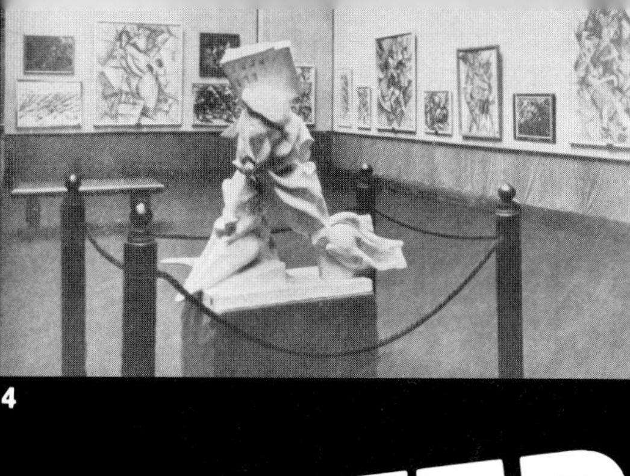

4

UNITED STATES

Although the manifestos and paintings of the Futurists received wide coverage in the American press beginning in February 1912, no work by a Futurist painter was shown in the country until September 1915, when an impressive group of works went on view at the Panama-Pacific International Exposition in San Francisco. Walter Pach had made a valiant effort to represent the Futurists in the Armory Show, which introduced the public of New York, Boston, and Chicago to a vast, international survey of modern art during 1913, but his effort failed, despite energetic support from Gino Severini. This did not prevent banner headlines accusing the Armory Show of Futurist extravagances, and Marcel Duchamp's controversial entry *Nude Descending a Staircase* (no. 92) became irrevocably identified with Futurism in the minds of American viewers. Several books published in 1913 tried to clear up the confusion, and Arthur Jerome Eddy's *Cubists and Post-Impressionism* of 1914 carefully distinguished between Futurism and other modern movements.

There is little direct evidence that American artists studied the Futurists' manifestos or catalogues, but many of the painters who exhibited in Alfred Stieglitz's gallery at 291 Fifth Avenue may have been familiar with the Italians' themes. John Marin's dynamic watercolors of Manhattan expressed his sense of "great forces at work, great movements." Although Futurism went relatively unregarded in Stieglitz's *Camera Work*, which published many advanced theories of art, its radical offshoot, the *291* magazine, reflected Futurist innovations in typography by 1915. Another provocative little magazine, Robert Coady's *The Soil* (1916–17), catalogued all of industrial America as a Futurist work of art.

Joseph Stella's *Battle of Lights* (no. 130) was without doubt *the* Futurist masterpiece by an American and was received with an appropriate uproar when first exhibited early in 1914. Born in Italy, Stella had immigrated to New York at the age of eighteen and his exposure to Cubism and Futurism occurred simultaneously on a visit to Paris in 1911–12. His works of 1913 to 1916 were unabashedly Futurist and he arrived only later at a more stable, geometric mode. Max Weber's relationship to Futurism is more difficult to characterize. A sophisticated observer of modern trends during his Parisian sojourn of 1905 to 1908, Weber remained in touch with European developments and his dynamic abstractions of cityscapes (begun in 1913) were a major contribution to Futurist imagery. Interested in the relationship of music to painting and in theories of the fourth dimension, Weber remained surprisingly isolated, notwithstanding the fragmented groups of American modernism.

There appears to have been only one American painter enlisted directly in the Futurist cause. Frances Simpson Stevens lived in Italy before the war, knew Marinetti, and contributed to the Free Exhibition of International Futurists in Rome in April 1914. She subsequently turned up in New York with twenty-one works and a militant catalogue preface for a show at the Braun Galleries in March 1916, and later vanished from view.

Among the Americans most concerned with international movements were Morgan Russell and Stanton MacDonald-Wright, who had settled in Paris before 1910 and who, together, proudly constituted Synchromism. Inaugurated in Germany in June 1913 and later introduced to Paris and New York (March 1914), Synchromism was a complex mixture of color theories (related to those of Robert Delaunay) with a profound study of sculptural form. Russell's *Synchromy in Deep Blue-Violet* (no. 127) is based on the twisting rhythms of Michelangelo's *Dying Slave*, a choice of subject Umberto Boccioni would have found sympathetic if "passatist." Russell assembled one of the most complete collections of Futurist manifestos and documents to survive, and the Synchromists' concern to achieve a rhythmic interplay of colors without foregoing solid construction was not far removed from Boccioni's own late chromatic studies of nude figures.

In March 1917, the first original examples of Futurism finally reached New York with Severini's one-man show at the 291 gallery, the last exhibition of a European artist in Stieglitz's gallery, which was to close its doors in June.

1. Frances Simpson Stevens with her *Battle of Gorizia* (from *Every Week*, April 2, 1917); 2. Stanton MacDonald-Wright with his *Study in Violet after Rubens* (from *Every Week*, April 2, 1917); 3. "Moving Sculpture Series: A Sellers Ten Ton Swinging Jib Crane" (from *The Soil*, January 1917); 4. Futurist gallery at the Panama-Pacific International Exposition, 1915

James R. Daugherty

1 8 8 7 – 1 9 7 4

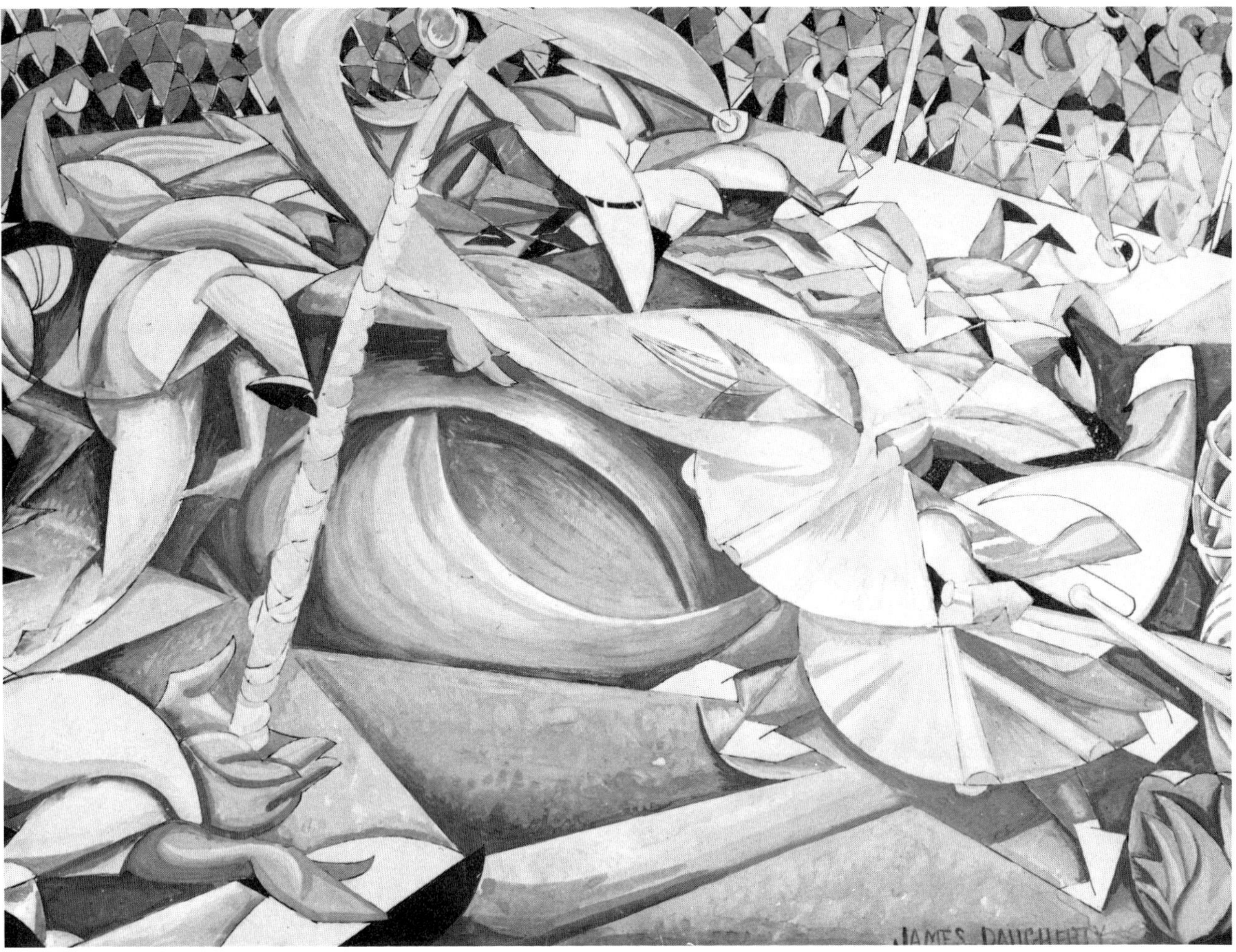

123

123. Three Base Hit (Opening Game), 1914
Gouache on paper, 12½ x 17½" (31.8 x 44.4 cm)
Whitney Museum of American Art, New York

Stanton MacDonald-Wright

1890–1973

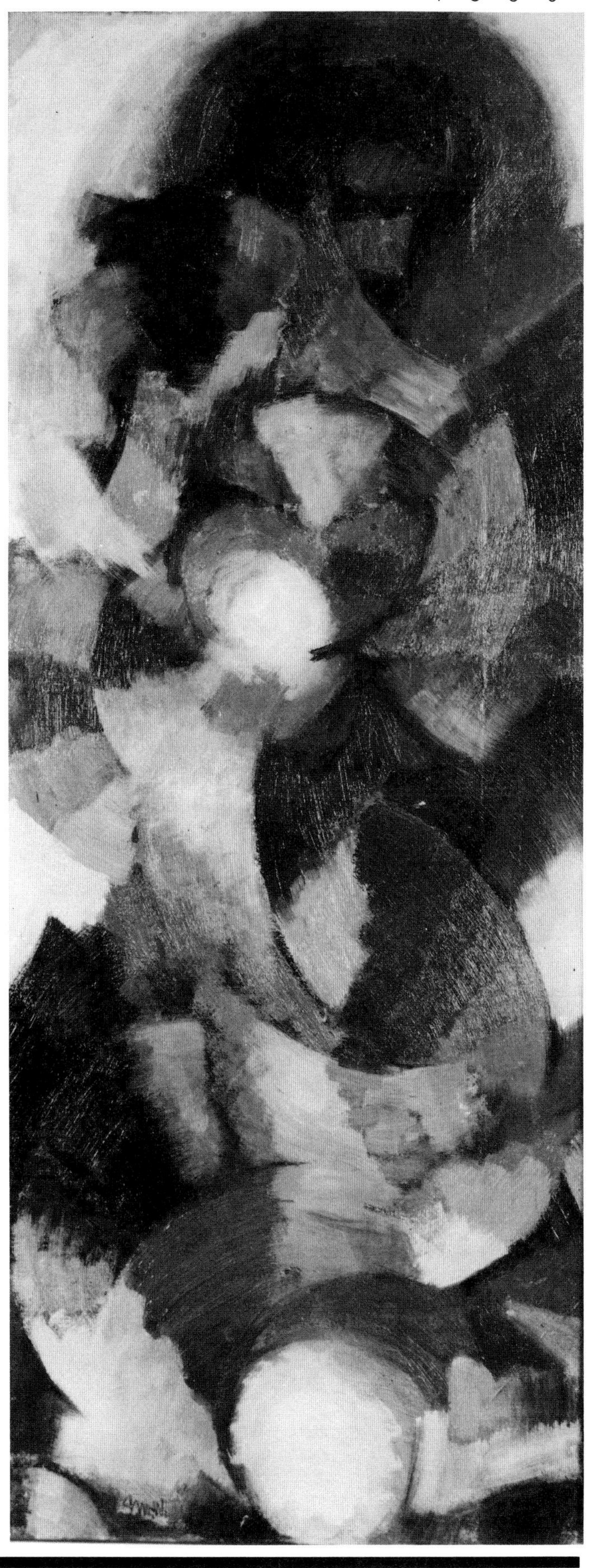

124

124. Conception Synchromy (Conception Arm Organization), 1914
Oil on canvas, mounted on cardboard,
29¾ x 11⅛" (75.6 x 28.3 cm)
The Lydia and Harry Lewis Winston Collection
(Dr. and Mrs. Barnett Malbin, New York)

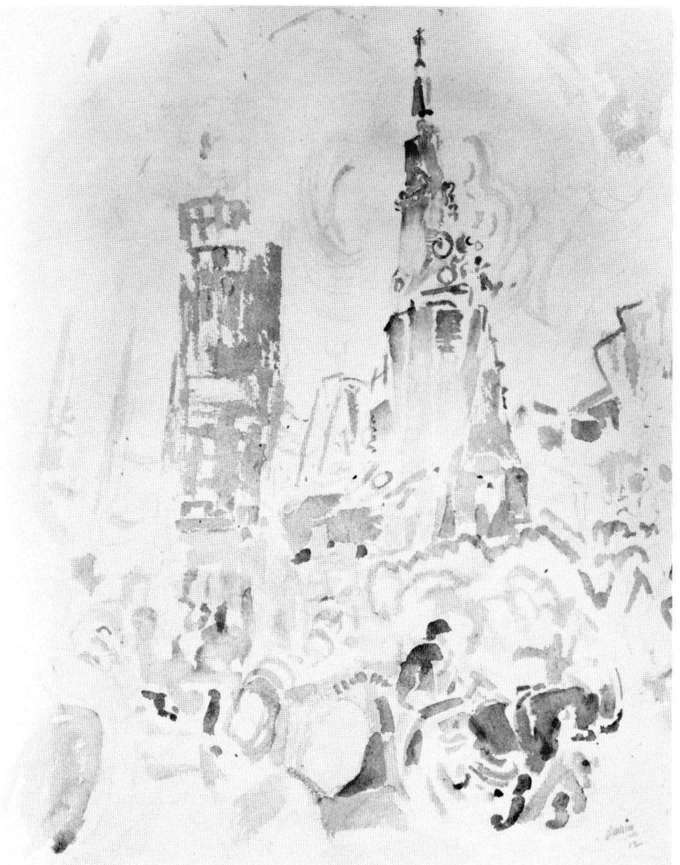

125

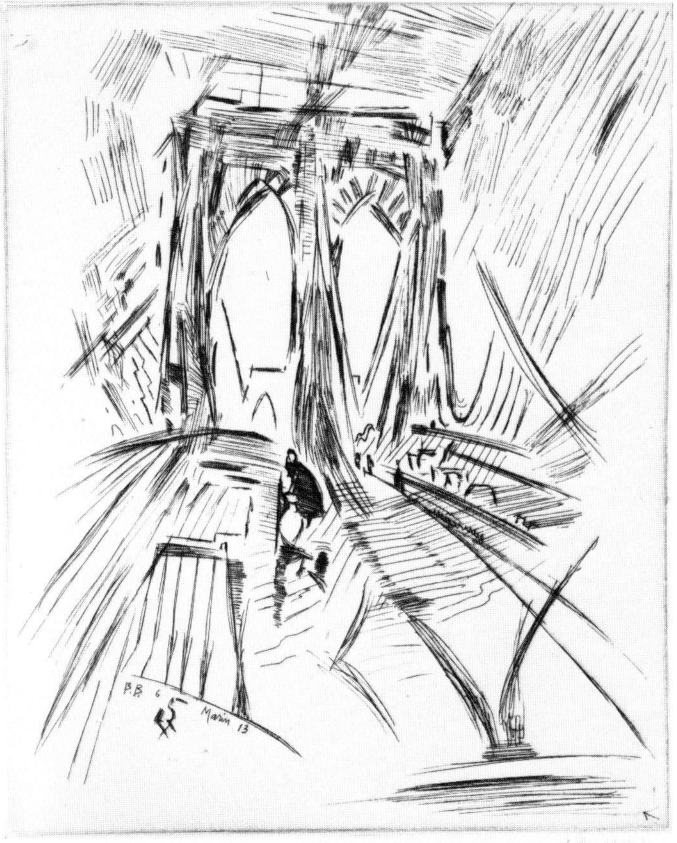

126

125. Saint Paul's, Lower Manhattan, 1912
Watercolor on paper, 18¼ x 14¾" (46.4 x 37.5 cm)
Delaware Art Museum, Wilmington
Gift of John L. McHugh
Exhibition: New York, Armory of the 69th Regiment, *International Exhibition of Modern Art,* February 17–March 15, 1913, no. 144

126. Brooklyn Bridge, No. 6 (Swaying), 1913
Etching, 10¾ x 8¾" (27.3 x 22.2 cm)
Philadelphia Museum of Art
Purchased: Lola Downin Peck Fund
from the Carl and Laura Zigrosser Collection

Morgan Russell
1 8 8 6 – 1 9 5 3

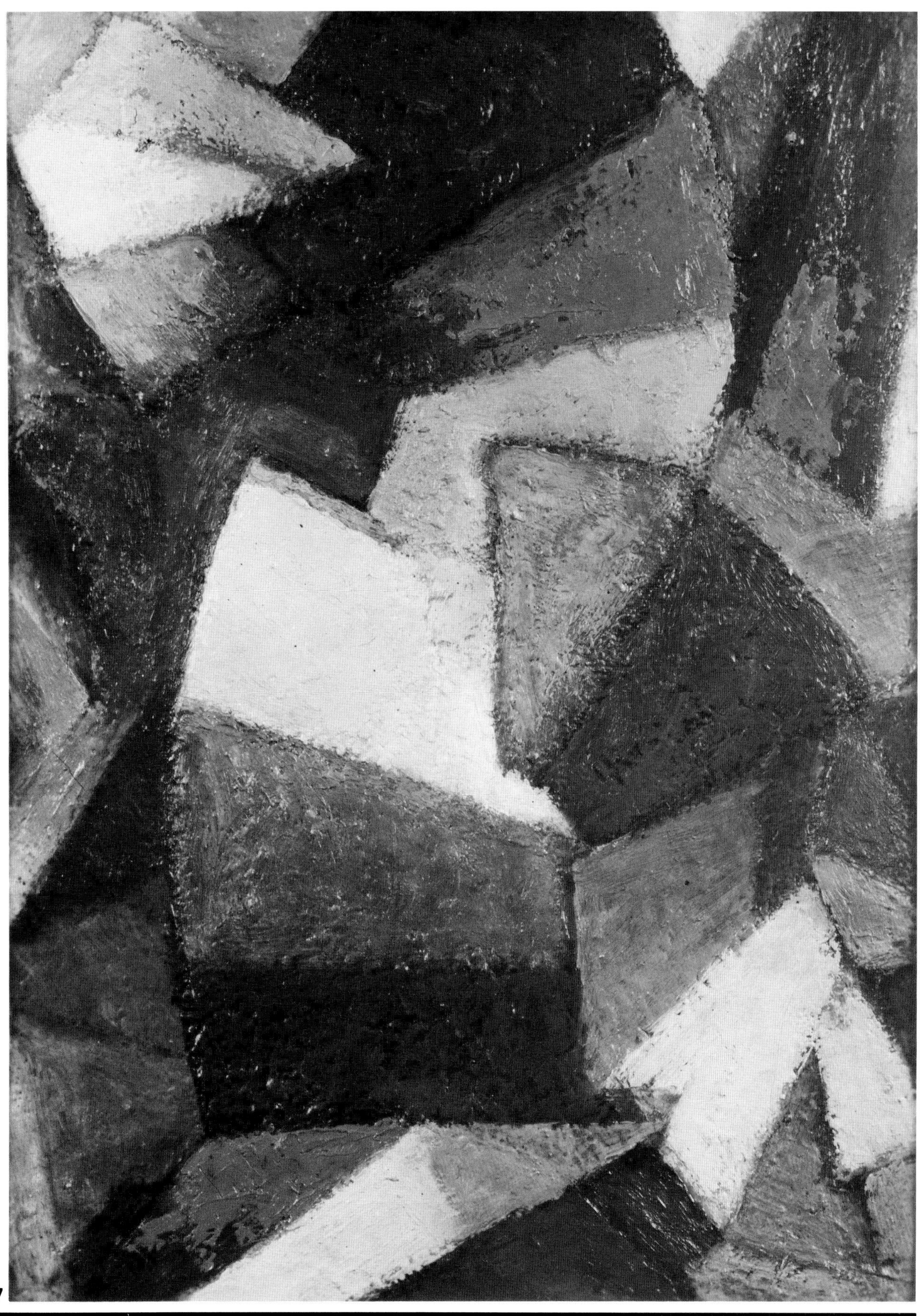

127

127. Synchromy in Deep Blue-Violet (Synchromy to Light, No. 2), c. 1913
Oil on canvas, mounted on cardboard,
13 x 9⅝" (33 x 24.4 cm)
The Lydia and Harry Lewis Winston Collection
(Dr. and Mrs. Barnett Malbin, New York)

Joseph Stella

1877–1946

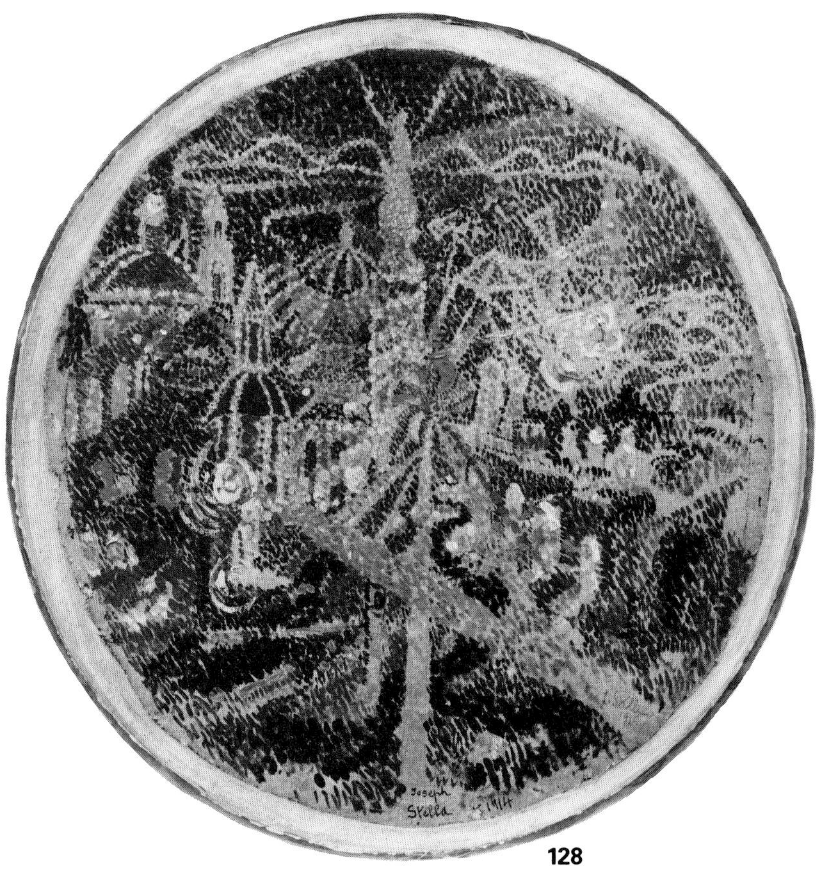

128

129

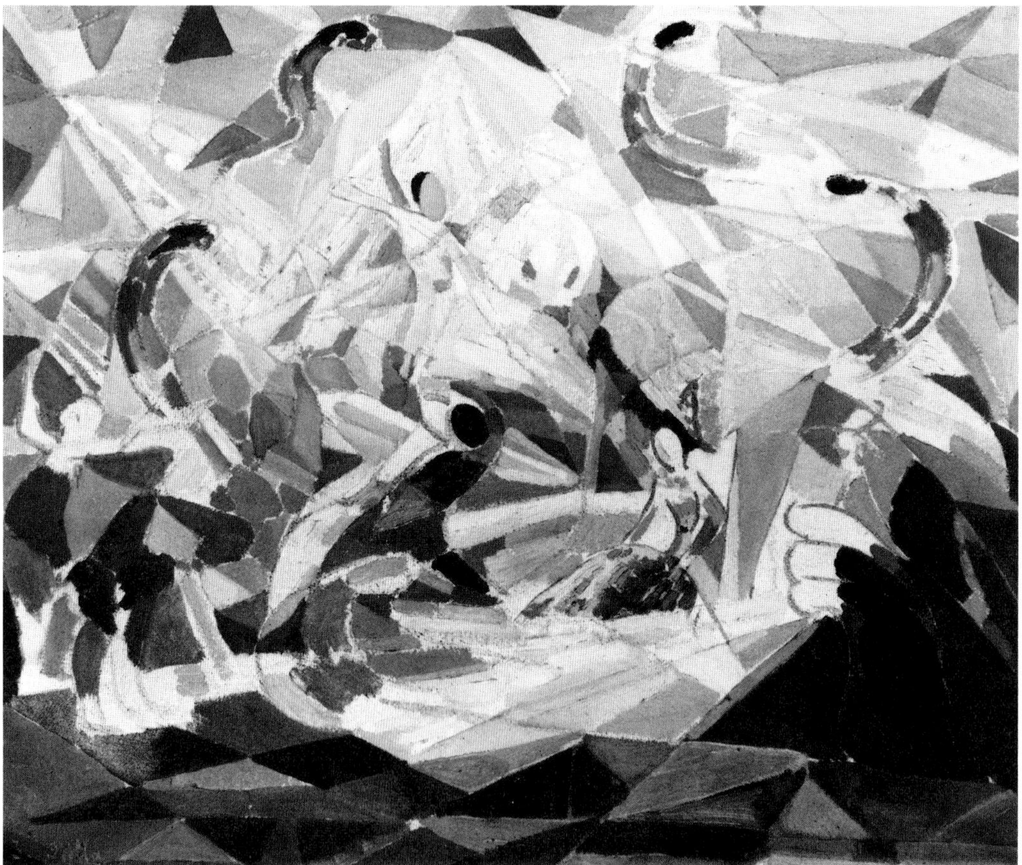

128. Battle of Lights, 1913–14 (?)
Oil on canvas, mounted on cardboard, diameter 20¼" (51.4 cm)
The Museum of Modern Art, New York
Elizabeth Bliss Parkinson Fund, 1958

129. Der Rosenkavalier, 1913–14
Oil on canvas, 24 x 30" (61 x 76.2 cm)
Whitney Museum of American Art, New York
Gift of George F. Of, 1952
Exhibition: New York, Montross Gallery, *Paintings and Drawings by Modern Americans,* February 2–23, 1914

Joseph Stella

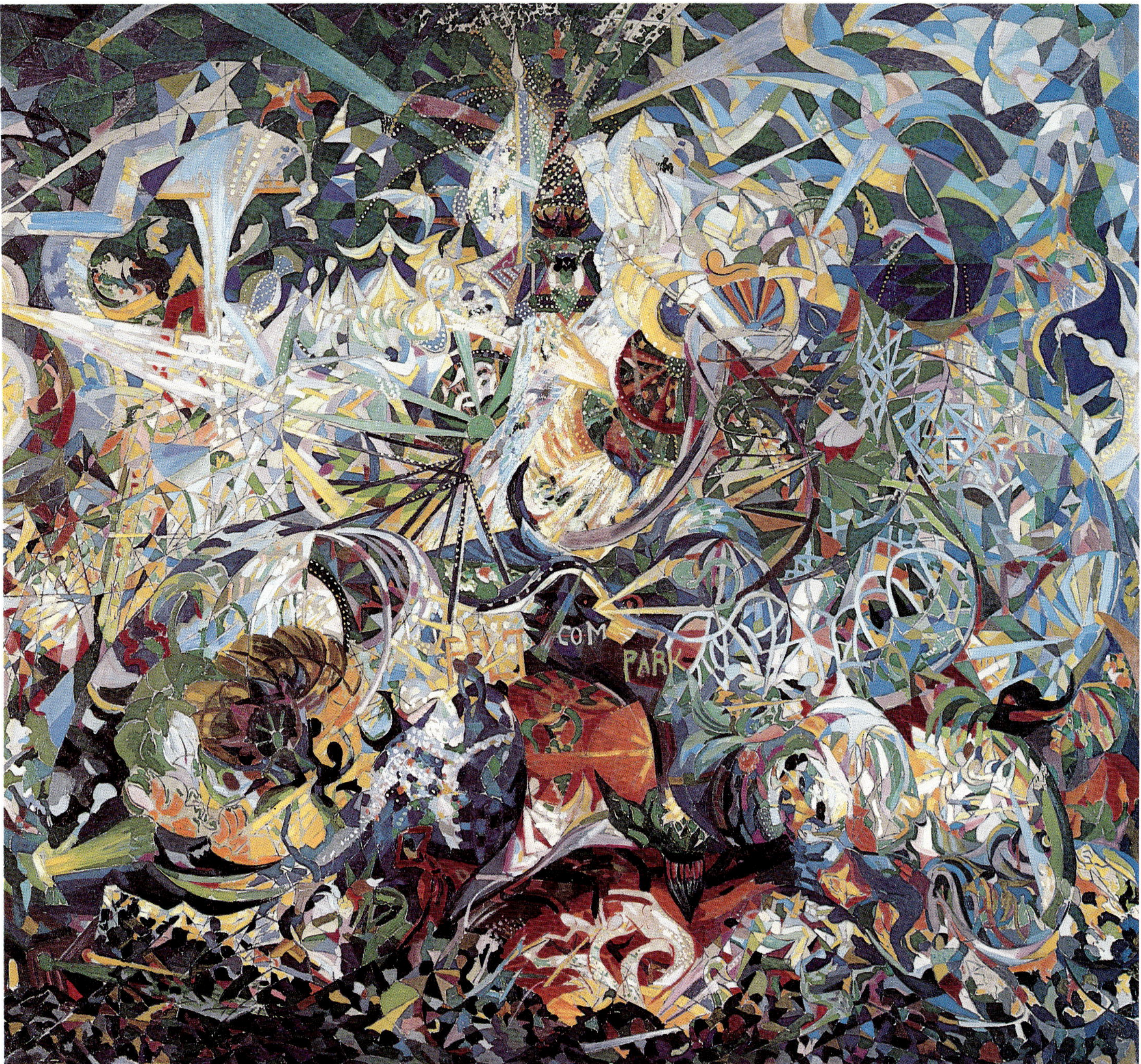

130

130. Battle of Lights, Coney Island, 1913–14
Oil on canvas, 75¾ x 85" (192.4 x 215.9 cm)
Yale University Art Gallery, New Haven
Gift of Collection Société Anonyme
Exhibition: New York, Montross Gallery, *Paintings and Drawings by Modern Americans,* February 2–23, 1914

Frances Simpson Stevens

1 8 8 1 – 1 9 6 1

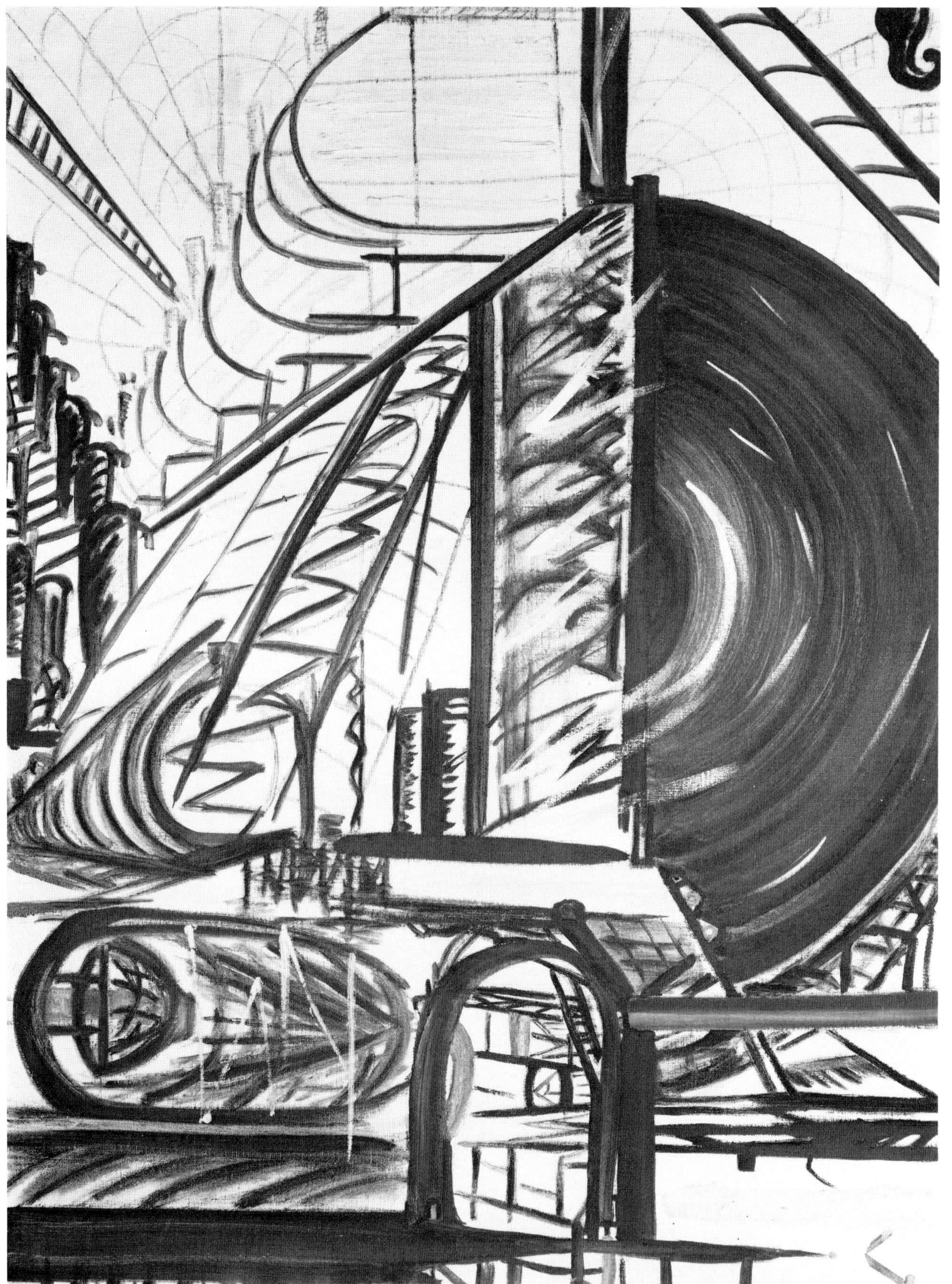

131

131. Dynamic Velocity of Interborough Rapid Transit Power Station, c. 1915
Oil and charcoal on canvas, 48⅜ x 35¾" (122.9 x 90.8 cm)
Philadelphia Museum of Art
The Louise and Walter Arensberg Collection
Exhibition: New York, Braun Galleries, *Futurist Paintings by Frances Simpson Stevens,* March 8–27, 1916, no. 2

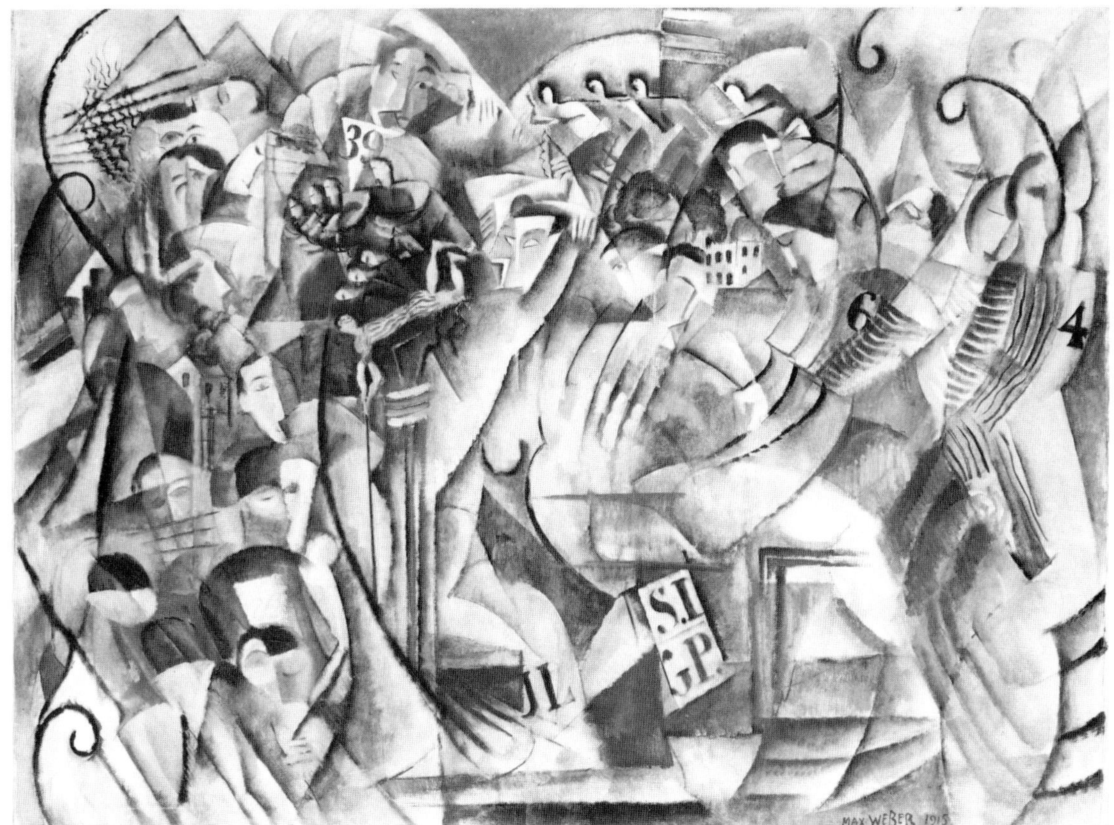

132

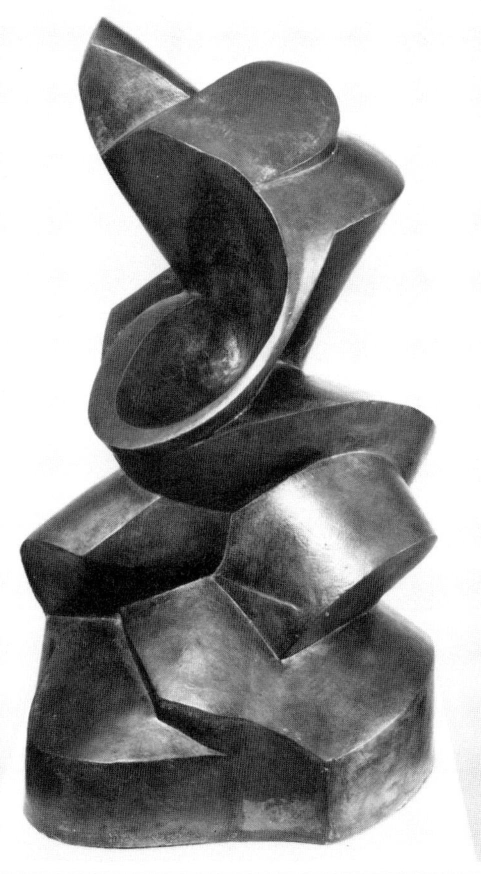

133

132. Athletic Contest, 1915
Oil on canvas, 40 x 60″ (101.6 x 152.4 cm)
The Metropolitan Museum of Art, New York
George A. Hearn Fund, 1967

133. Spiral Rhythm, 1915 (enlarged and cast 1958–59)
Bronze, 24⅛ x 14¼ x 14⅞″ (61.3 x 36.2 x 37.8 cm)
Hirshhorn Museum and Sculpture Garden,
Smithsonian Institution, Washington, D.C.
Exhibition: New York, Montross Gallery, *Exhibition of Paintings and Sculpture by Max Weber,* December 14–30, 1915 (plaster version)

Max Weber

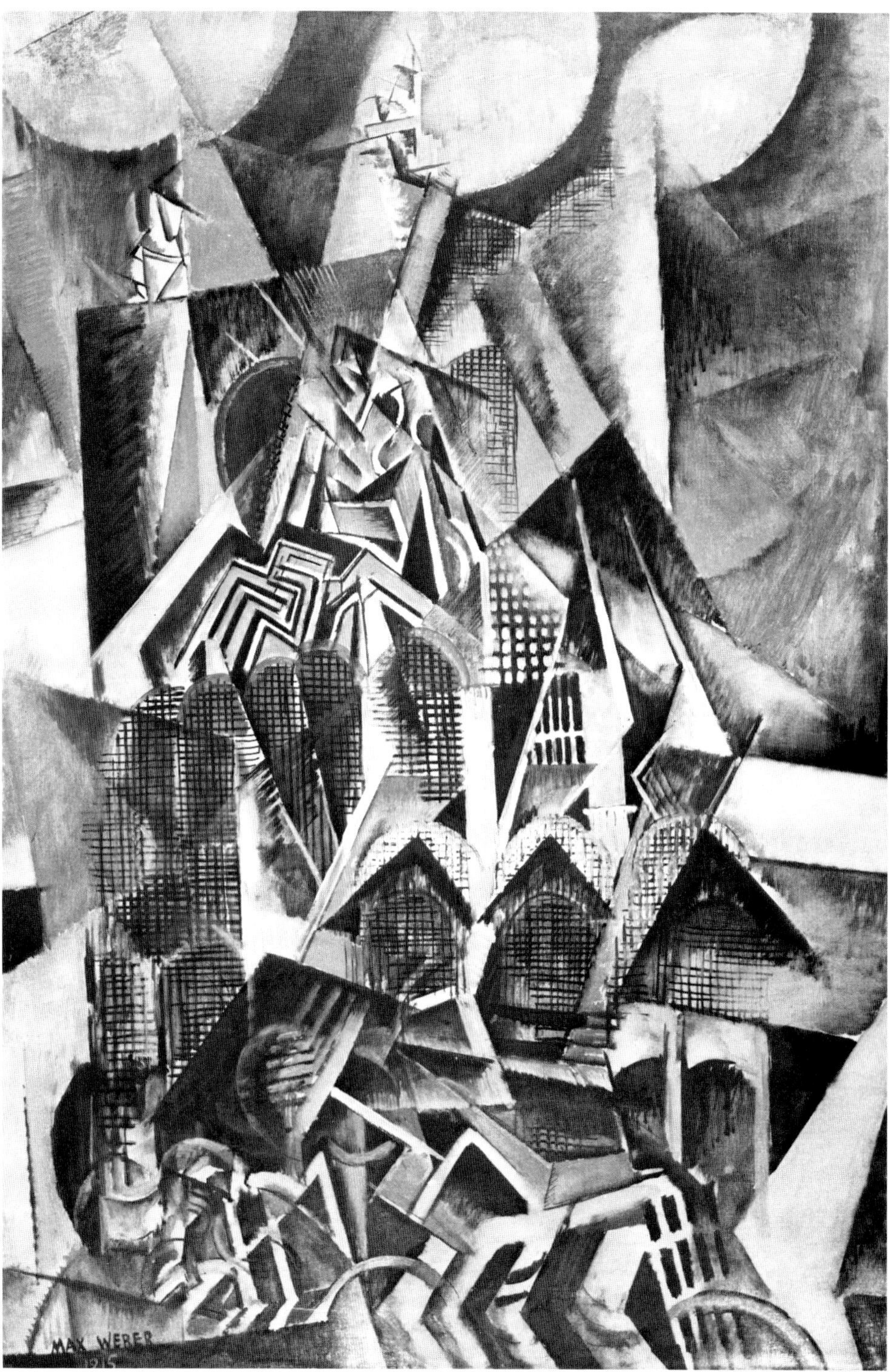

134

134. A Comprehension of the Grand Central Terminal, 1915
Oil on canvas, 60 x 40" (152.4 x 101.6 cm)
Thyssen-Bornemisza Collection, Lugano
Exhibition: New York, Montross Gallery, *Exhibition of Paintings and Sculpture by Max Weber,* December 14–30, 1915, no. 1